C000199879

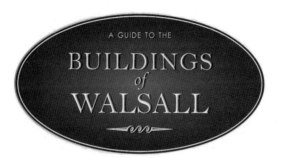

A GUIDE TO THE

BUILDINGS
of
WALSALL

WALSALL
Metropolitan Borough

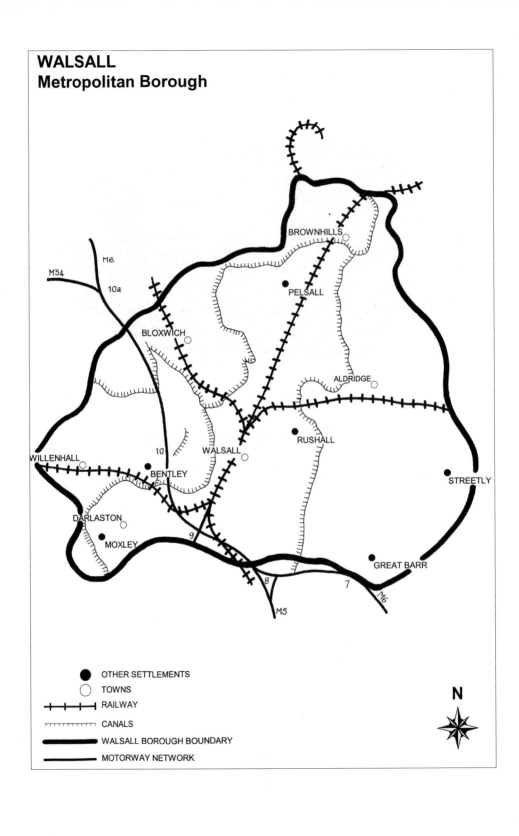

M6

M54

10a

BROWNHILLS

PELSALL

BLOXWICH

ALDRIDGE

WILLENHALL

10

WALSALL

RUSHALL

STREETLY

BENTLEY

DARLASTON

MOXLEY

9

GREAT BARR

7

M6

8

M5

● OTHER SETTLEMENTS
○ TOWNS
┼┼┼┼ RAILWAY
⊓⊓⊓⊓⊓ CANALS
▬▬▬ WALSALL BOROUGH BOUNDARY
▬▬▬ MOTORWAY NETWORK

N

PETER ARNOLD

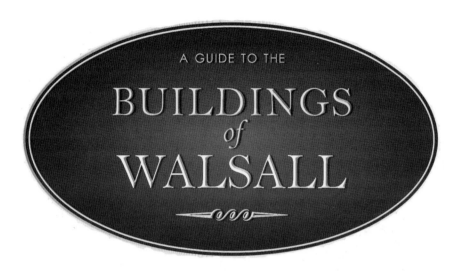

A GUIDE TO THE

BUILDINGS
of
WALSALL

AN ILLUSTRATED
ARCHITECTURAL HISTORY

TEMPUS

Frontispiece: Map of Walsall Borough.

First published 2003

Tempus Publishing Limited
The Mill, Brimscombe Port,
Stroud, Gloucestershire, GL5 2QG
www.tempus-publishing.com

British Library Cataloguing in Publication Data.
A catalogue record for this book is available from the British Library.

ISBN 0 7524 2498 x

Typesetting and origination by Tempus Publishing Limited
Printed in Great Britain by Midway Colour Print, Wiltshire

CONTENTS

Lodge, Memorial Gardens, Church Hill, Walsall. Architect, Geoffrey Jellicoe, 1952. At the time it was built building materials were rationed and so its first use was as a police house to secure a permit. The house acts as a Belvedere to the gardens. High up on the hill, it commands superb views to the north and west. The first floor is a rendered box with two windows and a balcony in each face. After a period of dereliction, the lodge is now a private house.

PREFACE

I was Principal Conservation Officer at Walsall Metropolitan Borough Council for thirteen years – from 1986 to 1999. In that quite short time, much changed. I fought many battles for the retention of the best of the borough's built past, but think that I lost far too many of them. Making the rounds of the borough four years later for the purposes of this book, much has changed again, sometimes for the worse. This book is partly a distillation of what I learnt in the thirteen years of my service and partly a snapshot of the borough's built heritage at a time when the forces of change – not necessarily benign change – have proven too powerful to be resisted.

Much of the visual character of the modern Metropolitan Borough is humdrum or downright poor. However, there are elements of national interest. There are over twenty-five miles of canal, with engineering structures and buildings to match, many of them in surprisingly rural settings. The industrial archaeology of the canal corridor is considerable, and, as yet, inadequately explored. The Industrial Revolution and the development of the Black Country as the 'workshop of the world' has left a wide range of significant industrial buildings – some architect-designed, others not. These, perhaps, are the borough's principal claim to fame – of international significance as the premises which supplied the world with leather goods, door locks and nuts and bolts.

Involvement of architects with national reputations over the past 200 years has left a variety of buildings of quality. Walsall Council House with its 'New Sculpture' bas reliefs is an important document of the artistic ideals of the early twentieth century. Geoffrey Jellicoe's redevelopment of Church Hill,

Walsall, in the 1950s created some of the UK's first 'post-modern' buildings. The Wolverhampton architectural practice of Lavender and Twentyman (later Twentyman Percy) designed three churches of national standing. Finally, Caruso St John architects of London put Walsall on the modern cultural map of the UK through the New Art Gallery.

Having got to know the borough as I thought intimately during my thirteen years as Conservation Officer, the preparation of this book took me into corners off the beaten track that I never previously penetrated. On one occasion I was trying to follow a green lane clearly marked on the map, yet very difficult to locate on the ground. I was aiming for an overbridge on Daw End railway cutting. I pushed my way through the scrub down the side of Rushall Olympic football club. Only when I got to the bridge was the line of the green lane clearly detectable. On another occasion, I went down a cul-de-sac. Unexpectedly, there was a footpath leading off the end. It led to another road with an intact Victorian house and the surviving gates to a now-vanished power station. On both occasions I was using a bicycle. An indispensable tool to covering a lot of ground in detail but quickly. In fact, I will keep a lot of memories of using a bicycle to travel around the borough's more inaccessible odd corners.

Preparation of the book proved unexpectedly difficult. Almost immediately after I agreed to do it I was hit by an extremely busy year. For this reason much of the work was done against the clock with little time for the careful checking of a number of facts. I therefore apologise to those who know better. Fortunately, my speaking notes for several seasons of architectural guided walks proved an invaluable quick reference for most of the essential items of information.

Particular thanks go to Marc Jones, Tracy Lister, Dan Roberts and Julie Wheatley of Walsall MBC for their help with the preparation of illustrations and the supply of various items of information. A 'thank you' also to Ann French, that experienced author on matters Walsall, for her general encouragement.

The aim of this book is to present the secrets and treats of the buildings of Walsall Metropolitan Borough to a wider audience. May the unknown be revealed – and relished!

Peter Arnold
Summer 2003

AN INTRODUCTION

The present-day Walsall Metropolitan Borough, with a population of around a quarter of a million people, is sited at the northern extremity of the Black Country, to the north-west of Birmingham. Like most modern, large, local authorities, Walsall is an uneasy amalgamation, imposed by Whitehall, of a series of individual local communities with a clear sense of their own identity – Aldridge, Brownhills, Darlaston, Walsall itself and Willenhall. These local communities were once politically independent with their own Urban District and Rural District Councils.

Community character is diverse. The west and centre of the modern-day Metropolitan Borough form part of the densely industrialised and built-up area known as the Black Country, the 'workshop of the world' as it once was. Other areas, particularly to the north and east, belong to rural south Staffordshire and are still farmed. The south-east part is largely residential in character and focused on Birmingham. Finally, the north of the borough belongs to the now-defunct South Staffordshire Coalfield, adding a further degree of individual character to the extraordinarily varied whole.

Topography

Physically, the western half of the borough area is rather flat, rising gently towards the north, with slight but noticeable summits at Darlaston and Bentley. Walsall town centre is marked by a steep limestone ridge running in from the south, with St Matthew's parish church sitting on top of a very steep escarpment overlooking the town centre in the valley below. North from

Upper Lichfield Street, Willenhall, a harmonious ensemble of a great variety of buildings from various periods.

Walsall, the land rises to a ridge at Birchills and then more gently up to another mini-summit at Bloxwich. To the south-east, Barr Beacon (227 metres or 745 feet) is one of the highest summits of the West Midlands and continues north as a lower ridge to Aldridge. This means that Pheasey and Streetly, to the south and east of Barr Beacon, are physically separated by high ground from the rest of the borough. Shire Oak, south-east of Brownhills, tops another distinct ridge (177 metres or 580 feet) which gives long views to the north-east over Lichfield. Another nearby summit is capped by the massive Iron Age embankments of Castle Fort, covered in trees.

Names

The area's place-names are largely Anglo-Saxon, but the 'Barr' of Great Barr Hall and Barr Beacon is a surviving Celtic word from an earlier past. Blakenall, Pelsall, Rushall, Walsall and Willenhall all incorporate the element 'halh', meaning 'sheltered place'. Another group of names – Bentley, Fishley, Moxley, Ogley (the ancient name of Brownhills), Shelfield and Streetly – contain 'leah' or 'feld', indicators of the ancient extent of Cannock Forest by means of its clearings and open fields. Streetly also refers to the Roman road known as 'Ryknild Street', which runs through Sutton Park just to the east of the modern borough boundary.

Industrial and Economic Development

The community that gives its name to the whole Metropolitan Borough, Walsall, has its origins as a trading settlement in the early Middle Ages, a market charter being granted in 1220. The market assured a modest and continuing prosperity, and the medieval town steadily expanded. However, the local geology was extremely important. Iron ore was present, as were coal and limestone. The local limestone is fossilised coral. In several places it outcropped to the surface, and was first quarried in the Roman period for both stone rubble and to make lime mortar. Limestone from the area of Rushall, one mile to the north-east of Walsall town, has been identified at the important Roman settlement of Letocetum (now Wall) on A5 Watling Street. In fact, limestone continued to be quarried – and mined – right up into the early twentieth century. It made very fine building lime, so the earl of Warwick's building accounts in the fifteenth century record the purchase of a great deal of Walsall lime.

Iron ore was also extracted and worked in the later Middle Ages. The local coal was used for smelting and was then worked. Walsall town possessed a large number of smiths, who seem to have specialised in the intricate ironwork needed for the harnesses of riding horses and draught horses.

This specialist ironwork has its own name – lorinery. The local specialism of lorinery was directly responsible for the arrival of the leather industry, saddlers and bridle cutters setting up shop to make use of the ironwork 'at source'. Tanners and curriers followed, to prepare and supply workable leather to the craftsmen. All this was just Walsall.

The combination of iron ore and coal available to other local communities led to a series of local specialities in 'metal bashing'. In fact, the whole Black Country is remarkable for the way in which individual products come from particular communities. So Bloxwich, to the north of Walsall itself, specialised in producing awls – useful, amongst other things, for making holes in leather. Willenhall, to the west, eventually became one of the world capitals for the manufacture of door locks. Darlaston, also to the west, specialised in nuts and bolts in a very big way. Large deposits of brick earth – Etruria marl – led to a developing brick and tile industry focused on Stubbers Green between Shelfield and Aldridge.

John Wilkinson, one of the pioneers of iron smelting in the Black Country, operated his blast furnaces at Moxley, in the extreme west of the modern borough.

The Industrial Revolution

Even as early as the end of the Middle Ages, there was a remarkable variety and quantity of manufacturing going on locally. But most of it was on a small scale, based on the output of individual craftsmen. The great local problem was good transport. Roads were poor and there were no navigable rivers. Everything manufactured had to be transported by packhorse or horse and cart, so weight and volume had to be kept down.

It was the introduction of new technology that resulted in the modern Black Country – the workshop of the world in the Victorian and Edwardian periods. The new development was canal technology. One horse on the towpath could pull several tons of raw materials or completed manufactures loaded into a narrowboat, and do so all day. John Wilkinson was one of the investors in waterways, his works being serviced by canal at Bradley (pronounced 'Braydlee' in Black Country dialect) and he built some of the first iron narrowboats.

Building Materials

Poverty, prosperity, development, redevelopment, industry, commerce, mining, quarrying and communications, have all shaped the townscape and landscape of the modern Metropolitan Borough, not least through buildings. In fact, its buildings are what give any community its special, individual character. They are the features on the community 'face'.

As always, the borough's buildings reflect the available building materials. Before the English Civil War in the mid-seventeenth century, half-timbering was the most common type of construction. A small group of such half-timbered buildings survives immediately to the west of Barr Beacon – one barn and three houses. In addition, there is one half-timbered gable in the Bell Inn, Market Place, Willenhall. By the time of Civil War, though, brick construction had put in an appearance, with three brick houses surviving in part, although none have been selected for protection by Listing. However, the White Hart at Caldmore Green, dating from just after the Civil War, is built of small, strongly fired bricks containing the characteristic local pebbles of rosy quartz.

The arrival of the waterways from 1797 meant that Welsh slate could be imported in quantity at prices that successfully competed with tiles dug and fired from the local Etruria marl. One such early graded slate roof survives in Ablewell Street, Walsall.

The boom in Victorian church building led to exploitation of the local limestone at both Christchurch, Blakenall, and St Michael's, Rushall. Being a coralline limestone there was no 'bed', but the stone could nevertheless be roughly shaped into blocks and it was of these that the two churches were built, using imported sandstone, probably from Hollington in north

33 Market Place, Willenhall, a large, late eighteenth-century town house with later, Victorian, sash windows and a slate roof. One early occupier was John Clemson, maltster, whose maltings occupied the building just visible to the left. No. 33 was later occupied by the solicitor who acted for the Willenhall Local Board, providing local government before the creation of Willenhall Urban District Council. There is a very fine staircase and good plasterwork internally. During recent repairs, some interesting public documents were recovered, having been stuffed through the cracks in the floorboards! The railings and arch are a modern recreation of ironwork removed for scrap during the Second World War.

Staffordshire, for all the carved work and dressings. St Anne's, Willenhall, is remarkable for being the only church to be built of the igneous dolerite stone locally known as 'Rowley Rag'. This stone came from a small quarry at Pouk Hill near Birchills, where a small igneous intrusion had pushed up through the coal measures. Most of this 'Rowley Rag' was used as road cobbles and kerbs. It has unusual weathering properties. Quarried a buff colour, use as roadstone gives it a distinctive glossy black finish.

South Staffordshire also developed a range of terracotta products, which appear in many late Victorian and Edwardian buildings in the borough. It is likely that Henry Boys, a local brickworks proprietor and philanthropist, was responsible for producing some of this terracotta, but research is needed to confirm this.

A by-product of iron smelting is blast furnace slag. It is a blend of the limestone used as a flux together with the impurities from the iron itself. Often, it has a sponge-like appearance because it was drawn off as froth. It was used as a building material, usually for boundary walls.

Architects and Designers

The master masons responsible for the chancel of St Matthew's church, Walsall (1462–71), were John Nightingale and William Wotton. No named architects and surveyors are known to have been involved in the buildings of the borough before 1800, though the famous landscape gardener Humphrey Repton, whose son John Adie Repton provided an architectural service to his father, is named in connection with the new landscape at Great Barr Hall. Francis Goodwin, a London practitioner, did much work in the West Midlands, including the wedding-cake Gothic of the nave of St Matthew's, Walsall (1820–21) and the Neo-Classical stucco St Paul's, Walsall, later replaced. A local practitioner, Joseph Ireland, was responsible for the dramatic, temple-shaped St Mary the Mount (RC), Walsall (1825–27). Another local architect, Isaac Highway, designed some borough churches at the beginning of Victoria's reign, including St John's, Walsall Wood (1837) and St Peter's, Stafford Street, Walsall (1841). A younger contemporary of his, William Horton, was responsible for All Saints Moxley (1851) and Holy Trinity, Short Heath (1855).

Of the 'big names' of the Victorian period, Gilbert Scott was responsible for several structures in Great Barr Park in the 1850s, of which two gate lodges and the 'Chapel' of the Hall remain. Anthony Salvin undertook some extensions at St Mary's, Aldridge, and Ewan Christian restored the chancel of St Matthew's, Walsall. John Loughborough Pearson designed the replacement St Paul's, Walsall, built (but without the intended spire) in 1891–93.

The rapid expansion of industrial Walsall following the arrival of the railway gave employment to several architectural practices, including those of H.H. McConnal, F.E.F. Bailey, Samuel Loxton and Henry Lavender. Of these, Bailey was perhaps the most prolific and accomplished, using terracotta detailing richly and effectively. The work of these architects survives in several works buildings, chambers and schools. However, the wider connections of the Established Church brought in J.E.K. Cutts of London, who designed both St Andrew's, Birchills (1887) and St Mary's, Palfrey (1902). C.W.D. Joynson of nearby Wednesbury designed a number of Methodist chapels in the south-west part of the borough during the Edwardian period, combining cream terracotta with fierce red brickwork and heavy, rich roof trusses.

In 1902 James Gibson of London (a pupil of T.E. Collcutt) won the competition for the design of Walsall Council House in Lichfield Street. His sculptor partner was Henry Fehr ARA. The result was a building of considerable interest and distinction, with a comprehensive array of bas relief sculpture. Gibson was also responsible for the Central Library next door.

The Wolverhampton-based firm of Lavender and Twentyman (later Twentyman Percy) was responsible for three important churches – St Gabriel's, Fullbrook (1939), All Saints, Darlaston (1952) and Emmanuel Bentley (1956). The practice's principal designer was Richard Twentyman, who worked in collaboration with the sculptor Donald Potter, a pupil of Eric Gill. In 1951–52 Geoffrey Jellicoe designed the Memorial Gardens, St Matthew's Close and St Matthew's church hall on a cleared site adjoining St Matthew's church, Walsall. This group of buildings has a particular claim to fame, being amongst the first UK examples of the so-called 'post modern' style.

Finally, Walsall was put on the modern architectural map by the New Art Gallery, the architectural competition for which was won by Caruso St John.

THE SIX TOWNS

The present Metropolitan Borough is an amalgamation of six different towns with their hinterlands – Aldridge, Bloxwich, Brownhills, Darlaston, Walsall and Willenhall. Each town has a decided character of its own.

Aldridge

The Anglo-Saxon meaning of 'Aldridge' is 'ridge with alders'. A spur runs north from Barr Beacon, dipping and then rising slightly. The medieval parish church of St Mary the Virgin is sited at the top of this rise, marking the focus of the medieval settlement. The High Street runs towards the church from the west. Six or seven ancient routes converge on the settlement, the modern town having expanded along them. With one exception. The north-east quadrant retains its original Georgian interface with the surrounding countryside. By some quirk, the settlement never expanded beyond the ancient back lane represented by Noddy Park Road. The footpath north out of The Green runs along an ancient hedge past the sports ground and joins the entirely rural Hobs Hole Lane, a hollow way.

The twentieth century has treated Aldridge cruelly. The High Street was entirely redeveloped in the 1960s, being replaced by a run-of-the-mill shopping centre. A number of half-timbered and Georgian buildings were destroyed. In addition, a new 'inner bypass' was broken through round the north side of the High Street, cutting deep into the grounds of the eighteenth-century Manor House, destroying its setting.

The might of industry: the south frontage of Shannon's Mill, George Street, Walsall, dating from 1887 onwards. Note the two water towers, one boilerhouse, tall chimney and a massive obelisk-shaped ventilator.

What has survived is the enigmatic public open space called the Croft, immediately to the south-west of the church. It has never been ploughed in modern times and its uneven surface suggests a hollow way aligned on the church tower and an assortment of house platforms. One dry summer, a strange, boat-shaped parch mark appeared on the grass. There surely must be much of archaelogical interest awaiting discovery here.

Aldridge is notable for its Georgian houses, there being five significant specimens – Shutt Cross House, Cedar Court, The Moot House, The Manor House and The Shrubbery, indicating that the rural and airy site was attractive to the entrepreneurs of the early Industrial Revolution in Birmingham to the south.

Bloxwich

The M6 motorway passes Bloxwich three quarters of a mile to the west. From that point of vantage, it is clear that the town is built on top of a shallow but recognisable hill. Bloxwich is also sited on a crossroads, where the ancient route from Walsall to Stafford meets the Wolverhampton-Lichfield Road.

The centre of the modern town is formed by the High Street. At either end of the High Street are two green open spaces. The southern end, Elmore Green, is an extension of All Saints churchyard, which has, unusually, a ha-ha along its eastern boundary. The northern end was once a patch of common called Short Heath, later converted to Bloxwich Park in honour of Queen Victoria's Golden Jubilee. A few much-altered eighteenth-century cottages overlook the park, indicating its comparative antiquity as a public open space. The Turf Tavern in Wolverhampton Street (also overlooking the park) is a traditional public house last altered at the beginning of the twentieth century.

The character of the High Street is very largely Victorian, despite much alteration. There has been no major redevelopment, but Bloxwich remains a lively retail centre with a market on back land to the west. Bloxwich's industrial specialism was the manufacture of awls, but few traditional workshops survive – one being on Park Road. In the Park, there is a cairn constructed of anvil-stones, specially slotted boulders used as tools for the trade.

The Midland Railway reached Bloxwich in 1858, passing to the west of the town centre. The station has recently been reopened. Because of the topography, the Wyrley and Essington Canal does not enter the town. Instead, it abruptly reverses course at Sneyd Junction to the west, and takes a deep and wide loop around Bloxwich to the south.

Brownhills

The label 'Brownhills' is modern. The ancient settlement name was 'Ogley Hay' – 'clearing belonging to Ocga'. 'Hay' refers to the local land-owning family. The community almost certainly owes its existence to being on a significant crossroads. Chester Road, the Anglo-Saxon herepath running along the Shire Oak ridge, comes in from the south east. It crosses the ancient Wolverhampton-Lichfield through route, running north-east, at Brownhills. Brownhills High Street is part of Chester Road. It has a slightly 'wild west' feel to it, being the only shopping street, straight, quite wide and with only low buildings on either side.

Coal seams are close to the surface and Brownhills Common, to the north, is said to contain traces of medieval bell pits. The presence of coal explains the arrival of the Wyrley and Essington Canal in 1797, looping around the south of the High Street along the contour line. The huge

Chasewater Reservoir to the north was opened in 1800 to supply water for the canal. In 1850, the feeder channel was widened to take narrowboats to the collieries next to the reservoir, creating the Anglesey Branch, which runs around Brownhills to the east. Along the Anglesey Branch is Ogley Junction – the head of a flight of locks that took the Wryley and Essington 'main line' down to the Coventry Canal at Huddlesford near Lichfield. Unfortunately, Ogley Locks were closed in 1954. The Anglesey Branch demonstrates that Brownhills actually tops a shallow hill, the waterway being cut into its slope.

The South Staffordshire Railway reached Brownhills in 1849, running in a cutting under the west end of the High Street. A siding ran from the station to a pair of canal basins for the transhipment of coal. One of the basins, with its sandstone retaining wall, is still there.

Brownhills contains one item of formal town planning. Church Road and Vicarage Road are precisely aligned on St James's church (Gothic, in crumbling

Former Brownhills Vicarage, Vicarage Road, Brownhills. It was probably built in 1851 to the design of architect G.T. Robinson of Wolverhampton, who was responsible for St James's church next door. A vigorous and lively Gothic design, using a purple brick characteristic of the time.

sandstone, G.T. Robinson architect, 1851). Church Road side-steps to the south of the churchyard linking the two alignments. This section of roadway preserves some unusual blue clay 'kerbstones'.

Darlaston

Darlaston is actually a hilltop settlement. The ground rises gradually on all sides to a summit crowned by St Lawrence's church. The church spire, because it is on comparatively high ground, is a very conspicuous local landmark. The original Anglo-Saxon meaning of Darlaston is 'Deorlaf's homestead'. The site is a more modest reflection of Wednesbury next door to the south, where two church spires crown a steeper and higher hill.

The town focuses on King Street to the south of the church and Church Street to the north, a rather bendy alignment running approximately north-south, indicating organic settlement growth with little or no conscious town planning. The through route from Walsall (to the east) and Bilston (to the west) runs approximately east-west at the south end of King Street. Camp Hill (to the west of Church Street) appears to be a medieval back lane.

Town growth was piecemeal. The London and North Western Railway ran a rather unsuccessful branch line in a cutting immediately to the east of the centre. The tracks have long since been lifted and the cutting is now a linear extension to Victoria Park. At the end of the nineteenth century a new civic quarter was created along Victoria and Crescent Roads, with the Council House, Post Office and Police Station, with the (very small) Victoria Park and a group of villas. The three main civic buildings are of architectural quality and make a good group.

James Bridge Station was opened on the Grand Junction Railway at the bottom of the slope to the east. The modern Station Road refers to this station and not the short-lived passenger station on the L&NWR branch in the town centre. Station Street became the focus of the large-scale manufacture of nuts and bolts (Darlaston's particular specialism) and several good quality late Victorian and Edwardian industrial buildings survive.

The late twentieth century has not served Darlaston well. The town withered and died as a retail centre, the west side of King Street was redeveloped, and much of Pinfold Street is unoccupied and ruinous.

Walsall

The largest of the 'six towns' is Walsall itself. It is the only one of the six to have the benefit of a full archaeological appraisal of its development. Like Darlaston and Wednesbury, it began life as a hilltop settlement. St Matthew's church stands on a narrow summit, with very steep slopes on three sides. Until the beginning of the twentieth century, the church was surrounded by a tightly packed 'old town' on the top of the hill. The present High Street, running north-west from the steps leading up to the west door of the church, is a medieval planned settlement contemporary with the market charter of 1220. The original section of the High Street is wide and straight, with regular burgage plots traceable. As the medieval town prospered and expanded, Digbeth continued the line of the High Street down to the small river running through the valley bottom. The modern The Bridge public square marks the place where the river was crossed. The medieval town then climbed up the other slope beyond the bridge on what is now Park Street. Burgage plots can be identified at Park Street too.

Upper Rushall Street and Peal Street, running north and south respectively from the bottom of the Church Steps, indicate the ancient routes to Lichfield and Wednesbury. Ablewell Street is a late medieval 'bypass' of the medieval town running round the north side of the hill top towards the bridge across the river.

The present Church Hill is partly artificial, terraces being cut out of it by limestone quarrying. (The industrial development of Walsall is described in Chapter 1). The Walsall Canal of 1799 became the focus for an iron-working quarter. The South Staffordshire Railway of 1847–49 was responsible for the formation of a leather-working quarter around the station.

Lichfield Street and Bradford Street date from the 1820s, and were originally lined by stucco villas and terraces. Larger detached villas were built further out from the town. Because the industrial area of the town was to the south and west, this meant, unusually, that the well-to-do residential areas were to the east, even though this meant that they were downwind of the smokes and smells.

Church Hill was cleared before and after the Second World War and the Memorial Gardens, St Matthew's Close and Church Hall, to the designs of Geoffrey Jellicoe, replaced the 'old town' on the hilltop. The Georgian and Victorian High Street and Digbeth were destroyed in the 1960s to make way

Lower Rushall Street, Walsall; a Georgian 'ribbon development' along a medieval street frontage. These houses were progressively taken over by the Eyland Buckle Works which occupied the land at the rear, for storage, office and light manufacturing use. The fourth house from the left had its two eighteenth-century upper floors amalgamated into one in the nineteenth century. The fifth unit from the left is a wholly industrial insertion with a ground floor coach arch serving the works at the rear. The terrace was gutted of its original interiors during conversion to housing association apartments.

for a shopping development. In recent years, with the arrival of the bus station and New Art Gallery, change has taken a turn for the better.

Willenhall

Church Walk footpath runs down the west side of St Giles' parish church. At one point there are brick walls on either side of the path. These walls are in fact the parapet of a bridge over the River Tame – now hidden from sight inside a culvert in an attempt to control flooding problems. This bridge may be a key to the origin of Willenhall as a settlement on a river crossing. The present St Giles' church replaces a medieval chapel-of-ease and almost certainly marks the focus of the early medieval settlement.

The street name 'Moat Street', at the north end of the present town centre, suggests the existence of a medieval moated manor site. The modern town centre is focused on Market Place, well to the north-west of the parish church. The disassociation of Market Place and church suggests that the centre is a separate piece of medieval town planning aligned on, and at the gates of, the manor. Certainly, Willenhall centre is laid out to an east-west and north-south grid, with a prominent back lane identifiable in Gower Street, Upper Lichfield Street and Cheapside. Burgage plots are traceable.

Whilst twentieth-century attrition has taken place (including the north-east corner of the Market Place), Willenhall centre retains its traditional built form, with occasional surviving seventeenth-century elements embedded in Georgian and Victorian construction. A particular feature is the dense network of pedestrian alleyways running east and west out of the Market Place. One or two of those notorious Victorian public health hazards – the residential 'closes' – still survive to some degree. And virtually all town-centre backyards retain some form of industrial workshop or other. The traditional local door-lock industry was often on a very small scale and

29 Bradford Street, Walsall. This is the end pavilion of a large Regency stucco terrace built by speculator John Eglington after 1832, shortly after the opening of Bradford Street. This end pavilion does not follow the usual architectural rules as the rusticated ground floor has pilasters! The upper floor pilasters have Corinthian capitals. No. 29 was the birthplace of the Late Victorian comedic writer Jerome K. Jerome. There is a little museum inside.

132 Lichfield Street, Walsall, built by John Walhouse, lord of the manor, in 1831, for his personal occupation, the first house to be built in the newly laid out street. It is a fairly modest Regency stucco design, with Corinthian pilasters and a parapet. The original main entrance was round the corner to the left. The present front door is probably a 1940s conversion from a window.

involved much outworking. So backyard workshops were viable right into the twentieth century. I visited one in the 1980s, shortly before it closed.

The New Road, a turnpike of 1820, bypassed the centre just to the south. The Grand Junction Railway, with a station, just to the south of New Road, arrived in 1837. A second railway, originally the Wolverhampton and Walsall Railway Company, was installed in 1876; it ran in a cutting to the north of the town centre, beyond Moat Road. No canal ever came close to the town centre.

The town has spread widely to the west, north and east, with much of industrial history interest, particularly to the east.

Other Settlements

Other, and smaller, settlements also have distinctive characters of their own. Bentley lies immediately to the west of the M6 on the north side of Junction 10.

Miss Jane Lane, daughter of the house at Bentley Hall, achieved fame in the seventeenth century as one of the helpers of Charles II during his escape after defeat at the battle of Worcester. She took Charles to his next place of refuge on the back of her horse, disguised as her manservant. Bentley Hall was demolished and rebuilt. The replacement hall was then demolished in its turn and overlaid with colliery spoil, landscaped to create an artificial summit. On the highest point today is a boulder surrounded by railings, erected as a monument to the site of Bentley Hall. The summit is now occupied by Emmanuel church of 1956. (See Chapter 10 for further details). The church was a benefaction of Alfred Owen, managing director of the Rubery Owen motor components firm. Two fragments of the old settlement remain – a battered seventeenth-century brick farmhouse immediately next to the Black Country Route and the early nineteenth-century Bentley House, also originally a farmhouse.

Great Barr is split between the neighbouring Metropolitan Boroughs of Sandwell and Walsall. The built-up part lies in Sandwell, leaving just the parish church of St Margaret, with a farm and cottages opposite, in an almost wholly rural setting on the Walsall side of the boundary. This is an ancient manorial site with some large field banks surviving from a deer park pale. The valley to the south-east of the church is the derelict Great Barr Park, laid out by Humphrey Repton at the beginning of the nineteenth century. Deep in the trees at the bottom of the valley is the wreck of Great Barr Hall (see Chapter 3).

Moxley, in the far west of the borough, is split in two by the Walsall Canal. On the east side of the waterway is the principal local landmark – the spire of All Saints church. On the west side is Moxley High Street with one or two Victorian buildings, including the former All Saints Vicarage. Away from the 'centre' to the south, though, along the A4098 Great Bridge Road, there is a small concrete obelisk in the corner of a playing field. It commemorates John Wilkinson's opening of the first Black Country blast furnaces nearby. The pub on the opposite corner is called the 'Fiery Holes' for this reason!

Pelsall is marked out by a huge common in the middle of the village, contracted at the mid-point to a 'waist' at the main shopping area. The village centre in medieval times was at the west side and moved over towards the east in the nineteenth century following the relocation of the church to a new site.

Rushall is in fact two settlements. Old Rushall is at the point where the urban sprawl of Walsall meets the countryside. There is a group formed by the medieval fortified manor house (a Scheduled Monument), a large sixteenth-century stone barn, and the Victorian St Michael's parish church. This group is at the end of a cul-de-sac off the beaten track. It is one of the borough's most important architectural secrets. New Rushall is on the main A461 Lichfield Road about three quarters of a mile to the north. There is a much-altered late seventeenth-century brick farmhouse, a fine pair of late Victorian almshouses with barley-twist chimneys and an operational 'tin tabernacle' – Christ the King, a chapel-of-ease to St Michael's, Old Rushall.

Above: Former Farmhouse, New Rushall. This much-altered, late seventeenth-century building preserves three steep brick gables from the time of its original construction, along with a classic upper string course.

Opposite: 3 Doveridge Place, Walsall. This late Georgian (probably 1820s) terrace is a great secret, being invisible from the street. The end house presents a blank side wall to Sandwell Street. All the surviving houses in the terrace have three-bay three-storey main frontages facing south. There is a fine view, the terrace being set high up on the Church Hill ridge. Some houses retain inner security shutters that slide into position vertically. Henry Newbolt, the poet, was born in the now-demolished end house.

HOME

Walsall is 'home' to something like a quarter of a million people. The twentieth-century architect Le Corbusier once remarked that 'a house is a machine for living in'. But, to most, the home is more than that. However small, it is the private palace on which care and attention is lavished. It is the place where we sleep, eat and relax. Usually, comfort and amenity matter more than architectural distinction. And, yes, there is a definite compulsion to 'keep up with the Joneses'. Why else should every second house display the chunky austerity of white UPVC glazing?

The borough's largest and grandest house is uninhabited. It is the wrecked shell of Great Barr Hall, tucked away out of sight in its own secret tree-lined valley within earshot of the immensely busy M6. Built in the wedding-cake style of architecture known as 'Strawberry Hill Gothic', the hall was assembled by three generations of the Scott family. Joseph Scott first built it in 1777 over the cellars of an earlier farmhouse, and called in Humphrey Repton, the then fashionable landscape architect, to plan the grounds, including two large ornamental lakes. His son Edward enlarged the hall and his grandson Francis added a Victorian Gothic chapel. Francis died young, and the hall was then stuck in a time warp until the death of his formidable widow in 1910. The improbable buyers of the estate after Lady Scott's death were the local Board of Guardians, who converted the hall into a 'colony' for the mentally ill, building a grand new Neo-Georgian mental hospital in the more far-flung reaches of the park. The hospital, in turn, passed its 'sell-by' date, and was progressively disposed of in parcels, the hall being bought by a property speculator who carried out various

Miner Street, Birchills, Walsall, a street of terraced houses dating from around 1900. The tiny houses are at the back of the pavement. Each has two rooms on each floor, with a rear extension containing a kitchen and a further bedroom. The front doors open directly into the front parlours. Construction is in brick with painted stone sills, lintels and keystones. The roofs are slate. The houses in Miner Steet have kept their original chimneys.

Great Barr Hall. The photograph was taken in 1991, when interim repairs were under way. The 'chapel', built to Gilbert Scott's design in 1859, is to the right. Gilbert Scott was no relation to the client, Sir Francis Scott Bart. Architect and client first met in Venice! Much of the stucco, Gothic, frontage visible in this picture was commissioned by Sir Edward Scott Bart, in the 1840s. The section of first-floor frontage immediately to the left of the chapel is probably part of the original hall built in 1777 by Sir Joseph Scott Bart.

29

preparatory works before going into liquidation. The end of the story is not yet known, hall and hospital growing ever more ruinous as time passes without any good news.

One of Walsall's best-kept secrets is Rushall Hall. It lurks out of sight at the end of a fairly ordinary suburban street, well off the beaten track. In fact, it is a small medieval castle. A battlemented wall with an arched gatehouse surrounds a very private garden. In one corner is the present house, a mixture of the seventeenth century and the mid-Victorian. The house is very much occupied and lived-in.

The White Hart at Caldmore Green began its life as a small manor house, built in brick on the site of an older manor house around 1670. Converted into a pub in the Victorian period, it miraculously survived a period of dereliction and is now housing association flats.

The towns of Aldridge and Willenhall still possess some large Georgian houses as signs of their past. In Aldridge they stand comfortably in mature gardens and people live in them. In Willenhall, they have long since been taken over for shop and office use and form part of the street scene in the town centre.

Rushall Hall; a view of the approach to the gatehouse, a fifteenth-century insertion into a thirteenth-century curtain wall. The dwelling house is off the picture to the left, a mixture of the seventeenth-century and early Victorian design.

White Hart, Caldmore Green, Walsall. It was purpose built as a manor house for George Hawe before 1679, in the 'Artisan Mannerist' style, represented by its Dutch Gables. The roof timbers visible in the attic have been recycled from a large timber-framed house, probably the earlier building on the site. The bricks were almost certainly fired from clay dug out from the cellars. They were extremely well-fired, giving them good weather resistance. The house became a pub in the mid-nineteenth century and fell upon hard times after a fire. It was compulsorily purchased by Walsall MBC to assure its preservation, and was repaired and converted to form housing association flats.

The arrival of the canals led to expansion in the size of the community, reflected in several stucco terraces and detached villas of the early nineteenth century. Two of these villas are now schools – Mayfield in Sutton Road and the present Blue Coat Infants School, Hanch Place, both in Walsall. There are two stucco terraces in Bradford Street Walsall, and another in Grove Terrace. Very little humbler housing has survived from the pre-1850 period, though there is one attractive block in Sandwell Street, Highgate, Walsall.

The terraced house is characteristic of the second half of the nineteenth century, right up to 1914. Despite much redevelopment in the second half of the twentieth century, they are part of the 'urban sprawl' of Bloxwich, Darlaston, Walsall and Willenhall. The standard pattern involved a building one room wide and two rooms deep, with a rear wing, usually two-storey. Stairs ascended between the front and back rooms. The smallest houses had a front door opening directly into the front room. Those slightly larger had a separate hallway. Cellars under the front room were common. Front bay

Left: A mid-eighteenth-century town house, Market Place, Willenhall. This grand frontage has end pilasters and carved stone first floor lintels, as well as a bracketed eaves cornice. The house was split into two and converted into shops around 1900, when the right-hand (sixth) bay was added in a matching Georgian style to take a staircase for the second unit. Some of the upper-floor rooms contain the original ceiling plasterwork.

Below: The 'Avenues Estate', Brownhills. Laid out by Brownhills UDC in 1922, all the original detailing – windows, doors and door canopies – has been lost. However, the overall shapes and the carefully planned layout survive

Shutt Cross House, Walsall Wood Road, Aldridge. A typical 'Staffordshire Farmhouse' built to the standard formula of three storeys and three windows wide, with end stacks and a centre door. It was probably built in around 1750, and 'gentrified' early in its life with the exodus of the wealthier from Birmingham to the south.

windows might or might not appear. Ornamentation was usually limited to painted stone windows and door lintels.

Darlaston in particular has a number of more elaborate semi-detached houses dating from the Edwardian period, with stained glass and terracotta decoration, as well as quite elaborate woodwork.

After the First World War there were two important new phenomena – the first council housing estates and, secondly, the ubiquitous commercial 'semi' built to a standard England-wide pattern. The first council estates built by Walsall County Borough involved a small range of standard designs, either semi-detached pairs or 'triplets'. The original windows were casements with small panes, giving an attractive cottage-like appearance now almost entirely lost through the use of bland UPVC glazing. A particularly interesting small estate was built by Brownhills

Police House, Dartmouth Park Avenue. Walsall County Borough built a series of Neo-Georgian police houses in the early 1950s. Almost all of them are semi-detached. This specimen, in Dartmouth Avenue, Coalpool, is one of only two to be built as detached houses.

RDC in 1922. This was 'The Avenues', using a mixture of Neo-Georgian and picturesque detailing. Layout was to a tight formal plan with carefully placed houses. Removal of the original detail has largely wrecked its appearance but the layout is still there. Interspersed amongst the estates are the larger 'police houses'. Those of Walsall were to an elegant Neo-Georgian design, with sash windows, pedimented doorcases with fanlight and steep pantiled roofs.

The 1950s marked a second phase of council estates, to carefully designed informal layouts with much greenery. Those of Walsall County Borough had steel casements, pantiled roofs and distinctive copper flashing, a particularly good example being Beechdale, near the motorway between Walsall and Bloxwich. Form involved extended terraces, with conspicuous arches giving rear access. Old Hall Estate, Bentley, by Darlaston UDC, included many Neo-Georgian semis with sash windows as part of its first phase. Architecturally, the most interesting house of the post-Second World War period is Geoffrey Jellicoe's cottage in the corner of the Memorial Gardens, Church Hill, Walsall. This is a rendered cube on a brick plinth, part-supported by pilotis, with a balcony on each of the four faces of the cube. A pyramid slate roof with a central chimney peeps above the cube parapet.

Public housing took a new turn in the 1960s. Large areas of terraced housing in Bloxwich, Darlaston, Walsall and Willenhall were flattened and replaced by tower blocks. In Walsall this was particularly unfortunate as several of the new tower blocks were sited high up in the hilltop area known as The Chuckery, wrecking the town's skyline.

Old Hall Farm, Old Hall Lane, Great Barr. The finest survivor of a small group of four half-timbered buildings tucked under the west slope of Barr Beacon. Old Hall was the seat of the Scott family, the local lords of the manor, before Joseph Scott moved down the valley to the present Great Barr Hall. Old Hall, dating from the seventeenth century, was once a much larger house, being cut down, probably at the beginning of the nineteenth century, into the smaller farmhouse that it is today.

Good quality private housing design post-1945 is conspicuous by its absence. Modern speculative housing continues to be built apace, but to standard UK-wide 'identikit' designs and layout, that do not add any visual value to the overall townscape.

Bridgeman House, Pleck Road, Walsall. An Early Victorian brick and stucco villa, with a strong Neo-Classical flavour. It became the dwelling of the founder of the South Staffordshire Waterworks Company and was passed by him into industrial use by the Waterworks. Surrounded by industry, it is now offices for steel stockholders.

Above left: A 'Moderne' villa, dating from the 1930s. Sited in Skip Lane, Great Barr, it features a bow-fronted staircase turret with a two-storey window as its main feature. The roof is flat and the window glazing is steel. It is now the only one of its kind to survive.

Above right: Sandwell Street, Walsall. The houses are probably Early Victorian, with simplified doorcase detailing. They are placed right on to the back of the pavement but are still of some architectural presence. To the right, out of the picture, there is a row of much simpler cottages at right angles to the street. The tall chimneys and pots survive.

Avenue Lodge, Chapel Lane, Great Barr (1854). One of a series of gate lodges designed by Sir Gilbert Scott for Sir Francis Scott Bart, of Great Barr Hall. The carriage drive from Birmingham Road crossed the public Chapel Lane, with a gate lodge on either side. This is the only one of the two that survives. It is a modest piece of work depending on its diapered brickwork and tiling for visual interest. It was recently rescued from dereliction for occupation as a private house.

Above: Henry Boys Almshouses, Wednesbury Road, Walsall. A benefaction by a local brick-and-tile manufacturer, using his own products. Quite a bold Queen Anne design by F.E.F. Bailey, architect, dating from 1887.

Right: St Patrick's Presbytery, Blue Lane East, Walsall (1909), architect Henry Sandy of Birmingham and Stafford. A very high-quality Arts and Crafts house, simple, but with great attention to detail. The guttering leadwork is noteworthy, as are the leaded lights.

St Gabriel's Vicarage, Walstead Road, Fullbrook, architects Twentyman Percy of Wolverhampton, 1957; a simple but elegant house forming a group with the church. The copper hood over the main entrance (in the left gable) is a trademark of these architects' work after 1945.

RECREATION

These days, much recreation takes place within the home. 'Going to the pub' or 'Going to the pictures' are perhaps more minority pursuits than they once were. But amusement and entertainment are what we human beings enjoy, so we do still leave the house and go to other places for our leisure. In the nineteenth and early twentieth centuries, the large, wage-earning populations looked outside the home for much of their recreation.

The Pub

First stop, the 'local', the pub. Then and now, an informal social club, with its community of 'regulars'.

Many of the pubs of the borough began life as farmhouses. Gradually, the built-up area reached and closed round them. Losing their farmland, a new use was needed. This was usually as a pub. The Manor Arms, Rushall has the Daw End Canal at its back door. But the building was there first. Probably built in the seven-teenth century, there are massive timber beams and joists inside, with a curious bar-serving hatch between timber-framing studs. With a small brick barn opposite, it was clearly a farmhouse. In an area intensely industrialised at the beginning of the nineteenth century, with limestone being quarried and burnt for building lime, involving quarrymen, kiln workers and boaters all generating big thirsts, it made business sense for the farm to diversify into selling beer.

The Shire Oak pub at the crossroads of the A461 Lichfield Road and the A452 Chester Road isn't much to look at now. It is a building that has been

The Lake, Walsall Arboretum, with the Edwardian boathouse on the farther shore.

so chopped, changed and refinished in its life that it has lost all character. But it has given its name to the whole area, so it must have been there a long time. It is at the top of a hill, an ideal place for horse and man to take refreshment.

Street markets are a particular feature of the Metropolitan Borough, those of Willenhall and Walsall being the most significant, the latter being the linear descendant of the first market founded by charter in 1220. Thirsty

Manor Arms, Rushall. An ancient farmhouse with the classic early eighteenth-century double-string course. The glazing and render finish are modern, but the building itself is older. Internally, the timber ceiling structure is exposed and is probably from the seventeenth century. Public-house conversion probably took place in the early nineteenth century after the arrival of the Daw End Branch Canal immediately to the rear.

stallholders and their customers gave good business to market taverns. The oldest survivor is probably The Bell at Willenhall, with its half-timbered gable embedded in later, but still Georgian, brickwork. The Green Dragon in Walsall High Street became the place where a tremendous amount of the Georgian borough's business was transacted. However, the built fabric of today's Green Dragon is largely the mid-Victorian shell, gutted and refurbished in the 1980s.

The 'gin palace' followed as the Black Country prospered during the nineteenth century. The finest examples date from around the turn of that century, with the Brown Lion at Pleck, the Borough Arms (now Flan O'Brien's) in Walsall and the Rose and Crown in Birchills.

The twentieth century was another good time for pub building, with the bigger breweries building pubs in their own house styles. Some of them were handsome efforts in Neo-Georgian, others in fashionable Art Deco, The Royal Oak on Chester Road, Brownhills, for example. Finally, the Wharf Bar of 1997 is one of the very few contemporary pubs to have won a design award. The architects were Sergison Bates of London. Unashamedly contemporary in style, the bar overlooks Walsall's canal basin next to the New Art Gallery.

Theatres

Few purpose-built theatres now survive in the Metropolitan Borough. Bloxwich Public Library (1960–64) has its own integral theatre. The most

The Wharf Bar, Wolverhampton Street, Walsall, designed in 1997 by Sergison Bates of London. It is one of the very few modern pubs to have won a design award. The glazed frontage facing the canal basin can be opened up in summer.

Shoepurmarket, Bradford Street, Walsall. This tall, striking brick building is in fact a purpose-built music hall dating from the end of the nineteenth century. Some stained glass survives in the upper windows and there is a fair amount of terracotta decoration. The shop conversion is on two floors and all sorts of fascinating features may survive above the suspended ceiling on the first floor.

significant survivor from the Victorian period is the former Imperial (now a Weatherspoon public house) in Darwall Street. Originally a Temperance Hall, it became the St George's Theatre and then a cinema. Some items of the stage machinery survived the cinema conversion and were recorded by the Metropolitan Borough's museum service before the present public house conversion took place.

The 'Shoepurmarket' shoe shop in Bradford Street, Walsall, is in fact a converted purpose-built music hall, now subdivided internally to provide ground and first floor levels. The gymnasium in High Street, Bloxwich, was also, originally, built as a modest music hall. It resembles a chapel more than anything else.

Cinemas

The cinema became popular and fashionable in the 1920s, not least in the populous (and quite prosperous) groups of communities making up modern Walsall. However, not one of the surviving cinema buildings is in use for its designed purpose. All, with the exception of the Classic in Caldmore which was converted into offices, were converted into Bingo Halls. The oldest extant cinema was the Imperial in Darwall Street, but the finest architectural specimen is the Avion in Aldridge. It is in the 'Moderne' style of the 1930s, with cream and green horizontal tiled stripes externally. The huge stained-glass window of the former tearoom is a feature of the frontage.

Sports Facilities

Deep inland, there was virtually nowhere to swim. Rivers were small, few and full of rubbish. The canals were in commercial use and polluted. Reservoirs needed to preserve good quality water. So the only real opportunities to swim came from artificial swimming baths, both commercial and municipal.

There is one rare survival of a commercial Victorian swimming bath. It is now the museum store at the rear of Walsall's Leather Museum. It was purpose built by the proprietor of the Littleton Street limestone mine, who filled it with the water pumped out of the mine. This very simple building has low walls of limestone rubble topped with a wide timber roof clad in slate and topped by a ventilating timber clerestory.

Bloxwich Swimming Baths, an early twentieth-century municipal effort, also has a slatted timber clerestory along the roof ridge for ventilation purposes. The main municipal baths in Walsall are an uninspiring effort of the 1950s, but

The former Avion Cinema, Anchor Road, Aldridge. The borough's finest surviving cinema building, in the 'Moderne' style of the 1930s. The exterior is clad in terracotta tiles. The huge first-floor window, with its stained glass, was originally that of the cinema café-restaurant.

Gymnasium, High Street, Bloxwich, purpose built as a music hall in 1857. It looks like a Free Church chapel, but isn't. The windows have been mostly reglazed.

the almost brand-new Darlaston Baths are an attractive contemporary design with a curving roof and decorative horizontal timbering.

Public Parks

There was also a widely felt need in Walsall for somewhere to sit and walk in the open air and sun, preferably without spending any money. So there is a borough-wide series of parks and public open spaces.

Walsall town centre's main public park is somewhat inaccurately called the 'Arboretum'. It was first laid out by a private company around a redundant limestone quarry, where the pits had flooded to produce two attractive blue lakes. The majority of trees, however, are quite ordinary, not the exotic types you would expect to find in an arboretum. The company failed to pay its way, and the new park was taken over and run by the County Borough. With its gate lodges and clock tower, its pavilions and boat house, the Arboretum is the most significant public park in the modern Metropolitan Borough.

The Memorial Park in Willenhall and Kings Hill Park in Darlaston were created by the imaginative landscaping of coal mine spoil heaps. But most parks are low-key organisations of path, grass and trees with little of architectural interest apart from a few park-keepers' lodges.

Gate Lodges and Clock Tower, Walsall Arboretum. This is the main entrance to the Arboretum, on the angle nearest the town centre. These, along with other original structures, were designed by the County Surveyor, Robert Griffiths, in 1874.

Sons of Rest Pavilion, Arboretum. This is the largest pleasure building in the park, Edwardian, combining a half-timbered top floor, with open cast-iron balconies to the lower floors.

SHOPS, OFFICES AND COMMERCE

The local economy was in a thriving condition from the time of the arrival of the railways until the collapse of the traditional industrial base in the 1960s. The various local industries served international markets as well as the local populace. All the six main urban centres of Aldridge, Bloxwich, Brownhills, Darlaston, Walsall and Willenhall were characterised by their shops and offices.

The first modern shops were simply the converted front parlours of houses, and some shops like these survive here and there in terraced backstreets. One of the Black Country's very few remaining Georgian shopfronts, a shallow double-bow with a central door, is at the former Ditchfield's bakery in Ablewell Street, accompanied by an array of bracketed signs.

Town centre trading has changed its retailing foci over the years, so that the secondary (or tertiary) retail areas of Walsall in particular have retained a number of original Victorian and Edwardian shopfronts. It is in Walsall too that upper floors over the shops were purpose built as offices, some with splendid timber and iron staircases and tiled stairwell dadoes.

Perhaps the most remarkable single shop is the former Taylor's Music Shop in Bridge Street, Walsall. It was purpose-built as a music shop in 1891, to the design of local architect Samuel Loxton. The building advertised the stock in trade, the whole frontage being faced with low-relief carvings of musical instruments, musical scenes from the Bible and busts of composers, interspersed with sunflowers in pots and scrolls of acanthus. The sculptor was John Lea, one of the tutors at Walsall Art College.

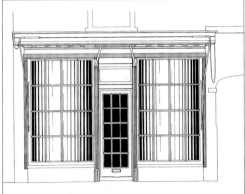

Above: Line drawing of Ditchfield's Bakery shopfront, Ablewell Street, Walsall. Late Georgian double-bow with thin reeded decoration.

Left: Solicitor's Offices, Walsall Street, Willenhall (*c.* 1850). A very unusual ground-floor frontage executed in stone.

Two-storey shopfront, Bradford Street, Walsall. The heavy terracotta on the first floor attempts to conceal the fact that this is an early steel-framed building from around 1900. Without some massive girders inside, the first-floor window would not have been possible. The present ground and first-floor glazing is modern but, inside, there is an intact barley-twist staircase.

Former Taylor's Music Ship, Bridge Street, Walsall. Architect, Samuel Loxton of Walsall (1891). This was a purpose-built music shop. A semi-circular gable has been removed. Apart from that, this amazing sculptured frontage is intact. John Lea, sculpture tutor at Walsall College of Art, was responsible for the carving, which features composers, musical instruments and musical scenes from the Bible – all in bas relief.

47

Bradford Street Arcade, a purpose-built shopping arcade with assembly rooms. The steel and cast-iron framing is partly exposed in this view. Architect, Jonathan Ellis (1897). The top assembly room still exists but is used for storage. It has magnificent coloured tile dadoes and doorcases. There are two malls with glazed barrel roofs inside.

Former Co-op department store, Lower Lichfield Street, Willenhall, in the 'Moderne' style of building, 1930s, with intact upper-floor frontages. The panels below the 'strip' windows use banded brickwork to striking effect.

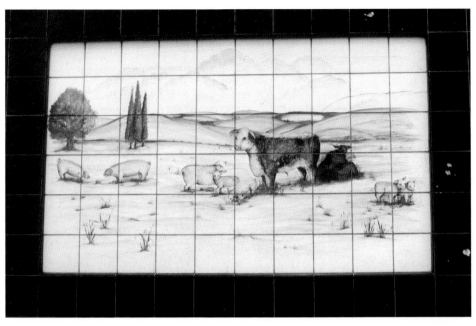

Hand-painted tile panel, Poxton's Butchers, High Street, Brownhills (*c*. 1930), displaying meat 'on the hoof' in a rural setting. The surround is in complementary glossy black tiling.

Above: Art Deco upper floor, Park Street, Walsall. The premises were purpose built for Woolworths in 1933. The elaborate render decorations include stylised lions' masks.

Right: Derelict 'Cleveland Discol' filling station, Park Lane, Fallings Heath, near Darlaston. Surviving sign and pumps next door to a disused nineteenth-century cottage.

Above: Lloyds Bank, the Bridge, Walsall (1904). The building is steel-framed with concrete floor slabs. Only the veneer is Portland stone – or, in the case of the plinth – granite. A purpose-built Edwardian Baroque bank, the bas relief carving on the canted corner is of a straw beehive, a symbol of the sweets of thrift and saving.

Left: Chambers, Darwall Street, Walsall. An elegant Edwardian Free Style building. The entrance door fanlight and the upper leaves of the first-floor sashes have leaded Art Nouveau flowers.

Opposite: Chambers, Bridge Street, Walsall. Architect, F.E.F. Bailey (1890). The building makes the most of its prominent corner siting. Bailey was something of a virtuoso in the use of terracotta, and this building is perhaps his finest. The style is a Dutch version of the popular Queen Anne with elaborate wrought-iron cresting on the roof (part of which once supported a flagpole). The first-floor windows have 'fans' of peacock-feather pattern stained glass. The extensive use of terracotta in this building inspired the choice of the ceramic cladding for the New Art Gallery, Walsall.

Leicester Buildings, Bridge Street, Walsall. A 1920s effort by the then borough architect, in a Neo-Georgian style with a distinct Art Deco accent, most noticeably visible in the clock turret.

COMMUNICATIONS

Communications were vital for the area's economic development 200 years ago, and remain so today. Without a means of transporting bulk loads cheaply, and later, quickly as well, there would have been no industry.

The Borough's Canals

The first canal to arrive was the Wyrley and Essington, opened to through navigation in 1797. It was a classic Georgian 'contour canal', wriggling its way from Wolverhampton in the west to Lichfield in the east by a series of extravagant loops. So loopy was it that boaters called it the 'Curly Wyrley'. The 'loopiness' avoided the high cost of cuttings and embankments. It also linked a whole series of coal and limestone seams, enabling them to be exploited on a large commercial scale for the first time. Entering the modern borough from the west, the Wyrley and Essington passes through the oddly named New Invention to Lane Head. East of Lane Head it goes under the M6 and runs round Bloxwich in a double hairpin, running thence north-east to Pelsall and then Brownhills. It now ends at Ogley Junction on the east side of Brownhills, the flight of locks there having been taken out of use in 1957.

Next to arrive was the Walsall Canal, open to navigation in 1799. It too was a contour canal, entering the modern borough from the south-west at Moxley, running round the north side of Darlaston. East of Darlaston, it was confronted by a natural obstacle – the valley of the River Tame. So, unusually for a Georgian Canal built on minimum capital, there had to be some large-scale

Left: Walsall Canal (1799) at Moxley. This is the view from the Holyhead Road Bridge looking towards the Moxley Road Bridge. In the undergrowth to the right of the towpath, there are the remains of lime kilns.

Below: Footbridge, Ogley Junction, Brownhills, a substantial cast-iron structure cast by the Horsley Iron Works. Used principally by tow horses. From Ogley Junction, the Wyrley and Essington main line connected to the Coventry Canal at Huddlesford beyond Lichfield. It closed in 1954.

Opposite: James Bridge Acqueduct, Walsall Canal (1797), a substantial piece of Georgian engineering taking the canal across Bentley Mill Lane (left arch) and the former course of the River Tame (right arch). The cast-iron date plaque over the centre pier is original.

engineering involving an embankment and an aqueduct – as well as a deep cutting to win the spoil needed for the embankment. The two-arch brick aqueduct is now Grade II Listed. One arch bridges Mill Lane and the other the River Tame itself. East of the aqueduct, the Walsall Canal is bridged by the M6. Immediately to the east of the M6, the canal passes through the traditional industrial landscape of a recently redundant copper refinery. The 1950s refinery office block actually bridges the waterway. The Walsall Canal then heads directly to Walsall itself, terminating at a brand-new canal basin in which is mirrored the twenty-first-century shape of the New Art Gallery.

These two Georgian canals were just the beginning. In 1800 the Daw End Branch Canal was opened, running from Catshill Junction at Brownhills south-east to the important group of limestone quarries at Hay Head and Rushall. In doing so, the Branch passes through the former colliery settlements of Clayhanger and Walsall Wood. So much coal was mined here that the ground level has dropped so enormously that the canal now runs along the top a tall embankment – having been first engineered as a ground-level contour canal! The banks were raised little by little as the ground settled, and the over-bridges were jacked ever higher and higher. East of

Walsall Wood the canal overlooks enormous pits dug for brick earth. Passing to the west of Aldridge, the Daw End Branch becomes quite astonishingly rural in character – hedges, meadows and the deep blue lakes resulting from the flooding of Park Lime Pits. It originally terminated at what is now Longwood Junction at Hay Head.

The unusual thing about Walsall's waterways is that they continued to be developed and extended well into the railway age. The reason? The convenience of the canal network for shipping coal. In 1841 the Birchills Branch of the Wyrley and Essington was linked to the Walsall Canal by a flight of eight locks glorified by the name of 'Walsall Junction Canal'. This enabled coal boats to come straight through to Walsall from the collieries around Brownhills. The Rushall Canal was opened in 1844. It used railway technology, running straight along embankments and cuttings (and down nine locks) from Longwood Junction on the Daw End Branch to the Tame Valley Canal (also of 1844). In 1850 the channel feeding the Wyrley and Essington from the huge Chasewater reservoir was upgraded to form the Anglesey Branch. As late as 1863 the dead-straight Cannock Extension Canal was put in, connecting the collieries at Cannock to the Wyrley and Essington at Pelsall.

Riddian's Bridge on the Daw End Branch Canal, which dates back from 1800. It is typical of several surviving Georgian brick bridges carrying farm tracks over the waterway.

Toll House, New Road, Willenhall (1820). The gate pier is the actual surviving pier of the toll gate on this section of turnpike, which 'bypassed' Willenhall's Market Place. The style is similar to that of Telford's Holyhead Road toll houses, with deep eaves under a shallow roof and cast-iron Gothic windows.

Lock-keeper's house and toll office, Rushall Locks, Rushall Canal (1840). The shallow roof of the cottage has a slightly Italian air.

Side pond and lock, Walsall Junction Canal (1841). In this application, the side pond was not used as a water-saving device when boats were 'locking through'. It simply acted as a spillway so that excess water flowing down from above (e.g. when it rained) bypassed the lock. The water flowed down the circular weir in the foreground. The road bridge in the background is an early twentieth-century rebuild.

Toll Cottage, Walsall Junction Canal (1841), an attractive little building with cast-iron Gothic windows to the toll office and a fish-scale tiled roof.

Stables, Pelsall Junction; a rare survivor of the provision for overnight stabling of tow-horses. The stable proper is to the left, with the 'tower' structure to the right containing a tack room under a hay loft.

Pelsall Junction, where the Cannock Extension (background) leaves the Wyrley and Essington (foreground). The Cannock Extension is dead straight. Immediately north of the junction is a bridge, stable block and lengthsman's cottage.

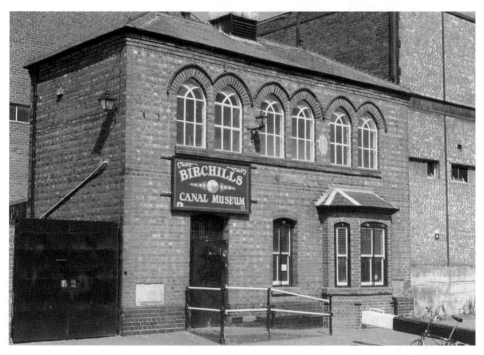

Boatman's Rest, Top Lock, Walsall Junction Canal (1900), erected by the Seamen's and Boatmen's Friend Society to care for the needs of the boaters and their families as the boats queued up to pay the toll and use the locks. There was a chapel on the upper floor and a stables, laundry and reading room on the ground floor. Converted into a Canal Museum, the Mission building is currently closed.

Railway Cutting, Leamore, opened by the Midland Railway in 1858 as part of their Walsall-Cannock line. The bridge in the foreground carries Forest Lane across the tracks. The bridge in the background is not a bridge at all. It is an aqueduct carrying the Wyrley and Essingtom Canal. The aqueduct is an elaborate cast-iron trough with an amount of decoration.

Railways

The first railway to enter what is now the present borough was the Grand Junction Railway of 1837 connecting Birmingham to Warrington. It enters the borough near the present Bescot Stadium (home of Walsall Football Club, alias 'The Saddlers'), parallels the M6 and then passes Darlaston at James Bridge running to the south of Willenhall. At James Bridge, sidings facilitated the large-scale manufacture of nuts and bolts in the factories on the east side of Darlaston.

Walsall was the headquarters of the now-forgotten South Staffordshire Railway, taken over by the London and North-Western Railway early in its history. The first section, terminating at Walsall, was opened in 1847. In 1849, it was extended to the north-west, passing Lichfield. The headquarters building on Station Street, Walsall has been long demolished. However, the railway was directly responsible for the huge expansion of Walsall trade in saddles and harnesses, enabling the industry to bid for, obtain and ship large

London and North Western Railway Departmental Offices, Corporation Street West, Walsall. The L&NWR absorbed the earlier South Staffordshire Railway. This complex building, with its variety of gables and chimneys, in the L&NWR house style, is largely in its original condition.

military contracts. The Crimean War and, later, the Franco-Prussian War, proved to be hugely profitable. Nineteenth-century warfare involved saddles and bridles for horse cavalry and the elaborate traces for horse-traction field artillery. These Walsall had the expertise to supply. It was no accident that a large leather-working quarter grew up immediately to the north of Walsall Station.

Competition from the Midland Railway – with a new line running in from Sutton Coldfield and crossing to the north of Walsall Town and Willenhall added to the borough's railway network, which was complemented by a mosaic of mineral lines criss-crossing the colliery areas in the north. The Midland Railway also opened an extension through Bloxwich to Stafford in 1859 that is still operational.

Roads

A5 Watling Street (the old Roman road) passes north of Brownhills, just within the borough boundary. Streetly, in the east, takes its name from the Roman Ryknild Street, which passes just outside the boundary.

Chester Road, running from Streetly north-west towards Brownhills, seems to have been an Anglo-Saxon herepath or 'military road'.

The basic borough road network is ancient and dates from the time of the earliest settlements. Hobs Hole Lane, just to the north-east of Aldridge, is an excellent example of the medieval 'hollow way', recessed into the landscape as a sunken road by the action of centuries of cartwheels.

Church Hill, Walsall, is closed to vehicle traffic and retains a traditional sandstone cobbled surface. This is very difficult to date, but it is probably nineteenth century in its present form.

An early 'bypass' was New Road, Willenhall. It was a turnpike, laid out in 1820 to take through traffic away from the narrow streets around Willenhall market place. Two toll houses still survive. The more intact of the two, with cast-iron Gothic windows, is just to the west of Market Place.

Cast-iron kerbs are Black Country specialities. They can be found here and there in odd corners, such as Albert Street, Walsall, where they appear in combination with blue brick pavers. Dolerite cobbles, a polished black, are also a local speciality. Malthouse Lane, Willenhall, has a good selection of dolerite and other cobbles. Church Road, Brownhills, has blue clay kerb 'bricks'.

South Staffordshire Tramways Electricity Generating Station, Darlaston Road, Pleck (1892). The Walsall Canal runs immediately to the rear of this building, which was connected to it by a pair of basins used for the delivery of coal to the steam-driven generating plant's furnaces and the removal of ash afterwards. It is an impressive building with a heavy temple pediment.

Walsall Bus Station, the architects Alford Hall Monaghan Morris (2001). The architects were the winners of a national design competition. The main feature is a huge elliptical concrete canopy with skylights, supported on slender steel pillars. This view shows the steps leading down to the public square in the foreground and the two-storey elliptical office suite.

The Motorway

The traditional manufacturing base of the Black Country, which had brought in so much prosperity, finally collapsed in the early 1970s, in response to the impact of worldwide trading competition. At the very same time, the M5 and M6 arrived, severing the western one third of the Metropolitan Borough from the rest, utilising the corridor formed by the flood plain of the River Tame. Today, the part of the M6 passing through Walsall is one of the busiest sections of motorway in the world. In a way, the impact of the motorway system has been to return Walsall to its early roots as a centre for trade – but this time through huge trading parks of warehouses and distribution centres.

A conspicuous feature of the motorway scene is the RAC Control Centre at Bescot, an exotic contemporary design involving an externally suspended monopitch roof.

Buses and Trams

The complex network of railways did not reach everywhere, yet people still needed to travel. Enter the arrival of the trams and, later, motor buses.

Walsall was one of the first English locations for an electric tramway, the second to use to use overhead electricity wires, opened in 1893. The former South Staffordshire Tramway generating station building still survives. Looking rather like a big chapel, it fronts Darlaston Road in the Walsall suburb of Pleck, with an inscription across the front proclaiming its function. The rear abuts the Walsall Canal and there are traces of the canal dock through which coal for the furnaces was delivered. Here and there, some highway lamp-posts were originally the supports for tramwires.

One of the modern borough's most spectacular new buildings is the Walsall Bus Station of 2001, designed by architects Alford Hall and Monaghan Morris. A huge elliptical concrete canopy is supported on slim pillars. In one corner there is a two-storey office suite, also elliptical in plan, tucked under the canopy. The new bus station flanks the handsome Neo-Georgian 1930s transport offices, headquarters of the former municipal bus company.

Manufacture

Raw materials were necessary before manufacture could begin. The borough's geology provided them. Coal, for fuel. Limestone, for building lime and blast furnace flux. Clay – Etruria marl – for bricks and tiles. Iron ore for smelting and thence for all the multifarious uses of iron and steel.

The face of the landscape remains marked by the quarrying and mining of these raw materials. The small spoil heaps of ancient coal mines sprawl over the fields in the north and west of the borough. The battered remains of lime kilns lurk in close proximity to the windings of the canals. Limestone quarrying made the pits that flooded to form the blue lakes of Walsall Arboretum and Park Lime Pits at Rushall. The vast clay holes of Stubbers Green sink deep below the Daw End Branch canal. For many years, derelict limestone mines under the centre of Walsall blighted all new development through the threat of progressive collapse. Much new building (including that of the New Art Gallery) had to await the laborious infilling of all these cavities by pumped rock-paste. The site of Pelsall Ironworks is now undulating grass, with limestone-loving plant species growing on the places where slag from the blast furnaces was tipped. Poured slag forms weird rock formations rising out of the pools in Moorcroft Wood, Moxley.

Much industrial production remained with small family businesses working in the backyard of the house. This still happens today with what remains of the outworking system – patternmaking for castings, elements of saddlery and bridle cutting. Just about every backyard in Willenhall had its workshop, the family producing either whole locks or specialist lock components. One such family business lock workshop has been preserved as

Above: General View of Station Street, Darlaston, looking east towards James Bridge Station, after which the street was named. Saw-toothed factory roofs are visible on either side. The manufacture of nuts and bolts – the Darlaston speciality – was much easier to mechanise than other local products, leading to large factories.

Left: Bradford Ironworks' Tall Chimney, to the rear of Charles Street, Walsall and fronting the towpath of the Town Arm. The early nineteenth century saw the development of an iron-working quarter along the towpath side of the town arm and this tall chimney of 1882 is one of the few physical survivals. Mr J.N. Lester, commemorated on the stone plaque halfway up the chimney, was the managing director of the ironworks. This chimney is reinforced at regular intervals by tie bars secured to tie plates close to the corners.

part of the Lock Museum in Willenhall, but there are many picturesque and now derelict survivors nearby. Whilst Willenhall had the greatest concentration of such workshops, there are survivors in Bloxwich, Darlaston and Walsall too.

The leather industry of Walsall has always been craftsman-based, the processes being too difficult to mechanise easily. So, whilst bigger firms emerged to handle large military saddlery and bridle-cutting contracts, they did so by recruiting teams of saddlers and bridle cutters who continued to work largely by hand, only some of the sewing being simple enough to mechanise. Natural daylight was important for the best craftsmanship and so leatherworks in particular were characterised by their continuous ranges of large windows, backed up by roof lights on top floors. Many of the bigger Walsall leatherworks were architect-designed, with imposing frontages, perhaps the finest being the Brooks Works in Leicester Street immediately opposite the Town Hall. An important landmark, clearly visible to travellers

Right: Workshop, Union Street, Willenhall. Two highly ornate (but non-matching) cast-iron chapel-type windows have here been recycled to glaze a simple vernacular workshop.

Above: Leatherworks, now a riding-wear clothing factory, Charles Street, Walsall. It is of the 'Industrial vernacular', occupying a corner site, and probably erected during the third quarter of the nineteenth century. The office suite is distinguished by the ground-floor sash windows. The continuous rows of windows provided natural light to the work benches. Some reglazing has taken place but this building is otherwise quite original.

Opposite: Brooks Works, Leicester Street, Walsall. Architect, F.E.F. Bailey (1882) in the Queen Anne style. It was purpose built for W. Brookes & Sons, saddlers, bridle cutters and coach ironmongers, specialising in the American market and has a very grand street frontage immediately opposite the former County Court and the Town Hall. There is stone detailing on the ground floor, with terracotta dressings above. Some original timber shop fronts (and their stained glass) failed to survive an unsophisticated ground-floor conversion into a public house.

arriving in Walsall by train, is the Ravenscraig Works of 1903, with its five storeys, water tower and chimney, purpose built for the currying trade – the processing of tanned hides to make them ready for the workbench.

Lock making and the manufacture of nuts and bolts proved easier to mechanise, and big factories were built in Darlaston and Willenhall. Eastern Darlaston in and around Station Street is an impressive nineteenth-century industrial estate.

The biggest traditional factory in Walsall is Shannons Mill in George Street. It was built progressively from 1887 for the rag trade – industrial

Leatherworks, Upper Bridge Street, Walsall, a fairly late nineteenth-century building. Two rows of cast-iron 'fanlight' windows on the upper floors make a calculated contribution to a main street. This building occupies a whole block, with another frontage to the next street. After disuse for many years the frontage block has been converted into a pub.

Ravenscraig Works. Detail of Bridgeman Street frontage showing plinth and shallow pilasters.

Right: Furnace building, Temple Bar, Willenhall. The precise use of this unusual industrial building, on backland, has not yet been identified. Each floor contains a set of ovens, all using the big flue emerging at the back of the ridge.

Below: Albion Flour Mill, Wolverhampton Street, Walsall (1849), a purpose-built steam mill originally built as two blocks on either side of Canal Street. The roadway was later incorporated into the mill and bridged over. The offices occupied domestic-style premises to the right. The left-hand block flanks the Walsall Junction Canal (1841) and includes a covered dock enabling narrowboats to offload grain and load flour in the dry. It has recently become redundant and is now awaiting a new use.

Above: Albion Tannery, Hatherton Street, Walsall, the only surviving purpose-built tannery building, comprising the office suite, warehouse and workspace. It was probably built in around 1850. The office suite is 'coded' by the sash windows to the left of the coach arch. To the rear was a tanyard, fed with water from the local Ford Brook watercourse. The rear elevation has a first-floor oriel window, used by the proprietor to oversee the work. Tanned hides were the staple of the Walsall leather industry.

Left: Ravenscraig Works, Bridgeman Street, Walsall (1903), Bailey and McConnal, architects. It is the largest surviving building of the leather industry in Walsall, and was purpose built as a tanners and curriers premises. Tanning is the process of preserving hides and currying involves their preparation for the workbench. The upper floors were used for drying hides after processing. This was a landmark building by reason of its bulk, water tower and tall chimney.

Above: Leather Works, Bath Street, Caldmore. This building dates from the late nineteenth century. It has small but well-detailed corner works, and a corner entrance door under a corbelled stone bracket that has suffered badly from modern HGV collisions. The brickwork has been carefully modelled.

Right: Homer Pressings, Charles Street, Walsall. It probably dates from the 1890s, purpose built as part of a harness furniture factory. Impressive but quite plain, with variations in the glazing patterns indicating uses, it was demarcated vertically by pilasters at irregular intervals.

Opposite: Crown Works, Marsh Street, Walsall, architect, Samuel Loxton (1889). It was purpose built as a saddlers and bridle cutters and is one of the grandest surviving leatherworks. Now it is under residential conversion with inappropriate concrete slabs replacing the original clay tiles on the roof.

Right: Former Glove Factory, Glebe Street, Walsall; Edwardian, purpose built, with an unusual 'cottage' appearance. The gloves were, of course, leather.

Right: Centaur Works, Green Lane, Walsall, a purpose-built Edwardian saddlery in a simple but elegant Free Style, with a slight Art Nouveau accent.

clothing – employing 2,000 people at its zenith. A large steam plant provided power, two water towers gave a head of water and arrays of big ventilators cleared the atmosphere. On the north slope of Church Hill, Shannons dominates the southern part of the town centre.

Perhaps the biggest factory of all was the Rubery Owen motor components works in Darlaston. It is no longer there. Its site is occupied by modern speculative housing, with just an office block surviving from the huge industrial operation it once was.

Brewing was and is an important local industry, with a thirsty local working population! Highgate Brewery of 1898 is a classic tower brewery still at work producing a traditional recipe mild beer using some of the original machinery. A management buyout from a big brewing combine some years ago has reinstated Highgate as an independent brewery producing an increasing range of traditional beers.

Printing is also a significant local industry, originating from the fact that the production of type required casting skills, readily available in the Black Country. However, the most conspicuous element of the large Walsall Lithographic concern is the 'International Modern' industrial block at the top of Bradford Street, Walsall, with continuous bands of steel windows alternating with brick.

The modern Metropolitan Borough's location straddling the M6 has given rise to a new growth industry of warehouses and distribution centres, almost invariably large steel-framed sheds with sheet metal cladding.

Lockworks, Lower Lichfield Street, Willenhall. This was a purpose-built works occupying a corner site, designed in the local 'industrial vernacular' and now in use as a furniture store.

Lock Museum, New Road, Willenhall. The house dates from around 1850, and the lockworks at the rear slightly later. It was run as a family lockworks by the Hodgson family for many years, then was acquired by a charitable trust for conversion into a museum of the Willenhall door-lock industry. It is a good example of a small, traditional lockworks, and is largely unaltered.

Lock Works, Upper Lichfield Street, Willenhall; late Victorian and, unusually for Willenhall, architect-designed. This view, showing the bold chimneys and terracotta keystones, is taken from the pedestrian Bell Alley.

Opposite: Shannons Mill, George Street, Walsall, a huge flatted factory built in increments from 1887 for the manufacture of industrial clothing. The largest industrial building in Walsall town centre, it had 2,000 employees in 1905.

Right: Shannons Mill, view from Upper Hall Lane, Walsall, showing the boiler-house tall chimney, second water tower and larger pyramid ventilator, as well as the cast-iron eaves catwalk. The whole mill was originally powered by a stationary steam engine driving a series of shafts, from which drive was taken to individual machines by belts.

Right: Highgate Brewery, Sandymount Road, Walsall, a classic tower brewery built in 1898. Some of the original machinery is still used.

79

Above: Walsall Lithographic Company, Wednesbury Road, Walsall, a 'Moderne'-style factory of the 1930s with continuous bands of glazing on each floor, a steel frame and a flat roof.

Left: Victoria Provender Mill, Long Acre Street, Walsall. It was purpose built for the processing of animal feed, both milling and chopping. This view shows the hayloft and stabling wing in around 1890.

PUBLIC SERVICES

Council Houses

There are no 'town halls' in the Black Country. Or rather, the 'town hall' is the main hall for public meetings. It is not the place where public administration is undertaken. This activity takes place in a building called the 'council house'. The borough has five surviving Council Houses – those of Aldridge, Brownhills, Darlaston, Walsall and Willenhall. Only Walsall Council House is now in full use as such. Aldridge now forms part of the police station and Willenhall accommodates the public library and museum. Brownhills is redundant and empty awaiting a new use and Darlaston remains in desultory council occupation.

Walsall Council House is in a class of its own. Aldridge is a modest Neo-Georgian building of the 1930s. Willenhall is an extraordinarily eclectic building dating from as late as 1934, combining elements of Neo-Classical, Arts and Crafts and 'Modern'. Brownhills, well-sited at the west of the main street, is in a striking Neo-Elizabethan style. Darlaston is a good, competent 'Queen Anne' building in dark red terracotta and brick, with leaded glass.

The former seat of local government in Walsall was the Guildhall in the High Street. The present building Italianate (Venetian Renaissance) building was built in 1865–67 to the design of George Nichols in brick and stone with urns and sculptural embellishments, including a figure of Justice and the keystones. Having become redundant after the magistrates courts were moved elsewhere, the Guildhall was converted into a shopping arcade. It is now a restaurant.

The Tower, Walsall Council House, architect, James Gibson (1905), sculpture by Henry Fehr.

Council House, Walsall Street, Willenhall. This very eclectic design was actually built as late as 1935. Detailing is in terracotta and the windows are steel. The main doors and fanlight have stained glass. Inside, there are a number of 'Moderne' features. Now it is occupied by the public library and a small museum.

Guildhall, High Street, Walsall (1867), architect George Nichols, in a 'Venetian Palazzo' style. This building is on the site of the original late medieval borough Guildhall. Little more than the shell now survives. After becoming redundant as magistrate's courts, the building lapsed into dereliction and was eventually converted into a shopping arcade, a commercial failure. It is now occupied by a restaurant.

Brownhills Council House, Chester Road North, built for the Brownhills Local Board in 1882 to the design of their surveyor, John Siddalls. The style is vaguely Elizabethan. The bracketed clock dates from 1911 and commemorates George V's coronation. The bell on the end wall was for summoning the volunteer fire brigade. The building ceased to be in local government use following the amalgamation of Aldrige and Brownhills UDCs and was used as commercial offices. It now awaits a new role.

Former Town Hall, Victoria Road, Darlaston, architect, Jethro Cossins of Birmingham (1887–88). It was built for the Darlaston Local Board and taken over by Darlaston UDC in 1894. It is a large but fairly subdued Queen Anne Revival building with mullion-and-transom windows and leaded panes.

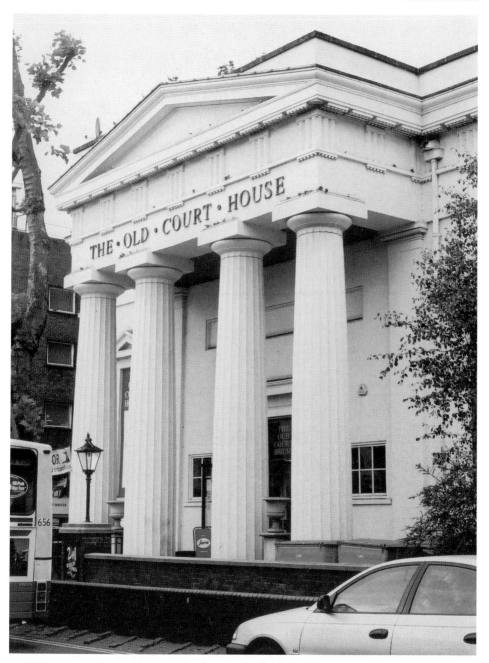

Old Court House, Lichfield Street, Walsall. This building has had a varied history, being built in 1831 as a private subscription library. It was then acquired as a property speculation and converted into courts, becoming the Walsall County Court. After the County Court moved out, it was converted into a public house. It is one of the very few pure Neo-Classical buildings in the borough, with its massive Greek Doric portico in stucco.

Walsall Council House

This is a very high-quality building. The design was the subject of a national competition, won by James Gibson of London. Gibson was a pupil of the Arts and Crafts architect T.E. Collcutt, responsible for one of the most significant buildings of the day, Lloyd's Register of Shipping, London, of 1898. There, Collcutt combined elegant Neo-Baroque architecture with very high quality sculptural embellishment by Sir George Frampton and Frank Lynn-Jenkins. Gibson's winning design reflected what he had learnt from his master, combining the Neo-Baroque with sculptural decoration.

Dating from 1902–05, Walsall Council House combines a symmetrical main frontage with a tall tower to one side. Sculptures crown the portals and pediments, and there is a frieze of low-relief carvings illustrating local trades and manufactures. Gibson's sculptor partner was Henry Fehr ARA, a frequent exhibitor at the Royal Academy. Fehr produced a series of plaster models and panels, which were transferred onto the building by a team of masons headed by George Hardie. Hardie had previously worked for Hamo Thorneycroft and Henry Bates on the very important Institute of Chartered Accountants building in London.

The result is a building that meets London levels of sophistication in design, layout and adornment. Fortunately, the exterior cladding of Staffordshire Hollington sandstone has proved reasonably erosion-resistant, so that the splendour of the carved decoration is largely intact. The Council House is probably the best of its kind in the West Midlands region. Certainly, in design sophistication, if not for sheer sumptuousness, it greatly outperforms that of Birmingham itself.

Schools and Colleges

Historically, Queen Mary's Schools date from 1554. They were endowed from former chantry lands. However, the oldest building now occupied by schools of this foundation is the present Queen Mary's Girls' School of 1850 in Lichfield Street, Walsall. This was designed in a plain Jacobean style by the architect of the new South Staffordshire Railway headquarters office in Station Street, Walsall.

Council House, Lichfield Street, Walsall. This view shows the tower, which contains a
carillon. The architect, James Gibson, won a national design competition in 1902. This
Edwardian Baroque building was erected 1902–05. Henry Fehr ARA provided the
substantial quantity of decorative sculpture that forms part and parcel of the design. The
sculpture, in particular, has elements of Art Nouveau. The exterior is finished in Hollington
sandstone from north Staffordshire, which has proved quite durable.

The next-oldest surviving school building is that built for the former St Andrew's Schools, Hollyhedge Lane, Birchills, in 1855. There is a schoolroom with cast-iron Gothic windows joined onto a modest school house, also with modest Gothic detailing in brick and stone. The school is now in industrial use.

A particularly fine selection of purpose-built schools was created at the end of the nineteenth century. Their design is in the 'Queen Anne' or 'Arts and Crafts' manner with much painted woodwork, complemented by decorative terracotta. These schools were not designed in-house but by local architects. Several were located in the landscape through quite complex towers. Brownhills Schools, Chester Road North and Whitehall Schools, West Bromwich Road, Walsall, are all good examples.

Good quality school buildings continued to be provided in the twentieth century. The present Darlaston Community Association Education Centre at Kings Hill, Darlaston is a sophisticated Neo-Georgian design complemented

Whitehall Schools, West Bromwich Road, Walsall (1899). The architect was probably F.E.F. Bailey of Walsall. The clients were Walsall School Board. It is a large and striking building occupying a whole block between two streets. The style is a dramatised version of the Queen Anne. This particular view shows the tower. Construction is in brick with extensive terracotta detail, all the windows being large, and sometimes elaborate, timber 'grids'.

Kings Hill School, Old Park Road, Darlaston (1931), a very refined and elegant Neo-Georgian building, with matching gate piers and railings. The detailing is a grey terracotta.

by elegant railings. Another good Neo-Georgian school is Moxley Infants, Moxley Road, Moxley, of 1927.

The other school of the 1554 foundation, Queen Mary's Boys, occupies premises dating from 1961–65. The central feature, the school hall, has a lively gabled roof clad in copper, the architects being Sir Robert Matthew and Partners, designers of the Royal Festival Hall in London. Unfortunately, this spectacular modern building is largely invisible to the public, being set deep into its site away from the highway.

Higher education has also made its mark architecturally. Walsall School of Art in Bradford Place, Walsall, dates from 1888. It was designed in the Gothic style by Dunn and Hipkiss of Birmingham. Much of the detail was executed in terracotta rather than stone.

The Walsall Campus of Wolverhampton University was opened in 1963 as the West Midlands College of Education. The architects were Richard Sheppard, Robson and Partners, who created a large, contemporary design building complex of high quality.

School of Art, Bradford Place, Walsall (1888), designed by G. Dunn and W. Hipkiss, architects in a Venetian Gothic style. All the detailing is in a biscuit-coloured terracotta. The royal coat of arms in the apex of the central gable has a polychrome finish.

Queen Mary's Boys' School, Sutton Road, Walsall. Sir Robert Matthew and Partners, 1961–65.

Moxley Infants School, Moxley Road, Moxley, a Neo-Georgian school of 1927. An elaborate fanlight is visible in the end gable. The entrance gate piers have their original gates. All the detailing is in pale fawn terracotta.

Former Brownhills Central Schools, Chester Road North, Brownhills; the architect, G.H. Cox (1893). The client was the Norton Under Cannock School Board. The building is a bold Queen Anne Revival design taking advantage of the prominent corner site, with lively use of dormer and bay window roofs. Now it is Brownhills Activities Centre.

St Giles School, Walsall Street, Willenhall, a boldly gabled Edwardian school executed in orange brick with matching terracotta dressings.

A former school, Midland Road, Walsall. From the late nineteenth century, it is a tall 'château' style building on a small inner urban site. The staircase tower is a striking feature.

Hospitals

The Walsall Poor Law Union Workhouse was built in 1838, in plain brick with a slight Elizabethan accent. As is the usual English pattern, the workhouse infirmary eventually took over the whole complex and was taken into the new 1948 National Health Service as a hospital. Today, only the St John's Wing, used for teaching, survives from the original workhouse. The purpose-built workhouse administration block, architect Henry Lavender, dating from 1898 and constructed in a rich Neo-Elizabethan style, survives on the campus of the modern Manor Hospital, albeit redundant and disused.

Walsall's Sister Dora was the virtual founder of Walsall General Hospital. This was built from 1878 on a site off Bradford Street, Walsall. The hospital became redundant in the 1980s and was subsequently destroyed by residential redevelopment, the only physical survivor being the elaborate brick and terracotta frontage of the former nurses' home, on Wednesbury Road. The architect was F.E.F. Bailey of Walsall and the style 'Queen Anne', though the ironwork of the main doorway is Art Nouveau.

The present Goscote Hospital was built, in a subdued Neo-Georgian style, in 1930 as an isolation hospital. Bloxwich Hospital occupies a converted and extended early Victorian Italianate villa at the south end of the High Street.

Police Stations

The original Walsall Police Station was built as part of the Guildhall 1865–67, round the corner in Goodall Street. The design is Italianate, with painted stucco detailing. It was vacated in 1966 when a new police station opened outside the town centre. It is now a restaurant.

The purpose-built Bloxwich Police Station of 1882–84 was redeveloped in 2000. The replacement building (architects Mason Richards of Wolverhampton) aimed at a high quality design but was let down by a bland choice of facing materials.

The finest surviving Borough Police Station is at Darlaston in Crescent Road. This is an accomplished Edwardian design using cream terracotta detailing on a brick structure. There is an area basement and the original area railings. The style might be described as Neo-Georgian with a heavy Arts and

The late nineteenth-century former board room and offices, Walsall Board of Guardians, Pleck Road, Walsall; the architect was Henry Lavender. This Neo-Elizabethan building was effectively the administration block of the workhouse. Internally, it has fine polychrome tiled dadoes and an impressive board room with a heavily coved ceiling. The workhouse became the present Manor Hospital and this building is now empty and waiting for a new use.

Darlaston Police Station, Crescent Road, Darlaston (1902). It is a very handsome Edwardian Baroque, with all the dressings in cream terracotta. The original wrought-iron railings have survived because there is an area basement behind.

Crafts accent. It forms part of the 'Civic Complex' at Darlaston in association with the Council House and the Post Office.

Willenhall has a fine Neo-Georgian police station dating from the 1930s, executed in brick. Aldridge Police Station, in a rather more subdued Neo-Georgian, incorporates the old Aldridge UDC offices.

Libraries and Art Galleries

The Walsall Library, a private subscription body, was founded in 1800. It moved in 1831 to a purpose-built Neo-Classical stucco building, with an imposing Greek Doric portico, at the junction of Lichfield Street and Bridge Street. This building was converted and extended to accommodate the County Court in 1855. It is now a public house.

George Nichols, the architect of the Guildhall, designed the public library built in Goodall Street, Walsall, in 1859. This was in a slightly exotic Italianate manner in brick with stucco detailing.

The present Walsall Central Library (1905–06) was built in Lichfield Street to a design by James Gibson, architect of the Council House.

Rusticated sandstone contrasts with smooth red brick. The upper windows feature some unusual joinery with 'floating' pediments.

The upper floor of the Central Library was converted in 1973–74 to accommodate the Garman-Ryan art collection, donated by Kathleen, Lady Epstein, widow of the sculptor Sir Jacob Epstein. By the end of the twentieth century, it was recognised that this important collection was not being housed and displayed to the best advantage. There was a national architectural competition for a new art gallery, won by architects Caruso St John.

The resultant New Art Gallery, on a canal-side site off Park Street, Walsall, was opened in 2000. The building is a tower, clad in overlapping slabs of creamy terracotta. The ground-floor finish is stainless steel and the windows are green-tinted. Window openings are irregularly placed and respond to the needs of the galleries within. The ground floor of the building is cut out and cantilevered to create an entrance porch.

Darlaston Post Office, Victoria Road, probably designed by the Office of Works in 1912 to a handsome design in a simplified Neo-Georgian with dressings in stone and terracotta. The frontage retains its matching pair of traditional K6 telephone boxes.

95

Police Station, John Street, Willenhall, a handsome 1930s Neo-Georgian building, executed almost entirely in brick.

Former Aldridge UDC Offices, Anchor Road, Aldridge. Now it is Aldridge Police Station. The building is in a restrained 1930s Neo-Georgian.

Post Office, Darwall, Street, Walsall (1926), designed by the Office of Works. A very
sophisticated and elegant Neo-Georgian design with a Vanbrugh-style 'quirk' over the end ground-
floor openings – a keystone separates the fanlight from the opening below. The mansard roof
with its pedimented dormers is clad in green Westmorland slate. Inside, the modern suspended
ceiling conceals a fine plaster ceiling.

Fire Engine House, Crescent Road, Darlaston, part of the Town Hall complex of 1887–88. A stylish street frontage in brick and terracotta adds to what is essentially a large coach house.

DEATH

Members of the twenty-first-century 'Consumer Society' find it hard to come to terms with death. This inescapable fact of human existence is somehow regarded as a tragedy, a failure of medical science. With earning, spending and enjoyment being the main social objectives, death doesn't fit. It has become the 'great unmentionable' of modern society. But, because it is a part of life, it continues to occur, however much we might wish otherwise. Bereavement is a painful process, sometimes guiltily so. Funerals and memorials are all about responding to the pain of bereavement. A good funeral and a costly memorial help to assuage the inner hurt.

Traditionally, all burials took place in churchyards. But, with population growth accompanying the Industrial Revolution, this became less and less possible. And, before modern hygiene measures were introduced, there were serious epidemics of such diseases as cholera. One such epidemic in Willenhall necessitated the opening of a series of emergency burial grounds, one of which (the Doctor's Piece) survives today, with its battered, crumbling memorial inscription. Some Free Church chapels opened their own graveyards – for example, at Little London Baptist chapel, Willenhall. Similarly, a great new series of municipal cemeteries opened.

Walsall's Queen Street Cemetery, opened in 1857, was once the finest of them all, with the rich memorials erected to the County Borough's great and good – and to Walsall's uncanonised saint, Sister Dora. She was a nun under simple vows and a professional nurse, who ran the cottage hospital, fought disease and patched up the terrible consequences of

Brownhills War Memorial, St James's churchyard, Brownhills. The Celtic cross is in white marble, with its lettering set into polished granite slabs (1919).

industrial accidents, with dedication and determination. However, Queen Street Cemetery has been totally devastated – first by the demolition of the chapels and then by clearance of almost all the memorials to create a smooth, bland greensward. Sister Dora's own headstone, surviving, continues to suffer repeated vandal attacks. Even the cemetery entrance gates are modern replicas.

The oldest of the surviving public cemeteries is James Bridge. This is a borough landmark, sited just to the west of the M6 and immediately south of the Walsall Canal, signposted by the spire of its redundant chapel. Here, the chapel, the keeper's house, the massive Gothic wrought iron gates and a wide range of good Victorian memorials survive. Bentley Cemetery, dating from 1898, is also in good condition, with entrance lodge, gates, railings and chapel as well as its full complement of memorials. Willenhall Town Cemetery has suffered through the loss of its railings in the Second World War and the demolition of its chapel, along with the ravages of Black

Right: Gothic wrought-iron gate, James Bridge Cemetery, Cemetery Road, James Bridge. It probably dates from the 1860s.

Below: Bentley Cemetery chapels, architect, Benjamin Baker (1898). The clients were Willenhall UDC. The chapels are in a plain Gothic style in brick with minimal stone dressings. They conform to the standard layout, with a central coach arch to accommodate the hearse, flanked by Church of England and 'other denominations' chapels.

James Bridge Cemetery chapel (*c.* 1860), with its unusual use of blue engineering brick laid in English Bond. Here is the south-west porch tower with the spire. The chapel spire is clearly visible from the M6.

Rycroft Cemetery chapel (1894), a Lage triple structure in brick and stone. The central chapel was Church of England, and the wing chapels Roman Catholic and Free Church respectively. The chapels became the borough's first crematorium, before that function was transferred to a purpose-built crematorium at Streetly.

Country polluted air and vandals on the stone of its memorials. Even so, what remains is of historic value.

Rycroft Cemetery, Walsall and Bloxwich Cemetery have kept their full complement of memorials. Rycroft, dating from 1894, retains some fine cast-iron railings along its Coalpool Road frontage. The chapel complex at Rycroft is unusual because it is triple, with a large centre chapel and two smaller wing chapels. Some of the openings have quite ambitious carved foliage decoration and there are abstract stained-glass patterns. As with almost all cemetery chapels in the borough, however, these are effectively redundant.

Early twentieth-century land warfare, with its earthen field fortifications reinforced by barbed wire and concrete bunkers, and defended by machine guns, trench mortars and magazine rifle-fire, gave defence great superiority over attack. The only known methods of attack proved hideously costly in human life. Almost every family in the country was affected by the huge casualty lists of the First World War. It was a dreadful, emotional experience that had to be coped with somehow. The erection of war memorials was part of the healing process. These memorials remain today as part of the borough townscape.

Perhaps the Metropolitan Borough's finest war memorial is at Willenhall, with its large, solemn Portland stone obelisk. Walsall has a 'cenotaph', also in Portland stone, capped with a replica of Napoleon's sarcophagus. The architect Reginald Blomfield designed a 'standard' war memorial involving a chunky Portland stone cross on a stepped octagonal plinth, with a bronze sword fixed to the face of the cross. Examples appear at Bloxwich and Rycroft Cemetery. War memorials were also manifested in bronze sculptures – a fully kitted soldier at Darlaston and a bust of Ordinary Seaman Carless VC in Lichfield Street, Walsall. Aldridge has a clumsy Celtic cross in granite.

On top of Barr Beacon, there is an eight-sided domed temple in Portland stone. It is a memorial to the dead of the South Staffordshire Regiment, which recruited in the area. Another memorial to the regiment's dead appears as a stone cross at the side of the steps leading up to St Matthew's church in Walsall.

The hilltop next to Walsall parish church was cleared of its old housing and redeveloped in the early 1950s. One element in the redevelopment was the Memorial Garden of 1951–52. This was a rectangular walled garden with a series of entrance gates, with a lodge house at one end and a chapel under a complex copper roof in one corner. An elegant and beautifully lettered slate roundel, laid almost flush with the paving, records the fact the garden was created in memory of the dead of 1914–18 and 1939–45. The architect was Geoffrey Jellicoe.

Above left: Willenhall War Memorial, Field Street (1919–20). The upright slabs flanking the Portland stone obelisk bear bronze plaques with the names of the fallen.

Above right: The Cenotaph, Bradford Place, Walsall (1920). A fat Portland stone pillar topped by a version of Napoleon's sarcophagus in the Invalides, Paris, with a Union Jack draped over it.

Right: South Staffordshire Regiment War Memorial, Barr Beacon (1920s). A Portland stone rotunda set as a landmark on top of Barr Beacon (227 metres or 745 feet high).

Opposite: Darlaston War Memorial, Victoria Park, Darlaston (1919). It is a bronze soldier in full kit on a tall stone plinth, the sculptor R.J. Emerson of Wolverhampton.

Above: Foundation Stone, Memorial Gardens, Church Hill, Walsall (1951), architect and landscape architect, Geoffrey Jellicoe.

Left: Memorial Gardens, Church Hill, Walsall. Architect, Geoffrey Jellicoe (1951–52). This is the north wall of the enclosed gardens, showing the drop to the street below and the second bay of the remarkable 'chapel' projecting over the street.

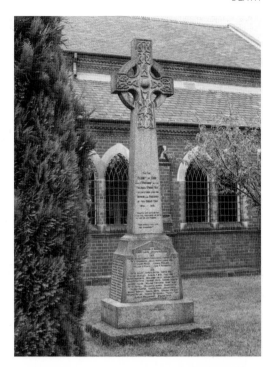

Walsall Wood War Memorial, in St John's churchyard, a granite Celtic cross with leaded lettering.

Rycroft Cemetery War Memorial, a standard design by Reginald Blomfield, architect. The chunky Portland stone cross rests on a tall plinth, with a bronze sword set against the stone cross.

RESURRECTION

The 'Consumer Society', with its acutely materialistic concentration on the gratifications of life before death, resolutely ignores the claims of the world's great religions about life after death, or 'Resurrection'. Four of these religions are strongly represented in the modern Metropolitan Borough, by both worshippers and buildings – Christianity, Islam, Hinduism and Sikhism. The claims of these world religions are strong and assured. Their buildings – churches, mosques, temples – are a silent but very visible reminder of the claims made by the worshippers who use them. They are not always so silent, either, when bells ring!

The place-name 'Walsall' is enigmatic. Its original Anglo-Saxon – earlier spelt 'Waleshale' – bears two possible meanings: 'Sheltered place of (man named) 'Weala' or 'Sheltered place of the Welshman'. If the second meaning is the right one, it refers to the continuing presence of a native British community. Native Britons, after the fall of the Roman Empire, remained Christians. So Christianity in Walsall could pre-date the missionary activities of St Chad (who was resident Christian bishop in the kingdom of Mercia 667–672).

Chad was the effective founder of the Christian Church in Mercia and he systematically organised it on the model of the Celtic Church in the north of the British Isles. He established a series of 'minsters' – communities of monks and priests who ministered to the wide area of country about them. The local 'minster' serving the modern Metropolitan Borough area was St Peter's, Wolverhampton. The 'minster' organisation proved long lasting. Until well into the Middle Ages, Christians were required to be baptised, married and buried at St Peter's. The present network of Christian parishes

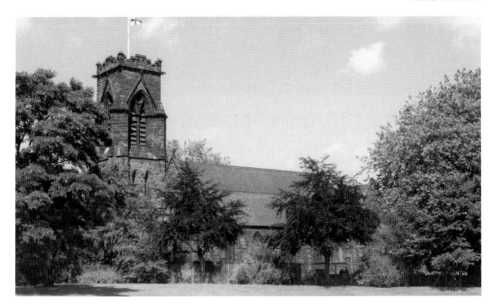

Parish church of St Giles, Willenhall (1866–67), W.D. Griffin, architect, built on the site of a medieval predecessor.

only slowly came into being during the Middle Ages – first as chapels-of-ease to St Peter's and only much later as independent units where baptisms, marriages and burials could take place.

Only two parish churches retain medieval fabric above ground – St Matthew's, Walsall, and St Mary the Virgin, Aldridge. Holy Trinity, Bloxwich, St Lawrence, Darlaston, St Margaret's, Great Barr, St Michael's, Rushall, and St Giles', Willenhall, are Victorian rebuilds on medieval church sites. Whilst Pelsall possessed a medieval chapel-of-ease, the present Pelsall parish church of St Michael is on another site. The stone plinth of a medieval churchyard cross survives at St Michael's, Rushall. Bloxwich too has an ancient churchyard cross – an enigmatic shaft with a ball finial, which probably dates to the seventeenth century.

Georgian Churches

There is only one significant Anglican example of Georgian church building – the nave of St Matthew's, Walsall, designed by the London architect Francis Goodwin 1820–21, with cast-iron columns, huge cast-iron Gothic windows, and a delicate Gothic plaster fan-vaulted ceiling of great refinement. The north

109

St Mary the Virgin, Aldridge, west tower and north aisle. The tower was built around the thirteenth and fourteenth centuries. The lower two stages with local limestone rubble, irregularly banded with red sandstone, are probably thirteenth century. The top stage, executed in red sandstone alone, is fourteenth century. The north aisle is Anthony Salvin's work and dates from 1853.

and south brick walls at All Saints, Bloxwich, do in fact date from 1791–94, but the building's overall character comes from its Victorian transformation.

The former Little London Baptist chapel (now the Mount Olive Apostolic chapel), Willenhall, probably dates in its present form from the early Victorian period 1840–50, but is in a 'Georgian Survival'-style with a pilastered stucco frontage and round-headed windows.

Georgian Neo-Classical design is powerfully represented by St Mary the Mount Roman Catholic church of 1825–27, architect Joseph Ireland, in appearance a pure classical temple with Doric pilasters and end pediments, beautifully sited on top of a steep spur to the south of Walsall town centre. Inside, there is a shallow coffered vault in plaster. Catholic emancipation in Britain only dates from 1829, so the church is historically interesting on this count, too.

Victorian Churches – Anglican

There was a boom in church building in the early nineteenth century, as industrialisation gathered momentum and the urban population rose sharply.

Tower and spire, St Matthew's, Walsall, which date from 1465. The tower received a cosmetic reskinning in Bath stone by Francis Goodwin, 1819–21, the new work including the cast-iron tracery of the bell-stage window. The spire retains its medieval stonework but was in fact dismantled and rebuilt in the 1950s. Despite its quite modest height, the spire is a conspicuous landmark because of the siting of the church on top of Church Hill.

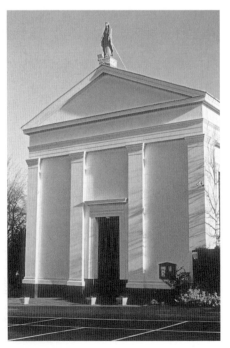

Above: Mount Olive Apostolic chapel, Little London, Willenhall. Founded as a Baptist chapel in 1792, the present stucco-fronted building probably dates from around 1850. An original pediment was removed in 1970 but the interior, with galleries around three sides, remains intact. The chapel is most unusual in the Borough context as it has its own small graveyard.

Left: St Mary the Mount Roman Catholic church built in 1825–27 by architect Joseph Ireland, who was also responsible for SS Peter and Paul Wolverhampton, of the same date.
St Mary's is a pure classical temple in shape. This view shows the west front.

St Peter's, Stafford Street, Walsall, of 1841 (architect Isaac Highway) is a classic Commissioner's church – a vaguely Gothic brick box with galleries. With a Georgian practicality untouched by the spiritual principles of the new Oxford Movement, the orientation is back-to-front – with a plain brick 'west' tower at the east end fronting the street and the chancel to the west.

Architect William Horton of Wednesbury designed two other Commissioners' churches – All Saints, Moxley (1851), and Holy Trinity, Short Heath (1855). Both have a strong Gothic character, using fairly accurate detailing in grey and red sandstone. All Saints has an imposing north-west spire with incongruous clock faces below. Both have steep, inventive timber roofs internally.

St Lawrence, Darlaston, and All Saints, Bloxwich, are oddities in that they have nave galleries set in double-height aisles, whilst being full-blown Gothic in style. St Lawrence has a fine sandstone spire whilst All Saints has to make do with a stumpy pyramid roof on top of the brick west tower. St Anne's, Willenhall (Revd H. Jeavons, 1858) is also an oddity because it is a double-nave design with a tiny west tower between the two nave gables. Yet the chancel opens off the south (and smaller) nave!

St Peter's church, Stafford Street, Walsall. A Commissioner's church of 1841, designed by Isaac Highway it is subdued Gothic in style, built in durable brick. There is a later Victorian Gothic chancel. Only one out of three galleries remains internally. The building is 'back-to-front', with the tower and porch at the east end facing the street. The chancel, at the rear of the site, is to the west.

The present St Paul's, Walsall, replaced an earlier Georgian stucco church in 1891–93. The architect was John Loughborough Pearson, one of the 'big names' in the English Gothic Revival, designer of Truro Cathedral. St Paul's is a late design with several characteristic Pearson trademarks – the face-like label stops, the height with steeply pitched main roof and a small transept chapel apse flanking a much larger chancel apse. Unusually for Pearson, though, the fenestration uses Decorated tracery rather than his favourite lancets. The nave porch was designed to carry a tall tower and spire, but these were never built as the money ran out. St Paul's was radically converted and subdivided at the end of the twentieth century, with an added roof ridge lantern and new stone Gothic entrance doors in the nave and transept frontages.

The real treasure of St Michael's, Rushall, is internal. The walling over the chancel arch and the transept east wall faces is covered by a huge late pre-Raphaelite fresco of angels – artist Reginald Frampton, 1905–06.

The Oxford Movement made an impact on the borough's church building, but not, largely, until the end of the Victorian period. St Michael's, Caldmore, an inner suburb of Walsall, was built in 1871 to the design of an obscure local architect, J.R. Veall. The client was Revd John Fenwick Laing, Walsall's first Tractarian vicar, backed by his family fortune. He belonged to a wealthy Newcastle mercantile family. The exterior is a stodgy, bland effort in soft sandstone. Inside, there are vigorous columns to the nave arcades and the remains of what was once a magnificent decorative scheme, devastated by fire in 1964. The Laing fortune also helped to pay for St Mary and All Saints Palfrey, another Walsall suburb. Built in 1902, St Mary's is an interesting effort in an Elizabethan style with some Renaissance details. The architects were J.E.K. Cutts of London. Following redundancy, St Mary's was acquired by the Greek Orthodox Church.

St Andrew's, Birchills, another Walsall suburb, was also a Tractarian venture. It dates from 1887 and the architect was J.E.K. Cutts (as aforementioned). The building is tall and in brick, in a plain lancet Gothic style. A bell-cote caps the ridge. The roof trusses are inventive and the stained glass is good.

Victorian Churches and Chapels – Other Denominations

Willenhall has a remarkable number of Free Church chapels still in use, albeit not by the original denominations. Little London chapel has already been

All Saints, Moxley, architect, William Horton (1851), a later type of Commissioner's church. For the sake of prestige, a cheap red sandstone was chosen. However, the tower and spire make an excellent local landmark. The clock face gablets at the foot of the spire are a distinctly 'rogue' detail.

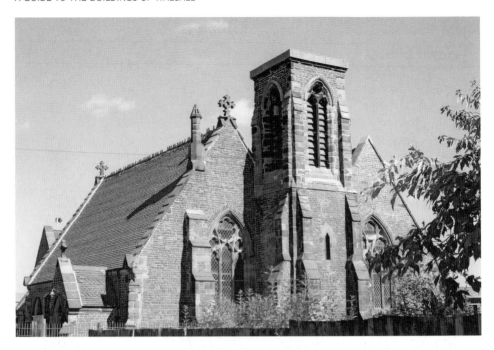

Above: St Anne's, Ann Street, Willenhall, a strange design by the first vicar, Revd H. Jeavons, dating from 1856-58. There is a double nave, with a small west tower in the middle. The church is the only known building to use 'Rowley Rag' dolerite stone in its construction, though all the dressings are in sandstone.

Left: St Paul's, Walsall, architect, John Loughborough Pearson (1891–93). It was built on the site of an earlier 1820s church and boasts a fine pair of apses characteristic of Pearson's work. The strange construction on the roof ridge is a recent skylight associated with the modern multi-purpose conversion of the interior, only part of which is now a place of worship.

St Michael's, Rushall (1856), with tower and spire of 1867–68. James Cranston was the architect. Walling uses limestone rubble, with all the dressings (and spire) being executed in sandstone. The tower has a curious appearance because the tops of the buttresses are at the same angle as the spire broaches. St Michael's was one of the few buildings to suffer damage during the central England earth tremor of 2002. Some stones were dislodged from near the spire apex.

Above: St Andrew's, Birchills, Walsall. 1884-87 by architects J.E.K. Cutts of London. It is a large, tall brick building with Early English lancets. There is a good quality Anglo-Catholic interior with attractive stained glass.

Left: Spire, St Lawrence, Darlaston. The present tower and spire are an 1872 stone recladding (architect, A.P. Brevitt) of an earlier Georgian brick tower.

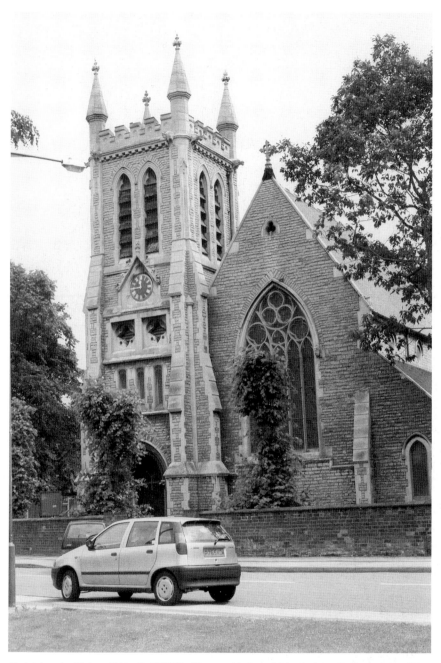

Christchurch, Blakenall Heath (1872). Thomas Naden of Birmingham is the architect. The tower was added in 1882. It is a simple, rather clumsy Gothic design. The walling is in local limestone rubble, the dressings are sandstone.

mentioned. Providence chapel in New Road was built for a local congregation in the 1860s. It is a large gabled brick box with cast-iron fanlight windows. There are galleries round three sides internally.

Trinity Methodist church dates from 1863. It was rebuilt at this date to the design of Samuel Loxton. The result is remarkable, with many features being drawn from the work of Sir Christopher Wren, including the main frontage with its two tiers of pilasters. Internally, the big arches are accurate replicas of Wren's work in London. The main front has odd 'sugar-loaf' domes at either end, which owe nothing to the Wren School.

The former Baptist chapel of 1862 is in Upper Lichfield Street. A stuccoed pediment with supporting pilasters faces the street. Down the sides are two tiers of cast-iron round-headed windows. Inside, there is an original gallery around three sides. Present occupiers are the New Testament Church of God.

The architect C.W.D. Joynson of Wednesbury had a large Methodist practice. Unfortunately, his work in the borough has suffered severe attrition, with the loss of two major Methodist churches, at Pleck and Darlaston, within the last thirty years. King's Hill Methodist church, Darlaston, another of his works, has recently been burnt out and faces a very gloomy future. Joynson designed in a very characteristic manner, using Perpendicular Gothic windows, buff terracotta dressings and bright red brickwork, with Art Nouveau glazing patterns and ironwork. He used massive, ornate hammerbeam trusses to support his roofs. Apart from Kings Hill, the only survivor of his work is the former Sunday school at Darlaston Methodist church.

In Walsall, the best surviving Free Church building is Hatherton United Reformed church (originally Presbyterian) in Hatherton Road. It dates from 1882 and was designed by H.H. McConnal working in partnership with a Mr Cotton. The exterior is fairly low key, being brick with friable sandstone dressings. The main frontage has a side tower, from which the stone spire has been removed. However, all the windows retain their original leading in contrasting grid and lozenge patterns. Inside, there is a huge and ornate timber roof, supported on two rows of piers creating a central nave and side aisles. At the front, there is a complex Gothic-style timber rostrum.

Methodist Central Hall, Ablewell Street, Walsall dates from 1859. The core is a very large pedimented chapel with a heavy plaster ceiling and galleries on three sides. The architect was William Horton of Wednesbury. This was converted into a Central Hall in 1929, with the addition of a

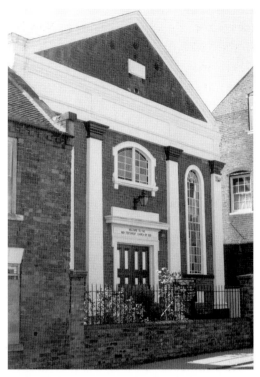

Right: New Testament Church of God, Upper Lichfield Street, Willenhall. It was originally a Baptist chapel, built in 1862. A large, impressive pedimented frontage faces the street. The inside has galleries around three sides although the ceiling plasterwork has been lost.

Below: King's Hill Methodist church, Joynson Street, Darlaston. A mature work by C.W.D. Joynson of Wednesbury, Edwardian. It displays his characteristic use of cream terracotta contrasting with bright orange brickwork using Perpendicular traceried windows. Now a shell following a devastating fire, King's Hill had a double hammerbeam roof and some attractive Art Nouveau stained glass.

Former Trinity Methodist church, Union Street, Willenhall. In its present form dates from 1863, designed by architect Samuel Loxton. The two-tier main frontage is slightly reminiscent of Wren's St Paul's. The twin 'sugar-loaf' domes are unique to the building.

Providence chapel, New Road, Willenhall (1865), in a simple vernacular style. It has a light and airy galleried interior with much straw-coloured woodwork.

forebuilding. Further alterations after the Second World War included the insertion of a floor at gallery level to provide function rooms below and a chapel above.

Mellish Road Methodist church dates from 1910. It is in an Arts and Crafts/Gothic design with a Portland stone frontage and a needle spire. The windows had elaborate Art Nouveau glass. Unfortunately, the building was abandoned following subsidence and was subjected to a prolonged dispute over responsibility for the subsidence damage, during which it suffered severely from arson and vandalism. It still stands on a very prominent site on the Lichfield Road approach to Walsall, but its future remains extremely uncertain.

Twentieth-Century Places of Worship

Richard Twentyman of the Wolverhampton-based architectural practice Lavender and Twentyman (later Lavender, Twentyman and Percy and later still Twentyman Percy) kept in touch with the latest continental developments, particularly those in Holland and Sweden, and seems to have been the practice's principal designer 1936–60. The practice was responsible for three high quality churches in the borough: St Gabriel's, Fullbrook (1939), All Saints, Darlaston (1952) and Emmanuel Bentley (1956). Of the three, St Gabriel's is the most visually massive, in substantial brickwork with Clipsham stone dressings. The style is 'stripped Byzantine' combined with a flat roof and a number of contemporary features. The east tower serves as the chancel internally. All Saints and Emmanuel have much larger windows and pitched copper roofs – gabled at Emmanuel and segmental at All Saints. All Saints has some rich stone carving by Donald Potter, sculptor, around the entrance door.

Jennings Homer and Lynch architects of Brierley Hill undertook much work for the Roman Catholic Church after 1945. St Catherine Laboure Beechdale (1963) is an octagonal drum with a central spike. St Peter's, Bloxwich had a twin-tower street facade added in brick (1954). St Patrick's, Walsall (1966) is by another practice, Harrison and Cox, and borrows some ideas from Coventry cathedral, particularly the canted side windows.

Finally, Brownhills Methodist church, St Martin's (Church of England) Sutton Road and the chapel at Willenhall Lawn Cemetery are all 'A-frame' buildings, the first being a sizeable local landmark.

Other Faiths

The classic pattern – a place of worship remaining a place of worship despite population change – is to be observed in Walsall. The former Vicarage Walk Baptist church, Caldmore Walsall (1878, architect W.F. Markwick) is now the Mandir Baba Balak Nath, a Hindu Temple. Externally, the chapel and its neighbouring Sunday school are little altered, presenting a pair of pedimented frontages to the street. St Matthias chapel-of-ease, Willenhall, is now a Sikh temple, as is a former chapel in Stafford Street Walsall.

Islam has made a positive addition to the Walsall skyline, particularly to train travellers approaching from Birmingham. The Masjid-al-Farouq in Wednesbury Road has a tall, conspicuous green plastic minaret and dome.

Opposite below: All Saints, Walsall Road, Darlaston (1951–52), by architects Lavender, Twentyman and Percy, an inventive modern design with a segmental copper roof. There is a shallow saucer dome at the east end, also in copper, with a star finial.

Above left: St Gabriel the Archangel, Fullbrook, Walsall. Built in 1939 by Lavender and Twentyman, architects, of Wolverhampton, it is a very substantial brick structure with an east tower acting as chancel. The bell turret is 'modern' in appearance but there are also round arches of a 'stripped Byzantine' character.

Above right: All Saints, Walsall Road, Darlaston. Detail showing the rich sculpture of the south porch – sculptor, Donald Potter, a former pupil of Eric Gill.

Emmanuel Bentley. Lavender, Twentyman and Percy, 1956–57, a benefaction by Alfred Owen, managing director of Rubery Owen Ltd of Darlaston. The church is sited on the top of a steep mound of landscaped colliery spoil, as can be seen from the picture. All roofs are copper. The tall, slim tower has off-centre openings in its west (left) face. An excellent contemporary design for its time.

Mosque, Rutter Street, Caldmore, Walsall, a crisp, elegant modern design successfully integrating the traditional Islamic minaret, dome and four-centred arch.

POSTSCRIPT

This book has more than one use. It is an architectural 'taster'. It provides a 'shopping list' for future Statutory Listings. It is an educational resource. It also can be used as a handbook by the enquiring tourist.

An essential tool for travelling around the borough is a copy of the A-Z Birmingham Street Atlas, published in various editions by the Geographers' A-Z Map Co. Ltd. The 1:50,000 Ordnance Survey Landranger series map 139 is also useful.

Walsall Metropolitan Borough is directly accessible from the M6 off Junctions 7 and 10, although Junction 7 has a non-standard layout that can easily deceive the unwary and land them in Birmingham or West Bromwich! For those who prefer to 'let the train take the strain' there is a half-hourly service from Birmingham New Street and an hourly service from Rugeley Trent Valley. There are four stations – Bescot Stadium (not all trains stop here), Walsall itself, Bloxwich and Bloxwich North.

The main bus station is in Walsall and there is an intensive bus service to all the major areas of population. A season ticket is a useful investment for those investigating the borough by bus. An expensive but very rewarding alternative is to hire a narrowboat and spend a week doing the circuit. There are only two lock flights (Walsall and Rushall) requiring much paddle-cranking and hand-blistering, though there should be a time allowance for clearing rubbish off the propeller. The canal ambience, even in the midst of the built-up area, is quite astonishingly rural. And it is possible to moor within a few feet of the New Art Gallery right in the centre of Walsall!

A bicycle is a useful accessory as it can take you on and off the towpath and into corners where a car can't reach. Walsall is located on National Cycle Route 5, for which there is a map available.

The borough has a wide range of hotels and bed-and-breakfast establishments, details of which are obtainable from Walsall Tourist Information Office in Walsall Bus Station.

A major tourist and visitor asset is the Local History Centre, Essex Street, North Walsall, with a huge array of accessible information about the borough's past. Walsall MBC's Leisure Services operate the New Art Gallery, Walsall Museum in Lichfield Street, the Leather Museum in Wisemore (Walsall) and Willenhall Museum, together with an extensive range of countryside sites with their own leaflets and trail guides. A charitable trust operates the Lock Museum in Willenhall.

As I hope this book demonstrates, there is more to Walsall than meets the eye!

Peter Arnold

Further Reading

Arnold, Peter, *Walsall Locks Trail* (Walsall MBC, 1998)

Currie, C.R.J., M.W. Greenslade and D.A. Johnson, *A History of Walsall* (Victoria Country History of Staffordshire, 1976 and 1988)

Department of the Environment, *List of Buildings of Special Architectural or Historic Interest*, Walsall Metropolitan Borough (1986). As amended

French, Ann, *Let We Goo Fer a Walk* (Walsall Local History Centre, 2002)

Pearson, Michael, *Canal Companion: Birmingham Canal Navigations* (J.M. Pearson and Associates, 1989)

Pevsner, Sir Nikolaus, *The Buildings of Staffordshire* (Penguin 1974)

Tildesley, *A History of Willenhall* (1950s)

DEATH ON THE STREETS

Cars and the mythology of road safety

by
Robert Davis

Death on the Streets

Published by Leading Edge Press and Publishing Ltd
The Old Chapel
Burtersett
Hawes
North Yorkshire
DL8 3PB
© (0969) 667566
Fax (0969) 667788

ISBN 0-948135-46-8

A CIP Catalogue record for this book is available from the British Library.

Editing and design: Tim Wright
Cover design: Ruth Abbott
Cartoons: Brick
Indexing: Tim Wright
Type: Leading Edge Press and Publishing Ltd
Reprographics: Ebenezer Baylis and Son Ltd
Printed and bound in Great Britain by Ebenezer Baylis and Son Ltd, Worcester.

Contents

Acknowledgements

Many people should be acknowledged here for helping me form my ideas. They include those I have worked with, interviewed, or debated with over the last ten years in my professional work as a transport planner, academic researcher or journalist writing on "road safety". They also include non-professionals, whether producing plain common sense arguments, or those otherwise intelligent and fair-minded people who are prepared to use the most inadequate or irrational arguments to justify a dangerous status quo.

Just some of them are:

My colleagues in the Transport Group at the London Strategic Policy Unit and the Transport Planning Unit at the London Borough of Ealing.

The Department of Geography at Lancaster University, particularly John Whitelegg; the library staff in the Transport Studies Group at University College London.

Help came from the following organisations:

Friends of the Earth, particularly Adrian Davis. Transport 2000, particularly Judith Hanna. Those around Radical Community Medicine, particularly Jane Hughes, Mark McCarthy, and Mel Bartley. The Royal Society for the Prevention of Accidents, particularly Howard Boyd. The Cyclists' Touring Club, London Cycling Campaign, Pedestrians Association, the Campaign Against Drinking and Driving, Automobile Association, Royal Automobile Club, Parliamentary Advisory Council for Transport Safety, Lex Services PLC, Gallup, Volvo UK, Porsche UK.

Steve Atkins, Dave Davies, Jane Dunmore, the late Dennis Gilbert, Mayer Hillman, Chris Hutt, Don Mathew, Melanie Miller, Martin Mogridge, John Morgan, Peter Murry, Steve Prower, the late John Roberts, Liz Speed, Heather Ward, the late Frank West-Oram, Simon Wolff in Britain; Andy Clarke (USA), Thomas Kraag (Denmark), Franco Zuppichini (Italy), Rene Kohler and Wiel Janssen (Holland) gave their help as professionals, academics, or simply those interested in opposing danger on the roads.

In the transport and road safety establishments, David Worskett, then Head of Road Safety Division at the Department of Transport; Murray Mackay at the Accident Research Unit, University of Birmingham and Charles Downing at the Transport and Road Research Laboratory gave up time for long interviews. The Australian Road Research Board (Ray Brindle) and the Accident Research Unit at Monash University (Peter Vulcan) sent material on cycle helmets, as did the Bicycle Helmet Safety Institute (Randy Swart) in the U.S.

BBC Radio 4 for permission to quote from the "Today" programme of 21 October 1991.

Renate, Albert, and Charles Davis gave much support. Special debts should go to Mike Donnellan and John Adams for their many discussions with me. Responsibility for the text is mine only.

Robert Davis, London, December 1992

Publisher's foreword

PICTURE the scene: a scene that will be re-enacted a dozen times tonight the length and breadth of Britain... A group of young lads take a fast car from a city car park and cruise the streets, looking for a police patrol vehicle. Once the cops are found, the taunting starts, and the fun begins. The joyriders speed off and the police, obligingly give chase. Quarry and pursuers become bit parts in a real-life enactment of a scene which is portrayed so often on TV that it has become part and parcel of a culture in which, if the car is King, then speed is the emperor of all. Of course, it is tragedy, not comedy, that tends to characterise this latter-day *Keystone Cops*.

Pick up the paper, turn on the telly: perhaps the loudest, and most expensive, single advertising message that appears is the voice of the motor manufacturing industry, exhorting us, on the one hand, to savour the speed and performance of the latest models while, on the other, reassuring us that the latest design of tyre or four-wheel steering will keep us glued to the road on fast corners. And if we should crash? Well, we've all seen how those delightful mannequins can survive almost anything, thanks to roll-bars, reinforced door panels, inflating air bags, etcetera.

The victims of joyriding aren't the only losers in this quest for speed. The persuasive argument that Robert Davis makes in this book is that what makes a road safe for speed, makes it dangerous for vulnerable road users. As those who sit snugly, or smugly, behind the impact-resistant bonnets of their "crash-worthy" cars take to the road, so exposed pedestrians and cyclists are sent reeling from the increase in danger.

Perhaps we should not be surprised when car builders sell the thrill of speed, but here is a remarkable account of how those supposed to be responsible for the safety of cars and roads have colluded with the roads lobby to promote speed not safety. At times, Robert Davis is like a lone moped rider battling the wrong way round the M25, but readers will surely find much that is persuasive in what he says. Few of us would dream of driving these days without a safety belt. But let us suppose there was a new law which actually banned the use of seat belts for a day. I suspect we would all protect ourselves by driving rather slower and more carefully — reducing the risk to vulnerable road-users as a consequence.

These arguments are, of course, like a red rag to a bull for many — not least to that group which has always been a close ally of the manufacturers in their quest for speed before the safety of non-car users — the motoring correspondents of the national and regional press.

We circulated details of this forthcoming book to those same correspondents on road safety day at the 1992 Motor Show at Birmingham. One — the *Daily Express's* David Benson — duly responded in his column of November 5, 1992. From beneath a review of a 150mph "gem of a car", he didn't mince words: "Personally, I shan't be reading his book," he fumed.

A pity, if not so surprising, for — as Davis himself points out in his lengthy critique of the recent work of road safety expert, Leonard Evans, at the end of this book — "There are none so blind as those who will not see."

Stan Abbott, Publisher, Hawes, North Yorkshire, December 1992

Photographs and Illustrations

Introduction

Then...

The suggestion was lately made in convention that it would help very much to make human life safer in New York if a suitable apparatus could be put up in Madison Square and a dozen reckless drivers could be hanged on it. Their reply was: 'A dozen? There are two or three hundred of those fellows that need hanging.'

Life Magazine, 1906.[1]

Men of England

Your birthright is being taken from you by reckless motor drivers... Reckless motorists drive over and kill your children... Reckless motorists drive over and kill both men and women. Men of England... rise up, join together, and bring pressure upon your representatives in Parliament, and otherwise make it unpleasant and costly to the tyrants who endanger your lives and the lives of your dear ones.

Poster circulated in London, 1908.[2]

...and now

Leicester Crown Court hears how a couple who work as driving instructors, Mr and Mrs A, chased each other at speeds up to 80 mph in L-plated cars and crossed to the opposite side of the road during their midnight race in a 30 mph zone. Each was disqualified from driving for one month and fined £150 for driving carelessly: Mr A was fined another £100 and disqualified for 12 months more for driving with excess alcohol in his bloodstream. The couple have now set up their own driving school.

Mr B is fined £200 for careless driving, £250 for failing to stop after an accident, and has eight penalty points endorsed on his licence after running down and killing a 16-year-old pedestrian at a speed estimated at 60 mph in a built-up area.

Mr C, a £54,000-a-year company director, is caught when twice over the legal alcohol limit at the wheel of his Ferrari. He has three previous drink-driving convictions and one for driving while disqualified. He receives a six year ban and a £1,000 fine.

York magistrates hear how a pedestrian is knocked down when a retired

7

solicitor, Mr D, loses his patience and pulls out of a line of cars on to the wrong side of the road. Mr D is fined £60 with £12 costs.

Some of the news reports collected in one three-month period by local branches of the Pedestrians' Association.[3]

THE CENTRAL THESIS of this book is that the dominant definition of "road safety" in modern society is wrong. Most books on the subject start by considering some numbers. Worldwide, between 15 and 20 million people have died and hundreds of millions have been permanently injured in road accidents since the beginnings of the motorised society earlier this century.[4] Britain's toll is just over 400,000 dead and 16 million injured in what have become known as "road traffic accidents", since official records started in 1926[5] (although because of under-reporting the latter figure should perhaps be increased to between 20 and 35 million).[6] Measurement can be made in other ways. What distinguishes deaths on the road from deaths elsewhere is their *prematurity*. Half of all male deaths in the 15-19 age group in Britain, for example, are from motor vehicle accidents.[7] As death from infectious diseases has diminished, death in accidents has come to form a much higher proportion of premature deaths. Looked at in terms of years of life lost and set against a notional figure of the age at which we expect to die, this prematurity greatly increases the significance of deaths on the road. So while far more people die of heart disease than from crashes on the road (about 30 times as many in 1983), the differential in terms of years of life lost comes down to a mere 1.7.[8]

As sobering as they are, however, these statistics do not do justice to the suffering and misery involved in road accidents. The injuries and deaths are sudden, and the psychological trauma produced, massive. In fact, road traffic accidents should be taken more seriously because they are often avoidable, and therefore, with hindsight, not really "accidents" at all.

Bringing the scale of harm to the attention of the public has long been the aim of road safety professionals and others in the road safety lobby. One way of doing this correctly is argued for by the mathematician John Allen Paulos[9], who points out the irrationality which can result from an inadequate assessment of the probabilities of different kinds of risk. The modern mass media are obsessed by risks of death — from berserk gunmen, rogue Rottweiler dogs or murder by strangers — yet these risks are very minor compared to those on the roads. Paulos argues that the media should be provided with an easily understandable "safety index" which they can use to accurately portray the chances of harm occurring, and thus clear up confusion. Similarly, a cry from the road safety lobby has often been, "If all these dead occurred at the same time and place, the public would take notice." Every day approximately 14 people die on British roads, and between 800 and 1,000 people go to hospital as a result of injuries sustained in what is classified as a road traffic accident. Maybe, these arguments suggest, if we were made more fully aware of the dangers, either collectively or individually, we would do something about them.

8

But these are naive arguments. The definition of social problems in the public mind, whether through the media, peer group pressure or education, has very little to do with the actual chances of harm occurring. The amount of attention and, much more important, the nature of the portrayal of the "cause" and "solution" of what has been defined as a "problem" are political and ideological issues. By "politics" I mean the power relations that exist not just between the state and the people, or between large pressure groups and government (although these are relevant), but also the power that individual road users have over the safety of others. By "ideology" I mean the attitudes and values generated by a system with certain power relations, which in turn support those relations through the formation of background assumptions and hidden agendas.

We tend to regard the death or injury of a loved one at the hands of another road user as different from a death from cancer or heart disease, particularly if we judge that other road user's behaviour to have been irresponsible. The point is not just the avoidable nature of the incident, but the abuse of potentially dangerous power. The abuse of power by a fellow citizen in a public place leading to sudden death or other harm is a feature which makes safety on the road a headline issue. Indeed at one time, this was how the issue was mainly defined.

The two quotations with which this introduction began defined the road safety problem as a motorist problem. This view continued to be a reflection of public opinion into the 1930s.[10] Private motorists were a minority of about a million in Britain, with about a quarter of a million motor vehicles on the roads in 1930. More mileage was covered and certainly more journeys were made by bicycle.[11] In 1935, after agitation by those most affected by the danger posed by motorists — Britain's cycling organisations, rail workers' unions and the newly formed Pedestrians' Association for Road Safety — supported by the voice of newspaper editors, legislation was brought in to control the danger (for example, the driving test). Road safety ideas, centred around the "three Es" of education, engineering and enforcement, were introduced. Road safety has since become the domain of various professionals: road safety officers, road and vehicle engineers, traffic police, doctors, lawyers and others. The anger and hostility towards the earlier abuse of motorists' power has become muted and "road safety" has assumed its blander, more scientific and neutral image.

Why is this? Part of the reason is that the road safety lobby claims success in its efforts. This success has, we are told, been achieved not by succumbing to anger, but by engineering vehicles and the road environment, by education, and through sensible attitudes to law enforcement. Part One of this book, however, shows that this is just not true. The view that the ordinary person might take, that there is more danger on Britain's roads than there was 60 years ago, is correct. To a large extent the dangers presented by motorisation have been legitimated. That is to say, that they have been made acceptable as part of a political and ideological process in which the dominant ideas of "road safety", and the activities of the road safety lobby, have played a central role.

To many professionals concerned with road safety, this may seem unfair comment on sincere efforts to reduce danger. Some approaches, if genuinely successful, such as those restricting the scale of drinking and driving, may have an effect on one particular area of dangerous behaviour. However, unless a wider, more radical approach is taken to the dangers posed by putting fallible human beings in charge of equipment with an exceptionally high potential for harming others, these benefits will be severely limited.

This is partly because of the way the aims and objectives of road safety are formulated. Part One concludes by showing the inherently discriminatory nature of the way "the problem" is conceptualised and quantified. Part Two shows how the road safety lobby operates to avoid going to the root of the problem and genuinely tackling the danger of motorisation. This is not just because of the ideology of road safety; it is also because of the political base of much of the road safety lobby. Its origins in organisations such as the Royal Society for the Prevention of Accidents (RoSPA) reveal that the motoring organisations and the road lobby played key roles in setting the agenda for the road safety movement. Indeed, it is a measure of their arrogance and ability to impose their will on others that they achieved this at a time when their members were very much a minority of road users. And, of course, a dominant role is played by the Department (previously the Ministry) of Transport(DTp), which has always supported motoring as against other forms of transport. [12]

In a further section the road safety lobby is analysed after consideration of one of its best-known victories — the implementation of legislation to make seat belt wearing compulsory. Such "victories" involve a failure to reduce motorist danger and, worse still, may actually make life worse for the more vulnerable road users. Most of the history of the last sixty years of "road safety" is one of this kind of deterioration, pseudo-restraint of danger from motorists, or minimal restraint (which, precisely because it appears to be serious control, may effectively become pseudo-restraint). Part Three gives some case studies of how this occurs.

Another reason is given for the acceptance of danger on the roads. We are now all motorists, and therefore we accept what motorists may do. Except that we are not. Most households in Britain did not include a car owner until after 1969, and 37 per cent did not in 1986. [13] 69 per cent of journeys are apparently made by car, according to the same official statistics, [14] but if the figures for journeys under a mile are included, the figure comes down to some 50 per cent. [15] None of this has prevented the dominant ideology from assuming for many years that "we are all motorists now". Even if the vast majority of journeys were made by car, it would still be difficult to justify the dangers posed to others. In fact, the advent of mass car use (in Britain, the time when car use first became a real possibility for working class families, in the late 1950s and 1960s) has created a number of problems, apart from the dangers, which are detailed in Part Four. Forecasted increases in car use throw these issues into sharper relief.

This book does not give easy answers. It is mainly concerned with clarifying the nature of the problem and helping to blow away the smoke-screens that have been set up around the issue of safety on the road. In analysing its practice, institutions and ideology, I sometimes refer to "road safety" in inverted commas. Sometimes, to fit in with contemporary understanding, I do not. There is another reason for this. If we want to modify existing practice slightly, it might be adequate to call for "real" road safety, rather than a travesty of it which belongs in inverted commas — and nowhere else. But if, as explained in Chapter 16, the association of the two words has become so irredeemably part of the problem rather than part of the solution, a civilised approach will simply have to separate itself from them altogether, whether they have inverted commas or not. One thing is certain: any confusion is the responsibility of those who collude with danger in the name of safety.

The task of demythologising involves stripping away layers of mystification which, like the layers of an onion, reveal others beneath. For example, criticising a particular "road safety" intervention because it does not "work" can lead to an examination of precisely what we mean by "work". This process of redefining and identifying the problem is not merely semantic — it is vital prerequisite for constructive discourse.

The book deals with some fairly sophisticated debates and ideas, and is intended to be read by professionals and campaigners in the area. However, where statistics and quotations are included, they have been presented with the non-academic in mind and do not presuppose any specialist knowledge.

The figures and data (including prices) used in the text apply for the dates given. They will change, and the latest editions of the relevant publications should be consulted: the nature of transport danger they illuminate should not. Similarly, while material drawn on is frequently international, most of it refers specifically to the British experience (and is so unless otherwise stated), but the main conclusions have a significance that goes beyond this country. Indeed, the aim of the book is to elaborate some basic universal and unchanging principles about human behaviour in the road environment.

Road-side memorial, Ripley, North Yorkshire

Part One

A question of definition —
what is road safety?

1.

Playing it by numbers

ALONG WITH CRIME FIGURES, the sober statistics of death on the roads make an annual bid for the nation's attention. And for many years there has been cause for some self-congratulation — or so we have been led to believe.

As the Department of Transport prepares to peddle another round of "good news" on road safety to the doyens of the press, we find ourselves trying to reconcile the official line that the roads are getting safer, with our everyday experience of a frightening increase in danger.

The key to the conundrum is fear itself. You may have heard someone say "that road's a death trap". As danger increases, so the trap widens its jaws and more and more non-car users get out of the way. With fewer pedestrians so there are fewer accidents. Only the fearless or the foolhardy would ignore the risk: between 1955 and 1990 a ten to 14-year-old's chances of dying on the roads nearly doubled.

❖❖❖

Numbers can be forbidding. The statements of government ministers, doctors and other members of the road safety establishment are couched in terms of the statistics of those killed or hurt on our roads. For the ordinary member of the public, the talk of rates and trends may bear little relevance to everyday experience. Or alternatively, the myths advanced by Britain's transport establishment may be

13

willingly swallowed — particularly if they present a rosy picture of "our" record.

But we need to overcome any fear of figures. The main principles involved in understanding the use and abuse of official statistics are actually quite easy for the lay person to understand. And this is essential for a proper understanding of what different definitions of "road safety" may mean. Given that there are alternative definitions, an analysis of the official statistics provides a key to suggesting which we should chose. At one level, provided they are treated with caution, the statistics might tell us what they are supposedly designed for — namely, according to the Department of Transport,

> to provide background information on such matters as roads... weather conditions etc, where road accidents happen. These statistics are used to stimulate informed debate on matters of road safety and to provide both a local and national perspective for particular road safety problems or particular suggested remedies.[1]

From this perspective, the basic facts about the circumstances of people being hurt or killed in the road environment can, in principle, give us a picture of the chances of being hurt or killed for different types of people, different kinds of travel, in different environments. A picture of probabilities is drawn. There is a sense in which we all assess risks for ourselves as we move about and such pictures can help us. But the official picture is deeply flawed.

At one level the quality of the data collected, such as the assessment of exposure to danger, is simply inadequate. Yet the problems are deeper. From the selection of particular categories, through the kind of analysis to which numbers are subjected, to their method of presentation in official publications and ultimately their presentation in the media, the official statistical enterprise is biased. The bias is in favour of a particular kind of transport policy, and a particular definition of the dangers to life and limb that this policy generates, which discriminates against the vulnerable groups of road users not travelling in cars.

This does not mean that official statistics should be rejected. Indeed, it opens up a fresh area, a study of the road safety industry and the way road safety is thought of today. In this sense I am following in the steps of modern criminology, which some years ago pointed out not just that crime rates as presented in the media were poor indicators of the true extent of certain kinds of crime, but that the production of the figures can itself tell us about the operation of law enforcement agencies and the media (as well as the whole society) in which those figures are discussed.[2] With few exceptions,[3] debate about road safety has not yet seriously considered this kind of question.

The statistics show that the chances of different kinds of road user dying or being hurt can, over time, be radically altered. Thus human agency, rather than fate, is involved. However, the statistics are also used misleadingly to indicate that "the problem" is at least partly being ameliorated by current policies. We are presented with the myths that Britain has a good safety record compared to most other countries, and that the record has been consistently improving. In many ways the

14

reverse is true because of official policies which perpetuate a particular transport status quo. The production and dissemination of official road traffic accident statistics legitimate and form part of those policies.

The production of official accident statistics

Official statistics are produced by the Department of Transport (DTp) in the form of "Road Accidents Great Britain" (RAGB), published annually. In 1986 the cost of collecting, storing and analysing accident data was estimated at £1.89 million.[4] There is clearly an enormous amount of effort involved in the production of statistics. Yet, despite the importance one would expect to be attached to them, these figures are not always available to the general public. It might be suggested that where figures are hard for the public to swallow because they don't match up with the received wisdom, it is easier for an organisation like the Department of Transport to exercise a little self-censorship.[5]

It is important to consider how the key terms are used in this process.

A. "Accidents"

The basic unit in the figures is the "accident", as recorded annually on some quarter of a million accident report forms, known as "Stats 19", completed by all the police forces in Britain and then sent to the DTp. There is some debate about the appropriateness of the word. "Accident" involves the notion of *unforeseen contingency*, which is somewhat at odds with the aims of road safety professionals and others who are keen to point out that much of what we see on the road today is avoidable.[6]

While connotations of randomness, unforeseen contingency and chance make "accidents" an unsuitable object for study by scientists concerned with non-random occurrences, the notion also implies a *lack of important responsibility* ("it was just an accident"). This clearly has moral and legal implications for people involved in acts leading to the injury of others. For this reason, organisations representing those whose relatives have been killed by drunk or other particularly irresponsible drivers have often opposed the use of the term "accident".

> **I get so angry when I hear the word 'accident'(used in such cases. Getting into a car with eight pints of cider inside you and driving into somebody and killing them is not an accident, it's a crime. It starts with the police using that dreadful phrase 'road traffic accident'... from the first stages of investigation, the idea that it was only an accident is part of the way society looks at it ...Crashes are incidents which may not just be slight acts of carelessness, and they should be recognised as such.[7]**
>
> *D Probart, Campaign against Drinking and Driving.*

This specifically refers to drunk driving. In terms of the intentionality involved, we could extend further the idea of wilful, avoidable action to all sorts of criminally negligent behaviour — through speeding to driving while tired, and on to official transport policy — should we decide that it is causally linked to more crashes.

The official definition of an accident excludes damage-only accidents, those with no known human casualties, and those which do not become known to the police or become known only 30 days or more after their occurrence.[8] The vast majority — between 80 and 95 per cent — of what lay people would call "accidents" or "crashes" thus become virtually invisible in the official statistics.[9] RTAs (Road Traffic Accidents) or PIAs (Personal Injury Accidents) are what the DTp, local councils and the road safety lobby are concerned about, not car crashes or what lay people may call accidents. The only statistical indicator of such crashes comes from published returns on insurance claims. This indicator has its defects; there is no substantial body of published research available to show how or why different vehicle owners make their claims. Yet in terms of presenting the statistician with particularly large numbers, better suited for statistical analysis, insurance returns would appear to be a very important source of information to assess the level of danger on the roads. However, in the 100-plus pages of *RAGB 1990* only one table and one-third of a page of text are devoted to this indicator. Indeed, before 1987 *(RAGB 1986)*,[10] there was no publication of aggregated insurance claim figures, and those published cover only the years 1981-86.

The figure for the total number of claims made increased by no less than 61 per cent, with the average claim per mile travelled increasing by 36 per cent, in the period 1981-89 as Figure 1 shows. A public perception of an increase in the number of crashes and therefore less safety in the road environment — informed by the sight of dented vehicles and carpets of broken glass on the streets — would be supported by a more prominent degree of attention paid to figures such as these, rather than the dominant picture of "improvement".

B. "Injuries" and "deaths"

Casualties produced by accidents are graded as "fatal", "serious" or "slight" injuries. "Deaths" are those deaths that take place within 30 days of the accident. Those that occur after this period are "serious injuries". Slight injuries are those "of a minor character, such as a sprain, bruise or cut which are not judged to be severe, or slight shock requiring roadside treatment." Serious injuries are those

> **for which a person is detained in hospital as an 'in-patient', or any of the following injuries whether or not he is detained in hospital: fractures, concussion, internal injuries, crushings, severe cuts and lacerations, severe general shock requiring medical treatment, injuries causing death 30 or more days after the accident. An injured casualty is coded as seriously or slightly injured by the police on the basis of information available within a short time of the accident. This generally will not include the results of a medical examination, but may include the fact of being detained in hospital, the reasons for which may vary somewhat from area to area.[11]**

Road Accidents Great Britain.

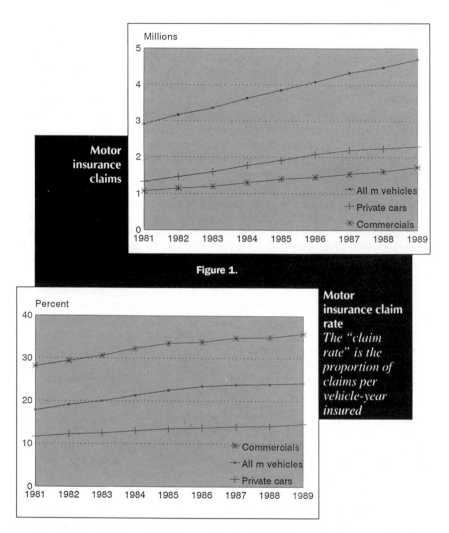

Motor insurance claims

Figure 1.

Motor insurance claim rate
The "claim rate" is the proportion of claims per vehicle-year insured

The numbers of casualties reported in the official statistics as being slightly or seriously injured bear a significantly inaccurate and unreliable relationship to those people who actually do fall into these categories. Leaving aside those accidents where there is no legal requirement to report to the police, a proportion of officially defined accident (RTA) casualties decide not to report to the police because of the chances of prosecution for road traffic offences, or because of the inconvenience to themselves or others. Hospital staff or doctors who treat them do not necessarily report to form fillers unless requested by police.

Three major studies of pedal cycle casualties, for example, which compared hospital admissions with data from Stats 19 forms, showed that most — respectively 83, 65 and 60 per cent — of those in the "seriously injured" category are not recorded on Stats 19.[12] For the purposes of statistical analysis it does not necessarily matter if a proportion (even a large one) is unreported, provided its size is known or, even if unknown, seen to remain consistent. But when there is such a degree of variation as is indicated in these surveys, meaningful analysis becomes difficult. Analysis becomes even trickier if we estimate that the possible level of under-reporting may be much lower. One smaller pilot study indicates a much lower level of under-reporting with as few as 35 per cent unreported for all casualties, and only 10 per cent missed for serious injuries.[13]

Even when casualties are recorded, the data — produced by medically unqualified police officers — may be wrongly recorded. The level of injury may be improperly recorded, with superficial injuries involving loss of blood recorded as more severe than those involving significant internal injuries.[14] One study that compared data from general practitioners with police records showed factual discrepancies in four out of five cases.[15] A British Medical Association memorandum states:

> The existing definitions on which records are based are misleading. Only one in four casualties classified as seriously injured are, in fact, seriously injured and many of those classified as slightly injured are, in fact, seriously injured. The existing definition of 'seriously injured' covers everything from a broken finger to total paralysis and to death occurring more than 30 days after the accident. Within these unsatisfactory definitions there is widespread under-reporting and misreporting of casualties and the distribution of these errors varies widely between different categories of road user.[16]

So even if the casualties were reported at a reliable and/or known level (which they are not), and were correctly allocated to the appropriate categories (which they are not), doubts would remain — even on the part of the road safety lobby itself — about the desirability of using these categories. For example, it appears that a "serious injury" to a motorcyclist is more likely to lead to a severe or very severe disability than one affecting other road users.[17]

C. "Accident/casualty rates"

With talk of "rates" we at last approach the question of chances of injury.

The first problem is what kind of denominator do we want? Are we interested in casualties per journey, per mile travelled or per minute travelled? Then other relevant questions can be asked. Is there a significant variation in chances according to weather conditions, hours of darkness, or region? And what kind of accidents/casualties record do different kinds of people have, on different kinds of road, using different modes of transport? In the following discussion it should be remembered that the evidence referred to involves numbers of accidents and casualties of different severities, about which, as already pointed out, we have very limited and flawed information.

(i) By kind of road

Official statistics are broken down by type of road: A-roads, B-roads, unclassified, motorways; and by whether they are in built-up (BU) or non-built-up (NBU) areas. It is useful to have an idea of the relative rates of accident/casualty if, for example, the choice is being made about whether to make a journey by motorway or other roads. But it is not as simple as that.

Consider the record of A-roads in built-up areas (with speed limits of 40 mph or less), compared with non-built-up area A-roads with higher speed limits. For every vehicle mile travelled on the built-up road, the car user has a three times higher chance of becoming involved in a reported road traffic accident than on the non-built-up road.[18] However, it would not be surprising if crashes on the faster roads were to occur at higher speed, being therefore more likely to produce a fatality. Sure enough, comparing fatalities shows that the chances of a car user dying on a non-built-up area road per mile travelled are twice as high as on the built-up road. Which type of road has the better record? Would you rather have a journey which gives you a better chance per mile travelled (although not necessarily per journey, as journeys in rural areas may be longer) of avoiding becoming a casualty, but a worse one of dying?

This is not simply a question for the prospective car user. The statistician and the traffic engineer concerned with road safety are keen to support accident-reducing measures. There is a tendency to deal with larger numbers, as it is easier to perform statistical analyses on them. A problem with official accident statistics is that the class of numbers preferred — since insurance claims are not used — is either "accidents" or "(serious) injuries", rather than the smaller number of deaths. As pointed out above, the former categories, which are more "statistician friendly", are far less accurate and reliable than the latter category. In the context of treating an accident "black spot" on remote country roads, where, in general, there are few accidents and even fewer deaths, there is an attraction in instituting measures which appear to reduce accidents and casualties but may have no beneficial effect (or may even have an adverse one) on the death rate. The changes in injury accidents may be what statisticians call "statistically significant"; but even with an increase in the death rate, the numbers will not be sufficiently large for proper statistical analysis to be performed.

An engineering treatment of a "black spot" or the redesign of a junction might involve exactly the kind of measure, such as a longer sight line, which leads to higher driving speeds. Such measures typify the difference between the two types of road being considered: one with higher speeds and fewer accidents per mile, but more serious ones; the other with lower speeds and more frequent but less serious accidents. Here another consideration arises, namely the fate of vulnerable road users outside cars.

Pedestrians are about 16 times more likely to be injured per vehicle mile on a

BU rather than a NBU road, but only 3.5 times more likely to be killed. The denominator used — motor vehicle mile — reflects the traditional bias of interest towards motor vehicle travel rather than vulnerable-road-user travel. If there were a measure of pedestrian traffic allowing comparison between the two types of road, and it appeared that pedestrian traffic were more than 3.7 times higher on BU than NBU roads — which is more than a strong probability — then the chances for pedestrians of being killed on NBU roads are worse. With cyclists, where an index of exposure does exist, the chances of serious injury are about the same, while the chances of death are some four times greater on non-built-up A roads. In other words, a road which appears to have a better record for pedestrians actually has a worse one when the more serious casualities (the ones more accurately known about) and a measure of exposure are considered.

This is one way of building discrimination into presentation of the figures. A rosy picture is painted of faster roads by selecting vehicle mileage as the denominator, and by choosing serious injuries rather than fatalities. This is exemplified in the official view of motorways.

In its guidelines for road safety policy into the next century, the DTp reassures us that motorways have "a generally superior record to other types of road", and that motorways are "eight times safer than other roads".[19] In fact, as is shown in Chapter 13, the chances of a car occupant being killed or seriously hurt per hour travelled on a British motorway are respectively either *greater than or the same as* on a typical urban road.

(ii) By mode of transport

Assessing the chances of being hurt for different modes of transport involves considering all the questions looked at so far — accident and casualty data, breakdown of data according to relevant variables such as type of road, as well as age of casualty, time of day, and so on. In addition, we have to consider the question of the *journey*.

As an illustration of the use of the journey as a measure of exposure, consider the experience of users of different modes in London:

> **If you compare the casualty rates by vehicle type per distance travelled, with the car as a unit of one, then walking has a comparative rate of 3.1, cycling has a comparative rate 8.9, motorcycling... 31. If we look at trips, because obviously trips are the important thing, walking actually becomes safer than cars, cycling is down to 1.3, almost on parity with cars, and motorcycling is down to 13.6.[20]**

J Brownfield, former Head of Road Safety at the GLC.

To take more recent figures, with killed car users at a unit of one, we have comparative figures per distance travelled of 15.6 for walking, 12.8 for cycling and 26.2 for motorcyclists.[21] These are national figures and are different for reported injuries of different kinds, which might of course be of different levels of severity within each category, on different kinds of road, at different times of day and in different weather conditions.

Another problem, considered below, is the breakdown among casualties by *age*. Children and elderly people subjected to the same kind of impact are more likely to die than less frail young men — so one would expect people in these age groups to be more likely to end up in the most accurate and reliable category, that of fatality. We therefore need to have a breakdown of exposure and casualty levels by age. This leads us into a difficult problem. When disaggregation of this nature occurs with the small cohorts (statistical groups) typical of fatality figures — which are already small with a group like cyclists — one is left with numbers which are too small to make statistical sense of.

There is an important prior problem. Rates by mile or journey include a measure of exposure. This means that we need to know how many miles and journeys, and preferably where and when, are made by people using different modes (and, if possible, the figures for different ages and other characteristics which may be relevant to a propensity to end up in road traffic accidents). These measures of exposure exist in a moderately accurate form for car mileage, less well for motorcyclists, poorly for cyclists and — most important — hardly at all for pedestrians.

Disability may be important from the point of view of survival chances in crashes. It is certainly important in terms of affecting the ability to walk in safety. Some 14 per cent of adults (6.2 million people) have some kind of disability.[22] For the purpose of the gathering of accident statistics, or inclusion in the National Travel Survey, people with disabilities do not appear as a specific category at all.

Pedestrians

The official attitude to the most basic form of transport is summed up in the first paragraph of the three pages (out of 87) devoted to walking in the DTp's National Travel Survey (NTS): "*Elsewhere in this report we generally ignore all journeys under one mile*. Al-

though they accounted for only 2.4 per cent of total travel mileage, they represented, however, *a third of the total if all journeys* over 50 yards were included" (my emphasis).[23] Another official statistical handbook, *Social Trends*, deals exclusively with powered travel in the transport section, with walking only appearing under "Leisure".[24]

Broken paving stones, frequently caused by parked cars, are a significant source of pedestrian accidents

In fact, this limited consideration given to pedestrians is an improvement on the otherwise virtually total neglect of pedestrian travel. Until *RAGB 1987*, where the results of *NTS 1985-86* are used, pedestrian exposure was considered only in terms of the overall number of people in the country, and irrespective of the number and length of pedestrian journeys. While the population has increased in size this century, the increase in journeys made by car and other forms of transport must have had an impact on the amount of walking done, yet this has not been taken into account until very recently. Even the rough count of pedestrian mileage is highly limited; any reasonable measure of exposure would refer to the amount of crossing of roads with different widths, traffic flows, speeds, and so on. Also — as is admitted in *RAGB 1987*, basing information on NTS — a periodic study with differences in definition and methodology between surveys, makes it impossible to construct a time series (an analysis of change over time) of average distances walked.[25]

Accidents to pedestrians appear to be under-reported to a large extent. Some 20 per cent of people have an accident as a pedestrian at some time in their life.[26]

Cyclists

The problems associated with non-reporting and misreporting of casualties, the inadequacy of the casualty categories and the doubt about when injuries should be reported have been mentioned. The small size of the reliable figures (fatalities) makes it difficult to carry out appropriate breakdowns. With exposure levels, we have the additional problem that until 1987 no estimate was provided of the number of cyclists in Britain.[27] The counts of bicycles carried out by the DTp suffer from lack of inclusion by automatic or manual counting methods, and are not disaggregated by the important variable of child/adult.

Motorcyclists

Despite knowing for some thirty years[28] that motorcyclist experience is a relevant variable for explaining accident involvement, and the ease with which it could be added to Stats 19 data, it is not included.[29] The pattern of motorcycle use, and in a more complex way casualty and accident involvement rates, probably varies according to engine size.[30] This, along with age and travel done at night, is a variable not included with mileage counts. The usual problems of under-reporting exist — a recent survey indicates that 35 per cent of casualties defined as serious, and 70 per cent of slightly injured two-wheeled motor vehicle riders, are not reported on Stats 19 forms.[31]

Car occupants

Motor vehicle mileage is easier than that of other road users to measure by automatic means. The main reason for an adequate index of motor vehicle, and more particularly car, mileage is, however, the role that these figures can play in supporting demand for road building. Given the massive funds available for supporting Britain's road system, and the technical sophistication of cost-benefit and other computer models used, a great deal more work on the accident record of different kinds of car could be done. It would, for example, be useful to investigate whether the drivers of company cars or more "crashworthy" cars (a car which is constructed in order to increase the protection to those inside it in the event of a crash) are more likely to get into accidents. At present it would not be convenient for the road safety industry to show that more crashworthy cars are more of a threat to those outside them,[32] or for the DTp to produce evidence suggesting safety disbenefits from policies giving additional subsidies to car use. I suggest that this is why research is not officially supported in these areas, or the necessary data created to facilitate it.

Car mileage also has another significance. The massive increase in car mileage is never referred to as a contributory factor in road traffic accidents, still less as a variable which should be restricted. However, whenever it comes to claims that "the problem", or "road safety" is "getting better", or "being solved", the massive increase in car mileage is quoted. (In fact, the relationship between increases in car mileage and casualty trends does not, for reasons examined in Chapter 2, suggest that there will tend to be anything like an equal increase in the number of overall casualties).[33] Changes in gross estimated casualties are regularly compared to other estimates for casualties at previous times (a comparison between numbers representing two quite different social phenomena) in the official statistics, with an unwarranted implication of improvement. Sometimes this particular denominator — vehicle mileage — is not even clearly referred to as the basis for the accident casualty rate, let alone properly argued for.[34]

An aside — Safety for whom?

Discussion about accident/casualty rates raises a question of central importance to this book and to any understanding of the official ideology of "road safety". This is the question of *what we mean by the term "safe"?*

There is an ease — hardly questioned, as are most of the background assumptions of everyday life — with which the two different meanings of the word "safe" are abused and distorted. These meanings are the *transitive* and the *intransitive*: "safe" as in not posin`g a threat or danger to others (transitive); or as in being in a situation or position not exposed to danger or threat from others (intransitive). Thus the extent to which a form of transport is "dangerous" can be understood as the extent to which the person using it is at risk from others, how hazardous it is (the intransitive sense); or as how much of a danger the person poses to others (transitive). This is not merely an abstract or semantic point — it can reveal the way particular road user groups are laden with, or exonerated from, the burden of being perceived or defined as a problem.

Consider the discussion of the "safety" of walking as described in the official statistics: "Pedestrian travel is roughly comparable to pedal cyclists in terms of the overall fatality rate, and is considerably safer than travelling by motorcycle. On the other hand, travelling by car or bus is much safer than walking."[35] Take that last phrase: "travelling by car or bus is much safer than walking". Safer for whom?

Leaving aside questions of which rate (per journey or mile travelled?), and the problems involved in disaggregating by age, and so on, consider the meaning of

23

fatality rate as a measure of "safety" for other road users. Nowadays the number of other road users killed annually in crashes where pedestrians are involved only just (if at all) reaches double figures, whereas about 1,500 pedestrians die in accidents where other road users are involved. In the case of cars, which the above quote assures us are "safer", in 1990 three users are killed in accidents involving pedestrians, with 1,014 pedestrians killed in accidents involving cars.[36] Most of us know that the threat from pedestrians, in whatever mode of transport we use, is far less than that from cars.

(iii) Rate by type or category of person

Accident/casualty rates cannot be assessed for different modes on different roads without taking into account the likelihood of different kinds of people getting involved in accidents, whatever the mode or location. The most common way of separating this factor is by age.

(a) Age

Children, for example, may have less of the skills and experience required to avoid an accident than adults. This means that comparison of chances of dying between walking and cycling, on the one hand, and driving, on the other, should ideally be made with the over-17-year-old groups of cyclists and pedestrians.

Younger motorists, in the under-25 and more specifically under-21 age groups, appear to have particularly high reported accident and casualty rates, due to inexperience and/or to a higher level of risk-taking on the part of people of this age. Above the age of 75, the rate of reported accidents and casualties increases, presumably due to disabilities associated with advanced age.[37]

The age factor is particularly relevant with vulnerable road user groups such as pedestrians and cyclists. When an accident occurs, the greater frailty of the very old or very young means that they are more likely to become reported as fatalities, and to appear on the most reliable and accurate of the indicators of casualties. An increase may occur in the number of cyclists killed in a year, for example, despite the same amount of cycling being done in identical conditions — if the proportion of cyclists who are very young or old increases, one would expect the number of fatalities to increase.

There are therefore two age factors to remember. The persistent tendency of young motorists to be more likely to be involved in crashes is the first — one of the few universally agreed upon road safety statistical facts. Since it is not just related to lack of driving experience,[38] it must be a product of higher risk-taking at younger ages. The other factor is the greater likelihood of the more vulnerable to appear in statistics once crashes have occurred.

(b) Gender

This is not a significant variable for most professional road safety analysts. However, it constantly appears in conversation among lay people. As in many areas of road safety, prejudices and ideology from other areas of life are allowed to determine discussion.

The available data for Britain indicates that women, with the exception of the youngest age groups, tend to be more likely than men to be involved and killed or hurt in accidents per mile travelled.[39] This tends to disagree with the American experience.[40] This data needs to be disaggregated further: men are more likely to travel on non-built-up-area roads with their different reported casualty and fatality rates; we do not know whether there is a differential of tendency to report, or of the kind of journey made, or of other variables such as vehicle size and time of day travelled.

However, much discussion about the difference between male and female drivers is limited to the attribution of vague characteristics.[41] Such discussion avoids consideration of the individual's potential to hurt others and concentrates on driving "etiquette". Categorising "bad" drivers is in general a useful way of fudging issues of danger and creating categories of deviants who can be scapegoated for their antisocial behaviour.

The "other driver"

> **What is dangerous driving? I have a tendency to believe that everyone's driving is dangerous, except my own.**[42]
>
> *George Bernard Shaw.*

The tendency to blame others for accidents is well known. A recent British survey of motorists found that 40 per cent of the sample rated the overall standard of driving as bad, with just two per cent claiming that *they* were bad drivers; 24 per cent rated the overall standard of driving as good, with 75 per cent thinking that *they* were good.[43] A survey of motorway drivers found that, on a scale of one (poor) to five (good), they rated themselves with an above average mean score of 3.9, with other drivers being rated with a mean score of 2.7.[44] Motorists' tendency to see themselves as better than other motorists is one of the stable features of discussion on road safety.[45]

This puts the question of isolating deviant groups into context. The legitimate purpose of road safety professionals in isolating deviant groups is eroded if the tendency for the rest of us to give ourselves a self-congratulatory pat on the back is reinforced by our readiness to distance ourselves from responsibility. The wider initiatives which might be pursued, involving fundamental changes in transport policy, can also be shifted from the focus of debate while specific target groups are isolated.

In the tendency to blame others more than ourselves, "badness" may be a reference to some features of driving behaviour which the individual genuinely regards as accident-causing and tries to avoid. But it might miss other accident-causing behaviour that the same individual engages in.

There is a more fundamental point. However misguided or unjust, subjective ideas about the cause of accidents may contradict objective ideas as to what constitutes "bad" or "dangerous" behaviour. After all, if all the "other drivers" were to behave according to the wishes of the individual driver concerned — or, better still, disappear from the road altogether, along with other road users and those physical features which are considered undesirable — *accidents would presumably not happen.* (The motorists' unique manner of attributing blame is discussed in Chapter 15.)

Are particular deviant groups more likely to be involved in accidents? While some groups of drivers are particularly accident prone in terms of above-average frequency of accidents for the relevant variables of age, type of road, and so on, they appear to be in a small minority. While isolating people who appear to be two or three times more likely than average to get into accidents could be possible, most accidents are caused by people who are "normal but fallible".[46]

Isolating particular minority groups is an absolutely classic way of maintaining the status quo by refusing to identify problems as being closer to home — it is always easier to criticise small groups than to generate and support the much more necessary self-criticism.[47]

Other categories might be considered. For example, approximately a million motorists are unable to pass the existing eyesight test — itself criticised as out of date and capable of being passed by people registered as blind — and about twice this number have inadequate visual ability.[48] Important as it is to examine this issue, however, and to consider official negligence of it, it can divert attention from more important questions involved in "seeing" other road users.[49]

At the time of writing, the latest problem group to be identified is people with nightime breathing difficulties (snorers) whose health problem results in daytime fatigue allegedly leading to an increase in likelihood of crashing by a factor of six.[50]

Different people display differing tendencies to behave safely in the road environment — their characteristics are those of certain states of mind that many of us have or display at various times in our lives.

(iv) Rate by states of mind

The main variable referred to here in official statistics is driving while under the influence of alcohol. However, while this is often narrowed down by age, the amount of drinking and driving, let alone on what roads, and so on, is more difficult to ascertain and therefore missing from many official statistics. Very little is actually formally stated about other states of mind which one can assume are related to proneness to accidents, such as fatigue, let alone more general questions of inadequate vigilance and alertness. Fatigue is admitted to by a substantial number of drivers, and in one of the few estimates, 20 per cent of motorway crashes are supposed to be related to drivers falling asleep at the wheel. These figures are not to be found in the official statistics.[51]

As with looking at types of person, the danger is that different types of expert can be brought in to develop their own field of interest, sometimes in competition with other professionals. Wider issues of danger will be avoided. How various kinds of fallible human being with various kinds of fallible state of mind come to be in a position of danger to others, and why they are not prevented from endangering others, becomes less likely to arrive on the public policy agenda.

26

(v) Rate according to weather conditions

One might intuitively assume that darkness, slippery road surfaces and inclement weather would make it more difficult to move safely on the road. To see if this is the case, and to hold these variables constant while considering the others referred to above, it is necessary to have the relevant data. This is listed in Tables 14, 15, 27 and 28 of RAGB. However, while the darkness/lightness, road conditions and weather conditions are all given, along with the differences in road user groups reported as being in accidents in the different conditions, this is not linked to the distance travelled by the road user groups in the conditions listed. In other words, these factors are not related to a proper measure of exposure for the road users who might be affected by them.

So if we take the most obvious feature — namely lighting — we see that there has been a slight but definite decline in the proportion of RTAs occurring in darkness in the ten years up till 1988. According to the official statistics, "There are a number of reasons for the fall in the number of accidents in darkness. It may be due to a decline in the distance driven at night, *but unfortunately, there is no traffic data to indicate whether this is the case.*" (My emphasis).[52]

Ice

In icy conditions we have to consider factors such as a reduction in traffic caused by the conditions. Slower speeds tend to result in a change in the proportion of crashes resulting in less serious injuries, once again raising the question of the relative importance of different levels of severity of injury.[53] It also indicates that motorists have more capacity to adapt to external changes — if they have to — than some might think.

Fog

Motorway crashes in fog have become something of a staple media highlight of road crashes. In fact, the proportion of casualties occurring in fog is tiny.[54] Of the limited work available[55] it appears that on roads in general while crash and slight injury rates per unit of traffic may go up, the fatal and serious recorded rates stay the same.

The picture is slightly different on motorways, where crashes are more dramatic. Nevertheless, there may still have been adaptation to more severe conditions by motorists not making journeys. Again, it may be the case that the most obvious feature of difficult weather conditions is just how well motorists can adapt to them. And, despite the media attention and the prospect of special psychological tests to study perception in foggy conditions, driving too fast for the conditions is likely to be not far less relevant in much of the vast majority of crashes that have nothing whatsoever to do with fog.

The myth of a good record

Official statistics are used to present two related myths: that Britain has a better accident record than other European countries, and that this record has been

27

steadily improving. These myths are used to show that the practice of the Department of Transport, which also happens to be in charge of the production of official road traffic accident statistics, is correct. The situation is slightly self-contradictory in that the complacency that accompanies these myths erodes the basis for more intervention. Yet, since most of the intervention consists of advocating a continuation of the tradition which has led to such a supposedly good state of affairs — namely increasing motorisation, road building, lack of support for benign modes of transport and low public transport investment — the myths serve their purpose.

As we shall see in Chapter Two, *a good accident record may not be a good indication of the levels of danger that exist for road users* — but for the time being we can show that even in its own terms the idea that "we" have a good accident record is flawed.

The UK and Europe

The UK has fewer road deaths per head of the population than any other European Community country.[56] This is the basis for the claims that "we" have a good record. However, this can be explained by the low rate of deaths for car occupants, coexisting with a particularly high rate for other groups:

≡ Moped and motorcyclist deaths per number of two-wheel motor vehicles (TWMVs) are one-third higher than the EC average. Out of 21 countries in the EC and elsewhere in Europe, only four have worse records.[57] (Most of the crashes involving motorcyclists and other vehicles leading to hospital admission are legally the fault of other motor vehicle drivers).[58]

≡ Pedestrian fatalities per head of the population are only significantly worse in three out of 12 EC countries.[59] These countries — Greece, Portugal and Spain — are at relatively early stages of motorisation compared with the rest of the EC and increasing car use levels rapidly. Both these characteristics are historically those of societies with high pedestrian deaths per head of population. In contrast to the UK, other European countries, such as Denmark, the Netherlands and West Germany, have made significant efforts to reduce the danger to pedestrians by traffic calming and speed-reducing schemes.

≡ Cyclist deaths per head of the population are lower in the UK than in most other EC countries.[60] But this is basically because a smaller proportion of journeys are made by bicycle; per mile or journey travelled, many of these other EC countries (such as Denmark and the Netherlands) have far lower rates. In terms of the percentage reduction in cyclist deaths between 1977 and 1987, only two out of 20 European countries have worse records.[61] While there is some doubt about exactly what a "pro-cycling" transport

28

policy would be,[62] the major study on policy and provision for cyclists in Europe puts Britain in the worst of four categories of the eleven countries surveyed.[63]

Other statistics can be quoted. A recent study comparing Britain with the Netherlands and Sweden finds that reported casualties per kilometre travelled are some three times higher among pedestrians and ten times higher among cyclists in Britain.[64] Even with car users, the decline in deaths per vehicle mile travelled between 1977 and 1987 is only average for the rest of Europe.[65] Britain's supposedly good record is made up of a majority of non-car-users, who, per mile travelled (or per head of population for pedestrians, as their other index of exposure), have significantly *worse* records than most of Europe. These non-car-users then are particularly vulnerable; so that even if their chances of being killed were to be reduced, if there were more of them about, the overall deaths per head of the population could well be higher. As far as individuals' chances of being killed are concerned, the position would be better, but for the compilers of official statistics the "accident record" would be worse.

Britain lags behind other EC countries in terms of providing support for the modes of transport which are the least dangerous both for those using them and for others — that is to say travel by train and, to a lesser extent, by bus and coach. From 1975 to 1985, bus and coach travel decreased more sharply in Britain than in any other European country. The share of road transport occupied by private motor vehicles, the most dangerous mode to others, is higher in Britain than in 11 of 15 other countries surveyed in Europe.[66] Out of 13 countries presenting figures on freight, only one lifted, and four moved, a higher proportion of freight by road.[67] Rail investment as a proportion of operating expenditure is lower in the UK than in any other European country presenting figures.[68] In 1986 a study showed that government support per train kilometre was two or three times lower than in Denmark, France, the Netherlands and West Germany.[69] In terms of the share of GDP devoted to railway financing, Britain is the lowest in the European Community.[70]

Chapter 2 indicates that on more densely trafficked roads, whether because of lower vehicle speeds, or because of greater awareness of the possibilities of conflict, the chances of death are probably lower than they would be otherwise. To put it more technically, congestion intensity (as one factor involved in accident causation) appears to have minimising effects on crash severity and/or likelihood. The UK, or particularly England, is characterised by high population density. *So fatal crashes are less likely anyway*. It may dent national motorist pride, but features such as the twice as high number of road accident fatalities (which has changed little over time) in more sparsely populated France, may be more due to geography than anything else.

Change over time: getting better or worse?

Year	Population (millions)	Licensed vehicles (millions)	Pedestrians killed	Total road casualties
1930	44.6	2.3	3,722	178,000
1960	50.9	9.4	2,708	341,000
1990	55.8	23.3	1,694	336,000

Table 1.

Source: *Road Accidents Great Britain, 1990*

Vehicle, death and injury statistics, 1930, 1960 and 1990.

The table[71] might suggest grounds for optimism. Despite an increase in the number of people available to be hurt, and a massive rise in the number of vehicles there to hurt them, the number of pedestrians killed has decreased. There is a negative side; the number reported as injured has doubled. This might reflect changes in recording procedures. It may, however, also reflect the changes in medical care which mean that many of those who died pre-war could have been saved by contemporary treatment methods. At present it is customary to argue that trauma centres and other forms of post-accident care could save some 20 to 30 per cent of all accident deaths.[72] This would be a continuation of changes in treatment which have occurred over the last sixty years. So although there are no estimates of how much the reduction in lives lost may be due to differences in medical intervention, initial optimism concerning the activities of the road safety lobby and the motoring public appears less well founded.

But there are other quite different grounds for being less happy. Anybody who remembers life in Britain 30 or 60 years ago will have memories of children playing in streets, of elderly or disabled people being able to cross roads and of pedestrians simply exercising their freedom more. With fewer journeys made by car, people were more likely to walk. There are no adequate figures on pedestrian exposure, but it seems reasonable to suggest that there were far more pedestrian trips and road crossings and more time simply spent in the street. We must conclude that the chances of pedestrians being killed — per journey, per mile walked or per hour spent crossing the road — have probably increased.

One way to show this is to look at changes in the fatality rate (per head of population) for children in the 10-14 age group of a much more recent period.

Manchester streets in 1962

Because these children are less likely to have changed their behaviour as much as younger children have (with increasing parental car ownership and pressure to avoid increasing danger on the roads), they are an important indicator of the pedestrian experience. Looking at this group of children who have continued to behave as children always have, we find that between 1955 and 1990 their chances of dying on the road nearly doubled.[73]

Similarly with cyclists. In 1988 the lowest number of fatalities among cyclists since records began was recorded, yet the chances of dying per mile cycled appear to have doubled since the early 1950s.[74] Of course, the absence of a reliable traffic index for cyclists means that precise figures are not available. Estimates of the amount of cycling going on change.

In 1989 the cyclist casualty rates for the year 1987 were officially re-calculated on the basis of a higher estimate for the amount of cycling in that year. The consequent reduction in the 1987 cyclist casualty rate was by no less than 32 per cent.[75] There is no evidence that this has happened because cyclists have become less alert or careful; on the contrary, given the massive increase in danger from four

31

to five times more vehicles, and the increased number of crashes, cyclists must on average have become *more* careful to suffer only a doubling of their death rate. Evidence of the increasing number of crashes comes from the relatively short period of 1981-89. When insurance claims from motorists and motorcyclists, who were mainly hitting each other or stationary objects, increased by some 61 per cent.[76] In terms of responsibility, the most recent study finds that cyclists were the least likely of all road user groups to be at fault in an accident (in 27 per cent of cases) in which they were involved.[77] This backs up all the other studies of responsibility, which allocate a minority of responsibility to adult cyclists in crashes where they are involved. Cyclists, it would seem, are a lot less blameworthy than prejudice against them suggests.

Conclusion: who counts in the numbers game?

On 13 July, 1989 the Government issued two press releases based on DTp figures.

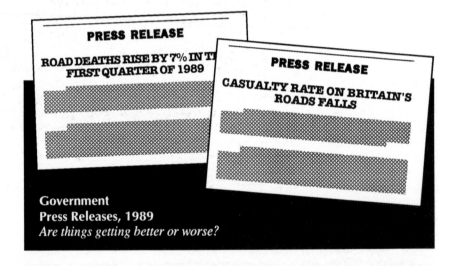

PRESS RELEASE

ROAD DEATHS RISE BY 7% IN T[...] FIRST QUARTER OF 1989

PRESS RELEASE

CASUALTY RATE ON BRITAIN'S ROADS FALLS

**Government
Press Releases, 1989**
Are things getting better or worse?

The reason for the difference in message can be attributed to different sections of the DTp bureaucracy deciding to give a different slant on the same piece of information. As should now be clear, there is no necessary conflict between the two headlines, and indeed there was none.

Right from the assumption that "the road safety problem" can be indicated in terms of the size of the overall number of casualties or fatalities, a pernicious process is started. It presents an image of progress — although, for vulnerable road users, even if safety is measured in terms of a fatality rate, life has got worse and is often worse than in other countries which are made to appear "worse". Even more insidious, official statistics present "the problem" as something "out there", divorced from the responsibilities of the road user.

This process of supporting an increasingly motorised transport system — one increasingly dangerous to vulnerable road users, if not to all — is bolstered by selective use of figures on the motorway accident record. Similarly, the use of "serious injuries" figures (and other measures) in preference to fatalities supports a favourable view of building or "improving" roads in ways which are discriminatory to the vulnerable.

The potential to hurt others is confused with the potential to be hurt. Most of the particularly vulnerable happen also to be less dangerous to others; and most of the dangerous happen to be relatively invulnerable. This fact, with all its moral and political connotations, is invisible.

Thus, when people are informed that the road user group they belong to has a "good" record, they tend to express a feeling of relief or even pride; their own responsibility is absent. Equally, the fact that a bad record may occur because of the dangers imposed by others also tends to be accepted as an unalterable fact.

In 1992, the Secretary of State for Transport, Malcolm Rifkind, commented on the gross reduction in deaths and reported "serious injuries" on Britain's roads by calling:

This continuing decline... a tribute to the motoring public and the quality of their driving.[78]

This at a time when there had been a steady increase in crashes and the chances of pedestrians and cyclists being killed, and where, if anybody was to be credited, it would be these road users, not motorists. Ultimately, despite evasive action being taken, the vulnerable will be unable to escape danger as long as there are still motorists. This could explain a particularly high child pedestrian fatality rate (measured by head of the population as no other figures exist) compared to Europe. Questioned about this Mr Rifkind offers the explanation:

It may be that more children are allowed out unaccompanied — young children who make their own way to school... whereas in many Continental countries they are maybe more likely to be accompanied by a parent...[79]

Yet research partially funded by his own department and published that year — the first of its kind seriously to assess the changing travel patterns of British children — showed not only a massive decline in independent school trips by children in the previous twenty years, but also far less freedom for children to cross roads independently than in a West German comparison.[80] When this was pointed out to the DTp's Head of Road Safety Division, his response was to suggest, on the basis of his daughter's Italian holiday experience, that the Secretary of State's guess was more accurate than the serious research.[81]

Much of the transformation in that motorist behaviour which did change was due to a factor politicians would rather not mention, namely a decline in economic

Pedal cars and pigeons in 60s Manchester before danger from increasing traffic cleared the streets

performance. Or to a factor like increasing congestion intensity producing spontaneous road user behavioural change (and which motorists generally regard as a problem). Congratulating all motorists on their driving behaviour is always dangerous, doing so when there is a continuation in a mounting trend of crashes is particularly so.

The business of defining problems, then, works subtly on the basis of hidden assumptions which acquire an increasingly unquestioned authority. "Accident reduction", as presently understood by the road safety lobby, is an inadequate approach to reducing the safety problems of road users, particularly if an equitable approach for vulnerable users is properly considered. It may even be just plain wrong. Chapter 2 uses the most reliable figures (for fatalities) to show what has happened in countries that have been motorised. It reveals some challenging data about the road safety industry's interventions and asks whether human beings have a right to "be safe". These questions push our consideration of the appropriateness of the statistics even further — do they, in fact, try to measure the right thing in the first place?

2.

A question of adaptation — risk compensation

WHAT COULD BE MORE DANGEROUS than announcing that as from tomorrow all traffic will drive on the other side of the road? It happened in Sweden in 1967 and the number of accident casualties fell dramatically.

If cars are marketed as "safe" or "crash-worthy" then should we be surprised if drivers become complacent and drive with less care? The drastic turn-around when the rule of the road itself was changed meant that, for a time, drivers had to sit up, open their eyes and drive more carefully.

❖❖❖

Everything that is supposed to produce more danger in fact produces more safety and... everything that is supposed to produce more safety produces more danger... Better roads, better sight lines, fewer bends and blind corners, less traffic, better lighting, better visibility, better weather conditions — all these that are supposed to make for greater safety in fact make greater danger. Worse roads, worse surfaces, etc... make for greater safety... because every 'non-restrictive' safety measure, however admirable in itself, is treated by the drivers as an opportunity for more speeding, so that the net amount of danger is increased... In trying to end the motor slaughter *we are perpetually chasing a factor we never catch.* It is a problem we cannot solve because X changes with every attempt at a solution (my emphasis).

JS Dean, Chairman of the Pedestrians Association for Road Safety, 1947.[1]

It is true that 7,000 people are killed in motor accidents, but it is not always going on like that. People are getting used to the new conditions... No doubt many of the old Members of the House will recollect the numbers of chickens we killed in the old days. We used to come back with the radiator stuffed with feathers. It was the same with dogs. Dogs get out of the way of motor cars nowadays and you never kill one. There is education even in the lower animals. These things will right themselves.

Lieut-Col JTC Moore-Brabazon, MP, later to become Minister of Transport, speaking against the 1934 Road Traffic Bill because it introduced a driving test for motorists and a 30 mph speed limit in towns.[2]

35

These quotations are from opposite sides of the struggle for power on the roads. Apart from their disagreement about the freedom that motorists should have to endanger others, there is another important difference. One side, despite protesting that it was being victimised, was in the process of winning more freedom, and the other was losing it. Moore-Brabazon's voice is one of wounded indignation on behalf of a threatened minority; in the debate he was to complain: "Over 6,000 people commit suicide every year, and nobody makes a fuss about that."[3] In fact there was great public anger at the danger posed by the less than 1.5 million private motorists in Britain. But Moore-Brabazon's protests — for example, that the Bill was unfair because it had been drawn up by a non-motorist — were unnecessary. The restrictions on motorists were minimal; motorist power was on the increase.

Dean's worries for the future were better founded. Not only were the restrictions on motorists in the 1935 Act minimal; to the extent that an illusion of control had been created, they would henceforth operate as a smokescreen. Motorists could claim that they had done their bit, so that minimal restrictions could become, in effect, pseudo-restrictions. Dean's contribution in his unjustly forgotten book *Murder Most Foul* (1947) was to show how the road safety lobby became part of the process which brought about the dominance of the motorist. This was shown partly by revealing its links with the motoring lobby, and partly by demonstrating how motorists would continually adapt to the changes in the road environment and the acquisition of driving skills.

On this point the opponents were agreed. *Road users would adapt to changing circumstances.* And both were right. Many people, as pedestrians and cyclists, would simply no longer be in the road environment. Those who remained in the increasingly dangerous motorised world might not be able to follow the lead of the "lower animals". They would have an increased chance of becoming accident statistics, even if their additional caution meant a rise lower than the rise in danger presented to them, and even if their overall annual toll were lower. As for motorists, the new road environments would reduce the need — previously enforced by the danger of poor sight lines and similar hazards — to be as careful, in terms of speed, alertness and vigilance. The road safety measures proposed by engineers and others would fail, as "safer" roads such as motorways were also to fail, to bring about a reduction in the chances of motorists dying[4] precisely because hazards had been removed.

The business of adapting to changes in perceived danger is part of everyday life. It is central to an understanding of what has happened, does happen, and could happen on our roads.

Risk compensation and the sociology of road safety

Sociology is often seen as composed of two different traditions. One looks at societies as wholes, forming more than the sum of their parts. Within these societies there is an orderly set of human behaviours; these may seem intensely personal, private and individual, but they occur in predictable and regular patterns. This tradition looks at the regularities in society — such as religion, informal moral rules or language — as facts which are independent from individuals, and have an unseen, coercive effect on them. These facts will tend to generate or modify behaviours — whether marriages, births or even the most private act of suicide — in ways which can be expressed statistically. The statistics absorb individual variation; "the average expresses a certain state of the group mind".[5] The resentment we might feel at the idea that our behaviours are to some extent determined by social forces beyond our immediate control can itself be seen as a socially generated belief. It is the idea of individualism, a product of particular kinds of society, which reached its ultimate statement with Margaret Thatcher's famous comment that "there is no such thing as society, only individuals and families".

The other tradition stresses the interpretive work which individuals perform in their everyday lives: constantly negotiating their way through situations they find themselves in; adapting and creating new ways of living with each other. It is wary of making statements about the social whole, or counting up features of human life or causality. The emphasis in this tradition shifts from the macro- to the micro-social. However, while it observes individual and small-group interactions more intimately, the differences between the two traditions are not so much of scale but of philosophy and belief about the nature of social science.[6]

There is a constant debate about the way these traditions can be used together, if at all. In the area of transport and safety, both can come to similar conclusions about the importance of the nature of risk-taking. Both approaches can indicate that there is a general tendency to take a certain level of risk, and that this is a central determinant of accidents. Because of this general tendency, interventions for "road safety" tend to redistribute danger and accidents, rather than eliminate them.

The role of ideology

So far, academic sociology has not tackled this area. Why is this? One part of sociology is the sociology of knowledge and ideas. I am concerned with the contemporary ideology of "road safety" as part of a society with a car dominated transport system. "Ideology" refers to a body of ideas and attitudes, generally in a derogatory sense because the ideology mystifies or distorts reality. It works as part of a particular power structure, in a set of social relations, and helps maintain that structure. Ideology sets hidden agendas of discussion, forms background assumptions about the nature of those discussions and, above all, makes certain features of a society appear natural or necessary. One might think that something generally described as important, because of the large number of deaths and injuries involved (not to mention the highly visible changes that have occurred in the road environment within the lifetime of most active academics), would have attracted sociologists' attention.

But ideology — in this case the ideology surrounding the hegemony of the car

— is very powerful. Challenging it means not only doing hard intellectual work and distancing oneself from the ways of thinking of most of one's peer group. It also means questioning privileges that some members of society have over others. Since academics are likely to belong to the group with the privilege (car owners), they tend to lose their imperative to reveal society's unstated rules. With research funds dominated by the institutions which produce road safety ideology, this imperative is further eroded.[7]

The macro-social analysis

In 1949 Reuben Smeed, for many years one of the central figures in the world of transport and road safety research, suggested that there was a relationship between a country's rate of road accident fatalities (deaths per registered vehicle) and level of motorisation (registered motor vehicles per head of the population) in a country.[8] There are problems with comparing accident statistics between countries, because levels of medical care and of reporting, and how long after an accident a death is defined as such, vary. However, there is a degree of reliability in the use of fatality figures, and the relationship suggested — the "Smeed law" — appears to indicate a regularity in all the countries that have experienced motorisation over many years.

Large differences exist in the death rate per vehicle between the least motorised countries (relatively high) and the most motorised countries (relatively low).[9] The differences are similar to those between the highly motorised countries at the early stages of motorisation and at their current levels. The implication is that a trend from high to low levels of fatality per vehicle is followed in all countries.

This fatality rate is different from the number of deaths per head of population. For example, in the early 1980s India had a fatality rate per head of the population about 2.5 times less severe than the UK, but per vehicle it was some 30 times higher.[10] Whatever the decline in fatalities per vehicle, the killing and injuring of people in motorised societies have remained persistent. Nevertheless, it might be supposed that if there are more vehicles on the road, there is more opportunity for crashes. A marked reduction may not be the only measure to consider; but might it not indicate some progress?

This is suggested in a poster on the wall of Smeed's old department at University College, London:

> A possible explanation why this formula [the Smeed law] should hold over such long periods and such a wide range of countries is that efforts made in a country to reduce road accidents depend on the number of vehicles and the existing accident rate. If this is so the formula gives an indication of the accident rate that countries are prepared to tolerate.

But what exactly is involved as "countries" reduce their tolerance of an accident rate? Part of the process could be what was suggested in Chapter 1, namely a move away from the vulnerable modes of transport. In other words, one accident rate (per vehicle) declines, while there is less change or even an increase in another rate (per head of the population); other rates still (per journey or mile travelled) increase for the vulnerable road user.

One important category — car occupants — has admittedly achieved a sizeable reduction in the chances of being killed per mile travelled. The orthodox explanation for this is that cars and the environment they travel in today present far less of a hazard to their occupants. With design features ranging from anti-burst door locks, through collapsible steering columns, seat belts and roll bars to crumple zones, the occupant of a modern car stands at least five times less chance of being killed in a crash than in a car built in the 1950s.[11] There has been a radical change in Britain's road environment during the years of increasing motorisation as junctions have been redesigned, sight lines lengthened and cambers levelled to remove hazards for motorists.

With these massive advantages that car occupants now have, however, the apparent success story is not so great. Albeit crudely, one might calculate that with these advantages and improvements in medical care (counteracted by a 3.5 fold increase in traffic), according to the official "road safety" view, the chances of dying should have decreased by anything between 3.5 and 8 per mile travelled for car occupants over the last 30 years.[12] But the factor is just 2.5.

There is another way of looking at the experience of motorists which contradicts this approach, while also painting a poor picture of the progress supposedly made. It suggests that motorists *have* adapted all too well to changes in their situation, and that the decline in their fatality rate (whether as in the Smeed formula or in deaths per mile travelled) would have occurred anyway *without the engineering changes mentioned*. The macro-social evidence for this comes from comparing countries now at the early stages of motorisation with those that achieved similar levels some 50 or 60 years ago, such as Britain and the USA. There is a similarity in their experiences of fatality rates per vehicle, as noted above; but the vehicles driven in Third World and other newly motorised countries, and to a lesser extent their roads, are a great deal less hazardous for car occupants than those in the pre-war years.

A mass of evidence shows that a variety of safety measures for motorists do not reduce accident chances but give motorists *safety benefits which are absorbed as performance benefits*. From seat belt legislation, to vehicle safety regulation,[13] it seems that there are minimal or no benefits in terms of the chances of vehicle occupants dying per mile travelled, and that the transformation of their behaviour as hazards to them are reduced means that additional dangers are posed to people outside their cars. In this sense motorists have indeed adapted to changing circumstances. The problem is that, however much this has been positive for them, moves to increase their safety have led to an exacerbation of the danger to vulnerable road users, already growing because of increasing motorisation. Some of the specific ways whereby risk compensation on the part of motorists occurs are detailed below and throughout this book. The society as a whole appears to create a general level of "accident" deaths which obeys laws of risk creation and restriction that are more powerful than even the most effective of regulations or "road safety" initiatives.

This process may not be necessarily amenable to psychological, micro-sociological or any other small-scale type of analysis. It might be said that there is a hidden hand of aggregate risk-taking in a society which affects our behaviour and is constituted by it in a way which cannot be understood by summating individual instances, even if it were possible to identify and measure each act. Where the Smeed law is not fully capable of explaining variations in fatality rates, another model based on a national economic index — something which refers to the behaviour of a society as a whole — seems to fit.[14]

Another way to consider this is to think of all the risk-taking decisions that occur in the road environment. All of us assess situations and make a variety of judgements about which route to take, how fast to go, where to cross the road, and so on. These involve numerous elements, such as how long and often to look in a mirror, through to differing degrees of concentration — any of which can contribute to a crash occurring. These judgements are in turn perceived and acted on by others. Out of this complex set of interacting decisions, the number of potentially disastrous consequences nationally runs into millions, if not billions, daily. Yet there is something predictable about the national outcome. Some people are very cautious, and others reckless, yet out of all their actions, and changes in transport conditions each year (weather, the mix of road users, distances travelled, changes in speed, and so on), the overall number of deaths can be predicted with a reasonable degree of certainty, falling within a limited amount of variation of on average 4.5 per cent, and no more than about 8.0 per cent.[15]

It is difficult to accept that causes can be so definite yet so intangible. One of the foremost figures in the contemporary world of road safety research describes "human infrastructure" as more important than components of the "engineering infrastructure" (the road and vehicles). He argues that the most important part of this is driver behaviour, which is: "culturally and socially determined... the prevailing social norm for driving in any society has a major influence on traffic casualty rates. Because social norms change slowly, it is difficult to quantify their contributions to traffic safety."[16]

Yet these intangible macro-social imperatives work through a society in a way that often is ultimately capable of being represented as statistics.

This applies not only in the area of road casualties, but for victims of accidents and violence of all kinds. Despite changes in the manner of death, there is a consistency here also; certain kinds of hazard are controlled, only for others to appear in their place.[17]

What is risk-taking?

Motorists regularly say that they do not take risks (although they observe other road

40

users taking them). This may be explained partly by a pride which prevents motorists from admitting their faults.[18] It may also be due to ignorance. But it is explained very largely by motorists feeling that they do indeed take a *level* of risk (or take risks on unusual occasions), but that this level is acceptable. The word "risk" therefore entails a variety of subtle and almost unwitting decisions made as part of everyday life; while it includes extreme risk-taking and recklessness, it also includes lower levels of carelessness. It might not always have the connotations of extreme irresponsibility that prevent people from admitting to it — although the lower levels it includes may also be less acceptable in a civilised society than most motorists might be prepared to accept.

As the Minister of Transport said in 1954: "Accidents in the main arise from the taking of very small risks a very large number of times. A thousand-to-one chance against an accident may not be rated very high, but for every thousand people that take it there will be an accident."[19] While the level of risk may be exceptionally low, it is still to some extent intentional, and therefore changeable, given the right incentives or disincentives. The official advice is therefore to "check your conduct... against the advice given in the Highway Code... If you habitually disregard what it says, you, or someone through your fault, will probably, sooner or later, be the victim of an accident which could and should have been avoided."[19]

Most motorists break laws and the regulations in the Highway Code as a matter of course.[20]

The micro-social analysis

Each of us modifies our behaviour according to the level of risk which we perceive as we perform any task. People change their levels of attentiveness, alertness and vigilance, and the operation of the skills at their disposal, according to the scale of the threat, which they think confronts them. Sometimes they may be more or less careless in similar situations than in others, but the general tendency to adapt to perceived risk remains. This can be observed in our personal behaviour. If we feel that a road has only a few vehicles travelling slowly along it, we are less hurried and watchful when we cross. Some of these changes in our behaviour are unobservable, but they are still there.

These alterations in behaviour are *interdependent*. Observation of a local shopping street reveals a change in collective behaviour. On busy mornings with stationary or slow moving congested traffic, pedestrians cross with more ease and at more places than they do with a faster moving flow. Motorists may in turn adapt their behaviour accordingly. The road environment, like nature, abhors vacuums. When space is vacated, it is filled by those who feel they have most right to it in the circumstances. There is constant competition for space, an ever-changing flux of movement involving the assessment of risk. When the judgements are faulty, "accidents" occur. These in turn form part of the basic set of assumptions about correct behaviour which we all have and constantly modify according to the light of our experience, our tendency to take different levels of risk, and to a lesser extent, the sanctions that may await rule-breakers.

A number of small scale studies show adaptation to the use of safety aids such as crash helmets and seat belts,[21] or other compensating action occurring in response to changes in perceived risk. One study shows adaptation to the use of studded tyres (designed to allow better road handling in icy conditions) in Sweden.[22] The safety benefit conferred by having the "safer" tyres tended to be consumed as the motorists using them drove faster round bends in the road. Sometimes the tendency to use "safety" benefits as performance benefits is anticipated by the manufacturers and incorporated in the marketing of the product. Television viewers might remember the first advertisements using a former senior police officer to sell car tyres with the slogan "The *Grand Prix S...* a major contribution to road safety." The *Little Old Lady S* might have sold less well.

Risk compensation can apply not just with the use of safety aids, but with the acquisition of skills.[23] Driver educational programmes can fail because people, particularly young people, may be introduced to driving earlier than they would have been otherwise,[24] or because they teach what Winston Churchill referred to as "undue proficiency".[25] The acclaimed ability to use speed to "get out of difficulty" — whether through training or by the use of "performance" cars — may be used to get into the difficulties in the first place.

The actual presence of other vehicles is in itself a factor affecting the risk-taking of motorists. In 1953 a study noted:

> **the number of accidents involving collisions between vehicles on two arms of 3-way junctions tended to be proportional to the square root of the product of the flows on the two arms, rather than to the product of the flows as would be expected if *the behaviour of the drivers was unaffected by the flows*.** (My emphasis)[26]

Looking at this and other evidence Smeed noted that: "in some circumstances at any rate — behaviour is affected by the amounts of traffic on roads".[27]

So with more motorists there are more fallible human beings in more potential collision situations to have crashes (and as such reducing their numbers would have benefits in reducing some crash potential); but the effect of increasing congestion intensity means that this increase is mitigated — although only partially — by awareness of increased traffic. I would suggest that this example of adaptation would be predicted by common sense. It has been studiously ignored by the transport establishment.[28]

Micro-social examination of risk-compensating behaviour can move up from study of individuals and small groups to road user populations, such as those affected by legislation governing the use of seat belts[29] or motorcycle helmets,[30] or the temporary transformation of motorist behaviour following drink-drive legislation.[31] All these cases indicate the tendency of what Dean called "X" — risk-taking by those in charge of motor vehicles — changing its form (or, as in the latter case, to be temporarily restricted, only to reappear).

Forms of risk compensation occur geographically (over space), and historically (over time). The first of these forms is generally known as *accident migration*. This phenomenon affects what has been a major part of the activity of traffic engineers concerned with safety, namely "black spot" treatment. A tendency has been noticed for accident frequencies to decrease at the treated "black spots" but to increase in the immediate vicinity. The explanation offered by two engineers describing this phenomenon was that, prior to treatment, drivers are likely to be involved in potential conflict, and so drive more cautiously as they leave the "black spot"; after treatment, the increased caution has disappeared, and accidents increase in the surrounding area. This work, operating on the basis of a rather straightforward idea, was first published in Britain in 1984.[32] It had been suggested as a possibility by a leading British psychologist nearly 20 years before that.[33]

The second, time-based, phenomenon is the regression-to-mean effect, first described in the nineteenth century, but not considered in the road accident field until 1980.[34] This refers to the tendency for particularly large numbers (in this case, of accidents at a particular site) to become smaller over time, or for particularly small numbers to increase. Put simply, if there are a particularly large number of accidents at a particular site, which is then treated, the resulting decline in numbers there would probably have occurred anyway. Investigation has shown that the regression-to-mean effect can produce apparent reductions of accidents of the order of five to 30 per cent at sites with observed frequencies in the range normally considered appropriate for remedial treatment.[35]

So, whether because of accident migration or the regression-to-mean effect,[36] "unsafety" — or risk-taking — shifts over time or place unless it is reduced at source. When properly assessed, the supposed benefits of black spot engineering can disappear altogether — a study of a county's record over several years shows that accidents are simply redistributed, not reduced.[37]

Dealing with the specific phenomenon of crashes where vehicles have skidded has been a concern for engineers for decades, with specific benefits claimed for laying skid-resistant surfaces.[38] Reviewing the last ten years of such measures, the Department of Transport notes no decline in the proportion of injury accidents in which at least one vehicle is reported as having skidded.[39] It claims that the overall decline is due to changes in vehicle design, more efficient brakes, lights and other machinery, and changes in road design. But the phenomena noted above, and other material suggesting that engineering the road environment does not affect collision rates, indicate that reduction in numbers of reported injury producing crashes can not be clearly defined back to such measures.[40]

Professionals are unlikely to minimise the beneficial effects of measures which they have demanded large amounts of public money to install. Establishing cause and effect is made even more difficult by the continuously changing interactive features of human behaviour in the road environment. But that is precisely the point: a reason for the disappointing lack of improvement in the proportion of skidding "accidents", which the DTp suggests is due to use of faster and higher performance cars, could be that motorists have accurately adapted to the change in road surfaces, knowing that they have less occasion to worry about the potential for skidding.

Risk compensation in society

There is, then, considerable evidence to suggest that processes of adaptation to perceived danger occur throughout human activity in the road environment, and are implicated in the causes of crashes, injury and death. One can take the approach of those sociologists concerned with the negotiation of everyday encounters, and look at the various subtleties of perception and avoidance that occur in actions as apparently simple as crossing a local road. Or one can use larger-scale studies of the effects of road safety regulations and the use of safety aids, or other measures to detect persistent and continual risk compensation. Finally, one can use studies of the society as a whole to see that there is a hidden hand of risk-taking, a spontaneous process of adaptation which occurs throughout that society, whatever happens in specific instances.

The significance of risk compensation has been debated among "road safety" professionals over the last few years. During this debate there has been some confusion over the meaning of different terms, and indeed an apparent confusion over the aims of the "road safety" enterprise. This is discussed below. But one of the main points about risk compensation and safety on the roads has always been implicit but often hidden: it is the question of *who experiences risk, from whom, and/or at whose expense?* This is essentially a question of the power of different road user groups, and can be illustrated by an example of risk compensation from an earlier time.

In 1815 Sir Humphrey Davy invented the miner's safety lamp, which, through its ability to reduce explosions, was what we would now call a safety aid. Far from reducing accidents, however, its use actually led to an increase in mining explosions and deaths.[41] The lamp was used by pit owners to send miners to previously unworkable areas. In this example of safety benefits being absorbed as performance benefits, the owners profited, while the miners were as badly off as before, or worse off. The invention was not simply appropriated by the owners for their own purposes; rather, they had actually suggested its development from the start. Similarly, much of the "road safety" industry's work has been an integral part of the transport establishment, supporting efforts to strengthen the hegemony of the car. The conflict between car users and others in the road environment is not identical to that between mine owners and miners; but deaths and injuries are equally involved and just as harsh.

Since there is no clear agreement about exactly what risk compensation refers to, it is necessary to reconsider the term, and the debates that have centred around its significance.

History of an idea

The idea that road users respond to changes in perceived risk by modifying their behaviour has been suggested since before the war — probably the first academic reference is an article in the *American Journal of Psychology* in 1938.[42] Smeed considered it in his 1949 paper.[43] Physiological studies of galvanic skin response measurements carried out on drivers in 1964 suggested that a response to driving conditions would tend to keep tension and anxiety levels stable.[44] Psychologists argued that "accidents are the product of a basically simple closed-loop process", or that driving is a "threat-avoidance" principle.[45]

The idea goes back to the earliest times. One element is the risk of harm caused by infringing social norms, which forms the basis of theories of deterrent punishment. An early example is that of Sennacherib, the Assyrian engineer-king, who set up the first "no parking" signs — posts along the processional way in Nineveh, inscribed "Royal road: let no man lessen it" — and decreed that a scoundrel who parked a chariot or other vehicle along this road should be slain and his body impaled on a stake before his house.[46] Like most legal interventions, this legislation probably served a mainly symbolic role. Nevertheless, one assumes that those charioteers capable of accurately assessing the risk modified their behaviour accordingly.

Theorists often approach the subject without any sense of previous attempts to generate theory. At present the best known risk compensation theorists are John Adams in Britain[47] and Gerard Wilde in Canada.[48] Much of the work is generated by political concerns, that is, an interest in the rights and safety of particular groups of road user, and mistrust of, or support for, the transport establishment. The politics are apparent in the generation of ideas, well before their dissemination and marshalling for lobbying purposes. Smeed plainly regarded risk compensation as an important possibility requiring consideration after reading Dean's work.[49] While Wilde does not ap-

pear to have started with a concern about the more political issues, his comments on the building of motorway-type roads have a relevance to transport policy.[50] Adams's work continues his criticisms of those contemporary transport policies which promote an increase in car hegemony.[51]

Risk homeostasis

Put briefly, the theory of risk homeostasis has the following components. First, everyone has a tendency to take risks; safety may well be desirable, but it is balanced out against other considerations. Why human beings possess risk-taking natures is a matter for metaphysical speculation.[52] Second, this propensity is influenced by the potential rewards and losses of risk-taking, which are realised from experience of one's own and others' accidents. The extent to which "accidents" occur is therefore both an indication of risk-taking *and* a cause of road user behaviour.[53] Third, there is a balancing act between rewards and losses representing a target level of risk, which is in turn set against the perceived level of risk. This can be summed up by saying that we have a type of "risk thermostat" in us which regulates our behaviour. Unless our willingness to take risks changes, accidents will be redistributed rather than eliminated by environmental or circumstantial changes.

Risk substitution may therefore occur across behaviour domains, thus accounting for the stability of gross violence and accident deaths in societies. Hell's Angels who stop motorcycling may engage in another similarly high-risk activity outside the road environment instead. Models of risk homeostasis feature "lagged feedback".[54] The amount of time required for compensatory activity to be completed is not specified. So there may be little compensation with one kind of road safety regulation, but a lot with another one at a later date.

Because concepts such as "target level of risk" or "perceived risk" are virtually impossible to measure, it is difficult to test risk homeostasis directly. There are also all the problems discussed with analysing accident statistics. Theorists such as Adams admit therefore that homeostasis cannot be refuted and is thus not properly scientific; but it has plausibility and, at the level of risk compensation — in other words at a level where some adaptation takes place — validity.

Some criticisms

One objection to the risk compensation idea refuses to engage with the macro-sociological theory. The idea that the whole is more than the sum of the parts is difficult for those outside sociology or anthropology to accept. An example is Broughton's rejection of the idea that "social learning" is a useful concept to explain the relationship identified by Smeed.[55] The debate involves fairly sophisticated discussion of statistics,[56] but the argument essentially comes down to disagreement about how changes in society occur. The sort of change described by

Smeed and Adams is explained by the intervention of road safety professionals; the fact that there may be a holistic process of spontaneous adaptation is not considered. Nor even is any macro-social conception of culture, norms or values, even if it involves no belief in social holism. Plainly it is difficult for road safety professionals to accept that change may occur by the activity of ordinary road users independent of them. A background in an individualistic human science (or supposed science), such as psychology, which avoids such explanation, provides appropriate ideological cover for doing so.

Another objection denies that risk compensation, let alone homeostasis, occurs at all. An example is the work of Lund and O'Neill of the Insurance Institute for Highway Safety,[57] which ignores or misrepresents the mass of evidence for risk compensation: "there is absolutely no evidence that the perceived risk of injury alters driving behaviour."[58]

Other objections deal with the imprecise nature of formulations of risk compensation or risk homeostasis theories. Not only are perception of risk and target levels of risk immeasurable, but it is unclear whether the theory specifies road users as a whole, the wider society, each individual, each group of road users or all four. It is difficult to say whether the risk of a crash, or actual physical injury, is the risk which people are concerned about. It may be that some reductions in hazards cannot be perceived, such as the changes that have occurred in the internal design of vehicles, or in more crash-resistant windscreens.[59]

The politics of the debate

Arguments about risk compensation can be usefully considered as arguments for particular kinds of transport policy — for supporting one side or another of the transport status quo.

To some extent, risk compensation was accepted by the transport and road safety establishment well before the interventions of Adams and others over seat belts. Over the years it has been quite common to hear engineers arguing against facilities for cyclists or pedestrians on the grounds that they might "encourage a false sense of security".[60] In using a concept of risk compensation, a negative hidden attitude towards the road user group concerned can be revealed. The view of Lund and O'Neill — part of that minority of road safety professionals who deny that risk compensation occurs at all — presents us with an image of rational drivers who simply want to get to their destination without an accident. "Risk" is a pejorative word which cannot apply to most drivers. But this is just an academic version of the defence of drivers who deny their fallibility.[61]

Modern risk compensation theorists are misrepresented. As one of the leading road safety researchers in Britain put it: "The trouble with risk compensation theory is that it's so negative... it says you can't do anything."[62] This is just not true. Risk compensation theorists have not argued against government regulation as such. Rather, they have pointed out the negative consequences of regulation, and that the officially stated aim is not going to be achieved. They have never argued against attempts to reduce danger — indeed, the justification for concern about road-building schemes, more crashworthy cars, and so on, is that they form part of a more dangerous environment for the vulnerable. Risk compensation theorists are all in favour of approaches which remove the burden of risk from the vulnerable.

Risk compensation theory is, in fact, positive in one sense — it is optimistic about people's capacity to be careful *if they really want to be*. Probably the most dangerous single change that could happen to a road system is the change of the rule of the road, from driving on the left- to the right-hand side. This happened in Sweden in 1967, and there was a quite dramatic fall in casualty rates (which disappeared after a time when presumably the target level of risk had been overreached).[63] Such dramatic achievements are made without the assistance of road safety professionals, or even in ways which oppose their dominant ideology. In this sense, of course, risk compensation theory is negative. It challenges their authority and reveals the supposedly neutral approach of "accident reduction" to be part of a system which increases the dangerous hegemony of the car.

A hypothetical illustration can indicate this. Motorised countries tend to demand public liability insurance cover for motorists. Consider a society where such cover was banned and where those responsible for accidents could be easily identified and made to pay damages (by removal of property and assets). My speculative suggestion is that if the inevitable motorist backlash could be withstood, a dramatic change for the better could be effected. Of course, as vulnerable road users became more relaxed in the event of safer conditions prevailing, their exposure and consequent casualties — but not necessarily per unit of exposure — would increase. This suggestion about the possibilities of more careful driving, and the negative role of insurance, might not win agreement from the theoreticians of the Insurance Institute for Highway Safety.

The risk compensation debate now

Risk compensation, in its broadest sense, suggests that there is a persistent process of adaptation to changes in the environment where there is some kind of threat. This casts doubt on a lot of the official road safety enterprise. Some criticisms, such as the point about unperceived risks made by McKenna[64] and others, may seem valid but are flawed. While some changes may be invisible, information about the results of crashes will ultimately reach the ordinary road user in the long term.

Other similar points can be discussed, but the real issue is that risk taking continually appears to change. Critics of risk compensation deal with this by arguing that provided homeostasis is not complete — as long as there is some net accident reduction — the necessary regulation should be supported.[65] This appears to be straightforward, but is not. The regulation may have negative effects on other road users — seat belts are a classic example.[66] Application of the normal public health criteria of refusing to allow, for example, drugs which have negative side-effects for a few, even if they are beneficial for the many, would block many such interventions. The longer-term and wider effects on risk-taking elsewhere in society are also not considered. The essence of safety on the roads is the interdependence of road users, and the effects of an individual intervention cannot easily be isolated.[67] The truth of this, however, is not readily accepted by the number-crunchers of road safety research. The tendency for further displacement can be indicated by looking at society at a holistic or at least some sort of macro-social level, which road safety theoreticians are unwilling or unable to do.

This discussion is essential in order to establish what has happened and what interventions are desirable. An understanding of the human tendency to adapt is crucial to understanding how people end up in crashes. So interventions which favour or indirectly collude with less care on the part of motorists are discriminatory against vulnerable road users. Many such points are raised in Chapter 3.

We finish this chapter by reference to a piece of theorising by a more important risk compensation theorist than any of the above, as he was then Minister for Roads. Referring to a roundabout and a crossroads in a city with high cycling traffic, Peter Bottomley said:

> Because everyone thinks that a roundabout is safe... they treat it as though it's safe and that leads to accidents. At the dangerous crossroads, appallingly dangerous, but the statistics say it is much safer than the roundabout, because everyone knows it's dangerous, we all take account of the danger and use the junction more safely.[68]

This is imprecise. The statistics do not say the crossroad "is much safer"; they say there are fewer accidents there. This makes the central point, not only that *accidents and danger are not only not the same thing, but that change in one may be associated with change in the opposite direction of the other*. Roundabouts, in fact, tend *both* to be dangerous for two-wheelers[69] *and* to have high accident rates for them. This does not oppose a risk compensation argument. Indeed, without some compensatory behaviour (most cyclists claim to try to take more care at roundabouts than at other junctions) the high accident rate would be even higher. Even with compensatory behaviour, after a while an accident rate simply cannot be brought down. The point is that roundabouts are a typical feature of a road system based on increasing vehicular capacity at the expense of the safety of vulnerable road users.

This raises crucial questions, which we can further illustrate by reference to the question posed above about the experience of car occupants and the change in their chances of dying. We have seen that with increased traffic density a factor as well, the decline in fatality rate is even less obviously a success story for the safety establishment than calculated above, and that the implication (along with specific evidence on engineering treatments and safety aids) is that measures it has advocated have not only failed in their alleged purpose, but further endangered the non-car users.

However, this factor, involving discomfort for motorists compelled to be more watchful, may be undesirable for them — the "safety measures" which allow them to relax may be more attractive.

The questions are: do we want low accident rates (whatever they may be) or do we want safety? And what kind of road-users should be presented with danger?

3.

Accidents, danger and accident causation — the politics of road safety

No one should be free to harm others.[1]

John Stuart Mill

We have been talking about this [the objectives of road safety initiatives] for years... and nobody can agree on what the goals are.

Frank Haight, editor, Accident Analysis and Prevention.[2]

RECENTLY a glossy advertisment showed a young couple gazing lovingly at a Volvo sports car beneath the ad agency's invitation: "Go on, lose your heart, the rest of you'll be safe enough."

A fast car which will keep the driver safe, no matter what, may be attractive to drivers, but it's not difficult to see what it holds for cyclists and pedestrians, or even for drivers of vehicles with less "armour". The manufacturers, who also preside over the Volvo Traffic Safety Awards, declined a request to reproduce the advert here.

Consider the following examples of how "road safety" is perceived:

I.   In November 1989 a junction between two motorways south of Birmingham was opened, to protests from motorists. The slip road from one motorway merges from the right into the fast lane of the other. The local MP described it as a "recipe for disaster", and urged drivers involved in a collision to sue the Department of Transport. (There was no suggestion that this course of action should be extended to pedestrians or cyclists involved in collisions on roads posing dangers to them and under the control of the DTp). The Automobile Association was reported as saying: "The new junction is going to call for the utmost concentration. From a road safety point of view, it's not ideal... It could be a nerve-racking experience."[3]

Studying this some four months later, with some 70,000 vehicles a day going through this junction which poses an unusual and particularly severe hazard to motorists, there had been no reported accidents. Local motorway police thought that this might be due to the additional concentration of motorists wary of a new hazard. Their experience of complex gyratory systems in Birmingham suggests that the problems come from local drivers who have become used to the risks, not

51

from drivers newly confronted with them.

II.   In 1988 *The Guardian* motoring correspondent warned prospective tourists about the Ruta del Sol in Spain. Because it was what she described as a "bad road" — with heavy flows of mixed traffic — motorists were advised to take the special precaution of avoiding having a "heavy alcoholic meal on a hot day" before travelling on it.[4]

III.   Also in 1988, the following observations were published in the journal *Ergonomics*:

> **On arriving in the United States or Canada from Britain, one is impressed by the large size of North American cars, and by the fact that they appear to cruise around in slow motion on wide roads, with wide shoulders and grass margins beyond. Pedestrian traffic in North America appears better behaved; pedestrians often wait at red lights when there is no traffic coming, and there seems to be more help for school children in the form of warning signs and crossing guards. Traffic in residential areas also seems much better managed, with many all-way stop intersections and more street layouts discouraging through traffic. On returning to Britain, one is impressed by the much smaller size of the average car and the fact that it offers much less protection to its occupants in a crash. The roads are much narrower — most of them were built before the car was invented — and separation distances between oncoming cars are much smaller. Speed limits on motorways are much higher and enforcement is minimal... vehicular traffic seems quick and darting compared with the more stately progression of North American traffic... Pedestrian traffic seems more anarchic... And the density of traffic is much higher: although Britain has fewer cars per head of the population than the US, it has twice as many per mile of road.[5]**

In other words, this quotations tells us that in terms of the relative lack of hazards presented to them — more regulations concerning vehicle safety, lower speeds leading to less kinetic energy dispersed on impact, easier roads to drive on, fewer obstacles when accidents occur, and so on — North America is "safer". But the average North American is about twice as likely to be killed in a traffic accident than someone in Britain, with fewer journeys or miles completed by the vulnerable modes.[6] On intercity roads, which are specially designed for modern motor vehicles, the chances of motorists dying per mile travelled are about 50 per cent higher than for all roads in Britain.[7] I am told by acquaintances returning from the USA that they resent driving in Britain again, and they proceed to tell me of the need once again to turn radios off, silence talkative child passengers, and so on. They have to concentrate more, pressured into being more careful.

Safety or leeway?

All this shows is that situations most of us regard as dangerous are not necessarily the same situations which result in crashes; *they may even be the opposite, as the perception of danger makes us more careful*. There is a persistently fluid set of reactions to perceived danger, continually modifying road user behaviour, which itself generates an interdependent set of reactions, and so on ad infinitum. This world of flux, of continual adaptation, is the world we are talking about when we consider safety on the road. The tension between danger and our reaction to it is the very stuff which concerns us; it determines how, when and where people are hurt. But it also tells us what people actually want in terms of safety. While the voiced aim might be that we want as little risk as possible, such claims misrepresent the nature of the situations that most motorists place themselves in. Attempts to reduce accidents tend to displace danger unless there is a fundamental change in willingness to take risks. People want to take the risks *they* want to take.

In terms of the above examples, motorists do not want unusual and tricky junctions near Birmingham, and they want more relaxed driving conditions whether in North America or Spain. They are capable of driving carefully if conditions remain hazardous, but they prefer to have the freedom to relax. They want *more leeway*, which they tend to use up mainly in an unconscious way. This may well be unobservable until the accident statistics are collected, if indeed they can be.

This presents us with an alternative objective for the aims of road safety: freedom from what, following JS Dean, I call *motor danger*. Those of us who feel strongly about the misery suffered by people hurt in crashes have often talked about "saving lives" and "injury reduction". Yet, despite being apparently obvious, there are problems with this concept, summarised below in discussion of it. [8]

When it comes to safety, we want a reduction in the danger that others present to us. Some are more vulnerable to danger than others — and they also happen to be less dangerous as well. [9]

We should be interested in the chances of people dying or being hurt as they cross a road, rather than in the net number of casualties at a particular road crossing. Scaring elderly or child pedestrians from crossing the road will reduce the number selected by the road safety establishment, but will not necessarily reduce the casualty rate. It might even be legitimate to argue for more freedom in crossing the road even if this does not reduce the casualty rate. More leeway, after all, is what the motorists quoted above appear to argue for, and the road safety lobby, particularly in engineering an easier environment, has obliged.

The difference between motorists and other road users is that, when motorists relax, they increase danger to the vulnerable; the converse is not true. [10] This crucial difference separates the approach of transport ministries and other establishment bodies, based around supporting the rule of the car, from the approach advocated in this book. Anodyne talk about "our accident record" pushes safety responsibilities away from the potentially dangerous road user and props up a system which discriminates totally against the safety of the vulnerable. There is nothing wrong with removing danger from road users — provided they do not increase their potential to harm others. This, unfortunately, is what the "road safety" movement has been doing for some sixty years.

The way we live (and die) now

(a) "Safe" cars:

One way in which danger has been increased in the name of safety is in vehicle design:

> Consider two fictional hypothetical vehicles at either extreme of a safety continuum. At one end... a hypothetical 'invulnerability vehicle' in which it is almost impossible for the driver to be hurt no matter how he drives. At the other end... a 'death trap vehicle' — one with, say, a sharp pointed steel spike positioned a few centimetres in front of the driver's forehead. This example has generated lively discussion regarding in which vehicle a driver would in fact be more likely to be hurt. However, there is *essential unanimity on the question of which car would pose a threat to other road users* ... When we consider car mass, which is closely related to engineering safety [sic], we find that *drivers in larger cars,* which are displaced towards the safer end of this continuum relative to smaller cars, *are involved in more crashes and constitute a greater two-car crash threat to other cars of all sizes* (my emphasis).[11]

So speaks a senior researcher employed by General Motors. "Safer" cars are more dangerous for those outside them, both because of transformations of driver behaviour and because the results of crashes are worse as more kinetic energy from

A Dutch campaigner's way of putting it

heavier vehicles is dispersed on impact.

This knowledge is not confined to technical discussion but is a foremost selling point of a number of major manufacturers, and therefore something likely to lead to reduction of motorist care. If a model (made by Volvo) is sold with its central advertising theme being that it can be driven out of a third floor window at 30 mph and allow the driver to walk away unharmed, it is absurd for members of the road safety lobby to say that driver behaviour will be unaffected by such knowledge. [12] A reduction in the *need to worry*, rather than safety in the proper sense of the word, is being sold and bought. The principal international road safety award, worth half a million kroner, given annually to senior members of the road safety establishments of different countries, refers to "the necessity of excessive concentration on the part of the driver" as a significant problem. Its full name is the Volvo Traffic Safety Award.

The quest for the more invulnerable car reaches its furthest expression in the modern rally driver's vehicle. Rally drivers were the first motorists among whom seat belt wearing became commonplace. Now they may wear fire-resistant suits, crash-helmets and the most sophisticated seat-harnesses in cars with additionally strengthened bodies. This is not because unwitting innocents may inadvertently turn their vehicles over and require protection; it is because the drivers want additional leeway to engage in a deliberately dangerous pursuit.

(b) "Safe" road environments

In 1988 a major conference on what "road safety" jargon refers to as Single Vehicle Only (SVO) crashes took place. [13] These crashes typically involve young men who are drunk and tired driving off the road late at night. A rational answer to the problem of SVOs, which constitute a sixth of all injury-producing crashes in Britain, might be expected to concentrate on the restriction of young people's driving, crack downs on drinking and driving, or the provision of public transport. The 1988 conference, however, advocated crash barriers on off-road objects, using "frangible, breakaway or flexible materials" in the construction of poles and other street furniture. As *The Guardian* motoring correspondent put it: "Badly sited traffic signals, telegraph or electricity poles, a tree or bus shelter, can cause injury or death." The general dangers of car use — regularly discussed in the prewar period — were nowhere in sight.

Following this approach, as bus shelters are moved over to the far side of the footway, pedestrians may be forced to desert the increasingly exposed areas which have been prepared for more danger in the name of safety. No statistics will show an increase in pedestrian or two-wheeler casualties, as the motorists' leeway increases again. What are the long-term implications of such a way of assessing "accident causation", of defining the problem of danger on the roads?

(c) Speed and "accidents"

Speed limitation has been a focus for safety campaigners for decades, and their efforts have been persistently and successfully opposed by the defenders of motorist power. Speed limits are ignored with impunity; on exceptional occasions infractions incur minor penalties. From time to time, however, the road safety lobby makes limited reference to the simple fact that kinetic energy dispersed on impact increases as the square of velocity — accidents at speed are much more likely to cause death. Speed is particularly important for pedestrians, and their chances of being fatally injured in crashes vary as follows: [14]

Speed	Proportion of injuries leading to death
70 kph (43½ mph)	83 per cent
50 kph (31 mph)	37 per cent
30 kph (19 mph)	5 per cent

This sort of evidence is part of the justification for the speed reduction element in traffic calming initiatives in Northern Europe. [15] Speeds can be automatically controlled with available technology. [16] In the era of the "smart" weapon, it does not take too much imagination to suggest the potential for other technologies which could, for example, automatically (or from a police vehicle) cut out engines altogether. The spectacle of high-speed chases, "joyriding" etc. could end immediately.

As early as the 1930s, campaigns for speed restriction included demands for speed governors which were resisted by the AA and RAC even more strongly than they opposed testing. As the pre-war gentleman motorist in Geoffrey Household's *Rogue Male* put it: "No driver has a right to average more than 40 [mph]; if he wants to terrify his fellows there are always a few wars going on." [17] Instead speed limits were introduced which have been more or less ignored ever since.

Speed has not been a high priority for transport academics. Two researchers on road safety in the 1980s claim they were advised to give a relatively low priority to work on the role of speed as a cause of accidents by the then head of the DTP's Transport and Road Research Laboratory, Barbara Sabey, a former rally driver. [18]

As with all other related questions, the attitude to speed depends on whose side you are on. Assessing the way people adapt to speed involves moral and political judgements about the transport status quo. For the DTp, speed reduction caused by congestion is bad because:

> **Frustrated by delays, the motorists react aggressively and irresponsibly — jumping traffic lights, attempting to overtake on the inside, etc. Pedestrians, too, may take liberties with slow moving traffic that they would not take with faster traffic. A mother who would never dream of wheeling her pushchair across an urban freeway may be tempted to do just that in a city street. [19]**

What assumptions are implied here? If cyclists or pedestrians were regularly to physically assault motorists they had seen breaking the Highway Code or law (such as speed limits), would the legitimacy of their behaviour be accepted, as the legitimacy of aggression among "frustrated" motorists seems to be in this statement? And where exactly does one decide what "taking a liberty" is? For parents, elderly people, people with disabilities and indeed any pedestrian, the DTp's insistence that they use a subway (with its own brand of safety problems) because it has built a freeway through their community is itself something of a "liberty".

(d) "Dangerous" children?

The following news appeared in my local newspaper in north-west London recently, meriting some three column inches. It indicates attitudes which are not untypical:

> **The death of a 9-year-old girl has prompted a coroner to call for all ice-cream van operators to display warning signs to motorists that they are trading.** [20]

The story is a familiar one of two children outside their home on a residential road who were knocked down by a motorist who "didn't have time to stop". Roadside observation in urban Britain shows most motorists breaking the speed limit (which is significantly higher than that automatically created by engineering methods on traffic-calmed roads in Northern Europe, with speeds reduced to less than 20 mph), and driving too close to the vehicle in front. Lack of proper training and a host of other failures in obeying the Highway Code are also commonplace. [21] The road in this case is not exceptional.

More specifically, paragraph 59 of the Highway Code is devoted to warning motorists about children near ice-cream vans, with an explanatory photograph. Readers can make their own observations of motorist behaviour in the vicinity of schools or in residential areas. A brief survey among colleagues in the road safety community supports my belief that no warning notice could make the slightest difference to ice-cream van incidents.

A "solution" to this problem can be advocated while ignoring the true causes of danger on the roads. The evidence of children's behaviour in traffic often suggests that: "it is the children who are anticipating danger and behaving responsibly, not the drivers." [22] Yet "education" of children is still pushed as a solution — despite these findings; despite the inevitable tendency of children, however massively policed by parents and others, to behave as children always have done; despite agreement elsewhere that adults and the less vulnerable should shoulder the onus of responsibility; and despite the fact that the determining role of those who are dangerous to others should be the focus of attention. Whether or not resultant changes in accident statistics occur after any programme of education, for sections of the road safety industry, and for the dominant ideology supporting the transport status quo, the cause of child pedestrian accidents is children.

In the 1960s, in one of the few mass circulation books on the subject published, one "road safety" analyst wrote: "To live at peace with his Frankenstein creation, Man now needs a national dodgems — a bumper-rink for bumper-cars — where the unconscious aggression, pride and envy of the community can hold sway without real danger." [23] This commentator correctly identified the adaptation to changing circumstances which has occurred, including the danger-producing characteristics of "safe" roads. He did not realise, however, how the crashworthy cars built for his "dodgem" circuit would both increase danger to people outside them and fail to reduce the chances of being hurt for those motorists who did not want to use the extra leeway created for them, but actually wanted lower risk. His book does not mention cyclists or motorcyclists, and in effect tells pedestrians to get out of the way. Other problems caused by mass motoring are not considered.

Such is the attitude of at least a section of today's "road safety" community. Leeway for motorists has been gained at others' expense and does not provide greater safety for the more careful driver. Apart from vulnerable road users being endangered, the more careful drivers do not get as much safety as they might legitimately expect. Under a smokescreen of misleading statistics and victim-blaming, the rhetoric of "road safety" lets motorists off the hook and leads to more danger for their victims. This support for car hegemony is implicated in the very process of constructing a transport system — including motorway construction and the use of cost-benefit analysis.

The alternative

So what is the alternative to the philosophy of the dodgems circuit ? To meet the basic requirement of reducing danger to others — an older and more honourable principle than cost-benefit analysis or the jargon of "accident reduction" — the emphasis has to go back to controlling the source of danger. This means controlling the way cars are used. Protecting people from others has to be separated from protecting them from themselves. Once the latter principle is invoked, vulnerable road users are subjected to more danger from "safer" motorists and have additional pressure focused on them to absent themselves from the road environment. As vulnerable road users are weaker politically, and more likely to get hurt in crashes, attempts to reduce their presence most easily fit the target of "accident reduction".

The alternative objective means implementing those measures which reduce danger in a non-discriminatory way, which do not create more leeway for any group at the expense of the safety of others. A classic example of present discrimination is speed. Motorists have often opposed lower speed limits on the grounds that higher speeds — in best risk compensation manner — tend to make them concentrate more. A non-discriminatory (or rather reduced discrimination) approach to road danger requires that the only form of acceptable risk-taking is that which is *not dangerous to others*. If tension is required by the potentially speeding motorist, it can then be supplied by the risk of punitive sanctions.

But why?

This approach poses an alternative to the myth that we are all in it together: the reality is more one of some endangering others. But, if it is indeed "them and us", what is so wrong with the powerful and less vulnerable having their way? It is not, after all, just the ideology of "road safety" and the weakness and division of those suffering which maintains the status quo. For a lot of people, things are just fine — if their increased freedom from danger is used up to endanger others, so what? If they already had excessive potential to danger, so what? The fact that the playing field has been uneven for so long can mean that it should stay that way, or get worse.

My argument (expressed in Chapter 7) is that even without the problems of mass car use,[24] even without the additional efforts made by non-car users to cope with motorisation, even without their increased chances of being hurt, right from the beginning, the introduction of the car has brought with it a danger which has never been properly coped with. If some people — and they should not even have to be called "vulnerable" — are using benign[25] modes of transport, they should have the right to move about in safety, with any threat properly controlled. That should also be available to the motorised — providing it is applied at source with reference to the discriminatory status quo. It may be a difficult aim, but stating it is preferable to the distortion of current practice.

"Saving lives" and the meaning of death on the streets

It may be difficult to assess reduction of motor danger in numerical terms, but then it is difficult to assess whether the "saving of lives" has occurred. We don't know how many people are hurt on the roads. Their chances measured retrospectively are only a rough guide to their future chances of being hurt, and may be inversely related to the danger confronting them. We only know that there will be a constantly changing inter-related web of presentation of danger and reaction to it, changing in virtually unknowable ways as an integral part of our culture. We value the lives of people lost on the road (by age attributed cause) differently. Their very presence there depends on the kind of transport system and society we want, and indeed the kind of danger that exists. In so far as some people's lives can be said to have been saved by "road safety" initiatives, others may have been lost. [26] Injuries are difficult or impossible to grade in terms of the suffering of those involved. People do feel a need to differentiate between those hurting and those who get hurt — "road safety" obscures this.

The very phrase implies a kind of separation from the world of danger, as if we were not implicated in it, but benevolent experts arriving from outside society on a mission of mercy. All that separation does is to remove us from our responsibility. Replacing "saving lives" (and "injury reduction") by the aim of reducing motor danger puts us in the tradition of all the civilised ideas about the intolerability of endangering others. That is more important than fitting in with the distorted number-crunching of the road safety lobby.

Consider an article in the traffic engineers' journal[27]: it describes how roads should be engineered to avoid certain kinds of crashes on curves in rural roads. Because the authors are aware of the tendency for accidents to migrate, they try to create a situation where accidents will happen in places where the car occupants are less likely to get hurt on impact with surrounding structures.

In the plan to create "safe" crashes they ignore the evidence indicating that risk compensation (of which the accident migration phenomenon is simply one manifestation) may still lead to injury-causing accidents to motorists somewhere in the system. But more important, because their work is based on the minority of crashes involving reported injuries, and because rural roads have a very low benign mode user level, the effects on people outside cars is neglected. In the event of any increase of use of the benign modes, the tendency to tolerate motorists crashing on bends would be disastrous. But this form of analysis and the overall approach of which it is part do not allow for that.

Death on the roads where we live is always more than an individual human being dying, or any kind of attempt to add up the sum of those hurt or killed. Even if the ultimate result of the existence of danger is most obviously seen when the worst has occurred, an equitable, human, civilised approach requires dealing with danger at source, and with the silence and mystification that surrounds it.

Meanwhile, the "might is right" philosophy of the dodgems circuit still holds sway. The cultural effect of discussing the "cause" of road accidents by the "road safety" establishment in the ways shown above must be destructive — although difficult in the first instance to assess through their methods of analysis. Coping with the destruction that has already occurred requires a fundamental change in attitudes and beliefs.

This should include the correct use of language. Motorists do not simply "lose control" through "errors of judgement" to drive off roads into trees. And these trees do not "cause accidents". Instead, motorists' use of a particularly dangerous form of transport which has always been out of control — or at the very least, inadequately controlled — has led to just one example of very many where their behaviour can lead to objects or people being hurt. Understanding this means moving beyond specific cases and returning to the basic wisdom of the early campaigns against "the motor danger". They would have regarded the blaming of trees as a kind of intellectual and moral degeneracy. If we want a civilised approach to danger on the road, we should too.

Part Two

The road safety industry

Introduction

THE ROAD SAFETY LOBBY is made up of different organisations and interests. Some of these compete among themselves for attention and funding; and some speak more openly than others for the interests of motorist power and privilege.

At one extreme are the motoring correspondents of newspapers, who often take up the only space in the press available for discussion of safety on the road. (Although not strictly members of the lobby, they popularise and support many "road safety" initiatives.) Their comments can include defence of drinking and driving, and bemoaning the introduction of computerised controls which could remove the possibilities of driver error.[1]

At the other extreme come representatives of pedestrian and cycling organisations. However, in terms of what becomes public policy and the dominant view of "road safety", their voices are of little influence.

The official "road safety" arena is occupied by the Department of Transport nationally and road safety officers and traffic and highway engineers locally. The DTp has long been linked with the road lobby, and these links sometimes involve the exchange of personnel. The head of the DTp's Road Safety Division when I began writing this book is now employed by the Royal Automobile Club. The personnel involved organise themselves in professional bodies — the engineers' institutions and the institutes and associations of road safety officers. These bodies are represented, along with the manufacturers of "safety aids", doctors, motorists' organisations, some academics and others, in lobbies for "road safety", principally the Parliamentary Advisory Council for Transport Safety (PACTS).[2]

The main "road safety" organisation has been the Royal Society for the Prevention of Accidents (RoSPA) whose road safety section was set up in the

61

interest of the motoring organisations. The Safety First organisation which eventually became RoSPA was based on an approach to workplace safety which emphasised purely voluntary measures and the responsibility of employees as opposed to control of employers. This ideology was continued in RoSPA, with the particular responsibilities of the potentially dangerous minimised. Organisationally, motoring and road lobby interests were over represented in positions of power.[3] The way it convinced the public that its enterprise was in the interest of all — although pedestrians' and cyclists' organisations left it in protest at certain times — is one of the victories of "road safety" ideology. In the 1980s RoSPA's star waned with the loss of substantial DTp grant aid and competition from some insurance companies that provide free "road safety" publicity material. These companies also give money for supposed research into road safety,[4] which, while appearing to be substantial in amount, should be compared with their turnover and advertising budgets. Their involvement is basically a form of advertising. It is difficult to see how their involvement generally leads to any real chance of reduction of road crashes, from which, of course, they derive a great deal of their revenue.

Some features of the road safety industry

Inter-dependence
Despite differences in emphasis and approach, there is a great degree of interdependence, with the same organisations meeting in slightly different permutations under different umbrellas, whether the Medical Commission on Accident Prevention, RoSPA or PACTS. Their activities will frequently be financed by motoring interests.[5] Through their meetings and publications the mythology of road safety is reinforced to achieve authoritative status.

"The wood for the trees"
The central facts of danger on the road are obscured by details of the road safety scene. The wisdom of the increase in motorisation is unquestioned and/or seen as something which should be accepted, particularly by those most vulnerable to the inevitable increase in motor danger. The adaptation by individuals — generally referred to as risk compensation — is only acknowledged if it is used as an excuse to avoid controls on motor danger.[6] The inability to see the wood for the trees also involves the following:–

Divide and rule
The problems originating from mass motorisation are separated from each other and distanced from their origin. Thus there are "pedestrian safety", "cyclist safety", "older road user" topics put forward for discussion and action. Apart from placing responsibility on to their own shoulders, non-car users are disunited by this process — while the source of their difficulties, meanwhile, fades into the background.

The illusion of objectivity

All road safety interventions are essentially political and moral acts. They create and use symbols we associate with danger on the road, which may in the first instance have little to do with actual chances of being hurt or killed on the road. From the point of pandering to motorists' desire to be carefree (as opposed to careful) onwards, the road safety lobby has tended to collude with motor danger. This has been covered up with the aura of scientific objectivity and professionalism.

Industry

Road safety professionals distance themselves from the origins of motor danger. This might seem particularly difficult in the case of the Department (and before it, Ministry) of Transport, as this dominates the car centred transport system. This process involves an almost obsessive production of "research', statistics, and other material, fuelled by a sense of purpose and achievement.

Numbers, numbers... and more numbers

The content of the road safety industry's output is a stream of statistics. Whether or not these figures bear any true relationship to the experience of ordinary road users, they continue to be released to show a record of progress. Because of the strength of contemporary "road safety" ideology, and the lack of power of the victims of motorisation, this core of road safety mythology is rarely penetrated. Its features are that "it", "we" or "the problem" is getting better despite the following facts:–

≡ Casualty rates for cyclists and pedestrians have — as far as we can tell — got worse over the last 40 years, even with, if anything, more care exerted on average by members of these groups.

≡ The one numerical indicator of danger, namely insurance claims, has been increasing steadily, both in aggregate and per vehicle.

≡ The decline in casualty rates among car occupants would have largely decreased anyway. Even if adaptation had not occurred, the decline should have been lower than it has been, given the amount of protection afforded them by vehicle and road engineering.

The mythology also claims that the supposed improvement is due to the beneficial efforts of the road safety lobby, in spite of the following:

≡ A general decline occurs irrespective of road safety intervention in times of economic downturn, such as in 1991.

≡ The process of spontaneous change by road users may involve "improvements" due to vulnerable road users absenting themselves from the road environment through sheer fear (for example, children not being allowed to cycle).

≡ Road safety interventions may not have beneficial effects (for example, because of accident migration and other displacement).

≡ These displacements can often involve increasing motor danger.

For any professional it is going to be hard to feel that his/her endeavours are simply failing, or indeed, even making things worse. Similarly, it may be difficult for him/her to accept that removing the vulnerable from the environment may no longer be regarded as a success. Helped by an ideology which separates out inseparable parts of the whole into different "problem areas", they can seal themselves off from responsibility for motor danger. Some will, with at least the merit of honesty, claim that they are only there to be part of the process of increased motor danger, pressurising its potential victims to take as much evasive action as possible, whether such action is possible or not.

This world of numbers involves values placed on units, where costs and benefits are supposedly related to road safety interventions.

The economist's tale — how much is your life worth?

There is a growing interest in cost-benefit analysis (CBA) as it is used in transport policy[7]. Government is officially committed to costing the effects on the environment of new development.[8] There has for some time been serious criticism of the DTp's COBA system (the department's own cost-benefit analysis system), which is used by it to justify road building, on the basis that all the costs and benefits are not properly allocated and assessed, particularly with regard to consideration of the more benign transport alternatives. Consequently one school of thought has held that CBA procedures should be followed which modify COBA or similar approaches, except with more consideration of the adverse effects of motorisation.[9]

It is certainly the case that the arguments put forward for CBA by its main proponents in the transport area should be properly considered, rather than simply resisting the idea of costing choices.[10] Nevertheless it appears to me that CBA will always have some inherent flaws which ultimately make it wrong to use. These are briefly summarised as follows:

A. Basic evaluation

As explained in Part One, there is no remotely reliable way of knowing the extent of harm which has occurred on the roads. We do not know the numbers which fall in each category, and those categories do not tell us much about the kinds of injuries sustained. In terms of the experience of those affected, even something apparently as uniform as a broken leg can have quite different effects on those affected if we consider factors like length of recovery time, extent of immediate pain, effects on differing numbers of relations etc. Societies tend to value the harm done to people in different age groups in different ways.

All the casualties should have the disbenefit of injury added up and given a value. In principle then a measure which, for example, saves some lives but takes some others (which is in fact what has happened with the introduction of certain safety aids)[11] could be properly assessed. Would we be able to properly balance up slight injuries (even if there were uniformity among them) against serious injuries? How many slight injuries equal a serious one?

B. Causality and changes in costs and benefits

Even if we could add up the cost of suffering, how do we know the reason for an apparent decline? As the following chapters indicate, despite the claims made by various professionals, interventions may not actually be responsible for savings. Indeed, although professionals will claim credit, reductions will occur because of a process of adaptation by ordinary road users which is too subtle and indefinable to be easily allocated a role in CBA — even if professionals were willing to include it, which they are not.

C. Adverse effects: who does what to whom?

Here we have a crucial point which the road safety lobby has persistently attempted to erode in significance. Lives are not simply lost, nor injuries sustained, in the road environment. Some road users endanger others. It is not just that some are more vulnerable, some are more potentially dangerous to all. Most people value an injury sustained by their own carelessness quite differently to one forced on them by the criminal negligence of others. While there is occasionally some reference to this in the literature,[12] CBA does not at present allow for this in calculations. This is also related to the point made against Pearce by Adams, that there is a vital distinction between willingness to pay for protecting something, and willingness to accept compensation for its loss. (The difference between giving and taking.)[13]

D. Negative reasons for "benefit"

The main reason for a decline in pedestrian — particularly child pedestrian — casualties over the last 60 years is the loss of pedestrian freedom created by motorisation. CBA will count this as a benefit. Should it be? This leads on to the next question:–

E. How is *danger* to be evaluated?

The main official text on CBA for road casualties is called "The value of life and safety: a search for a consensus estimate",[14] but as pointed out above, life and safety are not only different, but frequently mutually opposed. If greater safety leads to greater willingness to use vulnerable modes and greater ease of being hurt, is this a simple disbenefit? And by how much? We can estimate the fear of parents by seeing how much they are likely to refuse permission to their children to walk to school or cycle:[15] how much does this cost? Are the parents to be the ones to be asked, or their children, who are less likely to have *the ability to pay*?

F. The ability to pay

Most variants of CBA involve relating part of the cost-benefit equation to the ability of those likely to suffer costs to pay for those costs not to be inflicted. Frequently those most likely to suffer are those with the lowest disposable finance.

G. The relevance of CBA anyway

Consider the argument put forward by the defenders of the "moderated CBA" approach. If we put all the real costs of motorisation, including danger as well as accidents, into the equation, we will get a quite different result which will be better for motorisation's victims.

But will we? As I detail in Chapter 14, costs of motoring are — according to quite conventional forms of costing — a good £30 billion annually more than motorists pay. When road safety practitioners complain about the need to have CBA in order to prioritise the allocation of scarce resources, replies that the resources have already been allocated in the wrong way do not cut any ice. Playing the game properly, that is to say with a more level playing field and the goal posts the same distance apart at either end, is not on anyway. CBAs would not be used if they were. They are there to give a (pseudo)-scientific gloss to moves which have been planned to occur anyway.

It may be that the health disbenefits of mass car use are such as to dwarf the numbers of people killed and hurt on the roads[16], but not only are these costs not included in discussion, they have not had resources allocated to research them, as this might challenge the transport status quo.

On a more general environmental note, in a current textbook on transport economics, the section "Definition of the Environment"[17] does not include anything outside the immediate environmental effects of road and other developments, such as global warming, in which the transport sector is so importantly implicated.

H. The minorities question

But even if the dull costs and benefits (were we to stand any chance of equitably or even inequitably assessing them) to be properly added up, we have the question of what happens to the minorities. Even with an equal ability to pay, minorities might be squeezed out of the equation because of their minority status. Indeed, a classic problem with utilitarian philosophy — upon which CBA appears to be based — is precisely that failure.

I. The broader context

CBA fits into a wider economic system with environmental disbenefits of global implication.[18]

Those suffering most tend to be far away, and/or in unborn generations, and without economic clout in CBA equations, even if they are considered in the first place. We are asked by CBA to consider ourselves as consumers rather than

political citizens,[19] and to make decisions which are made as individuals when the only way they can be made sensibly is collectively. Indeed, the failure to make decisions collectively compels people to make individual decisions they would otherwise rather not have wanted to make.[20]

The benefits are counted in terms of indicators which are biased to certain kinds of economic activity and transport. Despite criticism that it is a poor indicator of the economic health of a society, GDP (gross domestic product) is a criterion of success. If its size depends on movement of goods, services and people by car and lorry, then the more cars and lorries there are, the better. The more obsolescent the better. Indeed, accidents can themselves be shifted on to the other side of the CBA equation as they are a form of economic activity (without them the crucial insurance sector would suffer). In short, if you have a car based economy, the rules of CBA will be bent in its favour to start off with.

Conclusion: should we play CBA?

In the satirical novel, *Catch-22*,[21] an American air force officer called Milo Minderbider engages in a ceaseless quest for profit through a series of enterprises with extraordinary ramifications. These include the purchase and sale of useless commodities, stealing desperately needed morphine from first aid kits, organising the bombing of his own base and alerting the enemy of attacks on them by his own side. These activities are justified by making his fellow servicemen shareholders, and when a profit is made "everybody gets a share".

But, in the case of road safety, we do not all get shares. Some get more than others, and at others' expense. The rules of the game are inevitably biased against those who are worst off, and changes in the rules will not be accepted if they involve a genuine alternative to the status quo.

There is something to be said for pointing out the contradictions in the CBA analysts' work. For example, where measures like skid-resistance are advocated by Pearce when evidence indicates no benefit from it according to their own criteria.[22] Here the poverty of their work can be demonstrated.

One can go further. On a motorway-type road there are fewer vulnerable road users present to be involved in accidents, and as a result the road is considered "safer". This leads to positive financial benefits being awarded to a road scheme of this type, even if its record in terms of the experience of its users is worse, and even if it generates more (unaccounted for) danger on adjacent roads.[23] This is a classic way in which money goes to a more dangerous system which we already pay for. We could argue that simple fiscal and legal controls, as outlined in Chapter 17, would not only suppress the demand for motorway building, but generate more use of the benign and vulnerable modes. From there we could argue that the danger from the remaining cars should be costed even more highly, because there are more potential sufferers from it.

But if we do not like their criteria; if we find that certain key notions are logically incoherent, and if we are concerned with minorities who are likely to be edged out come what may, should we be playing this game? There *are* quantitative criteria to be considered in transport policy — minimal standards for local public transport provision, standards of access to amenities for non-car users, levels of CO_2 and pollution emissions etc — and economic considerations which are stated in Chapter 17. But the fact is that decisions about endangering others are political and moral decisions which should not be fudged over by the language of economists.

4.

Clunk-click cover-up — seat belt myths and realities

THE SEAT BELT: crowning glory of the official road safety lobby, a prime example of common sense prevailing over reckless abandon. And yet, warnings were sounded about seat belt-use as far back as the late Seventies and early Eighties when legislation was beginning to look more likely.

Whether the Isles Report, *produced within the Department of Transport, was deliberately withheld is now hard to say. But its findings didn't fit in with a road safety quick-fix for which its advocates were making great claims. In fact, in the two years following compulsion, a marked shortfall in the expected number of lives saved occurred at the same time as an increased death rate of 40 per cent for cyclists — pedestrians and people in the rear seats of cars also suffered significant rises.*

There is no better single device available at the present time for reducing the risk of injury and death when automobile accidents occur.

Statement to seat belt hearings in US House of Representatives, 1957.[1]

This House elevates human life and practical considerations of pain and disability over pedantic obscurantism based on dubious theory. A vote for the Bill is a vote for sanity, compassion and common sense... for freedom and for life itself.

Jack Ashley MP, speaking for compulsory front-seat belt wearing, 1976.[2]

I emphasise that this is not the opinion of my Department alone or of any single group of experts, but the corroborated conclusion of many careful studies in several countries. It is really no longer debatable.

John Gilbert MP, Labour Minister of Transport, supporting the same legislation.[3]

It is time for anger, it is time to tell the Minister of Transport that his failure to enforce the wearing of seat belts is tantamount to being an accessory to murder... mass murder.

Speaker at British Medical Association conference, June 1981.[4]

Compulsory seat belt wearing, an eminently sensible and harmless measure which costs nothing.

Howard Boyd, RoSPA national bicycle safety officer, 1981.[5]

The quotes above summarise the conventional wisdom about seat belt wearing for occupants of cars, which became legally compulsory for front-seat passengers of cars and vans in Britain on 31 January, 1983, after some years of debate. According to this view, there was never any question to answer. Seat belt wearing would "save lives" with no adverse effects on any other road users. This was self-evident.

The conventional wisdom, however, is false and fundamentally flawed — fatally so for vulnerable road users. Evidence that compulsory seat belt wearing achieved anything like the benefits it was supposed to is either defective or absent. On the contrary, it appears that compulsory seat belt wearing led directly to a lower level of care on the part of motorists and a more dangerous road environment for vulnerable road users. Not only were there no benefits for the vulnerable, but *the level of danger became worse*. The move was justified by claims that it would "save lives". In so far as we can use these terms, it seems rather to have *taken* the most vulnerable lives.

Why discuss this issue now? Seat belt legislation, its effects on all road users, the evidence used to support it and the activities of those supporting it, represent a particularly important episode — if not the most important — in the history of road safety legislation.

The fact is that this oft-quoted victory for the road safety lobby had bad consequences for the so-called vulnerable road user — that is to say those human beings outside cars in the road environment, and those more frail people inside cars less capable of withstanding crashes whether belted or not. This episode is not just an instance of, but rather is symbolic of, how the road safety lobby has either colluded with or exacerbated these consequences, namely the increase in motor danger, since its inception.

The nature of the debate

For a measure which was supposed to have such obvious effects, the evidence in favour of compulsory seat belts was, and remains, inconclusive. Evidence which contradicted the official line of the Department of Transport was suppressed, and some findings by its own research body (the Transport and Road Research Laboratory) were released too late for debate. Other evidence which contradicted the DTp's preferred view was ignored or misrepresented. The Minister of Transport announced that "it is really no longer debatable" before a genuine debate could take place. Of course, for many of the participants in the debate, the evidence was irrelevant. Selected portions were used or misrepresented to back up already existing views, and the repetition of the same evidence eventually resulted in reinforcing its status.

The seat belt legislation was supported by a coalition of "road safety professionals" in the medical establishment, the Department of Transport, manufacturers of cars and "safety aids", "safety researchers" and others who more or less unquestioningly support the dangerous dominance of the private car. This already powerful alliance was supported by motoring correspondents who then, as now, controlled the outlet for "road safety" news in the media. Criticism came principally, but not exclusively, from some politicians on the right and from people concerned with the danger to road users of mass car use. The weakness of the doubters is an indication of the status of vulnerable road users in a car dominated society.

This episode, proudly referred to by the road safety lobby as one of its major triumphs, played a central role in legitimating its existence. It also, once again, let motoring off the hook. While the principal cause of danger to other road users continued to exist — or was even exacerbated in its severity — the powerful and privileged road users could bask in the glow of having "done something for safety".

Most of us, as car occupants, do not think twice about using seat belts. This fact is frequently invoked as a paradigm case of what "road safety" should be about. It is used to suggest that simple remedies can be "the answer", and it helps to confuse transitive and intransitive meanings of safety by initiating interventions into self-protection rather than the protection of others. Such a complacent view neglects the possibility of changes in human behaviour in response to changes in perceived risk. Accordingly, a number of serious disbenefits have to be set against the benefits which seat belt legislation might have brought.

A brief history of seat belt use

The car seat belt is a direct successor of the seat belt used in aircraft in the first decade of the century to prevent ejection.[6] During the Second World War the relevance of seat belts for car occupants was realised. By the late 1950s they were becoming available in new cars — such as Volvo models from 1959 — and the US road safety lobby was pushing for seat belt use.

In Britain, the 1967 Road Safety Act stipulated that seat belts meeting a British Standard (BS 3254, introduced in 1968) had to be fitted to new cars. For the next 14 years a flood of papers was published in medical journals and other outlets for the road safety lobby, claiming that seat belt use for front-seat occupants would reduce the chances of dying by up to 80 per cent.[7] The message was that seat belt use would "save lives" and that, as advice and education had failed to impress the majority of those who would benefit, their use should be compulsory. Persistent lobbying and debate led to the passing of the 1981 Transport Act, which made the wearing of seat belts by front-seat occupants of cars and light goods vehicles (vans) compulsory as from 31 January, 1983 for an experimental period of three years. In this Britain joined some 25 countries that had introduced similar legislation in the 1970s.

Some doubts about the effects of seat belt use were admitted inside the road safety establishment. For example, an editorial in the *Lancet* in January 1986 noted the shortfall between actual and predicted life saving and "the unexplained and worrying increases in the deaths of other road users." The editorial concluded: "There will be regret that the evidence on deaths is not more one-sided and

72

disappointment that the measure has fallen short of its promise."[8] Only a few days after this was published, and after parliamentary debate supposedly drawing on research on the effects of compulsion since the 1981 debate, legal compulsion was extended indefinitely.

The evidence

The justification for wearing seat belts in cars is simple. Occupants wearing suitable seat restraint do not suffer injuries incurred following ejection from the vehicle — or from making rapid contact with hard objects inside the vehicle — after impact, particularly if a crash is head-on. The literature contains discussion about the kind of restraint to be worn, and about various design refinements to seat belts, but the principle remains more or less the same.

Only two real objections were raised to seat belt use, right at the beginning of the discussion.[9] The first was that seat belt use might cause or exacerbate some injuries to their wearers. In fact, following the introduction of seat belt wearing, medical journals reported the existence of "seat belt syndrome", referring to whiplash neck injuries and thoracic and other injuries.[10] Wearers might also be trapped in a submerged or burning car, or otherwise hurt when ejection would have been preferable. Against this it was argued that the chances of worse injury being caused with a seat belt were far less than the chances without. While there must have been cases where belts trapped wearers in fires, and so on, it seems correct to argue that *when a crash occurs* the occupant is significantly better off wearing a seat belt.

The second objection was concerned with risk compensation, although it was rarely referred to in those terms; people spoke only of "a sense of false security" and "driving faster". This possibility — the adaptation of driver behaviour to a correct, not false, perception of security which could take many forms of which driving faster might be just one — was briefly considered as far back as 1957,[11] but not properly nor thoroughly until the work of John Adams in the late 1970s.

An extension to this objection is what I call *wider risk compensation*. Some objectors argued for more attention to reducing the chances of getting into accidents in the first place. The classic defence to this was that this issue could be considered, in addition to seat belt encouragement/compulsion, at a later date, and that the success of seat belts would enhance the reputation of the "road safety community" and therefore the prospects of any moves towards preventing crashes occurring. The worry was that, while motorists might not change their behaviour directly in response to seat belt wearing, attention would be diverted from more basic questions which in the long run would have adverse effects, particularly for the vulnerable. "Road safety" would become identified with secondary, post-crash, remedial measures and with measures whereby each individual would be expected to protect him or herself. Future efforts would become less attractive to car occupants who would have less to lose than previously. Reducing the adverse effects of crashes would therefore reduce, not enhance, the prospects for action in the future, particularly if additional care, self-control or self-discipline were required on the part of the motorist.

It should be stressed that diverting attention away from something is more negative than simply not paying attention to it. Also, wider risk compensation is virtually immeasurable, and occurs over a long period of time — it describes a kind of cultural change.

The nature of the evidence used in the seat belts campaign is relevant for other road safety campaigns, particularly those using "safety aids'. Casualties were examined after crashes to analyse their injuries, and to compare casualties who had been wearing seat belts with those who had not. This was in turn related to evidence available from laboratory tests intended to replicate real-life crashes using dummies and robots.

This mode of gaining knowledge, however, misses out on a crucial link between these kinds of evidence, namely the actual behaviour of human beings when using the safety aid in question. There is no allowing for risk compensation. Instead of formulations along the lines that "she would not have been killed/so badly injured if she had been wearing a seat belt", it needs to be considered whether additional crashes, or a more severe one in the case referred to, would have occurred if the seat belt had been worn, and the consequences of both the remedial effects of the belt and the hazards to other road users.

The debate centres on how this possibility was assessed. There are two ways of trying to do this. The first involves studying groups of motorists, either by watching certain features of their driving behaviour or by questioning them, to assess the way seat belt use may or may not change their behaviour. This small group type of study (small as opposed to whole populations of motorists) has some basic inadequacies. The second approach involves the study of road accident casualty (and in some cases insurance) data after compulsory seat belt wear was legislated for, principally on a national level. This constitutes the best kind of evidence, although it too has limitations.

Small-group studies

Assessing the possibility of less careful driving by actual or potential seat belt-wearing motorists faces an immediate difficulty. How does the researcher know what form of visible behaviour should be associated with propensity to crash? Obviously, certain forms of behaviour, such as driving on the pavement or the wrong way down clearly marked one-way streets, constitute high risk-taking behaviour. If such behaviour were to occur immediately after a previously unbelted driver, who had not displayed such behaviour before, started wearing a seat belt, then one could suggest that seat belt wearing would generate more careless driving (if such correlations showed a degree of statistical significance for groups of drivers representative of the motoring population as a whole). But there is no possibility that risk-compensatory behaviour would ever be manifested in such a clear-cut way.

This is partly because of the level of chance of accidents occurring, particularly with regard to the short stretches of road on which observations in this kind of study are carried out. The chances of dying in a crash on a British road now, albeit less than at the time of the seat belt debates, is about one in every 85 million vehicle kilometres travelled. This means that were behaviour to occur now which doubled the chances of a fatal crash, an additional one would happen for every few dozen million vehicle miles travelled. Thus, to compensate totally for (outweigh) the beneficial effects of seat belts, which were supposed to reduce deaths by about 50 per cent, we would expect to see an extra serious crash of this severity only once every few dozen million miles.

Yet the risk compensation hypothesis is still believed to suggest that an extremely high degree of obvious compensation — or rather over-compensation — occurs. As Lord Porritt, on behalf of the Medical Commission on Accident Prevention, put it in the House of Lords debate at the end of the experimental period:–

> I find that [risk compensation] an extraordinarily odd term. I should be awfully interested to know how many members of this noble House have felt so much happier and so much safer that they could drive much more joyously and buzz along and knock everybody over. I have never had anything like that feeling. I have never felt it. It is an amazing thought.[12]

Amazing indeed. Nobody, apart from those like Lord Porritt who were misinterpreting the concept of risk compensation, had ever suggested it.

This does not mean, however, that less obvious behaviour than that causing a serious crash cannot be observed. Less serious crashes occur more frequently. Even so, with insurance claims running at an average of one every three to six years per driver before seat belt legislation[13] it would still be difficult to base an assessment of accident-disposed driving on observed crashes. And to observe behaviour likely to increase motor danger by only partially compensating for increased security would be even harder.

Nevertheless, one might hope to gain an idea of a possible link of propensity to accident involvement with certain types of driving phenomena, which can then be reliably used as indicators. Indicators that have been used, with regard to investigating risk-compensatory behaviour and other forms of more careless driving, have included speed, headway length (distance between the observed car and the vehicle in front), gap acceptance of vehicles turning across traffic (the amount of time allowed for turning) and crossing or not crossing red signals. There is probably an association between the higher-level risk-taking observed in these different kinds of behaviour and a propensity to get into crashes.

Yet life is not so simple. Reviewing the question, two leading members of the US road safety community state:

> Since its beginnings more than 40 years ago driver behaviour research has sought such associations [between observed driver behaviour characteristics

and accident involvement] as one of its primary goals. Although common experience and intuition might suggest that such associations would be readily found, much research effort has yielded little.[14]

While the claim is made that a particular form of behaviour — giving shorter rather than longer headways on a freeway — is related to a record of accident involvement, other evidence quoted in the same article reveals no such significant correlations. Also, there is a stronger link between a record for traffic offences and the observed behaviour, but the decision to prosecute is itself based on observable behaviour selected by police officers.

Propensity to get into a crash is related to numerous factors which are at best only partly related to observable features of driving behaviour. Drivers may manifest a higher than average level of risk-taking with some behaviours, such as overtaking, driving with poor eyesight or inadequately maintaining their vehicle, but not with others. And hundreds, if not thousands, of kinds of behaviour, all of which have a degree of risk-taking involved, can result in crashes. Factors such as fatigue, or reaction times dulled due to illness or medication, are unobservable to roadside investigators anyway.

We also have to consider changes that occur over time in response to life crises, ageing and other effects which vary from motorist to motorist. This would add another difficulty, even if we had good knowledge of the levels of risk-taking across the spectrum of both observable and unobservable behaviour for a particular driver at a given time in their driving career. The change in the levels of alertness and vigilance are very small when we come to the question of less careful driving behaviour induced by a greater sense of security through wearing seat belts. We are therefore unlikely to get any reasonable indicator from this kind of study.

In the specific case of less careful driving behaviour induced by a greater sense of security through wearing seat belts, we are talking about a slight change in levels of alertness and vigilance of which we are highly unlikely to get any reasonable indicator.

We therefore have attempts to relate subtle changes, which may be manifested in a variety of different ways, to propensity for accident involvement, by referring to one of the multitude of potential accident-causing factors, when this factor (higher speed, shorter headways) has a dubious relationship to the proven propensity for accident involvement. This means operating on a very weak theoretical base indeed.

Yet opponents of the risk compensation idea have argued that: "For the risk compensation hypothesis to be relevant to consideration of occupant protection measures, its proponents must first identify *actual* behaviour changes that are related to fatality rates and that are the result of changes in perceived risk."[15] Because the changes are so small, manifested in a number of ways over a period of time and often not observable, we have a classic case of academics asking their opponents to do the impossible — or refusing to understand what those opponents are suggesting in the first place.

Studies claiming to investigate the possibility of risk-compensatory behaviour among belted drivers created a further theoretical problem. Small-group studies compared features of observed behaviour among voluntarily belted drivers to those who had not chosen to wear belts. During the years prior to legal compulsion, substantial effort was expended on convincing motorists to wear seat belts. Those who wore seat belts at the time of these studies were *ipso facto* probably more cautious drivers to start off with.[16] Therefore, even with risk-compensatory behaviour displayed after deciding to wear a belt, risk-taking behaviour might still be less in belt wearers than among non-belt wearers.

One curiosity is that some opponents of the concept of risk compensation claimed that it was never hypothesised for *voluntary* seat belt wearing. No risk compensation theorist ever said this, but it did not stop the most influential figure in this area of work in Britain's road safety establishment, G. Murray Mackay, stating: "Notice the distinction between voluntary and compulsory seat belt use. The hypothesis [he refers to the idea of risk compensation as "the Peltzman hypothesis"] only applies to those who unwillingly conform to a belt law." [17]

One would wonder then what the point of doing work in voluntary regime conditions was.

Discussing the difference of speeds between belted and non-belted drivers, and noting a difference in mean speeds of 0.94 mph, Mackay stated: "Clearly the difference in the mean speeds of less than one mph is of little importance." [18] Yet at the mean speed of 48 mph referred to, an additional speed of, say, ten mph might be thought by the average motorist as very significantly higher and indicating very high risk-taking; one mph would therefore be a significant increase, particularly with the sort of slight and subtle changes we are talking about. One study claims to show shorter gap acceptance by unbelted drivers when in fact at very low levels of gap acceptance — where risk taking is particularly high — the relationship is reversed.[19]

One small-group study performed research which this type of work should have tried to do, but in no other case actually did. This Dutch study isolated motorists who had been observed not wearing seat belts when they were driving in typical conditions. Under experimental conditions their behaviour was compared with that of belt-wearing drivers, and a comparison was made of their own behaviour when wearing and not wearing seat belts. It did not just look at speed and following distances (headways), but at eight different kinds of behaviour, much more than in other studies. The work concluded that *"Seat belt wearing leads to higher speed, more irregular maintenance of speed, and later braking."* (My emphasis)[20] In other words, the one piece of research which isolated non-wearers in experimental conditions, and used the most extensive range of indicators of behavioural change (albeit with a small sample), came to the opposite conclusion of all the others. It was carried out only after compulsion had been introduced in Britain as well as the Netherlands.

Another piece of small group research, a substantial study of attitudes of motorists in Europe with regard to belt wearing and associated questions, was done just prior to legislation in Britain.[21] Attitudes, rather than observed behaviour, were used to indicate future driving behaviour after legislation. The authors found that there was a lower perception of risk among those who always belted up under a voluntary regime and concluded that "the possibility of a significant decline in vigilance following enforced wearing of belts has not been fully considered."[22] Writing about their research later they claim to have "warned at the time that seat belt legislation... might unwittingly lead to an increase in collisions with other cars and with pedestrians and cyclists."[23]

Despite problems with relating attitudes to future driving, findings of this nature should have been referred to in the parliamentary and other debates that occurred on the seat belt question. Yet they were not, and even the opponents of the legislation were unaware of this research, even though it was financed by the major non-government fund supporting such research, the Rees Jeffreys Road Fund.

The effect of compulsory seat belt wearing legislation

According to Mackay's incorrect review of the evidence so far considered:

> **All the studies suggest that risk compensation does not occur and in fact, if anything, people who use seat belts, either voluntarily or under compulsion, accept *lower* levels of risk than people who do not use belts."[24]**

One would therefore expect the reduction of deaths and injuries following the introduction of seat belt laws to be at least as great as that suggested in the claims based on hospital and post-crash evidence and on experimental tests.

A number of countries introduced seat belt wearing legislation in the 1970s. In 1989 research was published in the Netherlands which involved the results of a time-series analysis performed on car drivers' and passengers' fatality rates for eight West European countries that passed seat belt legislation in the 1970s (Belgium, Denmark, Finland, the Netherlands, Norway, Spain, Sweden and West Germany). It found that "*There was no discernible effect of seat belt legislation on the fatality rate.*"[25] (My emphasis). In other words, bearing in mind our knowledge of the effect of seat belts after crashes have occurred, the legislation appears to have *led to motorists driving with less care than they did before.*

The principal evidence suggesting risk compensation came originally from John Adams.[26] Since the Dutch evidence was not available at the time of the British debate on seat belts, it was Adams's work — which comes to similar conclusions — which was discussed, and which we consider here.

Adams compared the record of 13 countries with seat belt laws with four countries that did not have them. The "law" group included only countries that had substantial increases in wearing rates following legislation. Countries that had passed laws but about which there was little relevant information were excluded.

The ones in the study included more than 80 per cent of the world's car population. The road death tolls of all the countries were converted to indices, with 1973 set equal to 100. (This was because 1973 was the year of the "energy crisis", with higher oil prices and publicity about the benefits of slower driving reinforced in many cases by lower speed limits; it was also when the death toll in the main motorised countries began to decline after rising for many years.) These indices included *all* road accident fatalities. Two composite indices, of the average of the indices of the 13 countries with laws, and the four countries without, were calculated. The index for the "law" countries fell by 17 points between 1972 and 1978, while the index for the "no law" countries fell by 25 points over the same period.

This indicates no beneficial effect from the introduction of seat belt laws in the 13 countries compared to the four countries which did not introduce laws; indeed, a worse record existed in those countries that introduced laws. Adams also attempted to control for the effects of the energy crisis by looking at changes in petrol consumption in the "law" and "no law" countries. Again, the alleged positive effects of seat belt legislation are not apparent. Because fatality statistics are more reliable than injury statistics (as explained in Chapter 1), Adams based his work on fatalities rather than injuries. However, he did refer to injury figures, showing that if they were used the same story would be told.

To back up his case, Adams looked at each one of the "law" countries in turn — Australia, Belgium, Denmark, Finland, France, West Germany, the Netherlands, New Zealand, Norway, Spain, Switzerland, Sweden and Israel — comparing their individual road death index to the "no law" index, and referring to the specific data (such as wearing rates) of each country. Again, there was no evidence of beneficial effects. Later work on Ireland and Canada's experience confirms this general picture.

What kind of study claimed success from the introduction of seat belt legislation? The State of Victoria was the first legislature (where road accident fatality statistics are reliable) to have a seat belt law, introduced in 1970. The studies of the effects of that law, and of the laws introduced in the rest of Australia the following year, were influential. Three of the main Australian studies referred to measured change by fitting a straight line to the trend that existed in the years prior to legislation — although no serious study of change over time can rely on simple before/after comparisons, or on an assumption that departure from a straight line fitted to the trend of a period immediately before the change being considered is a departure from the real trend. Departures from the increasing trend in fatalities in motorised countries in the 1960s were nevertheless attributed to seat belt laws in these studies, when in fact the trend from about 1973 onwards was downwards anyway. Making a before/after comparison on a downward trend, and attributing decline to the change at the point between before and after, is an elementary statistical mistake.

Some criticisms of Adams

Mackay criticised Adams's methodology and the reliance on aggregated fatality figures for all road user groups.[27] The first criticism, which has been answered by Adams,[28] appears to show a lack of knowledge about the use of indices in statistical analysis, and misrepresents some basic features of his method, as well as suggesting that Adams claimed that seat belt laws increased road deaths — whereas risk compensation claims that deaths will not be reduced in the manner suggested (if at all), which is different.

The second criticism is that, by referring to all road user groups, the effect of increased fatalities in a group unaffected by seat belt use will affect the overall picture. While seat belt users, and those who might be affected by worse driving if risk compensation occurs, constitute a significant proportion of all those killed, there are others to be considered in the total number. Mackay gives the example of motorcyclist single vehicle only (SVO) crashes (when motorcyclists come off the road irrespective of motorist behaviour); also pedestrians are hit by motorcyclists, and so on.

The problem with Mackay's criticism is that one would expect the effects of such other features to operate both in raising *and* in lowering aggregate fatalities, and for their effect to tend to average out over 19 countries. It is too much of a coincidence to suggest that confounding variables or unspecified factors could have been responsible for the lack of benefit shown in each country. One could equally argue that any significant benefit spotted by the advocates of belts was due to unspecified confounding variables.

The Isles Report

One other study should be mentioned here: the Isles Report,[29] which is distinguished by three features. First, although it restricted itself to a smaller number of countries than Adams, it used a more sophisticated method of disaggregating road accident fatalities by road user group. Second, it came to the conclusion that *claims for seat belt law effects were exaggerated, and that the likely effects in Britain would be either minimal or negative benefits for car users and an increase in deaths and injuries for people outside cars*. It claimed that the effect of seat belt laws in European countries had been to *increase* accidents in every country.

Third, this study was never published — perhaps because it was produced within the Department of Transport in Britain at a time — April 1981 — when the seat belt law was about to be passed. In fact it saw the light of day only when shown unofficially to the magazine *New Scientist* nearly four years later.[30]

Isles noted that "the predominance of positive effects [increased numbers of injuries] is alarming... Since pedestrians account for 20 per cent of casualties in Britain, and the effect seems to be significant for them, closer scrutiny is called for." Also:

> A simple model suggests no change in death rates, and an 11 per cent (+ or – two per cent) increase in injuries for all classes of road user, to have been the

effect of the law. However, comparison with two 'no-law' countries — and common sense — suggest that this increase results from the model being too simple, and that there is no significant law effect. A larger data base would be needed to test a more realistic model.

Despite this caution, Isles also noted that "the prior probability of obtaining eight positive results is $1:2^8$", or $1:256$.

The basis for caution is that the data base was too small. Yet it included Belgium, Denmark, Finland, the Netherlands, Norway, Spain, Sweden and West Germany, with Britain and Italy in the "no law" group. By comparison, most of the impetus for legislation had drawn on the studies based on Victoria and other Australian states, which provides a far smaller data base. The report also makes it clear that "international comparisons provide the only information about the effect of compulsory seat belt wearing." In other words, caution was urged on the basis of Isles's evidence, whereas it had been thrown to the winds on the basis of less complete, and wrongly analysed, information.

The British experience

Three studies were published in Britain on the experience of its seat belt law before the experimental period was extended in January 1986.

(i) The Rutherford Report

The first was a hospital-based analysis of road traffic accident casualties carried out under the authorship of one of the foremost seat belt campaigners, William Rutherford.[31] It dealt with car occupants only. As a one year before/after study it had the faults of assuming that the existing trend was not already moving downwards. It also assumed that there would have been an *increase* in casualties in 1983 without seat belt legislation, because of increased traffic and worse weather conditions.

As explained earlier, while greater numbers of vehicles pose increased danger for other road users, the increase in motorisation does not lead to a proportionally equal increase in lives lost (particularly over time) as people adapt to the increase in danger. In addition, with increased motorisation there tends to be a migration away from the more vulnerable modes to car use where travellers are less at risk. With a low increase in traffic growth, such as there was in 1983, there could therefore be an overall decline in fatalities. This can occur because of reduced speeds or other factors, such as greater awareness of an increased number of vehicles, associated with an increase in congestion intensity, as well as modal shift away from vulnerable modes.[32] A *decrease* in serious casualties may in any case be the consequence of snow and ice on the roads leading to reduced speeds.[33]

Rutherford noted that "The other measure in the 1981 Transport Act which might have led to improvement was the clause which sought to remedy deficiencies in laws which aimed at the control of drunken driving." In fact, some of the benefit claimed for seat belt law was instead a result of the drink-driving clause. This was the first report to refer to it, but it failed to treat seriously the possibility of the success of the anti-drink-drive measures (introduction of the evidential breath-testing machine).

First, it claims that: "the changes in the second year for Northern Ireland mirror closely the changes in Great Britain", and the law applied only in Great Britain. This contention is opposed by their own Table 66. Second, they point to differences between the experience on drivers and front-seat passengers as against rear-seat passengers and state: "It is difficult to see how they can be explained on the basis of controlling drunken driving." This is a good, and not isolated, example of a study completely missing the point. There never was a dispute about the effect of belts when crashes had already occurred, but about the tendency of them to occur. The balance between rear and front-seat passengers' fatality or other casualty rates has nothing to do with this.

(ii) The Scott/Willis Report

The Scott/Willis Report[34] used a more sophisticated form of analysis than many of the studies, disaggregating different road user groups, but it was still seriously flawed. The model used, which applied to the years 1979-83, cannot fit data existing before 1979. Rather than try to fit a more complex model to cope with the varying trend, the authors restricted themselves to a shorter period of analysis. As with many similar studies, the report relied more on injury than on fatality statistics. The reason, as usual, was that the larger numbers of injuries are more amenable to analysis than those of fatalities — even if they are utterly unreliable. Applied to the effects of the British seat belt law, however, the story told by injuries is the opposite of that told by the fatalities.

After complaining about the small size of fatality data, Scott and Willis reduce it further by using monthly data; they then exclude data from non-built-up areas when analysing vulnerable road users: "The vast majority of casualties among unprotected road users occur in built-up areas, and it was thought that the inclusion of casualty and traffic data from elsewhere might only serve to obscure any effects which existed." But in the year in question, 1983, 42 per cent of cyclist fatalities, 47 per cent of motorcyclist fatalities and 20 per cent of pedestrian fatalities occurred outside built-up areas. Hardly a tiny minority. If we take the case of cyclists, using a basic comparison of figures for 1982 and 1983 in *Road Accidents Great Britain*, we see that the one really significant change that occurs is in fatalities — up by 28 per cent — in non-built-up areas. (This is a classic example of the bias against vulnerable road users that appears when faster non-built-up (NBU) roads, which have more serious crashes where there are vulnerable road users involved, are compared to built-up (BU) roads.)[35]

So in two areas the report is biased against finding risk compensation effects: that is in the use of the wrong kind of data, and a model which does not cover the right time period. The Adams critique is not mentioned and the Australian studies are quoted without question. There is no reference to the Isles Report, available at the time and wider-ranging and more detailed than the other evidence quoted. Despite this, the savings attributed in the first year after the law were some 500 lives, which is significantly below the predicted amount. The possibility of a risk compensation effect "cannot yet be dismissed".

(iii) The Durbin/Harvey Report

This report, by two professors of statistics, was commissioned by the Department of Transport. It specifically includes vulnerable road users, and has a methodology which makes it one of the most — if not *the* most — sophisticated forms of time-series analysis ever used.[36]

Durbin and Harvey give good evidence that the risk compensation hypothesis is correct. The seat belt law had increased motor danger — it had had a worsening effect on driver behaviour, with dangerous consequences for people outside cars:

> **The large estimated increases of pedestrian and cyclist fatalities suggest the possibility of some change in driving behaviour by some drivers of cars and light goods vehicles after the introduction of the seat belt law.**

However, they do not follow this statement through to come out clearly in favour of the risk compensation hypothesis.

The problem with the Durbin and Harvey Report is that they did not properly consider the fatalities-versus-injuries question and the drink-driving question. Nor did they consider the shortfall between predicted savings and their own estimates, or refer to the European and other evidence. The fault in the report lies to some extent in not looking at some other relevant evidence, but more importantly in the quality of the data used and the absence of consideration of an important variable — the alcohol factor. The best method in the world will be useless if the wrong material is used in it. Durbin and Harvey's findings, and the criticisms of them, are as follows:–

(a) Increasing fatalities

In the two years after the seat belt law, the following fatality increases occurred for rear-seat passengers, pedestrians, and cyclists killed in two-party accidents with cars. They were increases above the prevailing trend identified in the report: pedestrians, up 14 per cent; cyclists, up 40 per cent; rear-seat passengers, up 27 per cent.

(b) Accidents with lorries and buses

While there was the above increase in deaths for two-party accidents with cars, the numbers of both pedestrians and cyclists killed in accidents with lorries (HGVs) and buses (PSVs) — for whose drivers the seat belt law did not apply — actually *decreased* slightly. If the reason for sudden increases in deaths for people outside cars is a tendency to behave more carelessly dating from 31 January 1983, why was this exhibited in the proximity of cars only, but not buses or lorries? Durbin and Harvey point out that this number is too small to use as a control against the two-party accidents with cars. I think that these statistics are nevertheless another element at least suggestive of risk compensation having occurred.

(c) Motorcyclists
New licensing regulations for motorcyclists were introduced at the same time as the belt law, and for this reason were not included in the report. However, despite the supposedly beneficial effects of the new regulations, and an apparent decline in drinking-and-riding deaths, motorcyclist fatality rates did not decrease for the first time in seven years.

(d) Fatalities versus "serious injuries"
We have the same problem that occurred with Scott and Willis: researchers relying on unreliable "serious injuries" data (particularly unreliable in the case of vulnerable road users) in preference to the fewer but more accurate fatalities data. Again, the two sets of data tell conflicting stories, with less or no significant change from the serious injuries or KSI (killed and seriously injured):

> **We found a large discrepancy between the estimates of the increase in numbers KSI and the increase in numbers killed which is hard to explain. Unfortunately we do not have hospital data for pedestrian and cyclists seriously injured which might be used to corroborate the findings for numbers KSI.** *Purely from the standpoint of statistical analysis we again regard the results from the analyses of numbers KSI as more reliable than the analyses of numbers killed .*(My emphasis)

Proper scientific study requires both exactitude in the handling of numbers with the appropriate methodology, about which Durbin and Harvey are experts, and also a good knowledge of the status of the data used — of what the numbers used reflect in the real world — about which they were inexperienced. This was particularly so with the rear-seat passengers, where "we find the large proportionate increase in rear-seat passengers killed hard to understand."

(e) The drink-drive factor
There appears to have been a marked drop in drink-driving related crashes in 1983, which is ignored in the report. The proportion of drivers killed found to be over the legal limit fell from 36 per cent in 1982 to 31 per cent in 1983. And the numbers killed between 10 pm and 4 am (the so-called "drink-drive hours" when drink-driving is particularly associated with crashes) decreased by 23 per cent, with only a three per cent decrease in other hours. This may be associated with the changes brought by the legislation introduced in May 1983, including a 20 per cent increase in roadside tests and prosecutions, as well as the new evidential breath-testing machine (intoximeter) which facilitated this.

This change is illustrated more specifically in a graph in the report by the Transport and Road Research Laboratory on this effect.[37] This shows a pronounced alcohol "blip" in 1982 for certain groups of car driver fatalities. The paper, by Broughton and Stark, suggests mixed effects of the drink-driving law changes, although there is a net beneficial effect in their fatal and serious casualty estimate. It is perhaps worth noting that their paper was not published until shortly after the final parliamentary debate on the seat belt law in 1986. The official silence on the drink-drive factor is in notable contrast to other initiatives on drink-driving, where any supposed beneficial effect will be widely proclaimed. In this case, of course, to do so would have taken credit away from the claims made for the seat belt law.

When pressed — but only when pressed — this silence became outright denial. The Parliamentary Advisory Council on Transport Safety claimed that the effect was small and subtle in nature and that fatalities declined "at all hours of the day and night".[38] Hardly very evenly. RoSPA's comment involved looking at averages over long periods of time, when the whole point about initiatives of this kind is that they have an effect over short periods.[39]

(f) The shortfall

The original claim made for the law in the 1970s was that 1,000 lives would be saved every year. Allowing for the wearing rate at the time the claim was made, and for changes in the number of cars, the number would come down to about 700. The claim made by Dr Murray Mackay at the time of the passing of the legislation was 600. The Durbin/Harvey Report gives two estimates, the higher not including what happened to road users other than front-seat occupants, and a lower one allowing for all road users. The figures given are 450 and 200 respectively for the two years after the law came into effect. The best estimate, which does not take account of an alcohol factor, is therefore significantly below the earlier estimate which was based on an enormous amount of laboratory and hospital study. The lowest estimate allows for the argument that even if some hundreds of pedestrians and cyclists are killed as a direct consequence of such "safety" legislation, this is acceptable provided the number of vulnerable road users killed is lower than those saved.

Another way of showing the shortfall is to use a simple formula advanced by the pro-seat belt road safety academic, Leonard Evans, to predict the proportion of "lives saved" among drivers:[40]

$$F = \frac{E \times \Delta u}{1 - E x u_1}$$

where E is the effectiveness of reduction in a crash, u_1 is the original seat belt wearing rate, and Δu is the change in wearing rate after the law. Using effectiveness levels of 73 per cent (the highest ever claimed), down through the 60 per cent quoted later, down past the 50 per cent claimed by the Highway Code to the 40 per cent claimed by Murray Mackay after the law was passed, I get figures of 43 per cent, 34 per cent, 29 per cent and 26 per cent reduction respectively.

But the actual proportional decline of deaths among drivers claimed by Durbin and Harvey *was just 18 per cent*. In other words, the shortfall is at best by about one-third, and at worst by three-quarters of what should have happened, according to the road safety lobby.

Besides, if an alcohol effect is included, and some allowance is made for the effect on motorcyclists, not to mention possible flaws in the modelling, we approach a minimal, or even zero, effect. (Incidentally, one might wonder, in the age of cost-benefit analysis, how this might be calculated. Are pedestrians of equal worth to car occupants, and if so, at what stage does one accept killing numbers of them in order to "save lives"?)

(g) Other countries
Even given less support for the risk compensation hypothesis, the report should still have referred to the Isles Report and other evidence, as the British experience in the two years after the law might have been an exception. This is supposed to be normal scientific practice.

The establishment response to the evidence

If the evidence for risk compensation by newly belted drivers had not been publicised by the vulnerable road users groups, it is dubious whether it would have been discussed at all. The road safety lobby had engaged in a process of misconstruing and covering up existing evidence which did not say the things it wanted to hear. This process continued in the parliamentary debates. The following account details responses made in Parliament and outside at the time of the final seat belt debates in 1986.[41]

The Isles Report
Speaking for the DTp in the House of Lords, the Earl of Caithness said:

> The noble Lord referred to a report that he claims was suppressed by my department. The report was not suppressed: it was not published because it was based on evidence of some European countries that was out of date because we were undertaking our own studies at the time. Now that we have the results of those studies and the independent studies, speculation on what the effects might be is no longer relevant.

The Isles Report dealt with the experience of seat belt laws in eight European countries. It was not "out of date". As a report on the effects of legislation in countries, even if more than ten years old, it still dealt with the effect of legislation in the years immediately after the intervention. It was therefore relevant at the time of the 1981 debate, when it was not published, and also relevant in association with Durbin/Harvey in the 1986 debate. It is difficult to know what "our own studies" were. Neither the Scott/Willis Report nor the DHSS Rutherford Report was being worked on in April 1981. Neither of them dealt with the European experience. Even if less important than Durbin/Harvey, bearing in mind the problems associated with this study which could have meant that the results were peculiar to Britain in the immediate two-year period after legislation, the experience of other countries should have been used as well.

PACTS stated that:

> the study was not completed for several reasons. Most important was the late appreciation that the methodology was unsuitable to isolate and describe the effects of seat legislation [sic] in a scientific manner.[42]

The study *was* completed: it has a reasonable methodology and no other study of this aspect of the effects of seat belt legislation was carried out by the DTp, then or since. One wonders how PACTS, a supposedly independent body, was able to produce any reasons, let alone several, in support of the DTp's holding back of research findings.

PACT's chairman, Barry Sheerman MP, seemed to have a different reaction to reference to the Isles Report in the Commons debate. It was to ask, "What report?", twice.

The alcohol factor

The Earl of Caithness claimed that the figures given in the Durbin/Harvey Report took "all the factors, including drinking, into account". This is simply not true. Durbin and Harvey did not allow for an alcohol effect.

Replying to the criticism about this omission, Durbin and Harvey admitted that "there is no doubt this [the effect of alcohol] is an important factor",[43] but were dissatisfied with the basis for the criticism: "If one looks at the series to which he [Adams] refers, 1982 appears to be an unusually high year compared to 1980 and 1981." But this is precisely the point. The kind of modelling used by Durbin and Harvey would have included this 1982 "alcohol blip" as part of the trend, so that when it subsided in 1983 (for whatever reason), this would appear as an effect of the seat belt law.

PACTS suggested that "reference to national statistics has led some to conclude that this drink-driving measure has made a greater contribution to car occupant casualty reductions than seat belt legislation." Nobody had said "greater" — but just sufficiently large to suggest that significant risk compensation by newly-belted drivers had occurred. Again PACTS seems to have had privileged access to the Transport and Road Research Laboratory (TRRL) report on the effects of anti-drink-drive measures which had yet to be published, by mentioning "preliminary study". The difference in casualty savings in the "drink-drive hours" and the rest of the day was 23 per cent compared to three per cent — yet PACTS sees this as casualty savings achieved "not... merely in the 'drink-driving hours', but at all hours of the day and night".

At least part of the establishment has made a volte-face. It is now claimed that the measures taken in 1983 *did* have an effect. The TRRL's annual account of its work states: "An evaluation of trends in drink-driving has demonstrated benefits from the new legislation, introduced in 1983."[44] And the main statistics bulletin for transport in London published by the DTp says: "There was a noticeable drop [in car user casualties] associated with the introduction of compulsory seat belt wearing *and tighter drink-drive regulations in 1983*" (my emphasis).[45] This apparent volte-face has taken place after the debate, when the need to remove conflicting explanations for fatality reduction is less strong. It is an indication of the Department of Transport's estimate of the value of proper debate, not to mention the safety of vulnerable road users, that such a reversal of views can occur so easily and so soon.

The shortfall

> My honourable friend and others say, 'We heard a figure of 1,000 a year.' That
> is true, but my honourable and learned friend will remember that, in those
> debates, many of us said that if only 100 lives a year were saved, it must be worth
> doing.[46]

Anybody commenting on the shortfall was made to appear churlish, as if uninterested in the fate of people killed on the road. The point was that if there were a shortfall, a measure had been introduced which had *taken* lives as well as "saved" them. One wonders why people so impressed by what would be, at the 100 figure, a two per cent reduction in road accident fatalities were not militantly committed to a whole range of measures which could have reduced the danger to all road users.

PACTS referred to the original estimate of 1,000 lives, made by Secretary of State for Transport, William Rodgers in 1979, as "in all probability" referring to the difference between 0 and 100 per cent wearing. This is unlikely. Based on wearing rates at the time, the claim would still have been well above 700. Mackay's own prediction in 1981 was "at least 600". The lowest one can get to on the PACTS new estimate would be 550, or at least 25 per cent from the higher of the two Durbin/Harvey figures.

The Adams study

PACTS produced a short piece trying to demolish Adams' original work, which repeated some of Mackay's earlier mistakes and showed more difficulty in understanding the use of indices in statistical analysis.[47]

The cycling fatalities

The increase in cycling fatalities was an embarrassment for the pro-belt lobby. As with other findings, it was misunderstood, and discussed in terms of a cycling problem about which something could be done in segregationist terms. The hypocrisies and contradictions of such a position are dealt with later in this book. The importance of the cyclist fatality figure was that, along with the other evidence, it pointed to a more dangerous road environment being created by the law, with more risk for all those outside cars, whether cyclists, pedestrians or motorcyclists. For Stephen Ross MP, the increase could be attributed to the growth of cycling in the late 1970s. In fact it had reached a plateau by the early 1980s, and the traffic index for cyclists had been accounted for in the Durbin/Harvey Report.

A factor said to be relevant by Mackay[48] and others was the allegedly increasing use of BMX bicycles by children in the years in question. No evidence relating BMX use to increased fatalities has been produced, and the increases in deaths were spread evenly across all age groups. With its stunt-cycle image, not many commuters or elderly cyclists ride BMXs.

Seat belt legislation had contributed to a road environment that was significantly more dangerous for cyclists and others outside cars

The politics of road safety legislation

The quality of the evidence presented to members of Parliament in the British debate was in one sense utterly irrelevant to the decisions made. As the one account of the debates puts it: "A large number of parliamentarians were content to disregard the available evidence either partially or totally... The work of such technical experts as John Adams or Murray Mackay has either been utilised very selectively or dismissed in favour of anecdotal evidence in order to support specific viewpoints."[49] There was a refusal on the part of the pro-belt lobby to seriously consider the implications of risk compensation. Either the vulnerable road user "problems" could be dealt with (got out of the way?) without any reference to motorist behaviour, or else the fate of the road user groups making up the majority of the deaths on Britain's roads was just not worth thinking about.

Reading through the comments of MPs such as Austin Mitchell, a key figure in the debates and also a supposed friend of vulnerable road users through his membership of the All Party Friends of Cycling, a clear picture of the official view of the debate appears. Motorists suffer danger, which is seemingly little to do with their responsibilities on the road, but more like the inevitable "hand of fate" casting danger on the innocent. Once this idea is accepted, the problems of danger posed to others can be pushed into the background, and the central issue of where the danger comes from in the first place is lost yet again. "Road safety", in this view, is something which well-meaning individuals can affect without having to question the dangerous consequences of the abuse of motorist power and privilege. From then on it was simply a question of portraying the opponents as dogmatic ideologists from, as Mitchell put it, "the provisional wing of the lunatic fringe of the libertarian lobby":[50] dogmatic ideologists, with just a hint of terrorism associated.

Mitchell, however, was wrong. Opposition, criticism and concern had come from every organisation specifically concerned with vulnerable road users. Pedestrians (Pedestrians' Association), cyclists (British Cycling Federation, Cyclists' Touring Club, London Cycling Campaign), motorcyclists (Association of Motorcyclists against Discriminatory Legislation, Motorcycle Action Group, British Motorcycling Federation) and bodies concerned with non-car users generally (Friends of the Earth, Transport 2000) had all expressed some concern about the effects of the law. In the vote, unlike the earlier votes which had featured such non-Tory "libertarians" as Michael Foot and Jo Grimond in the anti-lobby, opposition to the law came from some Labour MPs in working class constituencies (John Forrester, Eddie Loyden, Richard Ottaway, Bob Parry, Raymond Powell, Martin Redmond and Dennis Skinner) concerned about the worsening conditions for vulnerable road users.

Power

Whatever their proportion of suffering on the roads, in terms of *power*, the vulnerable road users were outnumbered. Barry Sheerman was keen to show that only three out of 48 members of PACTS did not support the law. But since only three organisations on PACTS were specifically interested in vulnerable road users, this is hardly surprising.

The power of the road safety lobby was further cemented by its *ideology*. One feature of this was its use of evidence. For Lord Porritt: "It is quite amazing that the figures one gets are almost the same, whoever produces them... All the bodies say very much the same thing." It is not amazing at all. The same report's findings had been recirculating for many years, repeated time and again until they had assumed the status of truth. All of them were seriously flawed, and counter-evidence had been suppressed, not produced at all, published too late or was not publicised or discussed properly.

Ideology

The road safety lobby was presented as a neutral body "saving lives". RoSPA had said that if risk compensation theory "stood up to scrutiny RoSPA could not possibly support legislation which aids one group — car occupants — to the detriment of others."[51] But, as this book shows, RoSPA, along with other sectors of the lobby, has been criticised for supporting moves which effectively discriminate against vulnerable road users since its close associations with the motoring lobby arose in the pre-war years.

The picture of innocent motorists threatened by mysterious external forces was reinforced by the persistent misconception of risk compensation. It was always going to be difficult, if not impossible, to get the idea taken seriously. This is partly because very slight changes in alertness and vigilance, longer term resistances and average levels of risk- taking are involved. In the context of individuals who in any case change their attitudes to risk-taking through the course of their lives, it is not surprising that many people find risk compensation difficult to accept.

Yet these are not the reasons why the hypothesis was rejected. Motorists, like all of us, do not like to think they are behaving without adequate care at the best of times, and there is also a tendency to see oneself as better than average. The idea of people behaving less carefully as they feel safer is extremely obvious; it is just easier to accept when *other* people are the ones whose social responsibility is in question. To some extent the best way of thinking about the issue is to picture yourself driving a small, evidently uncrashworthy car with no seat belt and a sharp spike through the steering column. Contrast this with driving a car advertised as being highly crashworthy, cocooned from the elements, and with a seat belt. Does it make sense to suggest that you will drive a little more carefully in one vehicle rather than the other?

This resistance to the idea of risk-taking is exemplified by the comments of long-time pro-belt campaigner George Robertson in the debate. For him, risk compensation was:

> a questionable, flimsy, tendentious theory [which] suggests that those who are belted have more confidence and start knocking down pedestrians, cyclists and motor cyclists... I am sure that the vast majority of the population would reject that theory, and they have shown that they have done so by the act that they continue to wear their seat belts.

In this formulation, the knocking down of vulnerable road users is almost a conscious, wilful act by deliberately dangerous drivers — not people like you or me.

The business of knocking down has, of course, been going on for some time, and has been done by ordinary, fallible human beings in charge of a singularly dangerous piece of equipment. The seat belt issue is just another feature of a balance between incentive to drive with care and respect for other road users' lives, and a lack of incentive to do so. Robertson's formulation is one where drivers are always highly skilled and careful. Apparently if they feel that an increase in the slight chances of them hurting somebody else will occur, this will make them abandon the cause of that increase, even if they are at risk.

My formulation is different. All of us balance risk against freedom. Motorists pose danger under the best possible conditions. Reducing that danger to, for example, the level of danger that vulnerable road users such as cyclists and pedestrians pose, involves restriction and restraint. The risk of damage to oneself is a major incentive to more care.

91

The situation is ably summed up by what appears to be a legal enshrinement of risk compensation. A report in RoSPA's magazine describes how the seat belt safety benefit is consumed as a performance benefit: "In Germany coaches with belts are allowed to travel faster than those without, thus allowing drivers to cover more miles in the hours they are allowed."[52] Increases in speed are usually regarded by the road safety industry as associated with a greater likelihood of crashes, and more severe ones. The implication of the German legislation is that because there is indeed less need to worry about crashes, a measure can be taken which will increase the likelihood and/or severity of crashes. In Britain in 1988, 150 people were killed in crashes where buses or coaches were involved; 136 of them were *outside* the bus or coach.[53] Even if the legal measure were not taken, if the experience of seat belt use in cars is anything to go by, it is likely that the safety benefit will be consumed, legally or otherwise, by increased speed or otherwise, in ways which are detrimental to those outside the coaches.

Other examples of a hypothetical nature could be thought of. For example, a move to increase the size, weight and general crashworthiness of some cars in a very obvious way, such that the remaining motorists would be increasingly threatened by some other drivers who had become "safer". Such cases are simply examples of what has happened with motoring over the last 60 years, aided and abetted by the "road safety" lobby, at the expense of those outside cars.

Conclusion: the importance of seat belt legislation

Adams refers to the Hans Christian Anderson fable *The Emperors New Clothes* to suggest that the road safety community has been taking part in a "grand conspiracy of self delusion".[54] There is indeed a naked truth of risk compensation: a common sense notion backed up by the use of the methods of that community, as well as alternative types of analysis. There is also a degree of acceptance of the thesis among those who have bothered to examine the evidence.[55]

But this is no fable where the innocent small boy can puncture a myth by simply telling the obvious truth. Or rather, in so far as the myth is seen for what it is, the brutal reality is that *those in power simply do not care whether it is or not*. This is partly a cynical disregard for the more vulnerable victims of motor danger, who happen to make up half of those killed on the road, and who were making the majority of journeys at the time the law was passed.[56]

But it is also because ordinary road users are not really interested in whether retrospectively analysed casualty rates decline against trends, or perhaps even whether their own individual chances of being hurt or killed change: what they want by way of safety is leeway to behave in the way they wish. The only problem is that the leeway was given to the people who are the source of danger on the road, rather than their potential victims.

Cannot the needs of the non-car users be ministered to now without worrying about this episode? Unfortunately there are problems without easy solutions, as discussed in the rest of this book. The problem is that with a continuing tendency to confuse the transitive and intransitive meanings of danger, the diversion away from the source of the problem continues. Also, those at the time who were genuinely interested in the vulnerable, but who wanted to devote time and energy to seat belt promotion, were in effect trying to pour petrol on the fire at the same time as water. In those situations the best you can get is a return to the (inequitable) status quo you had previously. Besides, the seat belt option was tried *precisely because* other means of protecting motorists were seen as undesirable or impracticable. These approaches which would have reduced danger to all road users by restricting the motor danger at source were eschewed because they would have been unacceptable to motorists.

The acceptance that motorists have a tendency to crash is an important landmark in the culture of tolerance of motor danger. A subtle, but definite, exacerbation of an already inequitable situation has taken place. As Murray Mackay put it some years earlier:

> **road accidents… occur with such frequency that they are a common function of the machine (a car). As such they must be considered as a normal event in the machine's life.**[57]

One could put it more bluntly by saying that motorists are accidents waiting to happen. We have been pandering to that idea as an acceptable normality rather than as a problem to be controlled. This process of distancing the motorist from their responsibility to others (by referring to a function of the machine, not the driver) has to be reversed. The tendency to crash has to be seen as a problem of those in charge of the capacity to hurt others, and one to be restrained. Starting that process properly — it has never *been* properly placed on the agenda — could happen with an admission of the truth about this most important episode.

5.

The engineer's tale

IN BEVERLY HILLS a taxi will drive you up a ramp and to the foyer of a hotel where a doorman will take your luggage. After you've unpacked, don't try and take a stroll, the doorman won't let you. You can only leave this hotel by car.

It's the logical extension of a "designing out" process that here in the UK routes pedestrians over or under roads; while recreational cyclists now head for the hills, claiming they've been forced off-road. Ultimately, it is dangerous driving behaviour that must be "designed out" if there is to be any real safety. Many engineering developments have done quite the reverse.

❖❖❖

The most important approach to what has become known as "road safety" is that of the civil engineer, traffic engineer or car designer. Engineers claim is that their approach is non-ideological, objective, unbiased, clear cut and above all, *scientific*. Yet this is not so. As with other occupations, engineers concerned with road safety are bound by norms and values formed by particular kinds of power relation, and which in turn reinforce those power structures. The underlying assumptions for road, traffic and vehicle engineers determine the definition of "the road safety problem", the measures to be taken and the assessment of the effects of these measures. These practices tend to be defined by engineers in ways which are biased against the non-car user and betray a fundamental misunderstanding about human behaviour in the road environment. They accept or promote dangerous forms of transport and/or deny the failures or adverse effects of engineering methods.

What is engineering?

"Engineer", in the present context, is the term used by traffic engineers, civil engineers, "biomechanics", vehicle designers and others. They are, broadly speaking, concerned with the structure of vehicles and the road environment. Their job is to engineer, or design, features of the road environment or vehicles in such a way as to achieve the objectives of "road safety". Mackay defines their project in a way which differentiates it from traditional educational and enforcement approaches:

> All people are as God made them, and often worse than that, and programmes for changing road user behaviour very quickly founder on the subtleties of human response and political limitations of the social manipulations of drivers

94

and other users of the highways. HL Mencken once remarked that for every complex problem there is a solution which is simple, neat and wrong. Unfortunately, many of the traditional road safety programmes aimed at behavioural changes come into that category.[1]

Putting it another way, we cannot do anything about the way people behave, so let us just make it easier for them to avoid crashes (by, for example, straightening roads for motorists) and cushioning them (and perhaps — to a lesser and inadequate extent — others) from the adverse effects of crashes when they occur.

The proposition that it is possible to eliminate or reduce a serious social problem by design — without any of the messy problems of coping with human behaviour — is seductive. In the world as described by Mackay, while others deal in the futile business of attempting to convince human beings to behave in a different manner, he and his colleagues proceed with the real business. These clear-eyed experts ascertain the "cause of accidents" and ways of reducing them without straying beyond the hard, unquestionable, physical facts of life. They scientifically establish a list of solvable problems prioritised in terms of costs and benefits. Unhindered by political or ideological considerations (but misunderstood by societies that starve them of finance and proper respect) they struggle on in their honourable endeavour.

This picture is a fiction. As with all views of social issues that ignore the distribution of power and influence in human societies, this approach is itself ideological and political. Indeed, the quote from HL Mencken describing "simple, neat, and wrong" solutions to complex problems is most appropriate for the approach advocated by engineers.

The world of the engineer

The way engineers talk and write about themselves and their work presents us with their view of the world and their position in it. The various features of this world, inextricably linked and interdependent, are as follows:

(i) The irrelevance of human behaviour

By changing the nature of the environment in which people find themselves, we do not have to worry about people themselves any more. This asocial view ignores the fact that human beings are intimately connected to the engineering project. It is implied that engineers, the holders of privileged knowledge and expert skills, are different from ordinary mortals.

More important is the assumption that people do not adapt to the introduction of newly engineered environments. By failing to consider *human adaptation to perceived changes in their environment*, engineers imply that human beings are passive — although it is a passivity that the engineers attribute partially and when it suits them.

For Mackay: "It does seem eminently sensible that where there is a direct, continuous feedback between the driver's input and the vehicle response, some sort of risk compensation relationship should exist."[2] When does "feedback", or the simple perception of risk, stop or start being direct or continuous? People tend to transform their behaviour in response to a change in perceived risk, and numerous factors contribute to the decisions we make. Why is it that something designed explicitly to change the danger we are exposed to will not involve people adapting to it?

Some 20 years earlier, Mackay seemed more willing to consider the possibility of risk compensation:

> "**Improvements in the accident prevention characteristics of vehicles do not *necessarily* lead to lower involvement rates. For example, the wet road adhesion of tyres has improved greatly in recent years. This is presumably an added safety factor, and yet one result may be that drivers are more confident when cornering or braking on wet roads now, and therefore drive faster and increase the risk to the same level as before. Indeed there is some evidence to suggest that road-users tend to drive so that in varying circumstances the 'perceived risk level' is kept constant. This difficult area I shall leave to more esoteric publications."[3]**

But little or no serious investigation into "this difficult area" has been made by engineers in the intervening years.

It is bizarre to suggest that changes effected by engineers will not contribute to the decision-making process. Even if these changes are not easily visible, or have not been made into selling points for vehicles or "safety aids", the introduction of safety aids and engineering schemes has a long-term effect. This long-term risk compensation effect involves the effects of pandering to motorist behaviour, while another aspect is the effect of constant claims that Britain's record is good and improving.

Some engineers *do* accept risk compensation ideas, but only for particular groups of road user, or for motorists in a direction which *improves* their performance. So engineering which removes some danger from cyclists should be treated warily because cyclists will develop "a false sense of security".[4] Provision for pedestrian crossings is treated with caution because it may "cause accidents" as pedestrians adapt to the engineering change of the installation of a crossing.[5] Motorists, on the other hand, not only are not so susceptible to changes which might adversely affect their driving, but will obey the principles of risk compensation when confronted by more danger.

This view is expressed in a particularly objectionable way by the former County Surveyor of Dorset, JJ Leeming, in one of the few attempts to give the public an explanation of the engineer's endeavour from the professional's point of view. Discussing local residents' pleas to change conditions at places which looked dangerous to them, Leeming writes:

> It can safely be said that places which look dangerous do not have accidents, or very few. They happen at places which do not look dangerous. The reason for

this is simple. The motorist is as intelligent as the 'local people'. If a place looks dangerous, he can see that it is so, he takes care and there are no accidents. He does not want to have an accident, and he will take care at an obviously dangerous place.[6]

This passage is particularly revealing. If motorists respond to perceived danger by taking more care, why is it that they might not take less care with less perceived danger? Then we have the comment that motorists "do not want accidents" — the classic defence of motorists' negligence, uttered with either wounded indignation or bewilderment.[7] At worst it accompanies demands on the vulnerable to lose rights — to get out of the way of the motorist — for their own good; at best it is a denial of the fact that, if accidents were genuinely "not wanted", greater care could be taken.

Although engineers claim to be unconcerned with human behaviour, or at least with changing it, there is here an implicit view of motorists as blameless innocents. For those who might wonder why there are any accidents at all, given motorists' capacity to spot danger, Leeming has the answer that there is "some trap in road conditions which is not obvious at a glance, or where the conditions are too complicated for the limited human machine to deal with in the short time available."[8] This trap (with its connotations of menace and cowardice) must presumably be eliminated, or at least be seen as "the problem". Thus natural features of the environment, or even human beings outside cars, are to be seen as problems for the innocent motorist (rather than the other way round). The "short time available" could be extended by reducing speeds, but Leeming proudly stands by his claim that he has spent 40 years of his life increasing traffic speeds.[9]

Leeming, of course, assumes one group of road users to be innocent and competent, capable of adapting to dangerous conditions, but somehow unlikely to adapt to safe ones. Their victims (when mentioned at all) are less innocent and competent — they tend to constitute "the problem". When they adapt to conditions by being scared off roads too dangerous to cross or cycle on, this is a step forward, as accidents are reduced. But when they (presumably unlike motorists) adapt to conditions being safer by venturing on to their roads, the "problem" is exacerbated.

The myth of neutrality

Engineers often claim, as part of their professional ethos, to be neutral. Yet they tend to be biased against the vulnerable road user. Part of this comes from the commitment to an idea of "road safety" which Part One of this book has shown to be biased, and which is integral to their professional training and practice. Part of it comes from aspects of their academic and career backgrounds not specifically concerned with road safety. Like other middle-class professionals, the qualified engineer is less likely to be disabled, working class, female or a non-car-user or non-driver than members of the population as a whole.

In the case of road or traffic engineering, his approach is concerned with road building. While lip service is paid to certain kinds of planning for the needs of people outside cars and for the environment, it is likely to be limited and to occur within a road-building approach. Any engineer advocating a fundamental shift of transport from car use to the more benign modes, as suggested in this book, swims against the tide. People interested in reducing car use and promoting public transport are unlikely to seek a training in road building or its associated disciplines.

Vehicle designers are also biased against those outside cars. They are unlikely to think in terms of methods of automatically governing the speed of cars, or of semi-automatic law-enforcing devices, as these may inconvenience motorists. Instead, vast quantities of expertise and resources are poured into "safety" features which protect motorists from their own or other motorists' mistakes, not to mention from the power and speed which make cars so dangerous. Despite the "Volvo declaration" of June 1989[10] (which anyway only applied to some kinds of urban settlement), it is unlikely that car manufacturers who employ designers will pay for developments which involve restricting the use of motor vehicles, or any real constraint necessary to improving the safety of people outside cars.

Sometimes the ideology of the engineer is made explicit in this respect. JJ Leeming's book is openly written as a defence of motorists, whom the author sees as unjustly accused of contributing to a dangerous road environment. The book cover states its purpose clearly: "an essential work for all who are responsible for our safety on the roads and should be widely read by all motorists whose interests he champions so vehemently and so persuasively."[11] For Mackay, writing at the same time: "The motor-car, it should be stated quite clearly, is now the most successful and most necessary of all engineering devices."[12] Mackay now acknowledges the anachronistic nature of car use in cities of more than half a million inhabitants.[13] However, in other respects his work is objectively opposed to the interests of the vulnerable road user. It is not denying Mackay's integrity to suggest that, were his findings more opposed to the status quo, he might be less likely to receive funding for work at the Birmingham University Accident Research Unit from the roads-dominated Department of Transport or from car and vehicle component manufacturers.

Simply because the status quo remains unchallenged, there will be a tendency to promote measures that make life worse for the vulnerable. This is partly because of a commitment to do what is easiest, avoiding questions of dealing with the fundamentals of car control, and placing restrictions (such as crash-helmets) on vulnerable road users who are less politically powerful than the roads, car and lorry lobbies.

Discussing this in the context of semi- or fully-automatic controls on the speeds of cars, Mackay says:

> **"The technology is basically there... but it's just far too Utopian... You're taking on the 19 million motorists in this country. If you are actually going to take away individual control from the motorist... that is so Utopian it's an absolute non-starter... The technology is there, you can do it tomorrow... An**

overbearing government could probably use it as a nice source of revenue... I don't think that as a professional I would be particularly effective going for that sort of extremist position. I go for the things that are possible."[14]

Given the current interest, albeit small scale and limited to some residential areas, one might be less pessimistic about the supposed "extremism" of, for example, on-board speed governors (which have already been used in pilot schemes on the continent)[15] gaining any kind of acceptance. It is also debatable whether the views of 19 million motorists (even assuming they all hold similar views) should be allowed to have such predominance over millions of other road users — and be automatically endorsed by "road safety" professionals.

Suggesting to Mackay that those who are not part of the solution may become part of the problem, I was told: "Well, I'm part of the problem."

The myth of being scientific

Objectivity and neutrality are supposed elements of a scientific approach to evaluation and assessment, which is claimed to be performed by engineers:

"One of the things that I have come to relatively recently, although I've always had it there, is to introduce some decent hard science into it. Everybody, from time immemorial... has been thrashing around with opinions, good, bad and indifferent... The thing that will change that is to get some decent science into the subject, get better data... Once that side of it evolves, then you begin to get facts rather than opinions, and then I think the subject will progress more."[16]

This claim — and here I quote Mackay — to a scientific status, is also a myth, failing in the following ways:

≡ By not conforming to its own supposed standards;

≡ By using theories and methods derived from simple notions of the physical sciences which may be incapable of making correct statements about human beings, transport and safety;

≡ By having an ideologically defined objective which is different from or opposed to the proper aim of scientific work in this area;

≡ By being inextricably linked to an unsafe transport system, and unable to explain adequately its relationship to the power structure of that system.

According to Mackay as quoted above, "the subject" is at present at a "pre-scientific" level. The quality of data examined in Chapter 1 is indeed "a shambles".[17] Yet the fact that we have not had adequate data reflecting levels of exposure to risk of different road user groups has never prevented Mackay and his colleagues from pushing forward various initiatives while claiming to have "scientific" justification for doing so. If it was important to know the chances of vulnerable road users being killed as a consequence of seat belt legislation before advocating such legislation, it was all the more important for someone claiming to be a scientist to be in the ranks of the doubters.

In Britain it has for decades been common practice for highway and traffic engineers to alter alignments of roads and otherwise engineer the road environment, particularly at identified "black-spots". The regression-to-mean effect has been known about by statisticians for over a century; but its discussion specifically in the context of the treatment of road traffic accidents dates only from the mid-1980s.[18] Similarly, the possibility that treating a site might cause problems elsewhere in the area — the accident-migration hypothesis — is in many ways common sense; yet its consideration in the relevant journals is equally recent.[19]

An in-depth analysis of the effects of engineering treatments carried out on a number of routes in Cheshire between 1977 and 1987, considering both these issues, was reported in the principal technical journal for highway and traffic engineers in 1989. It noted:

> If the effects of treatment on accident frequency [at the neighbouring sites] are ignored, then the effects of engineering treatment appear better than they actually are [ie, treatment effectiveness is overestimated or the adverse effect of treatment is underestimated]. If both the regression-to-mean effect and the change in accident frequency [at the neighbouring sites] is ignored, then treatment appears to have been effective for all cases.[20]

But when these effects *are* considered, there are appreciable regression-to-mean effects as well as effects on neighbouring sites, giving "the net *increase* in accidents which appears to have followed the application of engineering measures on the study network." (my emphasis)[21]

Engineering measures have long been carried out and legitimated by justifications of scientific assessment and evaluation of their applicability and effects. When basic scientific concepts are used to analyse these activities, they are revealed as inadequate or even counter-productive. The real question, however, is not how engineers can find the data and analytic techniques to bring their enterprise up to the level of sophistication required to justify its existence; but whether they should be carrying on in this way in the first place. As Part One shows, traditional number-crunching positivism in the social sciences has many problems inherent in its very theory and methods.

There is an inherent tendency to accept the status quo and neglect wider underlying social forces. Long-term cultural and macro-social characteristics cannot be identified and measured as simple "factors" to be entered into a computer model, nor can they be coped with theoretically or accounted for in engineering discourse.

Epidemiological approaches, by failing to recognise the way people adapt to changes in their perceived circumstances, are limited. Traditional approaches assume that the engineer or policy-maker's intervention in a complex social totality affects one feature but somehow avoids affecting others with which it is inextricably linked. This would be inadequate in any academic discourse linked to social policy, and changes associated with, or generated by, road safety intervention are widely implicated in exacerbating the problems of a car-oriented transport policy.

This can be summarised by considering a study of risk compensation by two American researchers.[22] Its purpose was to examine parameters under which risk compensation in driving can occur. The basis of the study was the establishment of links between certain observed behaviours (deviations from prescribed lane, speed, stated feelings of safety) and the wearing or non-wearing of seat belts in go-kart driving volunteers in an experiment set up by the researchers. The study found a degree of risk-compensatory behaviour which could be attributed to the wearing of belts. Besides giving support to a view continually dismissed by road safety professionals for decades, this finding raises other questions.

(a)   To what extent are the conditions for volunteers in go-karts on a US campus experiment applicable in other circumstances — for different kinds of individual, different kinds of vehicle, different kinds of "safety aid" or different countries with different traditions in road user behaviour?

(b)   Would the compensatory behaviour change over time as users became accustomed to the device, and how would such changes occur for different kinds of user in different vehicles, etc?

(c)   Given our inability to measure levels of alertness and vigilance directly, how could we tell what compensatory changes were occurring anyway?

To some extent these questions can be looked at by doing what was partially done in some countries: time-series analyses of the effects of compulsory seat belt wearing. This was limited by the poor quality of data, which the road safety lobby admits, and the fact that studies which came up with uncomfortable answers were covered up or misinterpreted, which it does not. But even the best-time series cannot produce answers to questions concerning the long-term picture: how has compulsory seat belt wearing, for example, affected any or all of the attitudes and beliefs, stated or hidden, which govern the way we behave in the road environment? Carrying out time-series analysis is difficult enough, given the problems of isolating relevant variables. What happens if there are underlying cultural variables, both affecting and being affected by a given intervention, which cannot even be fed into the best possible future model?

Then there is the question of the aim of road safety research. It is supposed to aid measures to "prevent accidents". But, as Part One showed, the realisation of such an aim can conceal increases in accident rates and it is based on attempts to quantify something which is difficult (because of inadequate data) or impossible (because it tends to make sense only in subjective terms) to assess. Even the chance of being hurt (the "accident rate" for specific user groups in specific situations) has to be seen in the context of the external danger implicated in causing that rate. If the quality of life is to be the concern of road safety engineers, it has to be seen as related to reducing danger. If a reduction in perceived danger occurs, the accident rate may not be reduced at all. When it comes to assessing danger and its perception we have to assess factors producing "accident rates", but different from them; the ability to quantify these factors is likely to be elusive.

Except in rare and distorted instances, the road safety industry has not considered such a way of looking at danger on the roads. Its view of the analytic or academic part of road safety — what Mackay calls "the subject" — tends to be different from and/or opposed to this approach.

The same holds for another area of supposed science which is intimately linked with the endeavour of the road safety professional, whether through the use of COBA or similar procedures in road building or the economic cost of accidents continually referred to by Mackay and others — namely cost-benefit analysis (see the introduction to Part Two).

Questions of how much danger there should be, for what kind of road user and how we should accept attempts (and who by) to alter our perception of it, essentially question the power and freedom afforded to different road user groups. The true nature of this power, and how the "road safety" enterprise is part of it, is obscured by the aura of supposed science which engineers draw round themselves.

Some engineers are aware that their work is related to general transport policy issues. Mackay wishes to develop a unified transport science, based on understanding the way transport, environmental and safety questions are interrelated: "No body of knowledge exists to measure, let alone judge, the effects of these interactions… The current structure… can best be described as a number of isolated islands of knowledge separated by an ocean of ignorance."[23] Certain aspects of a legitimate approach might not be very different from what occurs, or is supposed to occur, at present with some road safety academics. But as far as linking the existing "islands of knowledge" is concerned, we should be doubtful about the foundations of these islands, let alone their extension or linking, and in many cases we would be better off trying to float in the sea.

The myth of the expert

For the supposedly objective, neutral, scientific practices of engineering to flourish, it must be staffed by special people. These special people are called experts. One of the problems engineering has in being able to account for itself is that of adequately justifying the privileged status of these experts. Whatever their "expertise", to deal with questions of equity, energy, pollution, environment, public transport, and so on, means using tools these engineers are not provided with. It also means confronting a dominant ideology obsessed with car use.

In confronting this ideology they would have to explain their own role, a role linked with the engineer's conception of the ordinary road user or "lay person". As explained above, the precise view of human beings will depend on the degree to which the engineer in question sympathises with the type of road user concerned. For the overt supporter of virtually unrestrained motorist privilege, such as

Leeming,[24] motorists are competent and basically benign, although they require some assistance in making life more convenient. Other road users, even with less obviously biased engineers, will tend to be viewed with a more patronising tolerance, and with concern that any convenience or facility provided for them will lead to a "false sense of security". While some engineers genuinely do wish to provide more facility for the vulnerable, their efforts tend to be limited by the pressures of mass car use which they either wish to defend or see no way of eroding.[25]

Whether the road user is to be seen as basically sound — the same kind of person as the expert — or is to be patronised or controlled, at some stage the engineer has to relate professional practice to the subjective world of the lay person or ordinary (as opposed to expert) road user. The issue will be to determine how to relate their own subjective judgement to that of the ordinary road user. If engineering a "black-spot" to make it safer allows motorists to relax and cause accidents at neighbouring sites, where previously they would have been more careful — or if engineering a site causes motorists to relax even at the site itself, so that no reduction in accident rates occurs even there — what is the engineer to do?

Wright and Boyle, two engineers aware of risk compensation, accident migration and the illusions created by ignoring the regression-to-mean effect, worry over this in a review of the contemporary road safety engineer's practice.[26] In addition, they consider the interaction of "objective" and "subjective" risk. This question is the most basic of all: what is the causal chain leading to a given accident frequency? As they observe, there is a constant interaction between the danger presented to a road user, their perception of it, and accidents. Accident rates do not just represent the outcome of the interaction of the first two of these elements, they feed back in as part of a causal chain. Engineers attempting to assess risk have to consider what Wright and Boyle call "ambient risk", a sort of fixed external danger (such as a sharp bend) which poses a risk independent of the perception of the road user. Then there is the subjective assessment of that risk. Accidents will occur most often where road users' perceived risk underestimates ambient risk most often, or to the greatest degree.

Of particular relevance is the problem of assessing risk:

> There appears to be no immediate hope of finding a suitable measure of ambient risk... it would appear that the various components of ambient risk can only be assessed qualitatively through a visual examination of the site by 'experts'. These assessments are themselves subjective, and it may not be possible to express the results in terms which are directly comparable with the subjective assessments made by ordinary road-users.[27]

What, then, is the difference between the expert and the lay person? The profound implications of this question are masked under the cloak of supposed agreement on the meaning of "road safety". The conclusions to the discussion on the role of the modern engineer initiated by Wright and Boyle — who are radical in their attitude to contemporary engineering practice — is revealing. The road users specifically referred to are drivers, and the desirability of attempting to reinforce subjective risk as a means of reducing accidents while keeping ambient risk the same is objected to partly because it could make driving more stressful. The objective of the road safety engineer is still seen as "accident reduction" with all the problems that flow from that definition.

The discussion of the role of experts, who have essentially to make subjective judgements conforming to the likely subjective judgements of road users who are human beings like themselves, raises the following issues:

≡ Which road users are being considered? What is socially desirable about their form of transport and to what extent should it be controlled or regulated?

≡ Who should be entitled to intervene in these matters?

≡ What should the objective of "road safety" engineers be?

≡ What kind of science should they utilise?

These are questions about the power and freedoms of different road user groups, about transport policy and the environment. They are implicated in the everyday actions of engineers. On the rare occasions where they are openly addressed, they are generally dealt with inadequately and/or wrongly.

Conclusion

The culture of road safety engineering has a pernicious effect on any proper attempt to reduce danger on our roads in line with a rational and fair transport policy.

Engineers and road safety "experts" continue to press on with a "scientific method" which regularly fails to meet its own criteria. It may be investigating relatively trivial "safety aids", from additional rear brake lights through to reflective side-walled bicycle tyres. Or it may be the more important areas of vehicle crashworthiness or road engineering. The "research" will reflect, implicitly or explicitly, a view of the "road safety problem" tending to bolster a dangerous status quo and be biased against vulnerable road users.

Sometimes findings which do not fit in with the received picture are dismissed (or not published). At other times the criteria required to validate research which calls for speed controls for the benefit of all road users are expected to be far more stringent than those for research on protecting the occupants by wrapping them in more crashworthy vehicles.[28]

This may be explained in terms of the source of research funding or the pro-road and pro-car bias of engineers, or in the acceptance of the pervasive ideology surrounding car use. It may further be seen in terms of the refusal of any "scientist" to cope with evidence, however obvious, showing their activity to be based on false assumptions, or in terms of an inability to understand what a genuinely scientific approach to the problems — including, of course, knowing how to define the problem in the first place — would look like. Overall, the inertia of ideology combines with the vested interests of the powerful to resist the prospect of change.

People who claim objective, scientific expertise happen also to control policy. [29] Sometimes their ideas and practice coincide with what should happen, but we cannot be sure of this until the basis for a project to replace "road safety" has been properly constituted. This will indeed involve scientific expertise, but be based on a science which properly accounts for human behaviour—from risk compensation through to the professional ideology of practitioners. An endeavour of this nature should be open about its links to transport policies, and the policies themselves should be the appropriate ones for future societies. This science will have respect for the needs of members of the community who have so far seen more of the disbenefits than the benefits of mass car use, and whose common-sense knowledge of road user behaviour often has more insight than the "expertise" of the engineer. It need not abandon the positivist approach (there should be room for competing philosophies), but if it does maintain it, it must also consider approaches which examine the apparently seemlessly inter-related behaviour of road users, whether dealing with local behaviours or wider cultural changes. This science must be aware of compensatory tendencies (accident migration, smokescreening, risk compensation etc) and the effects of institutions and ideologies in the wider society. When this happens, the authority that engineers crave will be deserved.

Meanwhile, there is a need to be honest about what engineers achievements have been. The wrong group of road users have been pandered to in the process of "designing out" motor danger. Indeed, the danger, which could and should have been designed out has been reinforced — in effect, designed in. Engineering's legacies include the distancing of responsibility from the central fact that some human beings have the potential to damage their fellow human beings. When human behaviour is separated from "the problem", and when the arena of discussion becomes dominated by supposed experts dealing with cost-benefit and number-crunching, the evasion of responsibility becomes inevitable. As with other areas in "road safety", causing "accidents" has been discussed without really confronting this central fact.

6.

The educator's tale

CHILDREN PLAYING on a residential street: a problem? Well, yes, after all "Roads are for cars and lorries — not for pedestrians", says the Caring Parent guide to child road safety.
Does it really have to be this way? Have we created a society where only the occupants of cars and lorries count? And is the promise that road safety education holds out in reality a false one?

Few accidents arise... from ignorance of how to drive, and a much more frequent cause of disaster is undue proficiency leading to excessive adventure.
Winston Churchill, then Home Secretary, responding to a 1911 TUC delegation demanding the introduction of a driving test.[1]

If the reduction of the numbers of road traffic accidents involving children is taken as the ultimate goal, then the evidence that (their) training and instruction can achieve this must at the present time be regarded as only suggestive... The extent to which it can... remains unclear, and it is difficult to envisage indisputable evidence to support it being produced in the foreseeable future.
OECD, 1986.[2]

In terms of accident reduction benefits, very few studies have ever demonstrated any benefits of education programmes and publicity. Some would say the situation was even worse.
CS Downing, senior researcher at the Transport and Road Research Laboratory.[3]

Although there have been many studies of the influence of driver education on crash rates, none with acceptable methodology has shown that those who receive driver education have lower crash rates than those who do not.
Leonard Evans, Principal Research Scientist, General Motors Research Laboratories.[4]

Education — usually taken to refer to training and publicity for the different classes of road user — is traditionally one of the "three Es" of road safety, along with Enforcement and Engineering. It is probably the approach most commonly identified with "road safety" by the general public. Most of us are familiar with instruction on road crossing procedures at school and advertising campaigns in the mass media. For motorists there is the instruction required in order to pass "the test".

In terms of success, even as defined in the limiting terms of the road safety lobby, educational methods are the least promising. This was officially stated in the Department of Transport publication, *Road Safety: The Next Steps*,[5] but it has been known for years. Trying to reduce accidents by educational methods has a number of intractable difficulties.

While these are worth looking at, the main focus of attention should be the assumptions underlying the practice of road safety education. Like so much else under the name of "road safety", these betray an uncritical acceptance of the transport status quo with attendant discrimination against the vulnerable road user, and a failure to confront the source of danger. Of course, there is a genuine commitment from some educators to train road users to respect the safety of others; but the basis for success is lacking.

At best, road safety education leaves the central issues untouched; at worst, it bolsters present discrimination and danger. It fosters deference among users of vulnerable and benign modes of transport, while giving confidence to (without assurance of responsibility from) the users of dangerous modes. It creates an illusion, through advertising campaigns, that something is being done "for safety". And it plays a part in confusing the transitive and intransitive meanings of danger —the difference between one's own safety and that of others, often inculcating this confusion in impressionable young minds.

Why educational methods "fail"

Training does not achieve the formally stated objectives of road safety professionals because, in the case of drivers and motorcyclists, its present form *increases the potential number of people in a position to cause danger*. Were the level of educational achievement to be tested regularly to satisfy a high level of acquisition of skills, far fewer motorists would be legally entitled to drive — and such criteria would be opposed by the motoring lobby. Driver education is there to facilitate, not control, and therefore increases the risk to all road users.[6]

The second problem is that skills are acquired which can encourage the taking of additional risks. When confronted with the evidence of the failure of training schemes, the response of professionals is that some form of training should occur even if more people become road users of the type in question, as they will inevitably join that road user group anyway. The aim is, therefore, to reduce the level of danger for the amount of exposure that will occur in any case. Yet even here the evidence is not impressive.[7] Giving people more skills does not mean that they will use them - and they may absorb the safety potential as performance potential. As with a performance car, driving skills valued for their ability to help motorists get out of trouble can be used to get into trouble in the first place.[8]

There are enormous methodological problems in assessing the effectiveness of training schemes, above all in connecting what may be only change in one area of accident causation to accident frequencies, accounting for the OECD's verdict quoted above. This most extensive recent review of child safety education points out difficulties in relating knowledge accumulated and resultant behaviour. For behavioural change to occur and be maintained, it "requires programmes of instruction that are far more intensive than has conventionally been the case in the past. Even then... there are some instances where intensive instruction has not resulted in discernible change in behaviour."[9]

The problems of education succeeding are not simply the often-mentioned ones of the need to repeat training regularly and give it at an intense level. They are not even problems of assessing the worth of different programmes accurately in order to prioritise allocation of resources. The real problems are the deep-seated tendencies of human beings to take certain levels of risk, and to do so in a particular kind of transport system. The persistent tendency to balance risk against freedom means that education will have limited or no beneficial effects. More specifically the vulnerable will be at the mercy of the potentially dangerous, however carefully the vulnerable behave.

The potentially dangerous, whatever nuisance the vulnerable may cause them, will suffer principally at the hands of other members of the same road user group. Their behaviour will be affected by the extent of the loss of freedom associated with taking more care and less risk, and by cultural and ideological determinants of the appropriate behaviour of road users. Unless there is a constant altruistic commitment to the safety of others, there is no reason to suppose that people will accept the rules of safe behaviour which education might provide.

Road safety education, as presently conceived, is therefore incapable of seriously restricting the capacity of those with destructive potential to hurt others. However, in another sense it does indeed "work". It fulfils a particular social function as a set of practices underpinning the dangerous status quo. In this it operates against the aims of an equitable, decent or civilised approach to danger on the road.

Safety and "the test"

(i) The struggle for "the test"

The driving test which British motorists must pass in order to possess a valid driving licence was brought in only after prolonged campaigning, against bitter opposition. As early as 1903, debate in Parliament and elsewhere had mentioned the need for a means of testing people before they could be entrusted with a motorcar.[10] Along with associated demands—from a public increasingly concerned about a rising total of road deaths—for measures such as speed limits, compulsory insurance, law enforcement, licensing and the registration and numbering of vehicles, its introduction was fought with tenacity by the motoring organisations. As one account of this battle, which is not unsympathetic to the motorists' cause, states: "What they had to overcome in order to get the necessary legislation on the statute books was the determined, articulate and well-financed opposition of the powerful car lobby."[11]

Considering the road and vehicle conditions of the 1930s, the campaigners' case for a test seems irrefutable, and the opposition to it an example of how ruthless the motorists' lobby could be. Yet there was a good deal of humility in the approach of the campaigners, whether in organisations such as the Pedestrians' Association for Road Safety or leader writers reflecting public horror at a road toll which had reached an all-time high in 1934, the year before the introduction of "the test".

There was no basic opposition to mass motoring as such from the campaigners. Despite the fact that a minority of road users had completely transformed the road environment in less than two decades, their demands were moderate, to say the least. The call for a 30 mph speed limit, for example, has to be seen in the context of poor and unreliable braking capacity, less reliable road surfaces and road layouts far more difficult to negotiate than now. Private motoring was exclusively a middle- and upper-class pursuit,[12] cycling a predominantly working class one; but the issue was rarely seen as one of class politics.[13]

The campaign for "the test" was, then, a request for motorists to become a little more responsible, rather than a serious attempt at control. Part of a humble and placid approach, it was typified by those campaigners who tried to achieve their ends, like cycling and pedestrian safety campaigners today, by friendly persuasion using their own driving behaviour as an example. If they could drive with care and respect for other road users, why couldn't other motorists? Like other approaches skirting the fundamental problems of road danger, the campaign was always going to have limited — or even negative — results.

The dangers of the driving test — so accurately perceived by Churchill — were not (and are still not) appreciated. Instead the RAC complained that it would be wrong to demand a test for a driving licence when one was not required for a dog licence. In the event, driving tests became compulsory for new licence holders from June 1935. It was a double-edged victory. Benefits are not only inadequate in terms of screening out incompetent drivers or providing proper training, but are absorbed by encouraging feelings of pride and supposed fulfilment of responsibility.

(ii) The nature of "the test"

After a period of instruction, learner drivers are required to drive for about half an hour showing a knowledge of the Highway Code and the ability to carry out basic manoeuvres. This is probably the last time that many drivers seriously attempt to obey the Highway Code. Roadside observation indicates frequent and regular rule-breaking by many, if not most, motorists.[14] And spot checks reveal that most motorists are ignorant of basic elements of knowledge of driving that they may be examined on in "the test", such as ability to recognise basic road signs.[15]

The chances of being caught for behaviour which flouts the Highway Code is, as shown in Chapter 7, minimal, even for those potentially dangerous behaviours which can be seen. If there is no attempt to ensure that people obey the laws they are supposed to follow, why get them to display knowledge of them? Also, as the existence of so-called advance driver training indicates, why test at such a low level? And why the implicit assumption that — unlike for any other semi-skilled task — people's ability will not decrease over time (with 'the test' occurring once in a lifetime if driving)?[16]

There is a defence of "the test" against these charges. It is that about half of those taking it fail, and that therefore it must be a stringent examination of driving skills. The Department of Transport does not bother to compile figures dealing with long-term chances of passing. My impression is that those who are determined to gain a driving licence find it quite easy to pass "the test" by taking it again and again, without necessarily acquiring more skills. I would argue that a real indicator of chances of passing for those prepared to take a test, for example, five times, would be nearer 80 to 95 per cent.

These are not new criticisms. It should be obvious that taking "the test" is of little value in preventing motorists from being dangerous. Despite this it is still thought of as an important commitment, or even concession, made by motorists which cyclists (or even pedestrians) get away with not making.[17] Even a difficult, regularly repeated test would not close the gap in the potential to break regulations or inflict damage that exists between motorists and the benign road user groups. Not only is "the test" a weak control, then, *its social function is largely to provide a defence against accusations of antisocial behaviour, whether it actually minimises the likelihood of antisocial behaviour or not.*

The reason for putting inverted commas around the phrase "the test" is partly to cast doubt on its supposed function as a genuine restriction of dangerous behaviour. It also needs to be seen as an element in the successful completion of a rite of passage. Its role is to confer on the person who passes the idea that they have become a responsible road user, superior to others who have not. In this sense "the test" is dangerous — anybody seriously committed to a career of careful driving needs a sense of humility, rather than the pride associated with passing. It is arguable that its existence does more harm than good.

Nearly 60 years after its introduction, initial results were published of research on whether drivers who had passed "the test" would be able to pass it within the following two years. In a survey of 400 such motorists, just under half were unable to pass it. The main reason given for their failure was overconfidence.[18]

(iii) A proper test?

To meet the criticisms of inadequate training and testing, and that testing should occur after the driver has some experience of driving alone, various forms of advanced driver training have been introduced. They are also open to criticism.

First, there is doubt about the levels of effectiveness of the various tests for those who take them. Particularly at the level of the less sophisticated defensive driver training, there may be no benefit in terms of reduced tendency to become involved in accidents.[19]

There is, however, evidence that people who pass an advanced driver test will

110

have better accident records afterwards than those who fail it. The most frequently quoted is a 1972 TRRL study of the difference between successful and unsuccessful Institute of Advanced Motorists (IAM) test candidates. Those passing had 25 per cent fewer accidents over a three-year period after the test than those failing. [20] The IAM claims a conviction rate among its motorists of 1.9 per cent as against a national average of 10.4 per cent, although this is not corrected for age and other variables — those who want to take the IAM test may in the first place already be less likely to have accidents than a national average. For this reason the possibility of making such a test compulsory has been raised since at least the late 1960s. It has been opposed successfully on the grounds that "the cost of introducing and maintaining such a test is... unacceptably high."[21] But this is only part of the story.

Training which would teach people how to drive carefully is time-consuming, particularly if regularly repeated. Besides, a substantial proportion of the current licence holders at present on the road would lose their licences if regular testing at a proficient level were required. It is estimated that if the RoSPA advanced drivers test were to be compulsory for licence holders, some 30 to 40 per cent of current drivers would lose their licences, even after being offered appropriate training. [22] The motoring organisations are unlikely to support a measure which would sizeably reduce their membership, revenue and power.

More demanding training and testing are limited for the same reasons that limit all attempts to control the dangers which motorists present to others — namely the unwillingness of motorists to accept them. At present the membership of the IAM constitutes some 90,000, or about 0.45 per cent of all licensed motorists, with a smaller number of motorists having passed other similar tests. This tiny minority are a self-selected group prepared to admit that their skills might possibly be deficient. Central to the ideology of the motorist is the idea that driving is a personal, private matter. When added to notions of prestige and pride, this is hardly likely to lead to the kind of humility and self-criticism required to accept repeated rigorous training and testing.

The "elite driver"

There is a long history of the notion of the elite driver. It is linked to the prewar days when private motoring was outside the experience of the working class, and even to the earlier experience of motoring as an adventurous sport for the wealthy. Along with this sense of privilege came the idea that motorists should, out of a kind of *noblesse oblige*, behave in a courteous fashion towards other road users. In the era of mass motoring this spirit persists in the idea of the "knight of the road", linked to advanced driver training or to the use of high-prestige cars. Reducing the chances of hurting others is regarded as important, but as an act of a sort of feudal benevolence exercised by superior people, out of choice.

A good example of elite driver ideology is to be found in the book issued to new Porsche owners in Britain. [23] The expert driver is compared to a first-class sportsman or sportswoman; also: "The master driver shows by example that he or she is an expert... They are high achievers, people who are never satisfied with their own performance and always searching for perfection."[24]

It may seem churlish to criticise a guide which disseminates the rules of careful driving. The *Porsche Driving Book* reminds drivers of correct headways and the fact that "a car can be a lethal weapon",[25] emphasising the matching of braking distances to depth of vision and correct behaviour with regard to cyclists and pedestrians.[26] If all motorists followed this advice, they would be considerably less dangerous.

But will advising motorists to live up to lofty ideals work? For a small group it might. Without constraint and restriction, however, it is not enough, because it requires acceptance on the part of the vulnerable of a sort of benevolent dictatorship of the road by their betters. There are too many incentives, and insufficient disincentives, for the average fallible motorist to be placed in such an uncontrolled position. The plea of the expert teacher, that "efficient driving is created by consistent self-discipline, of the kind that comes from within *rather than the restraint imposed by speed limits and rules of the road*" (my emphasis),[27] is thus misplaced. Without real controls — more unpleasant but more real than an ideology of pride — these instructions will not be properly followed. It is so easy to pose great danger — voluntary codes of practice can never be enough.

Publicity

Many of us can remember the slogans of road safety publicity campaigns in the mass media. Along with being taught at school how to cross the road, the public perception is often that posters and television advertisements are what "road safety" is about. Millions of pounds are spent every year on such material.

There is no evidence that it has any effect in reducing road accident occurrence. Indeed, in a field where there is a good deal of debate about the effects of various measures, this is the one area where there is significant agreement, if not complete consensus — including among those responsible for producing the material — about the ineffectiveness of the measure.

This has been known about since the 1948 official Social Survey concluded that the public as a whole was immune to warnings about danger on the roads, and that visual propaganda affected neither the temperament nor the behaviour of the individual. This finding seems to have been ignored ever since.[28] To take the example of the 1988 police national motorway safety campaign, the research on its effects found that most motorists did not identify themselves with the target audience of drivers and that: "excessive speed and close following behaviour are extremely resistant to modification through traditional publicity techniques..."[29]

It is not simply a matter of public ignorance or forgetfulness. Official advertising and publicity play two important roles. The first is a smokescreen function; as with the official presentation of statistics, road safety publicity helps create the impression that something is being done. "We" — motorists in particular — are spending a lot of money on "the problem". In this sense we have a classic case of initiatives which may move over the fine line that divides an ineffective measure from one which, because of the impression given that it might be effective, is worse than useless. The second role of road safety propaganda is one whereby education, in its broadest sense, *does* take place. But the content is a victim-blaming ideology which diverts attention away from the source of danger and the problems which should really be looked at.

A history of controversy

The representatives of cyclists and pedestrians were critical of the road safety publicity of the 1930s and 1950s. Part of their criticism was directed at RoSPA, because of its apparent domination by the motoring lobby. The Pedestrians' Association expressed doubts about the National Safety First Association, which did not fade when it was granted the royal charter and became part of RoSPA in 1941, pointing out that in 1947 its chairman was secretary of the Commercial Road Users' Association, while the chairman of its road safety committee was secretary of the AA.[30] The effect of such opposition from the Pedestrians' Association was minimal — in 1954 the two posts were filled by the chairman of Vauxhall and the head of the legal department of the Society of Motor Manufacturers and Traders.[31] RoSPA's origins in industrial safety were such that it already had a commitment to voluntary, as opposed to compulsory, controls on the powerful, in defence of the status quo. This point is well made in the best account of the role of road safety education, the book *Murder Most Foul* (1947), by the Pedestrians' Association's postwar chairman, JS Dean.[32]

The criticisms were that publicity was implicitly victim-blaming, and that in so far as the correct objective was pursued, it was urging useless voluntary measures as a way of detracting from the need for compulsory restraint and controls on motoring. The Pedestrians' Association withdrew from RoSPA, and *rapprochement* was not achieved until the 1980s.[33] Similarly the Cyclists' Touring Club, the principal cycling organisation, collaborated with RoSPA for 25 years but seceded in 1950 after feeling that it would be assumed to be condoning a passive policy,[34] then rejoined a few years later.

The rift with RoSPA was the result of mounting anger over the inactivity, collusion with the motoring lobby, victim-blaming and educational smokescreening of the Ministry of Transport, which had been voiced since before the war by the representatives of the vulnerable road users. In an editorial in 1934, the weekly magazine *Cycling* said that the Minister of Transport, Mr Hore-Belisha,

> **must choose between the 'lesser important' enmity of the cyclists and the formidable opposition of the whole motoring community, which, financially and industrially, is now bound up with the life of the nation... He is anti-cyclist because he caters primarily for an age in which none of the leaders of public**

thought in transport matters are cyclists.[35]

This was when there were probably many more miles travelled by bicycle than by car, and certainly far more journeys.[36] Some 1,536 cyclists (the highest annual total ever recorded in Britain) and 3,529 pedestrians died on the roads.

In the same issue of *Cycling* a leading cycling journalist appealed to the Minister, sympathising with his efforts to reduce what Hore-Belisha had himself said was a situation where the roads were "like battlefields":

> But you cannot abolish battlefields by notice-boards. Once again, you 'appealed to the conscience of the community'; but you cannot cure a cancer by appealing to the patient's conscience.[37]

The dramatic metaphors are not untypical of the anger expressed in the 1930s. However, the writer, as other cyclists, did not place all the responsibility on motorists, instead assuming it to be community-wide.

Dean was to point out the contradiction of road safety being made largely the responsibility of the Ministry of Transport, when that ministry was responsible for having contributed so much to the danger on the roads in the first place. The same contradiction remains today. The content of official advertisements was persistently criticised, and the use of so-called "educational" methods was seen by the vulnerable road users' defenders as part of a cover-up. Meanwhile the motoring organisations advocated appeals to courtesy as an alternative to controls. Even mild publicity directed at modifying motorist behaviour was resisted — with the evidence even then indicating that it would have no beneficial effect and simply persuade the gullible that something was being done.[38]

How road safety education *does* work

In the 1940s JS Dean wrote:

> This 'education' is the worst possible training for the children as the drivers of the future, since it teaches them that the driver is the master of the road and the only role for other road-users... is to keep out of his way and that if they are killed or maimed through not doing so, this is something they deserve. Much of the motor slaughter may, indeed, be traced directly to the yearly appearance on the roads of young drivers brought up in this destructive belief.[39]

An apparent failure?

Education of children in road safety is something most people would appear to support. Road accidents represent the single major cause of death to children in European countries, accounting for between a quarter and a half of all deaths amongst children aged one to 14.[40] Despite its agreed importance, "provision [of safety education] in schools and by parents is limited and inadequate in most European countries",[41] involving "limited use of curriculum materials... limited preparation... inability to secure external assistance... lack of organisational structure... all further impeded by lack of co-ordination within schools and with external agencies."[42]

Yet this paradox is not strange. In post-war Britain, teachers have seen themselves cast as the defenders of society against juvenile delinquency, football hooliganism, vandalism, teenage pregnancy and all manner of social problems, generally with minimal resources. The cry for education is often nothing more than a buck-passing attempt to sweep the issue under the carpet. The fact that education does not work in reducing danger, or even fulfil the official objectives of "road safety", is not really the issue. In one sense, road safety education does indeed "work" — to ill effect.

Teaching them their place

"Road safety" education demonstrates to children the hegemony of the motor car. It is made clear, intentionally and otherwise, that "the road" — rather than motor vehicles on it — is dangerous. It is children's duty to defer to those who are not only less vulnerable, but more dangerous, and supposedly more capable of careful

Be sure that children know how dangerous traffic can be. Roads are for cars and lorries – not for pedestrians.

Not even when they're at a signalled crossing? As here in the *Caring Parent Guide* to children's road safety, children learn early that the car is king of the road, a message that carries over into adult driving attitudes.

decision-making.

It need not be this way. Restriction on children, as for the elderly and people with minor mobility disabilities, moving about in the vicinity of their homes is a recent phenomenon. Apart from the more heavily used roads, it dates back about 50 years, or, in many areas, not even as far as that. Photographs of urban Britain in the postwar years — for example, those taken by Bert Hardy, Oscar Marzaroli (in Glasgow) or Shirley Baker (in Salford as late as the 1960s)[43] — reveal streets available for play, for relaxed crossing by independent children, elderly and disabled people. The word "community" has become hackneyed, but these were indeed streets where a community could flourish.

In some European countries the domination of the car is not allowed the free rein it enjoys in Britain. A seminar paper on safety in residential streets in the Netherlands opens with a slide showing children playing by the side of a road with a car approaching at 30 mph.[44] For the speaker it is obvious that the problem is the existence of through traffic, or indeed any vehicles moving in that situation at that speed. The task is to design the road so that speeds are restricted to no more than 20 mph, possibly with additional legal commitment on motorists to give right of way to vulnerable road users. For many of his British audience, by contrast, the children are the problem.

Until this view changes, we are left with the onus of responsibility being put on those least capable of bearing it — with the prospect of a majority of motorists relying on children getting out of the way while braking is left until too late.[45] (Despite the assumption that child pedestrian accidents are due to the heedlessness of the children, evidence shows that they, not motorists, take most of the avoiding action against accidents.)[46]

It may be far fetched to relate the business of child pedestrian education to totalitarian social organisation, as Dean did in his analysis of road safety education.[47] But might there not be a link between an oppressive form of society and the schooling — through fear and guilt — of people into a relationship of obedience and deference towards people who are less vulnerable and more dangerous than they are?

What is without doubt is that road safety "education" breeds acceptance of an inequitable status quo with a lack of questioning on the part of the powerless which would have made a feudal lord envious. During childhood the transitive and intransitive meanings of danger on the road — the tendency to hurt and be hurt — are confused. "Road safety education" at this stage of life means socialising the impressionable into a society with a particular kind of transport system which they will be taught to see as natural. They are taught not just how to behave as children *but what they can expect to get away with a dozen or so years later when they are young drivers.*

Of all the accident and transport statistics, one of the most chilling must be that between 93 and 95 per cent of parents are regarded as being considerate drivers by their children.[48] The implications here for the behaviour of the next generation of drivers are profound and unsettling.

Conclusion: the education we need?

Safety on the road is, and always has been, a question of who defers to whom — of which road users are allowed how much road space, and what effect they are allowed to have on the safety of others. Discussion about appropriate measures to be taken for "road safety", whether in engineering, education or enforcement, is really a forum for the parade of views supporting the freedom of one or other group. Most official discussion of education, as with the other areas, is about supporting an unnecessarily dangerous and discriminatory status quo.

Sometimes the assumptions underlying what is supposed to be a common aim are hidden. At other times the dominant ideology is openly revealed. At all times there is an inability to accept that a situation which has changed dramatically in the postwar period in terms of levels of danger, and which is unusual with respect to other parts of the world, could be any different; or that demands for the vulnerable to get out of the way of the dangerous may not be the right solution.

Education is seen as unnecessary for the dangerous — unless it is for motor-cyclists, in which case it is "for their own good", rather than that of their potential victims. Where motorist education is advocated, this is to generate pride and skills without the necessary commitment to use them properly, to encourage young drivers into cars too early or to provide the smokescreen of "the test". Where education might do some good — at advanced driver level — it is hampered by the ideology of the elite driver. Advanced driver education is a possible benefit only if made compulsory, which, like other attempts to civilise car use, would be incompatible with the prevailing motorist ideology.

The idea that educational solutions can meet what this book sees as the real problem of danger on the roads is itself dangerous. These "solutions" represent a victory for those who in the 1930s opposed genuine moves for safety involving restraint of motorist power. Human beings may be benign, co-operative and amenable to education, but when they hold dangerous power — without sufficient incentive always to use it responsibly — the situation is different. This fact of human nature does not just apply to motoring in residential areas, or in the vicinity of child pedestrians, but everywhere. Road safety "education" systematically forgets this fact.

Another confusion arises from the idea of equality between unequals. If motorists are to be "educated", then so should the vulnerable. Schooling them to get out of the way has been advocated, for their own good. If this does not work, it only shows their incompetence and the need for stronger measures. The failure of driver education, particularly in terms of encouraging younger people to be more dangerous earlier on, is ignored.[49]

An alternative?

The above view, when expressed at a road safety seminar, meets with shock. Of

117

course there is a need to teach children to be careful crossing the road. But any educational approach must be part of a system that gives them a genuine chance of safety.[50] Driver education could be beneficial only if it moved from generating pride to generating humility, with properly researched programmes[51] in a context of fundamental change in motorists' underlying attitudes and beliefs — and in the danger they pose to others. It would not have any illusions about the ability of any teaching programme to transform ordinary human beings into particularly committed caring individuals with a high sense of altruism.

It would also involve an awareness of the problems of the present approach in the full context of the transport system we have. We need to understand that the few millions spent on publicity are not simply a waste, but that the publicity machine itself is an integral part of a transport system which squanders billions.[52] We need to ask why what was sometimes called the "licence to kill" is just given away with inadequate once-and-for-all information. We need to see the driving test in a context where the limited knowledge acquired is not, in fact, meant to be adhered to, and where the whole episode is wrapped up in a rite of passage which breeds a dangerous sense of overconfidence. We need to witness that otherwise intelligent and civilised people are able to support the system and spout its dubious mythology with so little opposition.[53]

An alternative safety education would also involve teaching children some of the knowledge about transport indicated in Part Three, while ensuring an ability to criticise injustice that real education should provide. It would create a different set of road values from today's prevailing philosophy that "might is right".

7.

The lawyer's and the police officer's tales[1]

"PEDESTRIANS cross at their own risk." A slogan of this kind might adequately describe a situation where dangerous drivers can kill and maim practically with impunity. There just isn't a particularly strong deterrent against antisocial and life-endangering driving.

The generous view taken by the courts of those whose driving causes injury or death has now prompted the relatives of accident victims to start a national campaign called RoadPeace.

Of the three "Es" of road safety, Enforcement has a particular importance. Enforcement refers here to the whole legal process, from policing (or lack of it) through to action in the courts (Magistrates', Crown and Coroner's). In this area, much discussion about "what should be done" takes place. Perhaps for this very reason, engineers and educators often argue that their approaches are more fruitful than one which relies on punishment. Indeed, both defenders of motorists' privilege and right to be dangerous[2] and the advocates of safer conditions[3] see their solutions as avoiding any of the cost or overtones of vindictiveness that enforcement implies.

Yet, as other chapters show, what we call engineering and education cannot satisfy even the official aims of road safety, let alone the aims of a rational and fair approach to danger on the roads. And, while law enforcement is a poor way to tackle most social problems — with punishment notoriously likely to fail in meeting its officially declared purpose — it could have a beneficial effect in reducing danger on the roads without the negative effects produced in other areas of human activity.

Also, in the discourse of the legal system, society articulates its assumptions about what kind of behaviour is permissible, and why, in the road environment. It both reflects and generates the ideas that underpin road safety ideology and operate in education, engineering and overall transport policy. The student of road safety in general, and road traffic law in particular, is therefore fortunate that Britain's most extensive official inquiry into road traffic law was completed in 1988. The Road Traffic Law Review Report, known as the North Report after its chairman, reviewed the basic principles which it saw as constituting road traffic law.[4] Virtually all its recommendations, with limited but noteworthy exceptions, were accepted in the government White Paper presented to Parliament in 1989.[5]

North's recommendations generally met with approval:[6] if implemented, they would both streamline the law, by giving less time to trivial offences, and crack down on the most dangerous drivers more effectively than had happened in the past.

In fact, even if new laws based on North are rigorously enforced, the effect on reducing danger on the roads will be minimal. Road traffic law and its enforcement have always had a minimal effect in the long term on danger on the road. We now have a continuation of that state of affairs, with (yet again) the added problem that any benefits will be eroded as the principal problems are obscured by the illusion that dangerous behaviour is being controlled.

A. Law enforcement now

Some 8 million road traffic offences are recorded each year, and also, as North puts it with great understatement, "a very great number go undetected and unrecorded".[7] The vast majority of these are committed by car drivers. Britain has some 20 million cars and millions of lorries, buses and other vehicles on the roads, and it is not easy to differentiate between the propensity of different types of vehicle driver to commit such offences. (For simplicity I look at the smaller number of car drivers alone, in fact some 18 million at the time of the figures in Notes 11-18.)

Proceeding with 8 million offences annually might seem like a massive display of law enforcement. In both intensity and in proportion to the rule-breaking that occurs, however, it is tiny. It results in the vast majority of cases in punishment that is quite trivial and hardly worthy of the name. This can be seen by considering the different penalties that can result from police action:

(i) Rewards for not breaking the law
We start with the inverse of punishment. Police in the north of England have given small gifts to motorists giving negative breath tests: this follows the example of United States Air Force personnel in East Anglia being given cash bonuses for not being convicted of drink-driving offences. I can think of no other area where not breaking the law receives officially sanctioned material rewards.

(ii) Written warnings
Written warnings are issued in some $3/4$ million cases. They politely ask the motorist to be more careful and typically wish them "happy and safe motoring in the future".[8]

(iii) Fixed penalty notices
Some five million fixed penalty notices are issued annually,[9] making up the response to two-thirds of offences dealt with by the police. They involve the payment of either £12 or £25. The severity of this can perhaps be assessed in the context of the total annual cost of running the average car (as calculated by the AA and other organisations, basing calculations on the full range of costs, including deprecia-

tion) of some £3,000 at the relevant time. The financial penalty amounts to approximately 0.4 to 0.8 per cent of the annual cost for the lower and higher fixed penalty notice respectively. There is the possibility of licence endorsement with the higher penalty.

(iv) Prosecutions

Prosecutions constitute some 20 per cent of the actions by the police, occurring two million times a year.[10] These involve:–

(a) Fines

For about 1,100,000 people each year the fine is the principal sentence for motoring offences heard at one court appearance. The average fine is about £50, with one-third being between £20 and £50. About 20 per cent of fines are for speeding offences, 25 per cent for offences relating to insurance and taxation.[11] The level of fining is supposed to bear some relation to ability to pay. In 1992 the richest man in Britain was fined £300 for his third speeding offence.[12] This does not involve particularly preferential treatment for the ultra-wealthy and in so far as it does, the fact is that fines tend to be of quite trivial amounts compared to the cost of motoring and personal income. Fines also accompany the other results of prosecution such as endorsements.

(b) Endorsement

Driving licences are endorsed with penalty points. This occurs about a million times a year. Licence endorsement can adversely affect insurance premium costs or prejudice potential employers who may require a "clean" licence. The main disadvantage is that if sufficient points are "totted up", the licence holder is disqualified from driving. But this happens only about once for every 60 times that a licence is endorsed; less than one in 1,000 motorists lose their licence every year due to totting up endorsements.[13] The licence holder starts from scratch again after three years.

(c) Disqualification

Disqualification occurs some 160,000 times a year,[14] affecting about one in 120 motorists. About 60 per cent are for drink-driving offences. Disqualification for careless, reckless or accident offences happens in 5,000 cases, or for one in every 3,500 motorists. Disqualifications for careless driving last for less than a year in about 70 per cent of the cases involved. Apart from for drink-driving most periods of disqualification are for less than a year.[15]

(d) Imprisonment

Nearly 15,000 motorists are given custodial sentences every year, of which the clear majority, some 70 per cent,[16] are for driving while disqualified. The length of sentence for the majority is three months or less in magistrates' courts, and six months or less in crown courts.[17] Press attention focuses on dramatic cases of causing death through reckless driving, a crime which carries a five-year maximum sentence. Just three people were sentenced to three years or more in 1986.[18]

Breaking down the recorded offences this way, we see that only a small

121

minority of motorists stand a chance of anything more than a small fine, with only the tiniest proportion likely to suffer some restriction on their freedom after conviction. Looked at in the context of the potential for destruction of other people's lives, health or property, the penalties for law-breaking seem small.

It may be that a 1-in-3,500 chance of being banned for careless or reckless driving every year reflects the law-abiding and rule-following behaviour of the average British motorist. Does it?

B. Rule- and law-breaking

Roadside observation indicates that rule-breaking such as driving too close to the vehicle in front, and failing to defer to pedestrians crossing roads which were entered from a junction,[19] as well as speeding are just some of the infractions committed by substantial proportions, if not the vast majority, of the motoring public. This does not include drinking and driving, which may be done by "only" a few million motorists,[20] or the inability of an estimated million-plus motorists to pass the current eyesight test.[21]

All these behaviours either involve breaking the law or, as in the case of breaking a Highway Code regulation, put the motorist in a position where he may be prosecuted for careless driving. It appears that the chances of being caught and prosecuted are therefore extremely small.

Estimates of the chance of being caught and prosecuted for drinking and driving vary from 1 in 250 to much lower (less likelihood) estimates, with the chances for driving under the influence of drugs — an offence under the same legislation — so far lower as to be virtually non-existent.[22] The chance of being caught for speeding is about once in a lifetime's motoring; but unlike drink-driving, in a number of surveys either a substantial proportion or a clear majority claim to break speed limits as a matter of course.[23]

In a typical recent case Prince Michael of Kent, President of the Institute of Road Safety Officers, President of the Medical Commission on Accident Prevention, sponsor of the Prince Michael Road Safety Awards[24] received his fourth conviction for speeding or careless driving after overtaking a number of vehicles at 104 mph. He was banned from driving for two weeks (his defence admitting that a driving licence was not essential for him) and fined £100 with £15 costs.[25]

It should be stressed that there is no evidence of preferential treatment being given here. Similarly, when Princess Anne's speeding career led to her receiving a one month ban and £150 fine (with £10 costs) for breaking speed limits by 28 and 55 per cent respectively on two occasions in 1990, the sentence was typical for this kind of offence. It is simply that these offences are so common that in order to qualify for newsworthiness the individual must have some sort of celebrity status.

It is generally argued that such rule- or law-breaking behaviour is not implicated in causing accidents, but the problems of talking about "accident causation" have already been referred to.[26] In so far as any isolated feature of driving behaviour can be specified as increasing the level of danger to others, most of these behaviours are illegal or careless in a way which increases that danger. If a quarter of all two-or-more-vehicle crashes occur when they are travelling in the same direction, it is difficult to deny that driving too fast for the conditions and/or too close to the vehicle in front is implicated in a signifi- cant proportion of such

These days you have to be a celebrity for your traffic offences to attract media attention. This cartoon by John Ireland accompanied a case history of "the fastest family in the land" which appeared in the Sunday Express Magazine.

accidents.[27] (89 per cent of motorists questioned in a survey significantly underestimated safe braking distances at 30, 50 and 70mph)[28]

Of course, some rule infringements are given more attention than others. Many, if not most, of us have seen motorists breaking the instruction of Paragraph 54 of the Highway Code in their use of car telephones. But should such behaviour be made a specific offence? In discussion about the need to support the necessary legislation, its advocates argue for "a law which specifically forbids something".[29] Yet the Highway Code specifically forbids the kind of misuse of car telephones that much of the special legislation would apply to, and prosecution for careless driving, or at least a written warning, would already appear to be a possibility. The problem is that the law is just not enforced in this area, as in numerous others where evidence suggests that rule-breaking plays a contributory role in accidents. Even if a specific law were created, as the same advocates admit: "Enforcement will obviously be difficult in view of the ways existing laws are ignored."

A more relevant rule might be in Paragraph 29. A survey among motorway drivers revealed that two in five of them had "nodded off" when driving on a motorway.[30] Leicestershire police published research in 1989 indicating that one in five motorway accidents were "a result of drivers nodding off".[31] Despite this, there is little evidence of fatigue being referred to in evidence against people who have caused crashes.

This raises the question of the difference between *potentially dangerous behaviour and the occasions when it actually causes a crash*. Spotting a tired driver is probably more difficult than identifying a crash which might have been caused by one; spotting a driver who is just not as vigilant as he/she might be is certainly more difficult than analysing the crash they cause. According to one viewpoint, because most behaviour which we might regard as dangerous, excessively risky or careless does not usually result in crashes, we should concentrate on those occasions when a crash or "accident" has occurred. An alternative view is that we should look at dangerous behaviour as essentially the same whether it results in bad consequences or not — why should there be a difference between the treatment of someone overtaking on a blind corner according to whether there is another road user behaving correctly on the other side of it?

This difference in viewpoint lies at the heart of discussion about road traffic law. My view is that there is lenience at both ends of the dangerous behaviour/ crashes-caused-by-dangerous-behaviour dichotomy. When attention is drawn to one side of the divide, a defence of the need for lenience is often made by referring to the other. Concern over loss of life following a crash is deflected by the legal establishment. It will point to behaviour which occurs regularly without such ill effects and when attention moves on to the behaviour itself, as isolated from the consequences, official interest fades away: unless a crash has actually occurred, the police and the courts are unlikely to be involved at any significant level — if at all. In this way road traffic law becomes a game where heads the dangerous driver wins, tails he or she also wins.

Let us take fatigue, lack of awareness, intoxication, inadequate vigilance, general carelessness etc. If looking at these when no crash occurs is too difficult, a middle way between behaviour, on the one hand, and severe consequences with damage to human beings, on the other, would be the examination of crashes where nobody is hurt with prosecution of those responsible. Most of the car crashes occurring are not reported as RTAs or PIAs,[32] but someone is very likely to have been at fault for the crash to occur.

Prosecution rarely occurs after a non-injury-producing crash because, among other things, the law does not require "damage only" accidents to be reported, barring certain exceptions.[33] The reason for this restriction of reporting of accidents to the minority with injuries and some damage-only crashes where there is very clear evidence of an offence, is stated in the Hendon Police College's training instructions to police cadets: "Police do not report every road traffic accident that occurs. If we did, we would do very little else."[34]

Even in crashes where there is obvious injury, the gathering of proper evidence, adequately supervised by an experienced officer, is supposed to occur only where death is thought probable. This is difficult to judge and frequently does not happen. Police at the scene of a crash are concerned about the removal of casualties and restoring traffic movement as priorities over investigation. Traffic police have a lack of prestige compared to other divisions of police forces, often serving as a reservoir for additional officers in the event of requests from divisions dealing with "more serious" matters, such as the CID.[35]

C. Why law enforcement?

Why could the law and its enforcement be beneficial? The justification for employing the police, with all this implies in terms of the use of authority over citizens, is based on the fact of the danger to human life which some road users can pose to others. Road transport is the major area where people regularly have the chance of killing or hurting, or being killed or hurt by, fellow citizens. Whatever the status of other offences in terms of deliberate intent, the chances of being hurt or killed by other antisocial activity are far less.[36]

The financial costs of employing the police can sometimes be recouped by revenue raised from fines, as with parking offences. The road safety lobby also argues that the financial cost of a measure such as random breath testing would be less than the cost of the crashes and their consequences which it would prevent. The problem here is the one of cost-benefit analysis, with all the difficulties of assessing the costs of suffering implied.[37] Besides, even without considering environmental disbenefits, the costs of motoring are not met by motorists.[38] This is another cost which could be presented to those who have introduced danger into the road environment, or those convicted of offences. It could be facilitated by a policy of fining, or out of general taxation as a necessary feature of a civilised society.

The following four supposed justifications exist for the punishment of citizens by the state and its institutions.[39] Consider them in the context of their application to other anti-social behaviours, particularly when the central element of punishment for crimes is thought of as custodial sentencing, whereas the most serious punishment (except in a small minority of offences) motorists face is the temporary loss of a driving licence.

(i) Retribution

Retribution is the least acceptable of all justifications, because it associates the use of the state with atavistic notions of revenge. Yet there may be a need for demonstration of social disapproval in the case of road traffic offences.

(ii) Isolation (incapacitation)

Protecting society by isolating anti-social offenders is dubious as a proposition for justifying custodial sentences. Apart from a minority of offenders likely to be dangerous, it involves the prospect of later releasing back into society people who have possibly been brutalised by the prison experience. Protecting society by disqualifying motorists, on the other hand, involves less suffering on the part of the offender and a more definite prospect of reduction of danger.

(iii) Education

Education is a highly dubious proposition for justifying custodial sentencing. For motoring offences banning could be allied to teaching of motoring offenders, as suggested by North, but this suggests that motoring offences result from lack of skills or knowledge, rather than from unwillingness to use skills or knowledge. Also, in so far as educational programmes may be beneficial, why should they not be there for non-offending motorists?[40]

(iv) Deterrence

Deterrence is difficult to prove as a legitimate justification for imprisonment for many crimes, particularly in terms of increasing length of sentences, although the prospect of being caught and given some form of punishment does seem to have deterrent potential. However, with driving offences, from parking offences and clamping, through to drink-driving and the breathalyser,[41] the threat of inconvenience through loss of licence can affect behaviour dramatically, with the experience of the introduction of the breathalyser a particularly dramatic example. If the threat of loss of licence can achieve results in one area of motoring rule- or law-breaking, there is no reason to suppose it could not have the same effect with others.

At every level, then, there is a remarkable suitability for the penalties of licence endorsement, provided it is linked to a genuine prospect of disqualification. Custodial sentences can be largely restricted to cases where licence disqualification has failed to prevent people from continuing to drive, or in cases of failing to stop after an accident. (At present people driving away from a crash they have caused when drunk may suffer no greater penalty if caught and sentenced for failing to stop than if they had stayed at the scene.) There is a degree of natural justice in the notion of a motoring punishment for a motoring crime. Unlike custody, this involves deprivation of something which is not universal. (Some 20 per cent of men and 45 per cent of women do not have driving licences, and even more lack access to a car for many if not all journeys.) [42] Its suitability is as a form of restriction on a type of criminal negligence which may not have a high degree of wilful intent against particular individuals, but involves an irresponsible failure of social duty with severe potential consequences.

D. Some arguments against

Speaking in the House of Lords in 1959, Lord Somers said:

> "There is too much of the view that the motorist is a criminally minded man out for himself and without any thought for anyone else. Most people are motorists now, and the British race is not criminally minded..." [43]

The use of the criminal law and associated enforcement has always been criticised as inappropriate by defenders of motorists' power and privilege. Motoring offences are not thought of as real crimes, although this is, in legal terms, largely incorrect. Motoring offenders are defended in the following terms:– [44]

(i) "Not basically criminals"

One defence is based on the idea that particular minority groups of people in society can be defined as "criminals". Their position in society ("the criminal classes"), their basic psychology or, even worse, their physiognomy predisposes them to "crime". [45] This appears to assume that those committing crimes, from sexual offences, through fraud to armed robbery, were all essentially similar *kinds of person*. However, the fact that motoring offenders do not have the same kind of wilful intent as those committing offences which have been recognised as antisocial for longer periods of time is no reason for failing to apply formal sanctions against them. [46] This misleading notion is linked to the idea that motorists and motoring offenders are:

(ii) "Not a minority"

A substantial proportion of households do not have use of a car; nearly half of all journeys are not made by car; and significant minorities of adults as well as all under-17-year-olds do not drive. [47] We are by no means all motorists. Significant proportions of motorists do not commit certain kinds of offence, and/or disapprove of them. [48] The arrogant claim that "we are all motorists" has always been accompanied by disregard for the facts. Lord Somers's remark that "most people are motorists now" was made in 1959, when more than 70 per cent of households were without use of a car and only just over five million cars were registered. [49]

But even if the proportion of motoring offenders were as high in the general or even adult population as is made out, this kind of populist defence is unacceptable. Various kinds of anti-social acts, from domestic violence to child abuse, are widespread and more likely to be committed by "ordinary" citizens than public attention might once have suggested. If something anti-social is regularly perpetrated by large numbers of ordinary citizens who are otherwise not regarded as criminal or anti-social, this could make it more of a problem. This is compounded by the fact that the powerful motoring lobby has been able to draw up a supposed consensus of opinion around its interests, even when it very clearly had only a minority status.

(iii) "Performing economically and socially necessary tasks"

Danger simply has to be accepted because motoring is necessary for society. (The converse of this view, that motoring for pleasure should be banned because it is not economically necessary, is less commonly expressed.) This argument fails on two counts. First, the various problems for the future development of viable societies are exacerbated by car use.[50] Second, even if special social advantages are gained by car use, this does not justify lack of an adequate level of controls and restraints. Legal controls on occupational safety in industries which are more economically justifiable than motoring are (in principle) far more stringent.

Associated with this is the idea that the role of the law should be to facilitate car use or, to use the famous phrase invoked in opposing all restraint, particularly over speed, "to keep the traffic moving". Bearing in mind the persistent failure to remove congestion problems by using motorist-friendly approaches,[51] the prospects for keeping traffic moving by law would appear to lie more with restraining vehicle use than by a permissive attitude towards motorists. The desire for a laissez-faire approach links in with an approach to safety based on convenience, ease and relaxation — which, as we saw in Chapter 2, is often associated with increased danger for those outside cars.

(iv) "Not intentionally causing harm to others"

Accidents are accidents. But are they? Most people know that they could be more careful. While there is an argument for providing superior education before motorists can be blamed for faults in their behaviour which they may have been unaware of, once that appropriate education has occurred, we are dealing with something which, while not necessarily involving a high level of conscious *intent*, can nevertheless involve a kind of *fault*. While the level of what lawyers call *mens rea* (criminal intention) is less in most motoring cases than for crimes which might carry a custodial sentence, we are talking about very real *criminal negligence*.

Any satisfactory legal approach to the use of potentialy harmful equipment must impose sanctions on departures from proper behaviour as well as on deliberate attempts to hurt others. What counts is the failure to perform the task with the required degree of care. This guiding principle can be summed up by the phrase often used for the offence of careless driving: "driving without due care and attention". A certain level of care and attention is *due*.

Exactly how far these duties extend, at least in terms of requiring what is legally defined as fault, is a matter for debate.[52] The fact remains — despite the tendency of legal experts suddenly to become experts on road safety and suggest that prevention lies elsewhere[53] — that legal controls involving the prospect of punishment must be a major way to prevent danger, given the difficulties with other methods.

All the above arguments in defence of motorist privilege are based around a picture of motoring as something which can be made adequately safe by polite appeals to conscience, or by engineering the environment. In so far as danger will not be adequately reduced by such measures, its victims must accept that it is inevitable because it is somehow necessary. Control may be exerted in certain extreme cases, but really only to give the impression that danger is being reduced, in classic smoke screening fashion. Most important of all, control is not a real option, because the current level of danger is a product of what people (motor-ists) want, and it would be undemocratic to control them against their wishes.

Frustration in the courts has led to some taking their campaign onto the streets

At the heart of the discussion is the question of acceptability and, with it, democracy. The argument runs that an unacceptable law will not work and is fundamentally undemocratic. If motorists are unwilling to accept restrictions, their large representation within the voting population will make law enforcement unworkable. Against this, however, there is evidence that many motorists are not alienated by their experience with the police,[54] and that some motoring crimes are seen as genuinely serious problems where law enforcement is appropriate.[55]

A second objection is more important. Democracy should not just be about what the majority feel is right, particularly if vulnerable minorities (or majorities with minority status, such as pedestrians) suffer as a consequence. Even if the majority status of motorists were as great as claimed, and even if the journeys have a greater importance to those making them, why should their convenience be allowed to infringe the safety of other road users? It could be argued that car transport should be restricted on a variety of grounds; the kind of criteria used by the Health and Safety at Work Act for occupational safety would probably make motoring illegal. Therefore, if motoring is to be allowed, it should be seen as a dangerous practice where inconvenience to motorists is justified in terms of reducing even slight chances of danger to other people. Given motorists' relative lack of interest in safety in their increasingly well-protected cars, compared to that of vulnerable road users outside, and what with risk compensation exacerbating an already high potential for danger, inconvenience would seem to be a likely characteristic of law enforcement and punishment.

Reckless driving, of the "boy racer" kind, for example, should not attract less attention from the police simply because it is not so widely perceived as antisocial as say minor property offences. After all, dangerous driving is no less important as a source of distress, and deterrence is likely to be equally effective against drivers as against burglars. If the law is supposed to protect the vulnerable, particularly given the ease with which the potentially dangerous can inflict harm and the lack of disincentive to do so (and incentives to be high risk-takers), everything points to the need for law enforcement and punishment which inconveniences at least a significant proportion of motorists.

These arguments are present in the reasoning of North; but what (partially) restrictive recommendations are made are so limited as to operate as a smoke screen for the danger they conceal and legitimate.

E. The North Report

North had the following main features: the replacement of the category of reckless driving by an offence (called "dangerous" driving in the White Paper) defined according to more objective criteria in order to prosecute more of the worst drivers successfully; the creation of a new offence of causing death through careless driving while unfit through drink or drugs; the use of a new driving test for some convicted offenders; the use of new technologies to assist enforcement; and the increased use of cautions in place of some prosecutions for careless driving.

North fails to address the problems in respect of catching offenders and deterring potential law-breakers.

Despite the availability of cheap speed governors to enforce motorway speed limits automatically, and/or speed alerters to notify police and other road users, these are mentioned but not recommended. It would be possible at a later date to install speed governors that automatically change their limits as vehicles enter different classes of road; it would ultimately be possible to produce vehicles fitted with the automobile equivalent of the aircraft "black box" to assess accident causation more accurately. Automatic control systems capable of monitoring or preventing manoeuvres, from inappropriate overtaking to flinging a car door open in the path of a two-wheeler, could be compulsorily installed, if what North refers to as "the enormous resources of the automobile industry" were diverted in that direction.[56] Although capable of removing much of the burden of policing and much of the prospect of high-speed police chases, recommendation of advances in this direction is minimal. North offers no support for random breath testing, but recommends the investigation of possibilities of automatic on-board drink-driving controls — one of the few recommendations opposed in the subsequent White Paper.

If most law-breaking activity continues to result in no prosecution, prosecutions that do occur will result in nothing more than penalty points for the vast majority when they are convicted. This will continue to be the case even with the use of objective criteria (quite what these are to be is not specified) to define the dangerous driving offence, with only a small proportion of those prosecuted standing a chance of losing their licence.

This situation is compounded by an interpretation of the difference between intentions (and/or behaviour) and consequences which is inherently biased towards the dangerous. When potentially dangerous motorist behaviours are unobserved or fail to result in actual bad consequences, there is very little chance of their being prosecuted. Yet when the consequences are severe, the argument for a lenient sentence is that intentions and/or behaviour are more important.

A sense of balance?

North and the White Paper balance the safety of road users against "the preservation of amenity and the efficient movement of traffic", noting with some understatement that "these three objectives often conflict with each other".[57] This neglects the difference between amenity and safety for different groups of road users; the increase of amenity and convenience for motorists has meant a decrease in amenity for others. The "efficient movement of traffic" might be best achieved by severe use of the law to reduce the numbers of motorists on the road; it might also be used to make crossing the road illegal.

North notes that people use cars for reasons other than objective ones of comfort, convenience and other quantifiable benefits. The "intensity" of such feelings as their "sense of freedom" and "sense of control [over a motor vehicle]" requires recognition from North.[58] North respects these feelings as worthy, rather than recognising that they constitute a basis for resistance to necessary measures. Nevertheless, North notes that acceptability of the law should not be measured solely on how readily motorists submit to it: "Law exists to serve the interest of society as a whole. There is strong feeling… that traffic law as it stands does not attach sufficient weight to the interest of those who use the roads other than in motor vehicles."[59]

How is this balance to achieve "the interest of society as a whole" to be set? One might be forgiven for thinking that anything which refers to "society as a whole" will tend to miss out on the requirements of the vulnerable if they have minority status, and North and the White Paper are no exception. (The environmental problems facing global society outlined in Chapter 14 certainly don't figure.)

The definition of the new offence of dangerous driving could in principle lead to a substantial proportion of motorists being prosecuted successfully for this offence on a regular and frequent basis: "It will be sufficient for the prosecution to establish that a competent and careful driver would have appreciated that some person or property might be endangered by the accused's manner of driving." [60] Although it depends what is meant by the word "might". The preceding paragraph reveals that: "It is not intended that the driver who merely makes a careless mistake of a kind which any driver might make from time to time should be regarded as falling far below the standard expected of a competent and careful driver." [61] How often is "from time to time"? How far is "far"? Are these decisions to be made by the non-motoring man on the Clapham omnibus or, as seems more likely, the man in the car overtaking it?

An illustration — what's wrong with shooting the lights?

The case prompting the formation of a grass roots campaign (one hope for a civilised alternative to "road safety") is instructive. A fellow citizen in charge of a high-powered motor vehicle goes through a red traffic signal at high speed and kills a child. His mother is informed that a charge of "causing death through reckless driving" is not to be made by the Crown Prosecution Service on the basis that progress through the junction was made "smoothly": only a charge of careless driving can be made.

The much vaunted change from emphasising consequences (actually, to be more precise, behaviour) rather than intentions of the offender in North therefore has no relevance. The new offence replacing reckless driving would not be applicable anyway because the objective standards were not bad enough. Moreover, unless the result (sometimes also referred to as consequences) of that behaviour involve at least a crash, and preferably an injury, there is unlikely to be a prosecution anyway.

Now, in the case of illegally crossing a signalled junction, there *was* the recommendation that automatic cameras should be used more at signals to prosecute offenders. However, even in the extremely unlikely event of all the signalled junctions in Britain being thus treated, and motorists in all cases subjected to deterrent penalties (also unlikely), what can we expect? Experience suggests migration of anti-social crossing behaviour to the vast majority of junctions which will remain non-signalled. Plus the usual smoke screen of complaining about naughty cyclists and pedestrians, in this case at junctions.

The smoke screen function

North does not significantly alter the chances of law- or rule-breaking motorists being caught or having available deterrent sentencing applied to them. Opportunities to change the law are missed with regard to: the low penalty for failure to stop (at present allowing one commentator to describe it as "positively encouraging drunken drivers to make a run for it"); [62] introducing widespread automatic or semi-automatic controls; breath-testing; addressing questions such as eyesight standards; and above all a genuine level of law enforcement and a significant chance of disqualification if convicted.

Yet the impression that something is being done has been created through the introduction of the new offences of dangerous driving and of causing death by careless driving while affected by drink or drugs. The problems with the new offence of dangerous driving have already been referred to: the difficulty and lack of likelihood of prosecution unless there are certain kinds of bad consequence, and defining where it differs from careless driving. The problem with the other offence arises from the intentions/consequences distinction.

John Spencer shows that the creation of the new offence is apparently in response to public opinion polls showing:

> An overwhelming belief that the consequences of... misbehaviour were important when sentencing a motoring offender, and, by contrast, little importance being attached to issues of *mens rea*. This particular revelation seems to have greatly influenced the Review when it considered the structure of the *more serious motoring offences* (my emphasis).[63]

In the case of drink-driving, then, the vast majority of offences will not result in any action by the police, and a few where there have been crashes will result in disqualification. The difference between the two outcomes will be a question of chance. In some of these cases where there are crashes, people will be seriously hurt, but there is no more severe category of offence for which the offender will be prosecuted. In a smaller minority of cases, somebody may die. Yet although there has been no difference in intention between the behaviour leading to this consequence and that leading to any of the three previous categories, and despite the fact that the largest of these categories involves an offence which is more easily detectable than, for example, burglary, a special offence is created, with prison available as a sentence.

There are good reasons for this. There is the desire of the bereaved to see those who, through an act of definite and wilful criminal negligence, cause the death of their loved ones, suffer a punishment of at least the same order as a minor property offence, rather than something less.(Although it might seem more appropriate to consider long periods of disqualification, rather than the periods of a few years that are common with current sentences for the causing of death through reckless driving.)

But again, why should the larger number of drunk drivers who permanently disable and maim be prosecuted for a lesser offence than those who have killed but behaved in exactly the same way?

Despite the limited amount of justification for different treatment, we have here a concentration on stiffer penalties for a minority of some of the more serious offenders on those rare occasions when they get caught, and generally only where there is a particular kind of bad consequence. The inevitable debate about the severity of those penalties, which may themselves be regarded as too lenient, should not obscure this. It is a simple question of generating the illusion that dangerously negligent behaviour will receive prison sentences or at least disqualification. And this is not the case at all.

F. Safety on the road — the controls we need

The present legal situation is characterised by a kind of lawlessness. For the less careful and/or less worried motorist, this is unlikely to constitute a serious problem. Indeed, as an argument for anarchy — for the ability of human beings to live without externally imposed restrictions — the present situation could serve as a good example. For those more worried and more careful motorists, and for vulnerable road users, the situation is different. There is for them no reliable control over the source of danger on the roads, whatever their own responsibility, and whatever engineering and educational methods are employed.

A more appropriate way of considering legal control would be to use the example of health and safety legislation in Britain and elsewhere. The most recent example of this is the Health and Safety at Work Act 1974, which extended the obligations of employers to responsibility for other members of society outside the place of work, as well as employees. This legislation places the onus of safety on the employer in the first instance; while employees have responsibilities, they must be provided with an adequately safe environment and a good enough chance to engage in safe work practices. Despite whatever limitations the legislation may have, at least it provides a more stringent framework than that which exists on the road.

Such a framework could apply at different levels in the case of road traffic law. At the closest level of similarity it would be necessary to ban cars as we now know them. As a system of transport, private cars are more dangerous than the industries covered by the Health and Safety at Work Act 1974; and although it would be necessary to provide reasonable alternatives to car use in such an eventuality, the economic justification for car use is less.

Taking a more tolerant view would mean that in any accident where a vulnerable road user was hit by a motorist, the motorist would be automatically responsible. With the "Albanian solution",[64] the behaviour of the pedestrian or cyclist could be used as a mitigating factor in sentencing, but the motorist would still be guilty.

An even more tolerant attitude would be to accept a more stringent view of the North Report — with mandatory custodial sentences for failing to stop and for driving while disqualified,[65] much higher levels of enforcement, automatic and semi-automatic controls and a far greater chance of motorists being prosecuted for offences, with a much higher chance of disqualification as a sentence. But even if this occurred in conjunction with an alternative transport policy to reduce car use, more stringent testing, and engineering of the environment to reduce danger, most acts of rule- or law-breaking would still go unpunished, often because they were unobservable. It would therefore be necessary to create an offence of strict liability where a motorist is involved in a road traffic accident in which a vulnerable road user is injured, with a likely (or mandatory) loss of licence if found guilty, and the right of defence by the motorist based on contributory negligence on the part of the vulnerable road user.

Nothing else even approaches an attempt to have a non-discriminatory system of road traffic law. Vulnerable road users are doubly discriminated against in that motorists are routinely allowed to be more dangerous, and in that they, the most vulnerable, have to suffer disproportionately from this danger. This discrimination would still exist even with the strict liability provision outlined here, although there would be better account given to more civilised conditions. As for their obligations, giving any kind of punishment to pedestrians and cyclists is inequitable while their environment is unsafe, in much the same way that it is inequitable to blame a careless factory worker until his or her work conditions are safe. Even discounting the most severe option outlined above and accepting mass car use as a fact, there is a good case for having no legal restriction on vulnerable road users until a quite different system of control is obtained.

Summary and conclusion

The trouble with the facts about the law-breaking of the motorists... is that there are too many: it is difficult even to grasp them. In fact, the position has long since passed far beyond the limits of ordinary law-breaking and become an exhibition of national degeneracy. [66]

JS Dean, Chairman of the Pedestrians Association for Road Safety, writing in 1947.

Most motorists are law-abiding. [67]

AA spokesman, Eurosafe 1988 conference.

Laws, and other official sanctions and their operation, are marks of the boundaries of what the dominant set of political and ideological interests regard as permissible in society. As such, there is actually no contradiction between the two above statements.

The latter is made in terms of what a substantial proportion of motorists deem to be "real" laws and regulations which they feel are appropriate for them to obey (although the stresses of life will tend to excuse or mitigate the breaking of even this rump of regulations). Sometimes the limit at which acceptable behaviour becomes regarded as deviant can be set on a statistical basis, particularly where behaviour is easily quantified, and indeed this is the frequently the basis for setting speed limits.

This means that a Parish Council requesting speed controls on speeding vehicles can expect the following reply from the Department of Transport:

You state that 'virtually every car' exceeds the speed limit through (your Parish) by a significant margin. If this is the case it implies that the speed limit may be set too low to be acceptable to the majority of reasonable drivers. [68]

On the other hand, if the boundaries are set in terms of restricting rule and law infractions which contribute to the motor danger, the former quote is correct.

135

If a restriction of motor danger is to be achieved then, while other means may help, there is no other way that this can happen than by transforming the operation of road traffic law. It cannot be emphasised too much that, without such a change, the basic conditions for citizens to move about without excessive danger from others are impossible to achieve.

One way of reviewing the basis for such a change is to consider the possibilities in terms of the response from aggrieved motorists — how do such changes fit in with attitudes towards errant cyclists and pedestrians?

In order of decreasing severity, the possibilities are as follows:–

(i) An idea proposed in the 1930s was to place the blame on motorists whatever the circumstances on the basis that it was they who had made the road environment dangerous.[69] If this seems bizarre, it should be compared to modern vehicle and road engineering designed to cushion the impact of a motorist's errors, even to the extent of further endangering others' lives. The application of this principle is simply being applied to the victims of motorisation — except that motorists are looking at legal sanctions rather than physical harm.

(ii) Less extreme, the application of a model drawn on contemporary Health an Safety legislation does make the vulnerable responsible in certain cases: but the prior responsibility rests with those who have made the environment dangerous in the first place. To fulfil this responsibility would in practice mean that no restrictions could be placed on the vulnerable until there were fundamental changes in access to car use and, after that, motorists' behaviour.

(iii) A much less extreme view suggests that the motor danger cannot be reduced to create as safe an environment as a workplace. Nevertheless, the principle long held in road traffic law, and implicitly supported by North, would be invoked. This is that, although there may be annoyance and inconvenience to other road users and that cyclists and pedestrians might legally be responsible for accidents,[70] they are "less dangerous to other road users" and should accordingly be less prone to punishment, at least in degree.

Consider this view in context. Examine the behaviour of an average motorist in terms of rule infraction, whether it be the Highway Code (say Paragraphs 47, 49, 50, 51, 54, 55, 60, 65, 66, 83, 84, 93, 110, 116, 124, 125) or the laws regularly broken as described above. If just half of that rule- and law-breaking behaviour which had a potential to cause harmful accidents was dealt with under existing law, most motorists would have been banned for some considerable period of time. The remaining half of the bad driving behaviour would still be potentially more severe than the non-motorist misdemeanours.

In other words, if instead of the law being invoked, even with its trivial level of penalties, to a tiny minority of its potential, it was invoked to half of its potential, there would be still be too little opportunity to seriously consider the relevance of non-motorist rule infraction. So, even without demanding the basis of law and its enforcement specified in (i) and (ii) above, it would still be necessary to give prior consideration to motor offences in a way which would demand making crashes where non-motorists are involved offences of strict liability, with motorists required to prove innocence.

This principle is more in tune with other European legal philosophies than with the English one — but is still quite capable of fitting in with the English system. All that has to be recognised is that there is something special about being in control of a motor vehicle. As the rest of the road safety lobby recognises, motorists are likely to commit potentially dangerous rule infractions at some stage in their careers even if they are highly skilled and careful. And, as shown above, even under existing law they are regularly committing easily observable infractions as a matter of course.

All this would inconvenience many motorists. But the current situation means that we all venture out into the road environment in effect at our own risk, with those using the benign modes even more so. Even the most extreme of the above views, which I reject, means having some danger on the road, and replacing this situation by one where the potentially dangerous venture out with a real risk of losing driving licences. The alternative is a continuation of the legitimised endangering of others sanctioned by the framework of the law and those who are supposed to enforce it.

At the most pessimistic, the offence of strict liability for motorists in collisions with benign mode users would mean an "unfair" situation for motorists running the risk of punishment (albeit with chance to prove innocence) in place of the really unfair situation of benign mode users having no real right to be safe on their own roads. Beefing up the legal status of Highway Code regulations for motorists, and legal and other controls on motor danger, is a necessary addition — but not replacement — so that we do not have to wait until the worst comes to the worst. The alternative is one where criminal negligence is tolerable and is exacerbated by the road safety lobby's insistence on targets, the implication being that such cts become tolerable when their number has reached some nominal level.

Meanwhile, it is possible to buy an insurance policy which gives chauffeur-driven car travel for those who have been banned for careless driving or speeding: [71] this constitutes a legally allowed incentive to break the road traffic law. The point is that unless we go beyond this particular legitimation of motor danger, negotiating a path through the layers of disincentive to behave in a civilised fashion, we will never properly consider the problem.

8.

The doctor's tale

MOST GPs rely on their cars: in a recent television documentary about a country practitioner, his round of visits was broken up by as much by interviews from the driving seat as from the surgery desk; and doctors were among the first groups to be car-users.

Perhaps it is because of this relationship of dependency that doctors have failed to grasp the nettle in the road safety debate. The British Medical Association could speak out about the damaging effects of mass car use, as it has done about other social issues.

❖❖❖

Like the other sections of the road safety lobby, the medical element has an incorrect idea of what safety on the road should be about. It has also been unable to give proper attention to the many other health problems of a motorised society. Its theory and method of individual epidemiology tend to concentrate on, and to blame, the victims of wider social processes which escape analysis.

Medical ideology — doctors

Like other professionals, doctors as a social group tend to be particularly unrepresentative of women, the working class, disabled people and non-car users. While some medical schools may now attempt to apply equal opportunity patterns of student selection, it is likely that doctors will continue a tradition of being more likely to be car users than the population as a whole, although the gap is narrowing with increased car use. It is important to note that doctors have long had a close affinity with car use. Indeed, before the war they were one of the few identifiable social groups (the others being the wealthy and professional drivers) likely to drive.

Doctors often claim that their job is not to question the social status quo. Yet in the post-war period they have formed a strong lobby on fiscal policies affecting alcohol and tobacco, and on the organisation of the National Health Service. These activities are an extension of the use of power involved in establishing their position in society through professional organisation. In road safety they play a role in lobbies, of which the most important is the Parliamentary Advisory Council on Transport Safety (PACTS), where they are represented by nine different groups, including the British Medical Association. Medical approaches are linked in with the work of engineers, providing a basis for initiatives such as seat belt legislation. Although the road safety lobby can decry the lack of involvement of departments of health in Europe,[1] the British medical establishment plays a pivotal role in "road safety".

Despite suffering a welter of criticism of traditional medical thinking from alternative complementary health advocates, feminist critics and radical doctors, doctors still manage to make their pronouncements with considerable authority. In their relationship with the media, they retain an unusual power to define problems and their solutions.[2] The traditional figure of the man in the white coat continues to retain much of its influence. Where this paternalist figure may have waned in influence it has been replaced by a more modern, media-conscious image, associated with ideas of individual self-help and consumerist responses to social problems.[3]

As with the engineers, the validity of the doctors' message rests on its claim to be scientific. As with the engineers, too, this assumption is frequently erroneous and has been criticised from a number of positions:

≡ The claim to a scientific status frequently founders on the failure of medical practice to meet its own criteria of scientific method.

≡ The theory and method draw on ideas derived from the "natural" sciences (known as positivism) which may be inappropriate to human society. Whatever the truth of this, the business of trying to isolate discrete elements from a complex societal totality has particularly severe short-comings when there is constant shifting about of risk-taking and danger from one part of the system to another.

≡ The approaches used fail to recognise commercial and wider social forces and the background assumptions of the professionals themselves.

≡ The objective of the enterprise the professionals are engaged in has not been fully agreed on.

Unlike with the rest of the "road safety" community, the criticisms of medicine are reasonably well established, often having taken root within medicine itself. Alternative definitions of the objectives of medical practitioners, opposition to victim-blaming and the need for wider social change have secured a presence in current thought. At the heart of the object of criticism is the focus on individual epidemiology rather than social ecology.

Medical ideology — individual epidemiology

Traditional epidemiology attempts to make links between morbidity and mortality among specific groups of individuals, on the one hand, and factors with some potential for being specified as causative, on the other. Why particular groups are chosen, or the causative factors investigated, may tell more about the ideologies of the society we live in than give a real causal link to disease generation. The wider processes that allow the prevalence of the causative factors (smoking, polluted food, and so on) are not examined and neither are the reasons why particular groups of people are associated with those causative factors in the first place. Emphasis on individuals can lead to a kind of victim-blaming, with unreasonable expectations for change placed on the afflicted individual. As the title of a critical paper says: "You are doing harm to your health: the ideology and politics of victim blaming."[4]

The argument is cogently expressed in a critique of epidemiological analyses of health problems associated with tobacco and alcohol:

> No theory based on a mathematical technique can satisfactorily explain the social, medical, and biochemical processes involved in the use of alcohol or any other drug... With such theories one cannot build one discovery upon another to form an even more comprehensive theory. One must always start at the beginning again or merely string together a number of disconnected statements.[5]

The charge is that without studying the underlying processes the researcher is caught up in a futile endeavour separated from the real issues. In fact it may be that radical methods are not required to deal with the above problems, however, with more powerful industries than the tobacco industry, and a central element of society such as the transport system being involved, something more comprehensive is needed. In so far as fiscal and legal restraint (such as the medical establishment advocates for tobacco and alcohol use) is an approach which I propose in Chapter 17, it has not appeared on the health professionals' agenda.

There is also debate about the objectives of practitioners, including discussion of the nature of health and the right of individuals to avoid paternalistic compulsion to be "healthy".[6]

The so-called new public health movement has made these issues visible to doctors using methods varying from curriculum design to institutional programmes (although the extent to which they are taken on board by the establishment is limited). Using a well-worn analogy of health practitioners as life-savers rescuing drowning people in a fast-flowing river (the classic medical interventionist), the public health movement seeks to pose questions about why people fall in the river in the first place. Such questioning could well be repeated in the "road safety" community. It might look at the nature of the present transport system critically, rather than accepting the transport status quo. It might listen to the people who are supposed to be served (although the view of the motorist ends up as the one heeded), and allow people choices with their own lives. The road safety community might also recognise the folly of attempts to quantify human suffering, and see the danger of cost-benefit analyses.

This leads to a picture of the requirements for health: the provision of safe and adequate food, shelter and sanitation, as well as such qualitative characteristics as freedom from poverty and fear, and a range of environmental prerequisites.[7] The relevance of this to road safety is to stress the removal of danger to create a life of higher quality.

While the input of the new public health, and of radical strands in medicine, could inform changes in road safety thinking, however, it needs first to go to work on the medical establishment. For even under the name of preventive medicine and public health, the medical establishment has not looked back upstream. For those of us who have been highlighting the ability to change those features of a road environment which lead to "accidents", it is particularly frustrating that when doctors intervene in the name of prevention they do not look at the real preventive approaches required. The medical establishment remains trapped by cost-benefit analyses and a refusal to question the transport status quo, or the realities of risk compensation. Confronted by the task of picking glass out of seat occupants' faces (a popular image invoked to campaign for seat belt legislation), doctors could think of seat belts, but not about the origins of the crash.

Here epidemiology is particularly vulnerable to criticism. Risk compensation shows that an underlying factor — risk-taking — is always there. The efforts of the road safety lobby have redistributed it. Epidemiology can take a surface analysis of the symptoms at any one time. But, failing to recognise that it will always be there means that measures are supported which could lead to epidemiologists some years later looking at another manifestation of the same cause. With road safety this has meant that danger has been redistributed on to those least capable of protecting themselves and who pose the least danger to others.

The inappropriateness of the epidemiological model to safety on the roads was suggested in Britain some 20 years ago by the psychologist, John Cohen. He argued that "black spot" removal might perhaps lead to "black spots" reappearing elsewhere (now known as "accident migration"). He wrote:

> The accident rate might be reduced, for a time or permanently, at the sites where the changes were made but this decline might be cancelled out by an increase elsewhere... To my mind the approach to road safety which seems... promising is one which attempts to identify the properties and shortcomings of the system as a whole.[8]

Doctors and road safety practitioners should heed this. It will mean questioning the use of categories, and ensuring that the subjects of study are often simply the most compliant and least powerful, that the wider social origins are studied, and that the object of good practice is redefined away from reducing costs to reducing danger at its source.

It would mean removing the danger from vulnerable road users, allowing them to make decisions which (barring danger to others and some consideration of nuisance) would still imply the possibility of their being hurt or killed. While one would expect casualty rates to fall in the first instance, they might not fall that much, and if safer conditions enticed more people into walking and cycling, one might expect higher net casualties for those modes, and (given their particular vulnerability) higher gross casualties for the population as a whole.

A healthy alternative

The aim for health professionals should be to properly consider the relationship of transport and health throughout society,[9] in order to assess the health problems detailed in Chapter 14. The critique of aspects of traditional medicine should be extended into medicine's view of danger on the road, with the move away from

141

individual epidemiology taken up by other professionals who have been concerned about road safety.

Good epidemiological work could be done — but it should be on the various health problems generated by mass car use, from the carcinogenesis and other disease generation by material in vehicle emissions, to the effects of lost public transport services, community severance by road building, and so on. In so far as strictly medical expertise is required, it could be provided in areas such as provision of trauma care centres in hospitals, where there are claims for the potential reduction of numbers in the order of 1,000 deaths a year.[10] Another similar area might be the less glamorous, but possibly just as relevant, issue of first aid and paramedical training.[11]

Indeed, apart from the statistical problems outlined above in this book, doctors' views are influenced by there being numbers of "accident" casualties which are apparently low when compared to those attributed to other health problems. However, by adding up the figures for the health problems of mass car use as a whole, or by calculating the numbers that doctors claim to benefit through using better medical intervention after accidents (and who do not appear on injury statistics therefore), the problem of traffic accidents could be much greater.

Contributors to the British Medical Journal can state:

> Doctors seem to spend their time these days exhorting their patients to adopt healthier habits... to wear seat belts, helmets... But perhaps the most important risks to health are beyond people's immediate control, caused by the unhealthy habits not of individuals but an energy hungry and throwaway society.[12]

But there is no sense in which the radical change called for in the article has really penetrated medical thinking. The much publicised support for cycling[13] involves no real commitment to the kind of measures required to support alternatives to car use.[14] Like so much else it tries to deal with the issue without touching the problem at its core. An attempt to back up the report at the BMA's annual meeting by calling for the need to discourage car use to be mentioned was dismissed.[15]

Doctors could consider transport safety issues in the same way that they claim to consider other aspects of health policy.

Why not examine the adverse effects of "road safety" policies in the same way that the side effects of new drugs are considered? And if a certain attitude is appropriate to advertising by the tobacco industry, why should it be different for car and petrol producers whose products also endanger public health?

If doctors were to reconsider their attitudes to motoring: from financing their own mileage allowances; to prescribing drugs to drivers; to the methods of analysis chosen for what they define as "accident problems", as well as the wider questions of health and transport, they may find that there is considerable scope for self-criticism.

Part Three

Case studies

9.

"Sorry mate..." The conspicuity con

VOLUNTARY TESTING and police surveys indicate that up to two million drivers in the UK would not meet the eyesight standard laid down by the current driving test. In spite of this astonishing figure, the road safety lobby continues to ignore the motorists' own back yard when it comes to apportioning blame for the high number of accidents which are passed off with the phrase "sorry mate... I didn't see you".

❖❖❖

A central focus of "road safety" campaigns and legislation has been the visibility of road users and objects in the road environment. Moving about without getting into collisions must include an element of seeing and being seen; but how vision fits into associated mental and behavioural processes — what "seeing" means in its full sense — is a more complex issue. So, too, is the question of what groups of road user are to be responsible for "being seen". As lighting on the road, and of vehicles, improves, we also have to consider adaptation of road user behaviour. This can mean the safety benefit being absorbed as a performance benefit by motorists so that they use less attentiveness, higher speeds, and so on.

The issue of visibility, like so many others, involves questions of the power and freedom of different road user groups. Its discussion by the road safety lobby, legislators and manufacturers has been an expression of these different interests and has strengthened the power of dangerous road users against vulnerable ones.

The efforts of the road safety lobby have been marked by absent or inadequate evidence, the influence of manufacturer pressure and a view of the problem which has confused understanding and diverted attention away from basic issues.

A brief history

Pressure for vehicles to carry lights existed in the nineteenth century, and after lobbying by groups including the Cyclists' Touring Club, the Lights on Vehicles Act 1907 compelled every vehicle to carry a white light at the front at night.[1] Emergency regulations during the First World War (later repealed) required cyclists to show a red rear light as well. From that time on till the Road Transport Lighting (Cycles) Act 1945, the cycling organisations opposed the need for cyclists to have compulsory rear lights. The grounds for opposition were that:

≡ The principle of road usage had been to place the onus of responsibility on the overtaker, and this was being reversed in favour of the "heaviest and fastest" vehicles — the opposite of the nautical principle of sail before steam.[2]

≡ The principle of driving had been for motorists' speed to be governed by the power of their headlamps. Pandering to the unwillingness of motorists to accept this principle — now expressed in Rule 50 of the Highway Code — was bad practice when there was a need to encourage correct behaviour, and would lead to higher speeds.

≡ These higher speeds, and/ or less alertness on the part of the motorist expecting to watch out for lights, would lead to disastrous consequences for unilluminated pedestrians and those cyclists whose lights had failed through no fault of their own.[3]

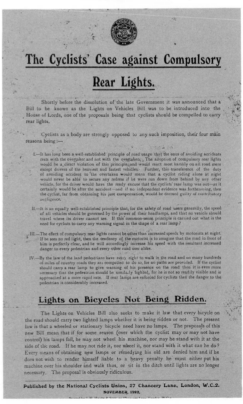

The Cyclists' Case against Compulsory Rear Lights.

Shortly before the dissolution of the late Government it was announced that a Bill to be known as the Lights on Vehicles Bill was to be introduced into the House of Lords, one of the proposals being that cyclists should be compelled to carry rear lights.

Cyclists as a body are strongly opposed to any such imposition, their four main reasons being:—

I.—It has long been a well-established principle of road usage that the onus of avoiding accidents rests with the overtaker and not with the overtaken. The adoption of compulsory rear lights would be a direct violation of this principle, and would react most harshly on all road users except drivers of the heaviest and fastest vehicles. Further, this transference of the duty of avoiding accident to the overtaken would mean that a cyclist riding alone at night would never be able to secure any redress if he were run down from behind by any other vehicle, for the driver would have the ready excuse that the cyclist's rear lamp was out—as it certainly would be after the accident—and if no independent evidence was forthcoming, then the cyclist, far from obtaining his just compensation, would be deemed guilty of contributory negligence.

II.—It is an equally well-established principle that, for the safety of road users generally, the speed of all vehicles should be governed by the power of their headlamps, and that no vehicle should travel where its driver cannot see. If this common-sense principle is carried out what is the need for cyclists to carry any warning signal in the shape of a rear lamp?

III.—The effect of compulsory rear lights cannot be other than increased speeds by motorists at night. If he sees no red light, then the tendency of the motorist is to imagine that the road in front of him is perfectly clear, and he will accordingly increase his speed with the resultant increased danger to every pedestrian and every other road user alike.

IV.—By the law of the land pedestrians have every right to walk in the road and on many hundreds of miles of country roads they are compelled to do so, for no paths are provided. If the cyclist should carry a rear lamp to give warning of his presence on the road then it is even more necessary that the pedestrian should be similarly lighted, for he is not so readily visible and is approached at a more rapid rate. If rear lamps are enforced for cyclists then the danger to the pedestrian is considerably increased.

Lights on Bicycles Not Being Ridden.

The Lights on Vehicles Bill also seeks to make it law that every bicycle on the road should carry two lighted lamps whether it is being ridden or not. The present law is that a wheeled or stationary bicycle need have no lamps. The proposals of this new Bill mean that if for some reason (over which the cyclist may or may not have control) his lamps fail, he may not wheel his machine, nor may he stand with it at the side of the road. If he may not ride it, nor wheel it, nor stand with it what can he do? Every means of obtaining new lamps or remedying his old are denied him and if he does not wish to render himself liable to a heavy penalty he must either put his machine over his shoulder and walk thus, or sit in the ditch until lights are no longer necessary. The proposal is obviously ridiculous.

Published by the National Cyclists Union, 27 Chancery Lane, London, W.C.2.
NOVEMBER, 1923.

It now seems that the concerns on which this opposition was based were well founded. Some 70 years later, cyclists still complain about the unavailability of cheap and reliable lights and the inability to prove that lights smashed in a collision were functioning. More powerful car and street lights are accompanied by higher speeds, widespread breaking of Paragraph 50 of the Highway Code and a general increase in danger from cars. Cyclists and motorcyclists are pressured to use reflective and fluorescent clothing and other supposed conspicuity aids. The main legislative thrust has been towards daytime motorcycle headlamp use.

The appeal to pedestrians has been more recent, although the 1970s saw the "Wear Something Light at Night" campaign (before widespread availability of reflective materials), which included advice to walkers to carry folded newspapers at night. The winter months typically see a national campaign mounted by the Department of Transport. The 1989 campaign had some characteristic features: support from the manufacturers of "conspicuity aids" (3M); a victim-blaming attitude towards vulnerable road users who failed to wear something reflective or fluorescent at night and during the day (called "dimwits"); an assumption of equal responsibility between motorist and the vulnerable (although most of the effort is directed at the vulnerable); and neglect of legal requirements for motorist eyesight, with advice to them instead to be more alert. Hard evidence as to the benefits of the adoption of such attempts to "be seen" was absent.

The business of "seeing"

When people talk about "seeing" they refer to a lot more than the process of receiving light from an object on the retina of their eyes. Seeing involves making sense of, and understanding, or perceiving, the image, and relating it to the correct programme of behaviour. Images do not just fall on a blank mental screen, but fit into preconceived ideas about the status of the person or object they signify. On the road, these involve ideas about how different road users should be reacted to. Also involved is an *active* element of watchfulness and the willingness to be aware of the different possible road users who may be around the next corner.

Being prepared to take the physical steps to look for these objects or people involves having adequate eyesight, looking in the right directions, leaving enough time to register the image, and so on. It also involves knowing how to react, and an initial willingness to react properly. After all, there are none so blind as those who will not see.

A. The ability to see

Evidence on the physical ability to see comes from voluntary tests taken by motorists, and surveys by traffic police. They indicate that between one and two million motorists cannot pass the existing eyesight test.[4] In one spot check, Devon and Cornwall police are reported as finding that the driver of a packed 53-seat coach was nearly blind; he informed them that he "suffered from terrible headaches", and was advised to seek treatment.[5] The eyesight test dates from pre-war times. It can be passed by some people registered as blind,[6] and has been criticised by the Association of Optometrists for not being scientifically based.[7] Little or no study has been made of factors such as unrestricted head movement or the psychomotor skills which dictate how the body deals with mental reactions. New evidence suggests that one in five drivers suffer from low luminance myopia or "night blindness".[8]

The official attitude has been to recommend that a right of appeal should be introduced for drivers who fail the present eyesight test.[9] The Guild of Experienced Motorists, supposedly concerned at what they estimate as one million motorists incapable of meeting the current standards, gives free roadside eyesight tests — on the basis that police will not be informed of negative results.[10] A leading member of the road safety lobby can suddenly become an advocate for the theory of risk compensation:

> **"deteriorating eyesight is not a significant factor in the cause of road accidents... People don't willingly put themselves in danger. They automatically compensate for their poor vision."[11]**

More important, the DTp has taken the approach that it is not the inadequacy of eyesight which counts, but the willingness of motorists to use their eyes.[12] This is an excellent example of a good argument being used for a bad cause, namely to avoid performing simple controls, such as eyesight tests after accidents, or other checks. It is also thoroughly hypocritical, as no real effort is made to achieve such willingness — and in fact most official effort effectively leads to *discouraging* it.

B. Observation

The next stage in the process of "seeing" is using visual ability to observe what is, or may be, in the road environment. Material instructing people to drive properly stresses the importance of "'seeing' that is not simply 'looking'".[13] It calls for *active* visual work: "making your eyes work" — an "acute sense of observation" that "requires intense concentration". This involves such details as the facial expression of other motorists, whether parked vehicles are empty, the position of pedestrians' feet and how other motorists hold the steering wheel.[14] It also involves anticipating road users who may not have emerged into the road environment, and all-round awareness far ahead.

Advanced driver training involves advice to change focal point at least every two seconds.[15] Willingness to anticipate visual signals — to *watch out* — is crucial. Research shows a major difference between the conspicuity of objects, such as road signs, which are searched for by motorists (search conspicuity) and those which have to catch their attention (attention conspicuity). Conspicuity in the former case is far higher.[16]

C. Acting appropriately

Paragraph 50 of the Highway Code states: "Never drive so fast that you cannot stop well within the distance you can see to be clear." Unless the instruction to match speed with vision is adhered to, there is no point having adequate visual ability or looking out for other people or objects. The same applies to the possession of driving skills, and the willingness to use them at all times, in general.

In context, then, the visual signals emitted by road users and objects in the road environment are a small part of the process of seeing. The process is not reducible to any one of its parts. Observation involves physical abilities such as the ability to move the head easily, and being able to respond in time to images depends on driver speed. What emerges is the importance of the active factor — the willingness to watch out determines the whole process. Even with a physical inadequacy, the determination to see others with adequate time to react properly would lead motorists to try and compensate by driving more slowly and with more general care. Where the physical defect cannot be compensated for,[17] one would expect a commitment for enforced testing and eyesight checks. While this willingness is absent, pressure on the vulnerable to "be seen" misses out on the central parts of this process and on the *determining* element.

This again raises the issue of something not just failing to address a problem, but making it worse by diverting resources and consciousness away from what needs to be done. On top of this, accustoming motorists to easier conditions can reduce alertness and make it easier to justify unwillingness to see.

Safety benefits consumed as performance benefits to increase motor danger

Consider the wording of an advertisement for 3M's reflective sheeting. It accompanies a photograph of a fatigued, elderly driver with half-closed eyes. The text refers to "drivers who are fatigued, suffering from poor night vision and those affected by age" and is headed: "He's tired, having trouble seeing, it's dark and starting to rain — his journey home could be a nightmare." This is basically encouraging people to break the Highway Code, or is at the least, collusion with

He's tired, having trouble seeing, it's dark and starting to rain — his journey home could be a nightmare.

He's going to need clear roadside information in a form which he can quickly recognise, understand and act upon — in good time. By day or at night.

With this in mind, 3M has developed Diamond Grade 'Scotchlite' reflective sheeting for all types of drivers — and road signs.

For drivers who are fatigued, suffering from poor night vision and those affected by age — for signs mounted on the right or overhead; Diamond Grade provides the high performance, bright solution.

Diamond Grade 'Scotchlite' reflective sheeting.

■ Colours	Sign identifying colours seen and recognised from further away.
■ Response Time	Readily visible signs add seconds to the response times.
■ Brightness	Effectively compete with complex and high ambient light backgrounds.
■ Performance	Levels of brightness that reach further down the road.
■ Angularity	Signs easily visible even when not directly in the headlight beam.

3M Traffic Management
3M United Kingdom PLC, 3M House,
PO Box 1, Bracknell, Berkshire RG12 1JU
Telephone: Bracknell (0344) 58495
3M and 'Scotchlite' are Trademarks.
© 3M United Kingdom PLC 1989

TRAFFIC MANAGEMENT

3M

It sounds like this driver's journey could be a nightmare for other road users as well. A well marked route could increase his speed.

those who do.

Easier visibility can generate higher speeds. The modern highway engineer's concern with long sight lines has led to the problems associated with motorways and similar types of road.[18]

The installation of reflector posts on roadsides in Finland "to increase optical guidance and help drivers to foresee the road alignment so that they can prepare themselves for the driving tasks ahead" and "to promote traffic safety" was recently studied. On one type of road there was no change in the accident rate. On the other: "the reflector posts increased driving speeds in darkness by 5 kph... [and]... increased the number of injury accidents by 43 per cent and all accidents by 20 per cent. Accidents in darkness increased most."[19]

The converse is also true: the research shows that "bad", or rather low, visibility reduces the chances of pedestrians dying when they have been involved in a collision with a motor vehicle.[20]

People see largely what they want to see. If emphasis on one part of the process of seeing results in unwillingness to tackle the more important aspects, the result could be no overall benefit, or even a disbenefit. This might be why there is little or no evidence as to the benefit of attempts to make road users more conspicuous.

The evidence

(i) Motorcyclists

Pressure on motorcyclists to have daytime lights, including legal compulsion, has been a preoccupation of the road safety lobby since the early 1960's. There is, however, no conclusive evidence for the benefits of daytime headlights legislation for motorcyclists.[21] Extrapolation from experimental studies fails, as with the use

Road fatalities in Britain

1938	6,648
1939	8,272
1940	8,609
1941	9,169
1942	6,926

A white-coated policeman shining his red torch to enforce the 20 mph speed limit during the blackout

The massive increase in road deaths in 1939 is often attributed to the blackout conditions, along with the influx of novice and overseas service personnel drivers. In fact, the increase in economic activity during the war may be more relevant. Policing of motorists was increased in 1942, but a more likely cause of the decrease—a 23 per cent drop in car, bus and lorry occupant deaths—is that motorists were quite capable of driving more safely in very dark conditions, but had to have the experience and incentive to do so.

of other safety aids, to consider how a change in the use of motorcycle lights might not result in less likelihood of crashes. [22] The possibilities of motorists looking for lights instead of motorcycles or of risk compensation by motorcyclists themselves being less careful, are not considered.

The real issues of motorcycle safety — the danger posed to vulnerable road users by motorcyclists, and the fault of motorists in the majority of accidents involving other vehicles — are ignored, just as they are with the helmet issue. [23] It is easier to compel motorcyclists to do something which has no proven benefit than to consider important questions relating to more powerful road user groups.

A US motorcycle researcher counted the number of "violations" (the number of times motorists carried out manoeuvres which impinged on his right of way and could have been defined as traffic offences) over three 30 day periods on the same route at the same time of day. In the first period he wore normal motorcycle clothing without reflective gear or the headlight on. In the second he had the headlight on, and in the third used reflective clothing and had the headlight on. The three periods scored 1.9, 1.8 and 2 violations per day respectively. During a fourth period of 14 days the experiment was continued with *no* violations recorded at all — he was dressed to resemble a police motorcyclist! (This survey uses a small sample of incidents and is highly subjective, but nevertheless instructive.) [24]

A major piece of research in Britain gives an unwitting example of the difference between search and attention conspicuity. [25] In the pilot test, the subject was tested for his ability to notice motorcycles with and without daytime lights after first being informed of the purpose of the study. Once aware of the purposes of the experiment, he had no problems in noticing all the motorcycles whether or not they used daytime lights.

(ii) Cyclists

In Britain the evidence available for the effects of conspicuous cyclist clothing is based on experiments where distances left by vehicles overtaking cyclists, [26] and the earliest point that a subject wearing different amounts and kinds of high-visibility clothing could be seen by observers, [27] were measured. These experiments found that passing distances left by overtaking motorists increased with spacers or full-sleeved jackets made out of high-visibility material, but the effect of clothing which was less bright (that is, without full sleeves, which cyclists could not be expected to wear in summer) was minimal. There is a criticism that the conditions in which the experiments were done were not fully representative of conditions which cyclists might find elsewhere; more important, that giving inadequate overtaking distance may be due more to misjudging distance rather than to the lack of conspicuity of the cyclist (as seen by considering the significance of the use of spacers in the experiment). [28] Then, as the report noted, drivers allow different overtaking distances in different conditions: the real determinant of whether cyclists would be given a wide berth or not was the width of the road. This backs up what many cyclists feel, namely that motorists know what behaviour they should engage in irrespective of the clothing worn by cyclists, but frequently are simply unwilling to engage in it. Finally, because not more than about one in ten of all cycling accidents involve motorists overtaking, such experiments are of limited relevance.

As the Department of Transport itself admitted when questioned specifically on evidence from actual accidents:

It is true that we do not have accident data which shows specifically that conspicuity aids — eg, lights and reflectors, bright and reflective clothing — minimise the number of road accidents involving pedal cyclists.[29]

Even the obvious danger of not using a functioning rear light figures rather less in reality than is suggested by the frequent citing of this behaviour as a major "cycle safety" problem. Only some 15 per cent of cycling accidents occur in the dark.[30] Allowing for a significant proportion of cyclists not having functioning rear lights (say, 25 per cent), and a doubling of the chances of being in a crash when not using a rear light, we would still have a cause affecting not more than 7.0 per cent of cycling accidents. And since a minority of cycling accidents involve being run into from behind, it is unlikely that the figure could be anything like as high as this. Other variables would have to be considered as well. More interesting is the old question raised by the cycling groups 60 years ago — the extent to which the absence of a rear light should be seen as the "cause" anyway. If motorists are watching out for unlit pedestrians on built-up roads (which are lit at night) where most cycling accidents occur, a cyclist moving away from them should not pose much of a "seeing" problem anyway.

Even this may be allowing too much importance to the lights question. Research material from the Continent indicates that the beneficial effect of lights is dubious.[31] In a study of the presence or absence of bicycle lamps in night-time accidents in Copenhagen, some 14 per cent of accidents involved non-light users. Leaving aside questions of whether this could have been a contributory factor — whether people without lights ride worse, whether it was not the cyclist's fault, and so on — it emerges that the proportion of cyclists without lights was *higher* than the proportion of cyclists in accidents without lights. The implication is that the absence of lights leads to cyclists being more careful, and/or that on brightly lit streets cycle lights are irrelevant. This is backed up by a report for Avon County Council which indicated that defective lighting was a contributory factor in some 9.0 per cent of all accidents in the dark, just one per cent of total accidents, with about one in three bicycles in the area having defective lighting.[32]

Much of the failure of conspicuity aids to reduce cyclist casualties is summarised by a voice of (partial) dissidence from within the road safety establishment. Describing their contribution as "limited", the long-serving national cycling officer of RoSPA, Howard Boyd, stated: "[A] highly successful campaign [to wear very visible clothing] would not make a great impact on cyclist accident figures...the author's view is that widespread use of any of the [conspicuity] aids would not have much effect on the annual total of cycling deaths."[33] Boyd points out that campaigns urging the use of such aids are "too easy" to mount because of the pressure of manufacturers and the ease of placing the onus on a group which is physically, politically and ideologically vulnerable. In his awareness of the pitfalls of encouraging high-visibility clothing, Boyd suggests that it "might encourage an unconscious attitude among other road users that cyclists are to blame if drivers fail to notice them."[34] (I would suggest there is little question of "might".)

One particular case is of interest: the bicycle wheel reflector. Describing the many resources spent on promoting what he calls "relatively ineffective visibility aids", Boyd says:

> **Pressure to include them in the International Standard... came from manufacturers and well-meaning legislators, not from accident researchers. In practice wheel-mounted reflectors must have a very low accident prevention value as there are few situations where one can visualise that a collision might be averted because of their use. No studies have been undertaken to evaluate the effect that their mandatory use is having on cycling accidents. Yet millions of bicycles in many countries all over the world are being fitted with wheel reflectors, at a cost of many millions of dollars, all because the International Standards Organisation committee followed the US Consumer Product Safety Commission in thinking it would be a good idea.[35]**

But even Boyd is perhaps not sceptical enough. He clings to the belief that some aids are "good", without considering the overall context and risk compensation by all parties involved. His attitude of arguing for other measures will have little effect as long as some support is given, as RoSPA has always given it, to such "aids". The fact is that accident research figures are not the deciding force in political decision-making, and will be used even if they are erroneous (as with seat belts and crash-helmets), as long as the measure taken fits in conveniently with prevailing attitudes. There is now some indication that research figures on the ineffectiveness of wheel reflectors are being used — to push for reflective bicycle tyre walls. A much firmer break with the ideology and practice of the road safety establishment is called for.

(iii) Cars

Using the criteria of the road safety lobby, it would appear consistent to argue for brighter-coloured cars. There is some evidence that different-coloured cars have different accident rates, and one study of fire-engines indicates that they had less accidents when they were repainted bright yellow.[36] The mandatory use of daytime lights on cars in Sweden may have been beneficial for cyclists (but not for motorists).[37] Common sense would suggest, however, that if motorists get used to a brighter environment — such as one where lighting-up hours are extended into twilight — their tendency to pick out the smaller amount of light from cyclists and pedestrians will be reduced. There is unlikely to be any study showing that this is the case. Evidence that the vulnerable had yet again been disadvantaged would only result in more calls for them to make whatever pathetic or hopeless attempts they could to keep up with a less attentive and faster-moving motoring environment. Also, with "better" lighting, the additional problems of glare and distinguishing between more and faster-moving lights increase.

(iv) Pedestrians

As predicted by the pre-war cyclists, pedestrians are the next to be victim-blamed.[38]

A court report meriting a few column inches in my local newspaper tells how a 21-year-old man was hit by a car near the brow of a hill on a road in a built-up area in north London and killed. A passenger in the car said they were doing just over the speed limit. The driver said it was dark, and his passenger that they "didn't remember seeing anybody until the impact". The police said the road was well lit.[39] Maybe this story can be looked at for the ease with which a young man's death merits such little attention; or the way, despite admission of rule breaking, no prosecution occurs; or the trivial sentence which no doubt would have followed if it had. My point is to show how easily the motorist can fall back on the "Sorry, mate, didn't see you" argument. If it was well lit, he should have been able to see; more important, *if it was dark he should have been slowing down*. The readiness with which the "conspicuity con" may be invoked implicates the road safety lobby and all the conspicuity merchants in deaths such as this one.

It can not be emphasised too much that this "ordinary" death has a particular importance which other more obviously grotesque examples — which graduate to getting a few column inches in the national press — do not:

≣ An 89-year-old driver without his driving glasses collides with a baby on a pedestrian crossing, causing the child probable brain damage, and fails to stop. He receives a ban and £300 fine.[40]

≣ An ex-ambulance driver who could not read a number plate at two metres

153

kills a woman on a pedestrian crossing: he had knocked another woman down seven months earlier and received a fine for careless driving with his eyesight unquestioned. He receives a ban, a suspended prison sentence and a £300 fine.[41]

These cases should show up the failure of the road safety lobby to consider defective eyesight a problem, as well as the usual trivial response from the courts when the worst comes to the worst. But it is much more important not to be drawn into long campaigns to institute random eyesight testing at the expense of cracking down on those who do not use what visual ability they have — and who are pandered to relentlessly and dangerously by the road safety lobby.

Conclusion

Advice to the vulnerable to attempt to be seen is unlikely to be of much use, because it relies on one small part of the "seeing" process. As this book argues throughout, a rational and fair transport safety policy would put the onus on the potentially dangerous and less vulnerable, rather than the other way round. The responsibility of the vulnerable should be far less (or perhaps not considered at all until the responsibility of the dangerous has been properly addressed) — not only because of their relative lack of danger to others, but because whatever they do they depend for their safety on the motorised, and the converse is not really true.

In the case of conspicuity, the aids suggested may be virtually irrelevant — such as reflective dog leads, thin strips of reflective tape on umbrella tips or rear bicycle wheel spoke reflectors (seen too late to avoid collision). Or their relevance may be minimal. As with all minimal controls on motorist danger, conspicuity aids detract attention from more important questions (motorist seeing); they "may encourage the idea that the vulnerable are to blame if motorists fail to notice them",[42] or they otherwise lower attentiveness and increase speeds. A minimal restraint becomes a pseudo-restraint, and the "solution" becomes part of the problem.

The traditional opposition to this line of argument is that concentration on motorists' eyesight is not contradicted by an attempt to "be seen", that there are attempts to discuss issues like night blindness, and that possibly vulnerable road users have to expect more careless and faster motorists. This view is taken up by cycling magazines trying to develop a sense of pride among cyclists (and to gain revenue from manufacturers of conspicuity aids). But, attempts to correct the "seeing" part of the process are somewhat poor and limited. The first effects of bringing night-time blindness to public attention have been for it to be used as a mitigating factor in a defence of causing death through reckless driving.[43] The implication of the failure of conspicuity aids is that "seeing" is becoming worse, not better. Thus we may not just have victim-blaming; not just pathetic attempts by the vulnerable to protect themselves, or even a necessary "something better than nothing" attitude which attempts to cope with an inevitable increase in danger. We may also have something likely to *make things worse*, when all the indications are for the need to reduce the danger at source.

The discussion about conspicuity is often little more than a symbolic statement about the rights of different road users. Motorists "notice" cyclists without rear lights, or pedestrians without bright clothing, as a problem. (Indeed, their readiness to "see" these people is an indication of just how easily they could pick them out if they really wanted to.) As elsewhere, this reflects the feeling that non-car-users are failing in obligations. While apparently a harmless enough suggestion, it is based on a dangerous misunderstanding about the real obligations of road users. None of this means that people should not be conspicuous, but neither does it mean that a higher level of obligation should be expected from the vulnerable than was required from, for example, pre-war cyclists. Efforts to pressure them into being conspicuous (beyond perhaps a basic minimum) are bound to produce misunderstanding and no benefits, with victim-blaming thrown in for good measure.

10.

"Does someone have to die first?"
Problems for pedestrians

*BECAUSE, over the last 30 years, there has been a decline in the number of
pedestrians reported killed on British roads, it is common to refer to the "success"
of the road safety movement. This ignores the exodus there has been of pedestrians
from the streets. Their habits have changed markedly: in 1971 80 per cent of
parents were happy to see their seven to eight-year-olds walk to school on their
own, by 1990 this figure had fallen to nine per cent.*

✤✤✤

Mr Tony Banks —The statistics show that one third of all pedestrians who are
injured in motor accidents, suffer injuries when they are on the pavement...

Mr John Maples — Presumably, as one third of pedestrians are injured on the
pavement, the other two thirds are injured on the road. *Where they should not
be* [my emphasis].

Debate on road safety in the House of Commons, November 1989.[1]

There is an extraordinary gulf in the motoring mind between intention and
action. What are we to do with these people with their split minds? As they kill
and maim pedestrians they chatter: "We are all pedestrians."

JS Dean, Murder Most Foul[2]

Walking is not just the most basic mode of transport. It is the most equitable, non-
violent, non-polluting, energy-conserving and generally benign way of getting
about. It is available to everybody, apart from a minority of those with physical
disabilities.[3] At present it constitutes about one-third of all journeys over 50 yards.[4]

Walking is also contemptuously treated and has low status in contemporary
society. Pedestrians killed by negligent motorists have their deaths recorded as
"accidents" in coroner's courts, however severe the offence recorded. The general
lenience to the dangerous behaviour of motorists when pedestrians are hurt or
killed, and the legal blind eye shown to the vast majority on behaviour which can
endanger others, has been discussed.[5] We live in a society where an MP can get
away with a statement which implies that pedestrians — whether or not they obey
the regulations or laws that he routinely breaks if he is a typical motorist[6] — do not
have the right to cross the road. Walking is regarded as not important, and the

adjective "pedestrian" has derogatory connotations. In 1976 the Press ridiculed attempts by the Greater London Council to provide for pedestrians. (Noting the problems pedestrians faced with traffic in London, research was done showing that walking comprised 7.0 per cent of total distance travelled, 38 per cent of total travel time, 41 per cent of journeys, and 60 per cent of travel time by value. The Daily Mail called it the silliest piece of research of the year.)[7]

This is no simple failure of courtesy or correct thinking. The trivialising of walking as a form of transport, or simply the absence of consideration for it, as with any form of denial or trivialising of the vulnerable by the powerful, holds the potential for danger. It is also comparatively recent. Until after the Second World War — with the possible exception of the USA and the fascist countries — it was assumed that, to a large extent, children would be able to make their way about in local neighbourhoods unaided. Street photographs in Britain up till the late 1950s or 1960s reveal not only children but all local residents able to move with a freedom and ease that are rare or non-existent nowadays.[8] Such a situation is still the norm outside the metropolitan countries, and even in parts of Europe serious efforts are made to reclaim space from car traffic for the pedestrian.[9]

This state of affairs occurs partly because the pedestrians most likely to suffer, whether in terms of the effects of being hit by vehicles, or because of their greater difficulty in coping with traffic in the first place, are elderly, very young or disabled. These social groups are relatively powerless and mostly unable to define authoritatively the nature of "the problem".Their problems in this respect are exacerbated if they are also in a weak class position. For able-bodied adults who do not have to put up with the personal security problems of subways or other features of modern urban road design,[10] the particular dangers of rural roads, the community severance of major roads or the difficulties of accompanying small children or disabled people across roads, life may not seem so bad. Nevertheless, accidents appear to involve anything up to 20 per cent of the population as pedestrians at some time in their life.[11]

Pedestrian problems are also not seen as serious — despite campaigns for pedestrian crossings and interest in traffic calming — because to take pedestrians' interests seriously would mean seeing them as in conflict with current motoring behaviour. The anger which follows an accident involving a pedestrian is often directed at the behaviour of a deviant minority rather than at car use in general. With the assistance of the road safety lobby, "the traffic", however fast, heavy or uncontrolled, is seen as something inevitable which has to be deferred to.

Motorists have been able to set the agenda of discussion on their own terms. Their classic denial of responsibility has been legitimated by the phrase so properly identified by Dean above: motorists feel that they cannot be accused of antisocial behaviour because, when they stop playing the motorist role, they may become pedestrians as well. The other variant of this is the acceptance (with a smile) that there is indeed a conflict between the two roles. Sometimes people are pedestrians worrying about the danger from motorists, sometimes they are motorists annoyed at pedestrians inconveniencing them. The fact that there are differences in the vulnerability of, and danger to, others of the two road user groups is forgotten, is held to be adequately controlled or is accepted as an inevitable fact of life.

General safety problems

The problems for pedestrians start with the absence of data on which to assess their chances of being hurt. As we saw in Chapter 1, little space is devoted to walking in the Department of Transport's National Travel Survey, which expressly ignores journeys under a mile, although these represent a third of all journeys over 50 yards.[12] The impact on the amount of walking done produced by increases in journeys made by car and other forms of transport was ignored until NTS 1975-76. The rough count of pedestrian mileage fails to refer to the amount of crossing of roads of different width, traffic flows and speeds. Figures on shorter trips are also not included in other official statistics on travel, such as Transport Statistics Great Britain or the Central Statistical Office's Social Trends.[13]

The information we do have tells us that about 60,000 pedestrians were reported hurt, with 1,694 killed, in 1990.[14] This indicates a chance of being hurt once every 900 years, yet the 1989 Gallup poll indicates that the chance is some three to five times higher, with apparently a high level of under-reporting. About a quarter of Gallup's respondents claimed to have had "near misses", and there was evidence of widespread anxiety about crossing busy roads and fearing for children's safety.[15]

The presentation of accident figures without a measure of exposure to danger which reflects the experience of walking, serves to create a false impression that things are better than they are for pedestrians. Over the last 30 years there has been a very slight reduction in the number of pedestrians reported killed and seriously injured. Yet during this time pedestrian habits have changed markedly; fewer pedestrian journeys are now made by elderly people and by children, who are now more likely to be ferried about by parents or prevented by them from making certain walking journeys.[16] A detailed survey of schoolchildren in five areas of England in 1971, followed up in 1990, showed that in the first survey 80 per cent of seven to eight-year-olds were allowed to go to school on their own, with 75 per cent of juniors allowed to cross roads on their own. These figures had dropped to 9.0 per cent and 50 per cent by 1990.[17]

We can obtain a useful picture of the pedestrian experience by looking at a group whose behaviour is likely to have stayed constant: the ten to 14-year-olds, who are old enough to have broken from parental control. Between 1956 and 1986 their chances of being killed or seriously injured (per 100,000 of the age group) *more than doubled*.[18]

This is not just a measure of the suffering of a vulnerable group, but an indication of the generally worsening situation for all vulnerable road users, along with the evidence on cyclists and the increasing number (and rate per vehicle) of insurance claims. Even this probably underestimates the rise in *danger*; for, whatever the complaints of bad pedestrian behaviour from motorists, pedestrians have probably adapted not just in terms of taking fewer journeys, but in taking more care over them. Photographs and film of pedestrian behaviour up till the 1960s show a more casual form of walking.

Britain fares badly enough in pedestrian accident rates per 100,000 compared with other countries in Europe.[19] But it appears that more journeys are made in areas which have traffic calming or in countries which have maintained traditions of child pedestrian freedom;[20] so Britain's comparative rate in terms of journeys made becomes even worse. In addition, British pedestrian behaviour is often *more* careful, not less, indicating that the amount of danger should be seen as yet higher still.

Any such consideration of how people actually behave is neglected or *opposed* by the DTp. Minimising the importance of pedestrian journeys allows the DTp, through the use of the NTS and other official statistics, to suggest that the proportion of car journeys is far higher than it is, and that the safety situation is far better than it is. All this provides ammunition for the argument that we have been moving correctly as we proceed down the road of increasing car use, and should proceed further in the same way.

Sometimes the question of the experience of pedestrians is raised in official discussion. In presenting its proposals for pedestrians in 1989, the DTp states: "People worry about walking. 'Perceived risk' has been identified as a significant deterrent to walking, just as much as knowledge of actual casualties."[21] It goes on to suggest measures which it is claimed will reduce the sense of risk among pedestrians, but it explains that the priority is casualty reduction. Consider the use of inverted commas here. They could well be removed from the phrase "perceived risk", which is all too real — as is the fear of crime — for those who suffer from it, and is also a consistent causative factor in the production of accidents. By contrast, inverted commas could be suitably applied to the phrase "casualty reduction", because the measure of casualty rate chosen is usually the wrong one for assessment of pedestrian experience, suitable only for serving the road-building, pro-car, policies of the DTp.

To talk about reducing the fear of danger as a secondary aim to casualty reduction is to talk about them as if they were complementary aims. But, reducing the fear of danger will often be *contradictory* to the aim of "casualty reduction". For when the fear of danger is a correct appreciation of actual danger, which it often is, if it is relieved by reducing actual danger, the change in behaviour it leads to (such as more journeys by elderly or child pedestrians) could well involve no overall drop in casualties. To me it seems that if the chances (per journey, or per unit of time, or per crossing) were reduced, even if overall casualties were not reduced, there would have been progress. Indeed there is a case to be made that if a greater sense of well-being existed, the chances of being hurt (which is only given by a retrospective statistic where both denominator and numerator can only

MY FATHER
MR BANNAN Lost
HIS LIFE ON THIS
RACE TRACK IN 1977

U-Turn: drivers in Tyne and Wear have to back-track in the face of protesting residents

Banner protest stops traffic on killer road

By PATRICK LAVELLE

CAMPAIGNERS brought traffic to a standstill on a killer Wearside road yesterday in their fight to get traffic to slow down.

About 50 banner-waving protestors blocked Premier Road in Plains Farm, Sunderland, just after 9am and urged motorists to support their campaign.

They are calling for the speed limit on the dual carriageway to be reduced after three people died in accidents on the road this year.

The latest victim was 84-year-old grandmother Margaret Morrison, of Perth Road, Plains Farm, who died last week after being hit by a car while on her way to a social club.

Local councillors have already met Sunderland Council's chief highways engineer Tom Ball and the residents have been promised

spy cameras and warning signs will be erected on the road in a bid to slow traffic down.

But Coun David Allan is also calling for a pelican crossing and roundabouts on the road, which splits the Plains Farm Estate in two and is crossed by scores of children on their way to school.

Among the campaigners were Ann Bulmer, 49, who launched a similar campaign more than ten years ago, and relatives of two of those killed in accidents.

Coun Allan said: "We support the residents who elected us and they have made their point this morning. It could have been a little dangerous but I will not condemn their actions."

● Two local men have been questioned by police over the hit-and-run death of Mrs Morrison. No charges have been brought.

Pat Catcheside's demonstration reveals personal tragedy

inadequately be assessed, if at all), let alone the over-all casualty number, should probably not be the sole deciding factor in assessing success.

The DTp's purpose of making perceived risk secondary to casualty reduction is to continue with a programme of reducing the safety of the environment for pedestrians, or at least to put a block on programmes which reduce danger. This view is clearly expressed in the ultimate example of confusing the transitive and intransitive meanings of the word "danger". When I asked the DTp's Head of Road Safety Division whether he would encourage policies which moved car users to rail or bus, since both modes are far safer for other road users and for the people using them, I obtained the following classic reply. It was that while people might have a lower chance of being hurt while on public transport, we would have to consider the negative effect of making more people pedestrians (walking to and from stations and bus-stops), as walking is the second most "dangerous" mode of transport after motorcycling.[22] Speaking transitively, of course, walking is hardly dangerous at all, and the reduction of danger to others when using public transport also counts.

Until this underlying philosophy changes, there will always be an inherent flaw in official road safety objectives. Any attempts made to help pedestrians are more than eroded by the policies supporting increasing car use — policies that could be seen as a "conspiracy against walking".[23]

The DTp's recent policy on pedestrians dates from the publication of the 1979 Policy Studies Institute report *Walking is Transport*,[24] one of the few attempts to consider walking seriously.[25] In response the then Secretary of State for Transport, Norman Fowler, acknowledged: "[W]alking undoubtedly serves all and that is going to be an increasingly important central Government objective."[26] A discussion paper was promised, but despite reiterating the promise, in 1983 his successor, Lynda Chalker, decided against it on the grounds of inadequate research data. Some ten years after the original statement in support of pedestrians' rights, with millions of extra vehicles on the road encouraged by government, we have *Pedestrian Safety: New Proposals for Making Walking Safer*.[27]

Besides the routine confusion over the meaning of "safety", we have the other usual problems. Drunkenness among pedestrians is wrongly targeted.[28] Conspicuity, apart from the usual mistake of blaming the victims of those who cannot or will not see, is brought up without any of the evidence which seems to matter so much when motorist behaviour is in question. Motorist education is briefly mentioned, despite the lack of evidence for its beneficial effects. And research on the reduction of danger accompanying speed reduction is not mentioned. Calling for research is a classic delaying tactic; if it criticises the status quo it is shelved or denied, whereas measures which have no supporting, or even some contradicting, evidence (such as on conspicuity) will be advocated anyway.

Then, of course, there are the problems of pedestrians suffering directly from noxious gas emissions,[29] personal security,[30] the diversion of funds [31] to road building which could be spent on repairing defective footways (implicated in a half-million estimated falls on the footway),[32] and so on.

Who needs a crossing?

Along with the desire to reduce or slow down traffic, the most common form of local pedestrian campaigning is for one of the types of pedestrian crossing. Sometimes taking up to ten years of lobbying, these campaigns have to be supported by local authority councillors for the areas concerned; crossings are installed only after investigation by council officers who will advise the councillors as to whether official criteria have been met. There is much flexibility in these criteria, and the outcome of an often laborious and time-consuming campaign is generally decided by factors other than the official criteria. In a survey of local authority practice in London in 1989, we found that the underlying assumptions about the freedom of different road user groups, as held by council officers, as well as the power of local residents and their representatives, are the deciding factor. [33]

(i) The official criteria

There are two sets of official criteria. The first involves squaring the number of vehicles passing the site in question and multiplying it by the number of pedestrians crossing there within a given time. If this product (PV^2) is above a value of 108, a crossing may be installed. The second is the number of accidents at the site. Provided certain design characteristics are met, local authorities then have the power to install one of the types of pedestrian crossing. But, apart from PV^2 and accidents, certain other criteria were listed by the DTp in its advice note TA 52/87. [34] These included relaxing the criteria outside hospitals and other kinds of residence where extra support needs to be given to pedestrians; in particular, one phrase referring to "other local considerations" [35] allows for local authorities to install crossings in ways which might depart significantly from PV^2 and accidents criteria.

(ii)...and their failings

By considering *actual* numbers of pedestrians crossing at a particular site, *potential* pedestrians — those who might be inhibited from crossing the road at that site because it is perceived as unsafe — are neglected. Similarly, the absence of accidents may mask very real dangers for pedestrians, who do not cross at a particular site *precisely because* it is dangerous. In both cases, low numerical values for the traditional criteria may reflect a suppressed demand rather than an absence of demand.

It would seem sensible, where delay is being considered, to have a formula which includes counts of both pedestrians and vehicles. But setting the particular relationship of P and V at PV^2, and at a threshold of 108, seems to have been largely arbitrary. Work was done in the 1960s at the Road Research Laboratory on computer simulation models for vehicle and pedestrian delays, and since then further work has been sponsored by the TRRL. [36] There are, however, a number of problems with such modelling exercises, for example: "[W]hile it would be possible to improve the accuracy of a model representing a particular site by including behavioural characteristics of pedestrians, any of these characteristics are site-specific and could not be built into a general model." [37]

Delay, facility and amenity

Delay costs, like much else in cost-benefit analysis, are contentious. The kind of delay we should be concerned with is difficult to assess. [38] It has been suggested that maximum delay rather than average delay or percentage of pedestrians delayed, merits attention. [39] The problem with excessive delay could be that the pedestrians thus affected would be tempted to cross at unsafe times, [40] but this might not be the only disbenefit. The effects in terms of amenity have received little attention, apart from in the works of Hillman and a handful of others. [41] There is little available material on whether the installation of crossings releases suppressed demand.

A fuller picture would require comprehensive information on factors such as length of specific journeys, width of roads crossed (with flows and speeds of vehicles) and available crossing facilities, plus the relationship of these characteristics with those of pedestrians (age, gender, (dis)ability, income, car availability, journey purpose, and so on) on a national basis. Compare the availability of figures on car use. A small survey carried out by the Office of Population Censuses and Surveys in 1980 is one example of the way to this type of data collection. [42]

Accidents and safety

With accidents, we have similar problems. As far as crossings are concerned, discussion centres on "rates" at different kinds of crossing, their relationship with flow criteria and the effects of installing a crossing on that "rate". The limitations of present knowledge are as follows:

≣ With under-reporting, we have inadequate knowledge of accidents in the first place. The numbers recorded appear to be three to six times lower than the actual number of pedestrian accidents. [43]

≣ The numbers involved are small at individual sites, with consequent difficulties for statistical analyses. It would be desirable to analyse data on an area-wide basis to consider factors such as accident migration. [44]

≣ The generally remarked claim that accidents tend to increase at sites where previous numbers of accidents have been below the mean following installation of a crossing may reflect a statistical artifact rather than the real effect of installation. The only reliable way of assessing a change at a particular site is one that allows for regression-to-mean effects.

≣ The "rate" generally referred to is one where the denominator is the site. It would be more appropriate, if we are to be concerned more with the experience of pedestrians, to consider rather the rate per trip, per road crossing, per pedestrian-mile, or per pedestrian-minute travelled. These measures would give an idea of the chances of accidents for pedestrians. If there is a release of suppressed demand, the rate per site might increase, while the rate per crossing stayed the same or decreased.

≣ The final point links up the consideration of amenity and facility with safety. It extends the consideration of the nature of the experience of pedestrians yet further. It is a simple point, but it seems to be difficult for practitioners to accept. This is that the main aim of safety initiatives should be to provide a reduction in danger, rather than a reduction in accidents. Reducing danger, as people adapt to the reduction in perceived

163

danger, may not have the effect of reducing accident rates, but will have the effect of producing a safer environment where people, in this case pedestrians crossing the road, will have more of a chance to go about their business safely. Provided the numbers of accidents (measured properly in terms of casualties per journey and taking into account different age and other groups) do not increase, and that more convenience and facility result, then it will have been a success for pedestrians.[45] If this is not the case, measures such as control on vehicle speeds, and other controls on motorist behaviour, should be considered.

11.

On your head be it — helmets

CYCLING through the British climate can be a punishing business, but in the 1990s cyclists must also negotiate a smoke-screen of "road safety" measures. The issue of helmet-wear has come to dominate the road safety agenda, and yet the new evidence from the State of Victoria in Australia, where helmets are now compulsory, suggests that there is no conclusive benefit to be gained from the move.

Other effects are less ambiguous. Apart from the role helmets play in deflecting attention away from dangerous driving, in one year in the Melbourne area the amount of recreational cycling fell by 41 per cent.

❖❖❖

People hurt in road crashes may suffer injuries to various parts of the body. When the injuries to a particular part of the body are severe enough, they (rather than the reasons for the crash) are referred to by the medical establishment as "the cause of death".[1] Head injuries are, for obvious reasons, capable of leading to serious long-term disability or death, and are critical in a significant proportion of all deaths. This proportion has been singled out for those on two wheels, although it is also highly significant for all road users. Indeed, the relevance of protective head gear (in terms of the criteria of the road safety lobby) could be greater for car occupants than for motorcyclists and cyclists.

After the Second World War the road safety lobby began to call for the wearing of helmets by motorcyclists. Subsequently it raised the question of head protection for cyclists. This tends to avoid the major underlying issue of the danger that some road users pose to others, particularly to two-wheelers. Bicycle crash helmet-wear (which even its advocates do not claim to be of relevance to more than a small minority of road accident casualties) has become one of the major — if not *the* major — "road safety" issues of the 1990s. Helmet campaigns are already having a negative effect in diverting attention away from the danger to cyclists and other road users created by the current transport system, which is the principal source of the danger they confront.[2] In the short-term a small amount of this danger may be reduced by wearing bicycle crash helmets: in the long term even this may be eroded by the phenomenon of helmet advocacy and its acceptance.

More certain than this is that according to the official criteria used by the road safety lobby — retrospectively analysed chances of increasing the "saving of lives" and decreasing injury severity (as distinct from my aim of danger reduction) — *the beneficial effects of helmet-wear are minimal, non-existent, or even negative*. The advocacy of helmets is therefore best explained by: the prevailing inability or unwillingness to confront the dangers arising from a transport system excessively organised around the private car; the political and ideological weakness of cyclists and motorcyclists; the tendency of the "road safety" lobby (particularly doctors) to be victim-oriented; the widespread refusal to accept the possibility of risk compensation or any similar evidence; and the power of the manufacturers of "safety aids". The central confusion in "road safety" ideology between transitive and intransitive meanings of danger and the responsibilities of the different road user groups is as usual a contributory factor.

A. Motorcycles

The evidence

Motorcycle crash helmets rank alongside seat belts in importance in road safety mythology. The same kind of extravagant claims are made for them that are made for seat belts; the total number of "lives saved" claimed for their use is less, but only because motorcyclists (in the highly motorised countries of the First World) are outnumbered by car users. As with seat belts, obvious benefits arise from their use once someone has been unfortunate enough to be in a crash. But, as with seat belts, the evidence that their use significantly reduces the prospects of dying or being hurt is slim.

The principal evidence comes from the United States in the 1970s, where over a period of a few years states containing about half the country's motorcycles repealed laws compelling motorcyclists to wear helmets. The road safety lobby uses this experience, of a kind of experiment in the effects of legal compulsion, to argue that it indicated how successful compulsion had been in reducing deaths and injuries which significantly increased after repeal. However, the evidence does *not* give grounds for compulsion. The main evidence used by the US National Highway Traffic Safety Administration was a graph showing a significant increase in motorcyclist fatality rates (deaths per motorcyclist) after repeal of laws. Yet the graph is of motorcyclist fatality rates across states, whether they repealed the law or not. In fact, the rate of increase was greater in the states that *did not* repeal their laws. Analysing this and the other studies used by the road safety lobby, Adams shows that "The evidence fails to support the widely accepted view that motorcycle helmet legislation has produced dramatic reductions in fatalities. In Britain, as elsewhere, legislation would appear to based more on faith than hard evidence."[3]

In Britain, compulsory helmet-wearing was introduced in June 1973. At that time it was estimated that some 80 per cent of motorcyclists, and 50 per cent of moped riders wore helmets.[4] In other words, some 25 per cent of motorcyclists started wearing helmets at or around the time of compulsion, with rider wearing being virtually 100 per cent. The Department of Transport's finding after the law was that it had achieved a reduction of just under 2.0 per cent of the 1972 total of motorcyclists killed or seriously injured in the year after compulsion.[5] It is not made

166

clear whether this is a doubling of the figures for the second half of 1973, and if exposure (mileage) of riders is included in the calculation. But even accepting it, given claims of at least a 30 to 50 per cent reduction in casualties,[6] with 25 per cent of the motorcyclists starting to wear helmets, a figure of some 8 to 12 per cent should be produced, not less than 2.0 per cent. Once again there is evidence that risk compensation occurred.

There is more evidence that risk compensation occurred in Britain. 1973 was an unusual year and a particularly interesting one for road safety analysts — the year of the oil crisis. One of the few points of general agreement is that more careful driving was seen in the motorised countries, with lower speeds, and perhaps reduced mileage, implicated in a reduction in deaths for all road user groups. All groups, that is, apart from motorcyclists. This can be explained partly by the increase in motorcycling (with more and more inexperienced motorcyclists on the roads) which occurred at this time. But the changes in motorcyclist fatality and casualty rates are not compatible with significant benefits from crash helmet-wear, and the fortunes of motorcyclists were in marked contrast to those of other road user groups.

Table 2 shows that the numbers of Killed and Seriously Injured (KSI) per hundred million vehicle kilometres (HMVK) declined by 3.0 per cent in 1974 from 1973, and by 5.0 per cent in 1975 from 1974. The changes in the Killed rate for these periods were +2.0 per cent and -15 per cent respectively:

Motorcycle injuries and deaths, 1970-75

Year	Distance travelled (00,000,000 km)	Killed	KSI	K/HMVK[†]	KSI/HMVK[†]
1970	32	652	13,894	20.4	434
1971	31	657	13,466	21.2	434
1972	29	626	12,374	21.6	426
1973	30	644	13,072	21.5	435
1974	32	704	13,445	22.0	420
1975	38	724	15,059	19.0	396

Table 2.

† hundred million vehicle kilometres

The only decline apparent in fatality rate is in 1975, after an *increase* in the first full year after compulsion. If the decline is due to helmet-wearing, it would be interesting to know why it should take over a year and a half for such a beneficial effect to be shown.

By contrast, consider the figures for all road users:

All road users — deaths, 1970-75

Year	Distance travelled (00,000,000 km)	Killed	K/HMVK†
1970	1,811	7,499	4.14
1971	1,917	7,699	4.02
1972	2,017	7,763	3.85
1973	2,123	7.406	3.49
1974	2,081	6,876	3.30
1975	2,098	6,366	3.03

Table 3.

† hundred million vehicle kilometres

Here we see a steady and persistent decline in fatality rate for all road users (with total motor vehicle mileage as the denominator) of 9.0 per cent in 1973 (over 1972), 5.0 per cent in 1974 and 8.0 per cent in 1975. Since the more careful behaviour of motorists should have *reduced* the danger to motorcyclists, there is yet more evidence for risk compensation.[7]

Advocates of safety aids have always claimed that those who use helmets and other safety aids only when they are compulsory are also the least careful riders. Achieving high, in this case virtually 100 per cent, wearing would therefore be particularly likely to emphasise the benefits of the aids in question. The existence of such benefits is not at all apparent.

Helmets and "the motorcycle problem"

The 1973 legislation was the first instance of road users being compelled to protect themselves, with the National Council for Civil Liberties and others voicing concern over it setting a precedent.[8] Understanding how this could occur involves an awareness of how motorcyclists could be seen as a problem to be dealt with by the professionals of the road safety industry.

In the post-war period, distinctive motorcycle subcultures developed in North America and Britain, with a strong anti-establishment and rebellious stance.[9] While the origins of "outlaw" motorcycle culture were in the US West Coast motorbike clubs which became known as the Hell's Angels,[10] a subculture extolling the bravado and machismo of motorcycling was also evident among working-class male youth in Britain. Although still in existence, it began to lose its constituency with the availability of cars to working-class families in the late 1950s and early 1960s. Industry support, so important in supporting motorist hegemony,

Motorcyclists campaigning against compulsory helmet-wear in 1973

was weak and declined further with the disappearance of the British motorcycle manufacturing industry.

Motorcycling groups were not opposed to helmet-wearing as such, although there was a strong feeling that compulsion was unjust. A minority group felt that it was being picked on. It resented the fact that the roots of the problem — causation of accidents, with motorists largely responsible — were not being properly examined. There had been a consistent rise in the number of people killed on the roads from the early 1950s to the late 1960s. The feeling among protesting groups like the Motorcycle Action Group was that they were expected to pay for the carelessness of motorists, and ineffectively at that. At this time most motorcycling was a kind of poor man's motoring; with its working-class base and lack of powerful economic interests, it could not field a well-articulated response to the road safety lobby.

A central feature of the public definition of motorcycling was the Mods and Rockers phenomenon of the late 1960s. Great publicity was given to the skirmishes between rival youth subcultures defined largely by their use of different kinds of two-wheel motor vehicle. Behind the publicity surrounding these events was a fear of the new-found mobility and disposable income of working-class youth. [11] The fear of mobile working-class young men was nothing new. The invasion of the young urban working-class male "rough" into genteel middle-class areas is a traditional source of fear. The "rebel" image, which some two-wheel motor vehicle users had assumed, could be easily imposed on motorcycling in general; motorcycling was "dangerous".

There is an important sense in which motorcycling *is* dangerous. Some 80 to

100 pedestrians are killed every year in crashes involving two-wheel motor vehicles,[12] which are also a potential threat to cyclists and even to people in cars. How dangerous motorcycling is to others in comparison with cars is difficult to assess.[13] But this is not the normal sense in which the word is used when the "danger" of motorcycling is discussed. Applying it in its transitive sense would mean returning to the subject of the main group of (potentially) dangerous road users, namely car drivers.

Motorcycling is dangerous in the intransitive sense of the word. Given high speed, high acceleration, and the presence of cars, motorcycling is — as one would expect — the most hazardous form of transport. If the power is reduced significantly, as with speed-governed mopeds, the hazardous, as well as the dangerous element, appears to decline.[14]

The legacy of motorcycle crash helmet legislation

Imagine the typical British reaction to the sight of a motorcyclist riding without a crash helmet, as is often the practice in countries without helmet legislation. The rider would stand out as doing something "dangerous". Yet the beneficial effects of wearing helmets appear to have been exaggerated, and the real hazards of motorcycling — largely those of the higher-powered vehicles, the people attracted to riding them and the danger posed by motorists — are obscured. The real danger, of posing a threat to other road users, has also been obscured, and *it appears to have been exacerbated*, as one would expect from a change in motorcyclist behaviour.

The effect on pedestrians

The Stats 19 data are shown in Figures 1.1 and 1.2.

In terms of pedestrian casualties per average month in 1973 after the law, the figures for killed, serious injuries, and slight injuries have risen by 54, 38, and 24 per cent respectively. This might, however, be accounted for by changes in levels of motorcycling at different times of the year.

Looking at the figures of pedestrian casualty rates — casualties per distance travelled by motorcyclists, (Figure 3) — we see a picture which could be accounted for *by more careless riding by helmeted motorcyclists*. With *fatalities*, there is an increase after 1973, although it is difficult to tell whether this is the continuation of a long-term trend. *Serious injuries* do increase, breaking a declining trend, until 1975. The *slight injuries*, and aggregate casualties, show a decline until 1973 — and then an increase.

Even given the reservations about official statistics expressed in Chapter 1, it is interesting to use the approach of the road safety lobby. We can use the Serious Injuries series, since the figures for Deaths are low, and since the reporting of Serious Injuries tends to be more reliable than that for Slight Injuries.

This leads to conclusions which tally with a risk compensation hypothesis: there is an interruption of a trend for a period of about two years after a change in danger, until adaptation to the change (by pedestrians) occurs. The deaths and slight injuries both tally with a similar interpretation, or at least do not contradict

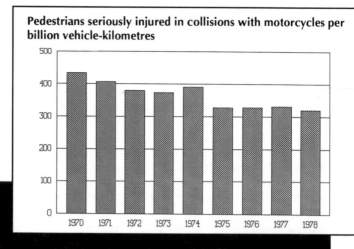

Figure 1.1

Pedestrians seriously injured in collisions with motorcycles per billion vehicle-kilometres

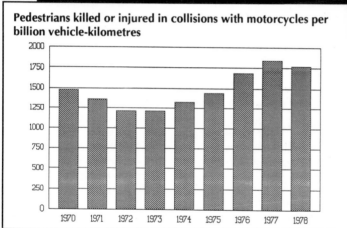

Figure 1.2

Pedestrians killed or injured in collisions with motorcycles per billion vehicle-kilometres

it. Indeed, looking at a graph of aggregate pedestrian casualty rates, there is a reversal of a trend which would lead any self-respecting statistician to ask: something seems to have happened in 1973, what was it?

All this occurred at a time when there was a *steady decline in total pedestrian deaths* on the road. Once again, even given caution about the status of casualty data, the evidence is that motorcycle helmet-wearing made motorcyclists less careful. I have never come across an attempt to assess the effect of compulsion in this way. Against all the (dubious) claims about "lives saved" by compulsory helmet-wearing, there is nothing about pedestrian *lives taken*. The official view, of unalloyed benefits from legal compulsion, has gone largely unchallenged and forms part of the basis for other moves such as compulsory seat belt wearing and, now, bicycle crash helmets.

171

B. Pedal cyclists

The racing cyclists' "leather hair net" type of crash hat has been around since the early years of the century. Its use probably arose from the exceptionally hazardous practices involved in the track racing of those days. The protection afforded by such hats is minimal. The interest in their adoption in the past lies in the way people who are thought to constitute a "safety problem" take up the use of a "safety aid". It is either done voluntarily, to create an impression of responsibility, or imposed by authorities anxious to feel that a problem is being controlled. Either way, the chances of cyclists being badly hurt or killed may be little affected in the long term. Meanwhile, the device helps those who are really linked with the danger avoid responsibility.

The modern bicycle helmet offers a genuine but limited capacity to absorb impact. Protection is afforded to those falling on their heads after crashes have occurred. Whether encouragement or compulsion to use the helmet would result in reduced chances of cyclists being killed or hurt in the long term, however, is another matter entirely.

Evidence

Bicycle helmets have been advocated since the 1950s and 1960s by "road safety" pundits, despite the fact that what we now know as a cycling helmet did not then exist[15] — the first example in this case of recommendation occurring irrespective of evidence. The basis for the claim that crash helmets are suitable is that a particularly high proportion of cyclist fatalities have head injury as the "cause of death". In the case of adult cyclists it is implicated in some two-thirds of deaths, compared to just over half of pedestrian and under half of car occupant deaths. Motorcyclists and their passengers, despite the use of helmets, still have head injury as cause of death in nearly half their fatalities (see Figure 2.)[16]

Figure 2 might in fact indicate that, in terms of total numbers of road users dying from head injuries, car occupants would be more likely candidates for helmet-wear. Even if restricted to drivers, the provision of helmets attached to magnetic strips on the inner surface of car roofs would appear — using the official road safety criteria — to be a great deal more relevant. Helmets such as those worn by rally drivers offer far more protection than bicycle crash helmets; there are fewer discomfort or storage problems; and the number of lives lost where head injury is listed as "cause of death" is some three times higher than with cyclists. The experience of motorcyclists should be cautionary, quite apart from the evidence of risk compensation and diversion from more important questions. The figures for head injury as a cause of death exist despite the far more sophisticated and impact-absorbing design of motorcycle helmets (although admittedly bicycle accidents tend to involve less kinetic energy dispersed on impact).

National figures are more reliable than those derived from small-scale local studies. Adams notes that the road safety lobby falls back on such small-scale studies in order to avoid the conclusions of work based on larger populations if they

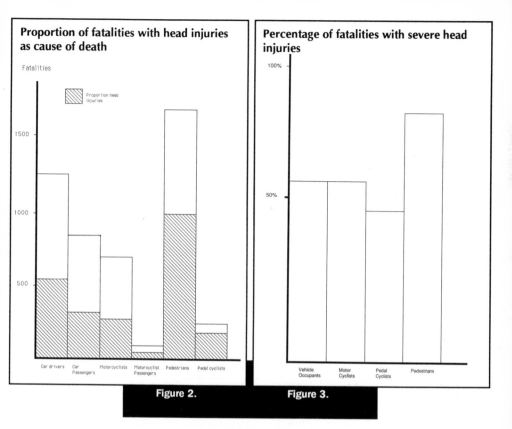

Proportion of fatalities with head injuries as cause of death

Fatalities

Proportion head injuries

1500

1000

500

Car drivers | Car Passengers | Motorcyclists | Motorcyclist Passengers | Pedestrians | Pedal cyclists

Figure 2.

Percentage of fatalities with severe head injuries

100%

50%

Vehicle Occupants | Motor Cyclists | Pedal Cyclists | Pedestrians

Figure 3.

fit its preconceptions.[17] In this case, small-scale studies based on hospital admissions, which were available to the road safety lobby during the time of setting up a British Standard on bicycle helmets and otherwise promoting their use, actually indicate a smaller proportion of fatalities than in all other road user groups with head injury as cause of death, such as 46 per cent or 44 per cent[18] (lower than for all other road user groups), with cyclists also showing the smallest proportion of those admitted who had serious head injuries[19] — see Figures 3 and 4.

The rule of the diminishing figure

The experience of the introduction of safety aids, with the typical case being seat belts, indicates that the presentation of evidence follows a pattern. Initially, claims are made for the aid of an extreme and exaggerated nature. This allows the reduced claims of the official road safety lobby, which tend to follow afterwards, to appear rational and sensible. The new claims are preceded by cautious statements suggesting that not all of the particular problem in hand will be solved by the use of the aid, but that since a lot of it will be, only a callous extremist would oppose its (preferably mandatory) use.

The third stage in the process occurs as even these more moderate claims are seen to be ambitious. The "only one life" defence may be used: if even one life is saved, this is justification enough. No relevance is accorded the fact that other lives have been forfeited by a process which has diverted attention from other measures, entrenched a victim-blaming approach and reduced the long-term prospects for a rational and fair safety policy.

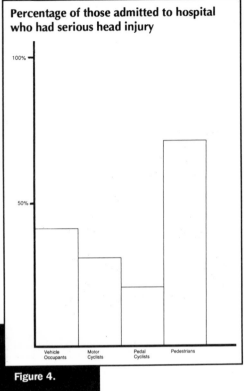

The final part of this process is when all the relevant evidence is gathered (generally some time after legislation to compel the use of the aid has been enacted) and it shows no discernible benefit. By this time, however, the adverse effects of adopting the aid, including long- and short-term risk compensation, have been working their way through for some time.

With bicycle crash helmets the process has been as follows:

Figure 4.

(i) Stage One

Here the claims made for bicycle helmets go up to the 90 per cent fatality reduction level. One example is the claim made by an Australian helmets advocate, who argues that no reduction in danger from motorists should be seriously considered as a possibility.[20] With unintentionally cruel irony,[21] he cites, as an example of the superiority of Australian as compared to British approaches to road safety, the earlier introduction of seat belt legislation. A better-known case of this kind of claim is the projected "90 per cent drop in injuries and death" claimed on the influential *That's Life* television programme. An analysis of this claim reveals it as a "piece of over-ambitious guesswork tacked onto an Australian accident survey which didn't involve a single fatality".[22]

(ii) Stage Two

While not necessarily responding to accusations of exaggeration, some studies are less ambitious. The first major attempt in Britain to put a figure on potential savings gave a modest "10 per cent reduction in fatalities and seriously injured casualties".[23] A study of minor head injuries claims some 50 per cent reduction potential.[24]

A summary of four major studies made by one of the foremost helmet advocates goes for a more easily defensible approach, allowing itself a broad range of reduction, from 40 to 90 per cent.[25]

The problem with the evidence marshalled by helmet advocates is that it tends to be post-accident analysis, using controls of non-helmeted against helmeted cyclists,[26] or self-report studies — one of which actually indicates *increased* accident involvement of helmet-wearers.[27]

Very little work looks at what happens over time when helmets are worn by people who did not previously wear them. In other words, there is no attempt to consider risk compensation, whether in the short or long term, by cyclists or changes in other road users' behaviour. One exception is Wood and Milne's study in Victoria.[28] However, it does not use mass accident data, and a decline in head injuries with increased helmet-wearing over the limited population of cyclists studied coincides with an increase in non-head injuries. Is risk compensation occurring, with a decline in some injuries as others increase, due to an increased likelihood of being in an accident? If so, are the non-head injuries less serious than the ones they replace? We are unlikely to find out, as the relative severity of the injuries is not assessed, and there is no cycle traffic index. We do not know about other factors which may be involved in generating bicycle accidents — such as what changes have been occurring in driver behaviour — nor about long-term trends in cycle accidents, all of which makes it difficult or impossible to assess the impact of helmet-wearing.

(iii) Stage Three

When there is examination of change over time the reduction figure not only diminishes nor even disappears — *it can become negative*. Looking at the USA, the main country where bicycle helmet use has increased over the period 1973-87, we find that:

> there is no statistical evidence that the growth in the use of hard shell helmets has reduced head injuries or deaths. In fact... *bicycle-related fatalities are positively and significantly associated with increased helmet use* (my emphasis).[29]

The author, Rodgers, himself a helmet-wearing cyclist, is surprised by the results of this study, and is forced to accept the likelihood of risk compensation by helmet-wearers. There is occasionally some acknowledgement of the possibility of risk compensation from helmet advocates in North America:

> [H]elmet campaigns locally and nationally have unintentionally created a new dangerous, monster attitude of 'If-I-wear-a-helmet, I-need-not-worry-about-my-safety-anymore.'[30]

(iv) Stage Four

The first large legislature to compel adult cyclists to wear helmets was the State of Victoria, on 1 July 1990. A draft report on the effects of the first six months of the law was produced by official road safety lobby academics in September 1991, [31] with a full analysis not due to be formally published for another year.[32] By this time the pressure to mandate helmet-wearing, particularly in the US, will have strengthened.

There is, on first glance, a success story here for the helmet lobby. Compared to the corresponding period the year before, the number of cyclists with head injuries fell by 46 per cent. However, the number of cyclists with other injuries fell by 35 per cent.[33] As the report states:

This is tentative evidence that the number of cyclists involved in collisions, either due to a reduction in bicycle use or a reduction in risk, has decreased during the post-law period.[34]

The report looks at the proportion of killed and hospital admitted cyclists who sustained a head injury over time. This proportion was no different from what would have been expected in the absence of a law.[35]

An earlier survey showed a 60 per cent decline in cycling in Victoria between March 1990 and just after compulsion was introduced three months later.[36] The author suggests the decline may be due to the usual reduction of cycling in winter months, which is on average 27 per cent in Australia, and might be higher in a colder state. However, the decline in cycling is likely to be primarily due to compulsion: the second survey was taken in fine weather, and the decline among those cyclists who were already helmeted was only 17 per cent. Other evidence that the decline was not simply seasonal is a 30 per cent reduction in the numbers attending a large local annual (allowing year-to-year comparison) cycling rally. Other reports support this hypothesis.[37] One more report was written on the basis of surveys carried out in the Melbourne area, this time comparing counts of cyclists in March 1990 and March 1991, thus correcting for the seasonal factor. It found a 41 per cent decline in recreational cyclists and a 37 per cent decline in adult commuter cyclists.[38]

The importance of assessing whether this effect occurred is twofold. Firstly, any reduction in cycling due to a law reduces the power of a cycling lobby and efforts to reduce danger to cyclists in the long term. Secondly, in the absence of good cycle traffic indices, we need to know if the decline observed, compared with three months before compulsion, was not purely a seasonal effect, not righting itself towards the end of the six month official study, if we wish to assess the chances of cyclists being hurt in the conventional sense. If the decline in cycling compared with the year before was of the order of 30-45 per cent, which is how it appears, then *there was no significant reduction, or even an increase, in the chances of cyclists, half of whom had now become helmet-wearers, sustaining injuries due to the law.*

There are problems in making definitive statements with the inevitable absence of really good statistics. Nevertheless, we can use one other piece of information to be certain that the law definitely failed in its officially claimed objective of reducing the chances of cyclists sustaining injuries of any type.

According to the authors of the draft report, the total number of road traffic injuries in Victoria in 1990 was about 20 per cent below the 1989 level, probably reflecting an often observed correlation between accidents and economic activity. (Actually, according to the official statistics which the writers of the report should have had access to, the reduction was notably greater, with recorded deaths and killed and seriously injured down by 29.4 per cent and 24.7 per cent respectively.)[39] No more than two points of this decline could be accounted for by what happened to the cyclists.[40] This decline indicates a reduction in danger from careless driving, which (until cyclists' compensation sets in some time later) would result in a *significantly lower chance of cyclists being hurt irrespective of helmet-wearing.*

But it appears that no such reduction occurred. Whether because of changes in the behaviour of cyclists or motorists, or both, *the chances of suffering injuries — including head injuries — seem to have actually increased as a result of the law.*

The creation, use and abuse of evidence

Evidence of the above kind tends not to be publicised. The Rodgers study is not discussed, despite full awareness of its existence, in the 400 entries in the largest bibliography about bicycle helmets,[41] published by the Bicycle Helmet Safety Institute, a body with an "active helmet advocacy programme".[42] It is not mentioned by sections of the road safety establishment, including the Department of Transport or the highway authorities with responsibility for creating or supervising a dangerous environment for cyclists in the first place. It is not mentioned by those in the road safety lobby who have pushed for a variety of safety aids, education, engineering or legal changes that have either had minimal effect or have made things worse for the vulnerable.

It is not mentioned by helmet retailers. For, while cycle traders are concerned about the loss of custom arising from an enforced helmet law, as the editor of the retailers' magazine, *Cycle Trader*, put it: "[J]ust consider the market: an accessory that is a genuine safety aid, that isn't particularly cheap and that millions of people *have* to buy."[43]

It is not mentioned by researchers whose work tends to ignore the determining context of bicycle crashes, and certainly ignores the effect of wearing helmets on cyclist and other road user behaviour. Instead we have, as with seat belts, studies of post-accident casualties and ergonomic studies of the impact resistance of crash-helmets. Research may involve "experiments to determine the mechanical impedance of the human head using accelerometers and pressure transducers in cadavers and monkeys".[44] But, as with seat belts, the real issue is what happens when the devices promoted by such "research" are perceived as a solution, and are then used and adapted to by real people in real societies, over a prolonged period.

It is not mentioned because the evidence is difficult to obtain. Even the American study by Rodgers does not have the kind of fully disaggregated data, let alone a good traffic index and material on the changes in danger in the environment, which one would want. This problem existed with seat belts, but with cycle-helmets far less is known about the effect of the device in crashes, or about the population being considered and the circumstances of accidents. More important, the population considered is far smaller, hampering statistical analysis. Besides,

177

full knowledge of the effects of helmets could be obtained only if there were sudden changes in wearing rates (such as could come only with legislation) among countries with very large cycling populations. By that time, it is too late to discuss the desirability of such legislation, and serious analysis would, as the seat belt experience indicates, not be carried out or be distorted, or even be concealed.

It is not mentioned because researchers generally have a commitment to promoting the use of the device which they study. Whether they be members of the road safety establishment or manufacturers, when they come together in places such as the committees of the British Standards Institution, their purpose is to encourage or compel the wearing of helmets, and they trade "research" figures reinforcing each other's prejudices. Sometimes a single individual plays several roles. Readers of the December 1988 issue of *Climber and Hill Walker* could read a recommendation that not only mountain climbers, but humble hill walkers should wear crash helmets.[45] The report was written by a university lecturer in fibre science who is a member of the BSI Helmet Standard Committee and who "after many years of helmet research" is now a manufacturer of mountaineering helmets for a number of British companies.

It is not mentioned by cycling organisations in North America because helmet use is seen as a symbol of respectability for those allowed into a road system where the domination of the car is accepted without question. Any suggestion that the origins and context of bicycle crashes should be seen in terms of a particular situation, and that less time should be spent on advocating helmet use, is considered "curious" or otherwise belittled.[46]

It is not mentioned by helmet-wearers who are unwilling to accept that they have advocated something which might make them more careless. Sometimes, however, this basic human characteristic is frankly acknowledged. The main British magazine for mountain bikers carries a feature on helmets entitled: "The Headbangers Survival Kit"[47] which "looks at the kit... to save us from ourselves..." [because] "We're going faster, we're going crazier, we're going out on the edge." It continues:

As a wise old biker... once said 'man who does not fall from mountain bike needs to try harder'.

This recommendation of assistance for higher risk-taking is extended to the advocacy of body armour:

Wearing the whole kit would undoubtedly slow you down but you would probably gain immensely in confidence and 'go places man has never been'.

The politics of helmet advocacy and use

The advocacy of helmet use depends not on the evidence produced, but on the beliefs of the road safety lobby, which in turn reflect background assumptions supporting the hegemony of the car. An element of this ideology, particularly evident in medical and engineering thinking, is the absence of helmet-wearing as a "cause" of injury or death.

An example of this is the case of the US sports car race driver Pete Snell, who was killed in a crash when racing in 1956. It is possible to argue that the "cause" of his death was the high-level risk-taking of men, particularly young men in most cultures. It could further be suggested that racing driving, and/or the behaviour of the driver who had driven into him from behind, is a particularly extreme example of this. It might further be argued that attempts to make these practices safer are inappropriate and self-defeating. Yet for his friends, the "cause" that mattered was the "failure of his crash helmet", and his death triggered the foundation of the Snell Memorial Institute which specialises in laboratory testing of helmets. Testing for standards for bicycle helmets is carried out at Snell by people who otherwise are involved in the design and advocacy of roll-bars and seat belts,[48] with all the implications this has for driver behaviour and its potential victims outside cars.

Along with the road safety lobby, the North American, Australian and New Zealand cycling organisations have promoted helmet-wear. It functions as an important symbol: the sign of the serious cyclist who buys their way into a car-dominated arena where tolerance will properly follow only if the emblem is displayed.[49] The use of safety aids or "tests" of one kind or another is not new in inspiring (false) confidence in road users. They will all continue along their uniquely human way in the road environment, assured that all is well (non-car-users tending to have less confidence in their rights than motorists). And, as they progress, the main difference between them is that the motor vehicle users kill others, while the vulnerable (more or less)[50] do not, and are more prone to being killed.

However, the emblem has (so far) not been so readily adopted by cyclists in the European heartland of cycling.[51] There is scepticism about the scale of benefits claimed, and concern about the diversion away from the origin of accident. The discomfort from a chin strap under tension and wearing any head gear when exercising in the heat (the difference in ventilation and discomfort between cycling and motorcycling helmets often not being appreciated), the inequality of singling out cyclists, and risk compensation are also cited by European organisations. While not opposing their use, they come out against mandatory use of helmets and are critical of the emphasis on recommendation.[52]

Whether these views will be able to stand in the way of the dominant ideology and resist the pressure of a road safety lobby which looks set on mandatory wear, is a matter for conjecture.

The danger from Victoria

There is a fascinating and tragic irony about the State of Victoria in this story. It was involved at the beginning of both research and mandatory use of that other safety aid, the seat belt,[53] which appears to have played such a negative role in the fortunes of cyclists. The story, right down to the same authors of the "road safety" reports, is running again. With the same unshakable (and uncontested) belief, helmet use has been introduced as the latest in a line of "road safety" initiatives.

179

Looked at in terms of the road safety lobby's own criteria, these initiatives have been remarkably unsuccessful. Measured in terms of recorded deaths or serious injuries per head of the population, its record is significantly and persistently worse than Britain's:

Deaths and serious injuries per head of the population: percentage higher in Victoria than Britain, 1983 -1990. [54]

	1983	1984	1985	1986	1987	1988	1989	1990
Deaths	+40	+37	+43	+39	+45	+44	+46	+25
Serious Injuries	+35	+34	+38	+41	+51	+53	+48	+33

Table 4.

Looking at fatalities per distance travelled for the most recent year available (1985), the rate is again consistently and markedly higher in Victoria than for Britain by the following approximate percentages: car occupants +20; motor cyclists +180; pedestrians +160. The 1985 rate is similar for cyclists in Victoria and in Britain, but some 50 per cent higher than for the 1990 figure in Britain. [55]

The impression continually given from the United States and Australian road safety lobbies is of alert and self-disciplined attempts to attack problems which just happen to have afflicted them worse than the "lazy or stupid Europeans". It is never suggested that those problems arise closer to home: not just *despite* the use of safety aids, but *because* of them, or at least because of a culture which attempts to pick up the pieces after events whose origins are not faced up to. A culture, indeed, of what we now know of as "road safety".

Conclusion

Of course, this book argues that casualty records cannot be the sole judge of success: they very often tell the opposite story to one of danger reduction, which I advocate. The purpose of showing the conflict between the facts and the claims of the road safety lobby is to reveal the lobby's ideological and unscientific bias. The continuation of cyclist casualties at this level also highlights that danger on the road is not being properly tackled.

If mountain bikers or other cyclists wish to "take it to the edge", eased on their way with extra armour on their heads or elsewhere, there may be no objection: the fact that the chances of getting hurt will stay the same or increase is a decision for the cyclist, providing no innocent bystanders are affected. In this kind of society, where individualist approaches become solutions at the inevitable expense of social transformation, it may simply be a desperate attempt to ameliorate a problem, however futile the chances of success.

The facts are, however, that in the real world of the road environment, the long-term effect of helmet advocacy and use may be to maintain or increase the level of motor danger.

This could occur because of changes in motorist behaviour or attitudes, or because of government policy being diverted away from real danger reduction. It could furthermore be brought about by a reduction in cycling following compulsion and weakening of the bicycle lobby, or by shifts in any of the subtle processes which constitute a society's culture and ideology. The point is that it is precisely these subtle, intangible, uncountable features which determine how road users end up on the receiving end of danger.

There is the familiar argument that helmet use is just something else to be added on to other more important measures which can be advocated as well. For example, the RoSPA Bicycle Officer in 1988 argued that:

> We would... leave ourselves open to accusations of irresponsibility if we tried to promote helmet usage as anything other than a very small part of a wide-ranging traffic education program. [56]

But, even if meant honestly, this does not mean that the helmet advocacy effort has had no ill-effects and that such other efforts will be any other than attempts to get back to the *status quo*. As with seat belts, the use of "secondary" methods or "safety aids" has arisen precisely because of failure to deal properly with the motor

danger: if it had been tackled properly in the first place there would have been little or no need to try such measures. The negative effects of a measure are as factual and real — and as negative — as the facts of particular kinds of injury taken in isolation. They erode the efficacy of any real attempts to control motor danger. And the fact that helmet encouragement is not just "a very small part" of what is happening indicates that those real attempts are not being made anyway.

At the end of the day decisions about safety are decisions about who should be doing what in the road environment. They are made on the basis of power and ideology. It is not so much that the road safety lobby's campaign in this area is hypocritical, inconsistent, or likely to fail according to its own criteria. It is that, like preventing street assaults on women by imprisoning them at home (or making them wear chastity belts)[57], it backs up the victim-blaming ideology which allows the problem to exist in the first place. It is not irrational — from the point of view of those whose power goes unquestioned — but it is just not the right approach.

Postscript

Shortly before publication of this book, a further analysis of the Victorian experience of compulsion was given by the road safety lobby. The new material includes a statistical analysis (a regression method using a linear regression model) of the proportion of injuries that were head injuries (PIHI) thus evading the problems of having no proper cycle traffic index and no clear picture of the changes in danger to cyclists, as the way of understanding the effects of compulsion. Despite claiming benefits, the material presents no real evidence for the benefits of helmet wear.

The regression model is first used to calculate the head injuries that should have resulted following the passage of the law. Looking at Transport Accident Commission (TAC is the sole insurer in Victoria) claims in Victoria as a whole, in Melbourne, and at hospital admissions in Victoria, the results confound the authors' expectations. No significant benefits are demonstrated.

The model is then used again to calculate the PIHI expected had the law not been passed. The TAC claims for Victoria and Melbourne fall outside the statisticians 95 per cent confidence limit (an indication of statistical significance). The only demonstrably significant change is in the case of hospital admissions. But 75 per cent of these involve accidents where no motor vehicle was involved: these are cases which do not refer to the principal problem facing adult cyclists, and all cyclists travelling on public roads. Focusing on cases such as these — typically child cyclists playing off-road — continues to play an important role in diverting attention away from motor danger.

But even if changes in PIHI could have been demonstrated, we have two other problems. Firstly, we are told that "the number of persons killed and admitted to hospital resulting from all road trauma" was 12 per cent below that of the previous year. Secondly, we have the figures for Melbourne of a 44 per cent decline for the 12 - 17 age group, and 36 per cent for all children, combined with the other figures quoted above to indicate the decline in cycling.

Making a calculation based on the report's graph for TAC claims throughout Victoria, we see an increase in non-head injury rates. Combined with their own calculations on the proportion of injuries which were head injuries, by the official criteria of casualty rates, things have become worse.

The report does not even consider the possibility of this. Compensatory behaviour by helmeted cyclists or changes in behaviour by motorists towards cyclists are not considered. The claims, which this book shows to be unfounded, of conspicuity aid and greater responsibility from newly helmeted cyclists, are made again. The fact that this should have made benefits dramatic, rather than minimal at best, or non-existent, or negative, is not mentioned. Any suggestion that things may not have worked out properly is "explained" by cyclists not strapping their helmets on (without any supporting evidence presented) or by the standard for cycle helmets with adequate ventilation being inadequate.

But road safety lobby's statisticians are too deeply compromised now to be able to consider the basics of human behaviour. The law, passed without the rudiments of proper research being available, has also resulted in a dramatic fall in cycling to the massive detriment of public health in both Victoria and now New South Wales. This should be seen as just the latest episode of dangerous and anti-social behaviour perpetrated in the name of "road safety".

12.

Drink-driving as a road safety problem

DRINK-DRIVING accounts for at least 18 per cent of deaths on the roads. To all intents and purposes the campaign against drink-drivers appears to be a genuine case of danger being tackled at source.

But in so far as breath-testing has been successful, it could go further. Health and Safety inspectors have the right to make random visits to premises: random breath-testing and stiffer penalties could be introduced to remove the "sporting chance" currently afforded those who drink and drive.

❖❖❖

Other things being equal, being drunk reduces the chances of a driver being careful. Alcohol is a powerful depressant which can have detrimental effects on reaction time, vigilance, information processing and visual and psychomotor skills, [1] as well as generally relaxing feelings of responsibility and loosening inhibitions. Motorists have accordingly been made aware of their tendency to become more dangerous under the influence of alcohol for some 60 years. Nevertheless, millions of journeys annually continue to be made by motorists who are over the legally defined blood alcohol limit.

The history of defining drinking and driving as a problem is important in three ways. First, drink-driving persists despite being seen as probably *the* road safety problem. The recourse to educational methods alone to dissuade people from drinking and driving, despite the evidence that this is ineffective, indicates the tenacity of the defenders of motorists' privilege in avoiding steps to reduce danger on the roads. [2] Second, the experience of attempts leading motorists to feel that they are likely to be caught if they drink and drive, and will suffer a loss of driving licence as a consequence, is dramatic. The initial effect of the 1967 Road Safety Act is probably the one single case of road safety legislation in Britain having a significant and unambiguous effect on reducing danger, albeit for a short time; the same applies to similar legislation in other countries. Third, while any attempt to reduce danger on the road must involve measures to control drink-driving, there are problems with the way drinking and driving has assumed the high profile of becoming *the* most notorious road safety problem. While not a smoke screen in the same way that other "road safety" initiatives are, by making drink-driving part of a general "alcohol problem" the basic dangers of the current transport *status quo* are obscured.

A brief history

The history of identifying drink-driving as a road safety problem (although, with doctors playing a crucial part in the defining process, it has also been defined as a public health problem) is similar to that of other road safety problems. The common-sense idea that alcohol consumption would tend to impede driving ability was stated and used in publicity campaigns some 60 years ago in this country. The first legislation against drinking and driving was in the State of New York in 1910. Legislation moved from talking vaguely about drunkenness, to the act of driving while under the influence of, or impaired by, alcohol; with instruments available to measure alcohol in the body, from 1936 (in Norway) laws have specified levels where this is judged to occur.

Experimental work on the effect of alcohol in laboratory conditions was backed up by the 1965 Grand Rapids study[3] to show that the difference in rates of involvement in accidents between drinking and non-drinking drivers could be explained specifically by the alcohol factor, as opposed to any other. This work, and commentary on it,[4] quantified risks for drivers with different levels of blood alcohol,[5] and assessed the average risk increase as occurring sharply at the 80 mg per cent level to twice the level at 0-10 mg per cent, although it occurred at 100 mg per cent for more experienced drinking-drivers and at about 50 mg per cent for those less experienced in either drinking or driving.

This research and other material[6] was used by the road safety lobby to inform the campaigns leading up to the Road Safety Act 1967, which provided for the breath testing ("breathalysing") of those in charge of motor vehicles whom police officers believed to have excess alcohol in their blood. The effect of the introduction of breathalysing was dramatic. While there should always be caution over road accident casualty figures, the clear indication is that there was a reduction in fatalities of some 15 per cent, and in casualties by 11 per cent, during the following year, with some 5,000 fewer deaths and 200,000 fewer injuries in the seven years following the Act.[7]

The difference between this and the ineffectiveness of other road safety regulations or initiatives of all kinds cannot be over-emphasised. The only other discernible changes on graphs of accident casualties that can be as easily spotted are those after the 1973 oil crisis, or after specific changes such as the changing of the rule of the road in Sweden, which were temporary and not in response to road safety measures. (The effects of seat belt legislation are both exaggerated and discriminatory, and those of the 1935 regulations introducing "the test" are similarly exaggerated or perhaps non-existent.[8])

Change occurred in 1967-68 because motorists tended to be less likely to drink and drive. Another cause for the decrease in accident casualties — one less favoured by the road safety establishment, but likely to have augmented the main cause — was that motorists near the legal alcohol limit took great pains to avoid the kind of behaviour which they felt might attract police attention. Either way, danger to other road users was reduced because motorists were deterred from some potentially dangerous behaviour by the prospect of temporary loss of licence.

As with any other changes which (partly) threatened to reduce motorists' freedom to be dangerous, and many that were pseudo-threats, the motoring organisations bitterly opposed the introduction of the breathalyser. They succeeded in weakening its chances of long-term effectiveness by pressure which resulted in the omission of random testing.

After 1967

The success of the breathalyser was short lived because after a while it became apparent to motorists that their chances of being caught for drinking and driving were negligible. By not allowing police more opportunity for their testing procedures, drinking and driving became a sort of game where the motorist had to be given a sporting chance. This omission — part of the continuation of a series of legal loopholes used to protect drunk drivers since before the war [9] — was the principal immediate cause of the legislation failing to fulfil its initial promise. It was highlighted in the Blennerhasset Report which had been commissioned to explain this failure. Rather than the lack of harsher sentences, including prison, for offenders, [10] it has been accepted that lack of police power to use the breathalyser is the most likely reason for drink-driving legislation to fail. In so far as any reduction in drink-driving results from a legislative move, the perception of the chance of being caught appears paramount. [11]

Educational campaigns had failed for the usual reasons, combined with the decreased chance of drunken drivers responsibly considering the message of campaigns unless they are backed up with a realistic possibility of being caught. By 1990, opinion polls showed consistent support among a clear majority of the public, including drivers, for the principle of random breath tests. [12]

The position now

At present some 20 per cent of motorists and motorcyclists who die in crashes have blood alcohol content (BAC) above the legal limit. [13] Looking at casualties where at least one driver was over the legal limit when breath tested, or tested for BAC following death, indicates that some 18 per cent of those killed on the roads are killed in drink-driving related crashes. However, this is an underestimate, which misses out factors such as hit-and-run (failing to stop) crashes where there is no chance to carry out a breath test. [14] From slightly earlier data we learn that some 10 per cent of all casualties from road crashes involve a drinking driver. [15]

Surveys asking motorists about their experience indicate that more than 20 per cent of men and 7 per cent of women claim to drink over the legal limit and drive, at least once a year. [16] About 5 per cent of men and 1 per cent of women drivers claim to do so more than three or four times a year. [17]

While some campaigners argue for lowering the legal BAC limit to 50 mg per cent for certain driver categories, there is a degree of unanimity among lobbyists that such measures, and others like imprisonment for drunk drivers, zero limits or education campaigns, will be red herrings unless accompanied by a genuine attempt at law enforcement. Everything points to a need to change the perceived chances of being caught by making them real. A review of international experience points to "blitzes" and other well-publicised attempts to detect drink-driving as the only initiative, producing noticeable results, both nationally and locally, albeit temporarily.[18] A programme of random breath testing (RBT) at roadside check-points, following the examples of New South Wales, Victoria, Sweden, Finland and elsewhere, is now on the agenda in Britain.

Has a reduction in drink-driving occurred?

There has been a decline in some indices, such as the proportion of dead drivers over the legal limit, which has lead to some opposition to random breath testing. This is a classic example of how reference to "our record", whether over time, or in comparison to other countries is used to downplay danger. But, the argument that claims a big increase in the proportion of motorists who are voluntarily refusing to drink and drive anyway, has other problems as well. Firstly, the decrease in dead over-the-limit drivers from one in three to one in five over the years 1978-1988 has to be seen in the context of a 41 per cent increase in motor traffic.[19] The amount of mileage by motorists under the influence of alcohol may have remained stable. Secondly, a decline in total numbers of dead or injured drunken drivers will, given the greater protection given to them over that time by seat belt use and changes in vehicle construction, involve less likelihood of them dying compared to the level of danger they pose to others — which will have declined less.

Thirdly, any actual decline in drink-driving may have occurred because *there has already been an increased perception of the risk of being caught*. Roadside breath tests in Britain increased from 142,000 in 1978 to 597,000 in 1990.[20] The police claim that from 1986 to 1991 the chances of being breathalysed have doubled.[21] And of course, the introduction of evidential breath testing in 1983 led more motorists to feel they would not be able to get away with drink-driving.[22] Fourthly, any supposed improvements are trivial compared to the impact of the introduction of the breathalyser.[23]

With public support and apparently good results behind it, the introduction of random breath test is on the cards. Could this be one case where the road safety lobby does not take the easy way out? Could it be that at least some of "the motor danger" is actually now to be tackled properly at source?

Some problems with random breath testing

The first problem is actually getting RBT introduced. Government has not yet positively responded to the campaigners, and RoSPA at present has not even supported the campaign. If, then, it is introduced, would it consist of sufficient visible chances to stop a large proportion of drinking drivers? If the number of checks that would be carried out are similar to those in Victoria, the average motorist would only be stopped by one once every three years. [24]

The evidence of the benefits of RBT are also not as conclusive as might be hoped. In Finland, where RBT was introduced in 1977, numbers of drunken drivers killed did not decrease until two years afterwards — and actually increased during the first two years. The proportion of all drivers killed who were over the legal limit does not appear, from a series going back before 1977 until 1986, to show a clear beneficial effect due to the introduction of RBT. [25] Similarly, a study of the experience in Victoria suggests that there is no obvious beneficial effect visible from time-series analysis. [26]

If RBT is not the panacea it is made out to be, there could be a reason other than inadequate implementation. This third problem is really the distinguishing feature of all road safety initiatives: migration, risk compensation and smoke screening. If there is a persistent tendency to endanger others through the use or abuse of the most potentially dangerous form of transport available to ordinary people, then trying to deal with one element of it alone will generally result in shifting danger elsewhere. This is relevant here in two respects: immediate driver response and longer-term ideological change.

Immediate driver response

Drivers do not just happily accept measures which are introduced to stop them doing things they were doing beforehand. Where there are well-publicised local crack-downs on drink-driving, offenders may choose to drive through neighbouring areas instead. Indeed, stories of drunk drivers taking alternative routes through adjacent areas have been used to show the positive effect of the harsher action taken; as in the case of magistrates in Grays, Essex, threatening offenders with a night in the cells. [27] A reason suggested for the poor results of RBT in Victoria is that a switch is made from alcohol to hedonistic drugs (such as cannabis), particularly by young drivers who seem likely to oppose authority anyway; all that has been achieved is to change the form of illegal behaviour without beneficial effects. [28]

Numerous variations on this theme could be hypothesised as likely behaviour changes, following the introduction of widespread RBT, by people who still wish to engage in high risk-taking, or by those who simply wish to use cars on their way for a drink. In the latter case the driving can be handed over to a family member whose licence is regarded as less important; even if the chances of apprehension were raised several times, given the small chances that exist at present, [29] increased chances of apprehension brought about by RBT could be a mere hiccup in the career of at least some of those wanting to drink and drive.

Long-term ideological change

Here we are dealing more particularly with smoke screening. The loss of what is, in effect, the right to drink and drive could be seen as a sacrifice made by benevolent motorists in much the same way as "the test" or other minimal or pseudo-restrictions are. Bearing in mind that drink-driving is attributable as a cause for only a minority of crashes, any advantages — in the event of RBT being effective — would be reduced by such feelings. As with other areas of restriction, genuine attempts to control antisocial behaviour will always produce a backlash unless the underlying problem is properly addressed.

Part of this longer-term diversionary effect might occur because of the way drink-driving is seen as an alcohol, rather than a motoring, problem.

Drink-driving as an alcohol problem

The basic tendency to avoid the underlying issue of the dangers posed by motor vehicle users to others is made worse by the involvement of the alcohol abuse lobby. One of the leading campaigners in Britain describes drinking and driving as "Simply another form of alcohol damage".[30] It slots into publications by health professionals alongside chapters on teenage drinking and alcohol and work.[31] Understanding the nature of alcohol use is obviously relevant for the study of a particular kind of abuse of motor vehicles, and there is nothing wrong with saying that certain problems should be defined as alcohol abuse. But there are enough problems with the medical establishment's view of road safety without the alcohol element of drink-driving being stressed.[32]

The dangers of looking at the issue as an alcohol problem rather than a driving problem are made worse by defining a specific problem group within the new problem area: the "problem drinker", alcohol-dependent person or alcoholic.

When the principal problems are those of the freedoms which the normal driver is allowed, picking on any sub-group and defining it as deviant, however much more it poses a threat, is dangerously misleading. With the "problem drinker", not just one activity but a *kind of person* is identified, with professionals vying for support in their struggle to deal with them.[33] The special problems of heavy drinkers[34] can detract from the wider questions of alcohol abuse, let alone the question of drinking and driving, and let alone the wider basic problem.

The effect of alcohol after crashes

A difficulty for those concerned mainly about the dangers that motorists pose to others, is that innocent victims are only part of the casualty toll attributed to drink-driving. Comparing the proportions in results of roadside screening, and the indications of coroners' records of dead drivers respectively, we find that 3.3 per cent and 28 per cent were over the legal limit, and 1.5 per cent and 20 per cent were more than twice over the legal limit. Discussing this, a leading medical expert on drink-driving comments: "The nearly 10-fold difference in the proportions with high BACs is intriguing... Apart from the greater risk of involvement in an accident, could those with high BACs be at greater risk of dying in an accident

189

because their injuries are more severe, because of the acute effects of alcohol, and/
or the chronic effects of alcohol?"[35] Part of the reason for this high factor could be
that drunk, particularly very drunk, drivers may go especially fast and have crashes
with more severe consequences. *But, part of it may simply be that alcohol or its
effects restricts recovery from trauma.*[36]

This question of survivability — how alcohol affects the chances of surviving
crashes — has only recently been studied, and constitutes a very small part of the
vast amount of literature on drink-driving. Whether because of a greater risk of
immediate death due to increased vulnerability to shock,[37] or other reasons, a reduction in deaths from a decline in drink-driving could involve, by comparison, a
significantly smaller decline in danger to others.

Drugs and driving

The legislation dealing with drink-driving dates back to the Road Traffic Act 1930
which made it an offence to drive while unfit through drink or drugs. The only
comment on this from Britain's most experienced anti-drink-driving campaigner,
John Havard, then Secretary of the British Medical Association, is that alcohol is
a drug.[38] This is undisputable, but neglects the millions of prescriptions for drugs
with the ability to impede motoring performance given by his members to
motorists over the years, with virtually no mention of this issue in the road safety
literature. Various types of medication are prescribed which affect the central
nervous system: tranquillisers (such as the benzodiazepines), analgesics, hypnotics,
antidepressants, hypotensives (for high blood pressure), antihistamines (for hay-
fever), and others. They could all affect the ability to drive properly. In one of the
rare references[39] given to the subject in official literature, the estimate of the
number of motorists taking prescribed medication which can adversely affect
driving exceeds 1 million.[40] This excludes any estimate of the numbers under the
influence of proprietary medications bought over the chemist's counter, such as
travel sickness pills, cough mixtures and cold cures. As one of the few reviews of
the subject notes: "[A]lthough... driving under the influence of drugs, including
medicines, which adversely affect driving performance, has been covered by
legislation in many countries for over 50 years, the number of drivers actually
prosecuted is very, very small, indeed so small that there are virtually no statistics
available."[41]

Control of this problem is basically restricted to recommending that doctors
warn their patients of the adverse consequences of taking the medication and
driving. Given the record of patients failing to heed their doctor's advice, even
when there is no disincentive to do so, this must rank as being an even more
ineffective road safety measure than publicity campaigns. It is further hampered by
the lack of study of the effects of different drugs, in marked contrast to the reams
of work on drink-driving.

If proportions indicated by recent work in Europe were similar for Britain, it would mean that some three-quarters of a million motorists were taking tranquillisers, with between 50,000 and 100,000 taking prescribed psychotropic (mood-altering) drugs.[42] A more recent assessment by a leading British expert in bezodiazepine use is even more alarming, suggesting that 10-15 per cent of the adult population take this type of drug, with one-quarter to one-half a million of them dependent on them.[43]

It is far more difficult to properly study the effects of drugs than the effects of alcohol, which itself involves problems of different kinds of response to different concentrations. Insufficient data exists on the number of users, such factors as predisposition to accidents among types of drug taker, the interaction of different drugs with each other, environmental features, and so on. We do not know, for example, the exact level of drug concentrations in the dead crash victims examined during a study in Switzerland in 1980, and found to have measurable levels of drugs — no less than 35 per cent had measurable concentrations.[44] Much of this was no doubt small doses of fairly benign drugs, and it would be a big mistake to create another devil — the drug taker — to take attention away from normal driver behaviour.

Although such studies could provide almost indefinite work for researchers looking for employment, they would come across the problem that studying this area, and recommending measures to restrict the taking of drugs by motorists, would bring into question (and possibly threaten) the power of doctors (Dr Havard's members), whereas concentrating solely on drink does not.

Although studies of this kind could provide researchers with an almost endless source of employment, they would risk finding themselves in conflict with the powerful medical establishment. Concentrating on researching — and restricting — alcohol avoids that kind of showdown.

Doctors do not like drunks. Alcohol can present patients with problems which doctors would like to see minimised. The law also refuses to see alcohol as an excuse for crimes committed by people under its influence. Unfortunately, whatever the desirability of seeing certain alcohol consumption patterns as a problem, alcohol is an easy scapegoat. In all the different, ambivalent attitudes to alcohol, one thing stands out: *we think that when we are drunk we are not our normal selves.* This commonly held attitude has an unfortunate corollary for those worried about the activities of people when they are sober. If we can put down much of our bad driving to times when we were *not our normal selves*, when we were under the influence of alcohol, then it is all too easy to forget just how bad our normal selves are. My view is that crashes are increasingly seen as something which *abnormal* people, or people in an *abnormal* state, cause. As with "the other driver", crashes become things which we, at least in our sober state, do not cause.

Prospects for the future

The prospect offered by RBT could be one of failure, or one which moves towards a real attempt to deal with the origins of danger on the road.

At present, failure is a more likely outcome. The chances of RBT being introduced are not certain. More importantly, it is unlikely that it will be brought in on a regular, intensive, or permanent level across the country. There is also the prospect of a shift to hedonistic drug taking, or other high-risk behaviour, occurring among drivers who would in the past have been drinking drivers. Even if this is minimal, and the intensity of RBT high, there are all sorts of migratory behaviours that could occur as risk-taking is taken out of one context only to re-appear in another. It could be a straight refusal of banned drivers to stop driving, as happens in some 20 per cent of cases now; [45] or an increased unwillingness to accept controls in other types of driving behaviour as part of a backlash; or a newly found self-righteousness among those who do not drink and drive which inhibits self- (or other) criticism about driving behaviour.

As risk compensation theory suggests, there would have to be a fundamental willingness for lower risk-taking, at least in the case of drink-driving, for the initiative to have a permanent effect. It would also require a basic level of social intolerance of the behaviour of the minority who would not conform, backed up by the commitment to prevent it. Will this happen?

Making the connections...

One constantly reads in the campaign literature that drinking and driving "is a 'freedom' which should be abandoned", and that "nobody has to drink and drive". [46] There is probably no need for the inverted commas round "freedom", because in terms of the severity of punishment and the chances of being caught, the freedom is all too real. More important is the wider question of what freedoms should be permitted: what should people "have" to do. The loss of personal convenience by making a journey by public transport rather than car may often, particularly for the keen drinker, be far less than that of giving up drinking before driving. And the reduction in danger to others is substantially greater.

People do not buy sports or "performance" cars because they *have* to get from A to B by car; nor do they *have* to drive at the speeds, or with the low level of care, they happen to choose. If they could drive more carefully, then they do not, strictly speaking, *have* to drive as they do. People state that they *have* to make journeys by car, but the perceived requirement is itself generated by the creation of a transport system with car use given pride of place. The history of transport has seen people placed in a position where car use is considered more and more a necessity. Reversing this would involve reducing people's ability to get away with stating that they *have* to travel by car at all.

If stronger drink-drive controls are to be applied, why should not similar controls exist on other aspects of driver behaviour? Campaigners have often called for the need for "server intervention" which places responsibility on those selling or serving alcohol to potential drivers. If this is to be advocated, it would be consistent for doctors to make a serious attempt to control drug taking and driving. Yet the idea of confiscating driving licences for a period over which a drug is prescribed (which could involve notifying the DVLC or re-introducing the need to carry a driving licence) is highly unlikely to be contemplated by doctors.

Campaigns against drink-driving have always been opposed by motorists accusing the campaigners of wanting to spread their net more widely. There is an understandable tendency on the part of campaigners to limit themselves to an extreme and obvious kind of dangerous behaviour by agreeing that sober driving should not be thought of as dangerous. Most people do not want to campaign against anything which might be considered a basic human right, namely the current levels of car use and typical driver behaviour.

Yet the nettle has to be grasped. It is simply not logical to assert that "anyone who drinks and drives is a potential menace",[47] unless it is recognised that an element of menace exists with many other behaviours in cars where alcohol is not a factor, and unless these behaviours are defined and dealt with.

...or a recipe for failure

The alternative to making these connections will be the production of a set of compensatory behaviours such as those outlined above. The best that could be hoped for would be a reduction of part of one limited kind of dangerous behaviour. Without extending the opposition to irresponsible behaviour into other areas, the possibilities of achieving results even just with drink-driving are few.

Defenders of motorists' privilege argue that RBT is an encroachment on civil liberties. The road safety lobby has countered that it is not radically different from existing police powers for checking, for example, on vehicle defects, or those for television licence surveillance, or on customs' random checks, and that opinion polls indicate that the public does not see RBT as a serious infringement of their civil liberties. The restriction on the safety of others is a more serious infringement anyway. For these reasons, bodies such as the National Council for Civil Liberties have accepted RBT as legitimate.[48] But this could go a lot further. Those in charge of motor vehicles could be seen in the same light as owners or managers of factory and work premises. Such people are in a position where they can adversely affect the health and safety of others in the workplace and of members of the general public; so we accept that health and safety at work legislation allows for random visits by inspectors.[49] Is the road safety lobby prepared to make this much of a connection?

Similarly, by using casualty reduction as an indicator of progress, the road safety lobby has made things difficult for itself. In any case a distorting and incorrect way of looking at safety on the road, this has also allowed opponents of anti-drink-drive measures to argue against them on the basis that "we already have a good record".

Then there is the hypocrisy of the road safety lobby over the introduction of the intoximeter (evidential breath testing machine), which, along with associated changes in the law, made it easier to secure convictions. As already shown, [50] the effects of this move, or at least a reduction in the incidence of drink-driving coinciding with it, appear to have reduced the incidence of drink-driving, but were covered up in order to make the benefits of seat belt legislation seem greater than they were. This kind of falsification — or the subsequent reversal of views — hardly serves a cause which depends on showing how intensifying law enforcement can have beneficial results. The Parliamentary Advisory Council on Transport Safety, which tried to minimise the possible benefits of anti-drink-drive legislation in 1986,[51] was by January 1989 arguing that a gradual long-term reduction of accidents resulting from drink-driving was due to a combination of factors — one of which was "the evidential machinery changes in the 1981 Transport Act".[52]

All of this is a recipe for failure, for which the road safety lobby appears prepared. Already the "solutions" posed consist of extensions of the "belt them up and let them loose" variety, such as simply altering the physical environment and accepting drunk-driving as a fact of life.[53] In this approach, anybody on two wheels or two legs ventures out at their own risk (as does anybody not inside a tank-like vehicle); this loss of freedom receives scant, if any, attention.

As part of the refusal to think of drink-driving as a driving problem, we have parts of the establishment pointing out the dangers of being a drunk pedestrian. Sometimes the drunken pedestrian is not portrayed as a problem on the same scale as that of the drunken driver, but this is not always the case.[54] The crucial difference between the potential danger to others of pedestrians and motorists — the dependence of the safety of one group on the other, consideration of which should precede any discussion of the responsibilities of the more vulnerable and less dangerous group — has already been remarked on.[55] One might also suggest that migration by drinkers to the benign modes is a sign of the success of anti-drink-driving measures. But one could go further. The danger of motorists has been accommodated by engineering measures which tolerate or even encourage more risk-taking.

Would the road safety lobby show the same sort of tolerance to forms of transport which have longer histories: would it accept that some people will walk when drunk and then try to protect *them* by slowing down and reducing the number of vehicles and otherwise shift the onus on to the powerful? I would not be particularly keen to meet more drunken pedestrians as I make my way about, (although accommodating the carelessness of pedestrians is a relatively small threat to others), but at least we could expect a debate stressing the difference between danger to others and danger to oneself.

To some extent this kind of view is coming from members of grass-roots bodies such as RoadPeace and Keep Death off our Roads (KDOOR), which look at other forms of irresponsible driving apart from drunk driving. Whether they will reverse a history of official tolerance for the abuse of motorist power is another question.

Conclusion

The technology available to law enforcers has been augmented by on-board automatic breath testing machinery which prevents drivers with excess BAC from switching on the ignition. It will not be used, either because motorists would find ways of evading its use (using compressed air canisters?), or because drivers will refuse to accept legislation making them mandatory. A less technologically based approach could be tried, which I have never seen mentioned: rewards could be given for "shopping" over-the-limit drivers.

Members of the public are asked to inform on various kinds of criminal, from armed robbers to illegal fly tippers. Rewards of approximately £200 to £300 could be made — balanced by larger fines if breath tests were negative (along the lines of penalties for wasting police time) — to people given a type of special constable status. Television programmes dedicated to solving crime by means of encouraging the public to contact the police receive massive popular support. The police are already legally entitled to stop and test on the basis of information received,[56] and both they and sections of the media have advocated either reporting, or at least attempting to stop, intoxicated people who intend to drive.

The reason why such a measure would not be adopted is nothing to do with fears of turning us into a nation of informers, or with the cost of such a step. It is because of the "sporting chance" mentality, based on the central idea that driving is a *personal* matter. Each individual motorist, subject to the behaviour of other road users, is to be the master, to virtually all intents and purposes, of his or her own decisions. Formal controls are minimal, non-existent or are pseudo-controls: the only real controls are informal cultural controls based on motorist acceptance of them (they are freely broken by substantial proportions of the motoring population), and the behaviour of other motorists.

The road safety lobby has not effected a move away from this, and much of it would not want to anyway. The opposition to drink-driving remains advisory when it is known that advice is not enough. Instead, a kind of half-hearted shadow-boxing occurs. A limited (although definite and obvious) form of motor danger is given special attention. It is specified as being distinctly different from other motoring problems — and then is not dealt with, despite a pretence that action is being taken. Hypocrisy and smoke-screening indeed.

13.

Getting out of whose way?

Segregation, traffic calming and the struggle for road space

OVER THE COURSE of the century various of the lobby groups have taken some unlikely positions in relation to the question of segregation. For example, in the 30s the Cyclists' Touring Club supported the construction of special roads for cars: later known as motorways. Whereas previously, motorists themselves, in the form of the Motorists' Union, were against the idea. They feared that such treatment would lose them the freedom of the roads, a response that we hear now from some cyclists as they face up to life on the margins of road transport — in cycle lanes.

As changes in car use lead to a doubling of traffic on motorways and other roads, what does allocating space to particular user groups mean today?

❖❖❖

In the public outrage against the misery caused by car use in the 1930s, a strand of thinking was developed by the defenders of motorist privilege which remains an important element in their defence today. Its seductive logic has led to its adoption by some of those genuinely concerned with the welfare of those outside cars. It also informs the practice of engineers confronted by problems of congestion and pollution, as they design the urban and other environments of the future.

The idea is simple. All of us have a view about which part of the road environment "belongs" to us. If this environment can be designed to organise the movement of different kinds of road user in such a way that the possibilities of confrontation are minimised, then there will be less need to worry about the danger posed by car and lorry traffic. This has meant the provision of a footway for pedestrians, and sections of the carriageway being marked out for cyclists. Footbridges and subways are built as "facilities" for pedestrians. The guiding principle here is *segregation*, as with the provision of motorways for motorists. More recently, certain kinds of "traffic calming" have stressed the proximity of vulnerable road users, to each other and to motorists, on streets where the emphasis is on lower speeds and cautious driving. However, even such environments, characterised by a degree of integration, exist within overall hierarchies where there is segregation from roads which carry heavier and faster flows of traffic. Their existence may sometimes even be made conditional on the construction of such larger roads.

Much has been written on how road space can be allocated to facilitate different road user groups. International conferences and codes of good practice produced by professional bodies and ministries of transport contain a welter of detail on everything from the width of shared cycle-pedestrian paths through to the desirability of chamfering the edges of road humps. How those possible design features are to be implemented, and in which areas, is another matter.

There have been attempts at allocating road space specifically for cyclists since the 1930s, with serious efforts made since the 1970s. The experience of pedestrianised areas and play streets dates from before the war. There has been considerable experience of traffic calming measures in Northern Europe since the 1970s.

Perhaps the least popular form of pedestrian segregation: the urban subway

Yet the only road user groups to gain substantially from road building designed specifically for them are people using lorries and cars.

Re-allocating road space may have some limited potential advantages for vulnerable road users. But these have to be balanced against what is referred to elsewhere in this book, and by other commentators, as a diversionary effect. A recent paper on traffic calming suggests it might be "a 'green' smoke screen".[1] For another commentator: "All palliatives are just that: when they are introduced they attract attention at a level quite beyond their real importance, and distract attention away from the real problem: over-production and use of the motor car."[2] Similar criticism has been made of a tendency to think of a safe environment for cyclists in terms of the provision of segregated cycling "facilities".[3] These criticisms apply to some extent *even if* there is widespread implementation of road space allocation towards vulnerable road users, which has not been, and is unlikely to be, the case in Britain.

The problem

Rather than analyse the numerous case studies or guides to good practice, it is more profitable to consider the difficulties associated with attempts to solve social problems through *segregation*. From Bantustans under apartheid, through to "special schools" for children with disabilities, the questions are the same. Who is defined as "the problem"? Who gets what share of the resources? What happens in the long-term throughout the wider society? And what are the consequences for the disadvantaged or oppressed group? Apartheid and "special schools" may seem dramatic analogies, but they are instructive. In each case there is a refusal to consider the true origin of the problem.

The provision of certain kinds of environment in certain areas can give a few road users in those areas some benefits. Balanced against these benefits are the following prospects:–

≡ *Most cycling and walking, particularly in rural areas, has to be unsegregated.* Even with good environments planned for cyclists and pedestrians in urban areas, there will be the proximity of motor vehicles.

≡ *There is a shortage of space to allow for satisfaction of existing, let alone future, demand for car use.* When applied to motorists, the idea that road users should have "their own" space which caters for their desires, produces an intolerable strain on the environment and adverse effects on society.[4] This could include eroding benefits gained from having special road space for the benign modes.

≡ We bring a set of culturally and individually determined values in our role as road users to any road environment. We feel that we have certain rights to be exercised, and should expect certain behaviours from other road users. *Changing the environment may not change the antisocial attitudes of the potentially dangerous.* Indeed, even if real benefits can be gained for the vulnerable in special areas for them, *necessary controls on motorists outside these areas and in society in general may become more difficult to achieve by stressing segregationist principles.*

Together, these prospects suggest that benefits from properly designed environments — which would take a long time to implement satisfactorily — could be eroded unless general controls were implemented as part of a programme to restrain and control car use. The importance of not forgetting basic attitudes and the proximity of all types of road user is crucial. Because this tends to be forgotten just when segregation (or traffic calming, which despite its initial emphasis on integration is still part of the same approach) is proposed, I doubt whether the "something is better than nothing" dictum can apply. Even where traffic calming, pedestrianisation, networks of cycle routes and a transport policy based on shifting transport modes away from car use are pursued vigorously, the unsatisfactory "something" may not be achieved.

A process whereby the benign road user groups are (if they are lucky) to be "given" something which was theirs anyway has been advocated and implemented as follows:–

A. Pedestrians

(i) The footway

The footway is a feature of the road environment which did not always exist. It can meet many of the requirements of pedestrians, and may therefore be one form of segregation which is satisfactory. Yet even here the story is not so simple.

First, a form of integration, where the boundary between space for pedestrians and other road users is blurred or absent, may be preferable. This has been a distinctive feature of the Dutch *woonerven* ("home-streets"), an early type of traffic calming introduced in the 1970s. With physical and legal obstacles to prevent cars from exceeding slow speeds, this can work to allow pedestrians, particularly elderly, young and disabled pedestrians, basic freedom to move around in their own streets. However, without these restrictions, or a culturally generated commitment to give way to the vulnerable, such integration fails because there is a general tendency, given the speed and width of cars, for motorists to assume that they should have legitimate control over far more space than other road users.

Second, footways need to be protected from encroachment by parked or moving cars, which they are not. Parked cars smash footway surfaces, contributing to a massive toll of pedestrian accidents.[5] In Britain, pedestrians are killed or injured by motorists when on the footway or on pedestrian crossings in about 4,500 cases every year.[6] Protection against this occurring can be effected only by continuous barriers which prevent convenient crossing by pedestrians.

Third, footways cannot exist on many rural roads.

Fourth, with constant possibilities of road widening, and demand for space for cars increasing, the amount of footway space may be reduced.

The provision of the footway is therefore not an unqualified blessing. It is under threat, is to a certain extent restrictive, and is far from universally available. The allocation of specific sites for crossing the road is also problematic.[7] More obvious problems of pedestrian segregation come with subways and footbridges.

(ii) Subways and footbridges

Personal security when travelling is often cited as a major problem. Certain environments present both real and perceived danger. A recent report states:

> **Of all transport facilities it is undoubtedly pedestrian subways that are the most disliked. They frequently combine the worst environmental features...**

often there is not clear visibility; there is virtually no surveillance... by its very nature the main passageway of the underpass is not visible to motorists and not overlooked by residents or workers; [they are] often poorly maintained; narrow constraining walls do not allow easy avoidance of confrontational situations.[8]

This does not include the physical difficulty of walking up and down steps, which, along with the security issue, makes subways a particular problem for young children and their carers, for women, for the elderly and for people with disabilities. There are limited possibilities for improving the design of subways, so:

Perhaps the most obvious solution to the design problem of subways is to avoid the need for them in the first place. Crossing the road at ground level on a fully protected signal phase is most pedestrians' preferred solution for busy highways.[8]

Similar problems of inconvenience, worsened for those who dislike heights, exist for footbridges.

Subways are very much a feature of the 1960s era of road building, sited at the periphery of city centres beneath ring or relief roads. They are thus features of inner-city landscapes, with their high incidence of crime-related and security-related social problems. The product of a particular kind of road building based around the idea of segregation for cars, subways are a graphic reminder of the inappropriateness of the word "facility". Even when wide, well lit and well populated — the best example being Birmingham city centre[9] — they place pedestrians in an unsatisfactory subterranean environment created by just one of the logical extensions of giving rein to the power of the car.

(iii) Pedestrianised areas

Making central urban areas places for pedestrians, with various kinds of access for cyclists, buses or trams, and service vehicles, is one way of segregating for, rather than against, the pedestrian. Continental experience indicates that this is a feasible possibility which often assists economic activity, with evidence of pleasant and popular environments in several cities.[10] There are problems, however, with the organisation of access for people with disabilities and the provision of public transport. The inner city pedestrianised area is untypical of the vast majority of areas where people walk. Some of these areas generate additional motor traffic towards them — high levels of car parking in them are a common feature — and such additional traffic can present very obvious problems to pedestrians in the immediate surroundings of the area.[11]

B. Cyclists

Cycle tracks, cycle paths, cycle ways or cycle routes: such terms are used, often interchangeably, to refer to supposed cycle "facilities". The sloppiness of the terminology reflects an attitude which, unconsciously or otherwise, is contemptuous of cycling and generally refuses to consider the adverse effects of motoring.

(i) Pre-war history

Pressure for cyclists to be segregated from motor traffic arose in the early 1930s, when far more miles were travelled by bicycle than by motor vehicle. Only some of those motor vehicles were cars, and with lower mileage per journey for cyclists, many times more journeys were made by bicycle than by car. [12] It is therefore a reflection of the arrogance of the car lobby at this time that the demand to move cyclists off the carriageway could be made. The demand should also be seen in the context of the wave of public indignation against the dangers posed by car use. The defenders of motorist privilege have often, under criticism for their danger to others, responded by criticising those who are both less dangerous to others and particularly vulnerable to their potential danger. Some approaches to psychology indicate that attacking others for the misdeeds one is accused of is a common form of human behaviour. [13] Characteristically, the attacks on cyclists (in print and in magistrates' courts, as well as the actual damage caused by motorist negligence) coincided with the public opposition to motorists' danger. As one historian of cycling put it: "The idea of segregating various forms of road traffic occurred as a way of getting them [cyclists] off the public highways onto separate paths: 'for their own good' of course!"[14]

Segregation involved the motorist lobby achieving its hegemony at the expense of the more numerous, less dangerous and more vulnerable cyclists (as well as pedestrians). It also involved motorists defending themselves by criticising and defining as "the problem" this group of their potential victims. Finally, it gave the appearance of a genuine defence against public criticism by creating the illusion that cyclists would be able to be safe from motorists now they had been given a "facility". It was a dangerous illusion, although few cyclists were taken in by it.

The first British cycle path was constructed in 1935 along 2½ miles of the Western Avenue (A40) in West London. Other short sections of track were built at a handful of locations for similarly short lengths, mainly along new trunk roads.

They were not very useful or safe for cyclists for a number of reasons. They only extended along the sides of (part of) roads and did not aid cyclists at junctions, where the majority of accidents occur; traffic turning left off the main road had priority over cyclists, making it both dangerous and inconvenient for cyclists travelling along the track... Cyclists had to give way at minor service roads and the tracks were frequently blocked by parked cars, and badly maintained. [15]

Cyclists were being moved off *their* roads for the benefit of the minority introducing danger into them. Motorists, becoming used to seeing cyclists off the carriageway, would be presented with them again at junctions or stretches of road where tracks could not be provided.

It was an attempt at a something-is-better-than-nothing approach. However, the lack of enough space for continuous tracks, the problems at junctions and the inferior status of tracks (in terms of their treatment by parking motorists, pedestrians and the local authorities responsible for their maintenance) meant that, in this case, something was definitely *worse* than nothing. Despite this, there are some, who should know better,[16] who can still think of them as desirable.

(ii) Post-war

A different kind of segregation was advocated with the post-war building of new towns. The low-density layout of the new towns had space to afford a segregated network of cycle and pedestrian paths or tracks and features such as grade separation at some junctions, without conflicting with the car-oriented layout of modern new town design. But the cycle facilities in new towns had severe limitations.

They were appropriate to new towns, but not in the places where the vast majority of cycling would occur in Britain. Cyclists continue to be told of the desirability of the Stevenage or Peterborough type of design which cannot be implemented in older towns, rural areas or other places dissimilar to new towns. The cycle facilities were also by no means as satisfactory as is assumed. Criticism of the facilities built integrally into the layout of Milton Keynes, for example, indicates likely or endemic problems concerning conflict with pedestrians, poor maintenance, loss of rights and safety on the carriageway, and so on. [17] In addition, the areas considered are typified by a planning and transport policy which is the *reverse* of what is appropriate for the future of the rest of Britain. It features distances too long to walk, isolated and dangerous environments for pedestrians, particularly severe obstacles to having adequate public transport and other problems associated with organising a society excessively around car use. [18] The kind of new town layout typical of Milton Keynes or Stevenage cannot and should not exist for cyclists or others in a society with a proper transport policy.

(iii) The 1970s and after

Modern cycle planning is somewhat more sophisticated, and has been developed with regard to contemporary environments since the decline in cycling in the post-war period was reversed after the oil crisis of 1973. Nevertheless it remains limited in its possibilities. These now include:

Off-road routes

The Bristol—Bath shared pedestrian and cycle path, built on the site of a disused railway, is probably the best known of these. Other routes use canal towpaths, bridleways and forest roads. Such "green" routes are exceptionally limited in availability, and when available are prone to appropriation by the more powerful and space-hungry forms of transport: Bristol—Bath has been threatened by light rail development, another (Parkland Walk) by a road building scheme.

Side street routes

The idea is to avoid heavy traffic on main roads by linking side streets through facilities such as road closures being opened for cycle tracks, or converting footbridges to shared pedestrian/cycle use. While there may be some scope for this, virtually all the cycling continues to be on ordinary roads in ordinary conditions. Often the only thing distinguishing a cycle route from a road which would have been used by cyclists anyway is signing. Much of the danger confronting urban cyclists remains, or is even increased, because there are more junctions and greater

distance than on the more direct main roads. Because increase in distance can make a
journey prohibitive, another
technique tried more recently
is:

Cycle lanes

These enable consideration to
be given for cyclists on main
roads. They tend to be hindered
by illegally parked cars — a
general problem on bus lanes
and elsewhere — and by hostility from motorists, or those
acting on their behalf, con-

cerning the real or imagined loss of capacity to cars. They cannot co-exist with on-
street parking and offer little or no protection at junctions.

Perhaps the most obvious feature of cycle planning is that it has hardly been
implemented in Britain. Yet if, for example, the 1,000-mile network of routes
suggested by the Greater London Council some ten years ago were to be implemented, the advantages would be limited. Some 93 per cent of London's roads
would not be cycle routes, and they would have homes, shops, workplaces and
other cyclists' origins and destinations on them. Even where a cycle route existed,
a more direct alternative could still be preferable for some cyclists. Most of the
cycle routes would still tend to be ordinary roads, albeit quieter ones, with similar
problems to other roads — and in the case of danger at junctions, perhaps even
more. Where cycle lanes exist, the general absence of enforcement becomes
critical.

The problems with planning for cyclists are actually quite obvious. Instead of
reading from the large literature on cycle planning,[19] one can simply think of the
possibilities on the last few journeys one has made by any mode of transport. If
there is no desirable or adequate space for cyclists moving from a typical origin to
a destination, they must belong on the road. If they cannot easily be accommodated
on existing road widths, they need lanes; but then road space has to be taken from
motorists. This means that even if very good facilities exist for cyclists, the vast
majority of roads will involve the proximity of cyclists and other road users, and
the segregation idea could have the negative effect of obscuring this fact.

This does not necessarily mean that good cycle facilities should be opposed.
Yet it suggests that, even if good and extensively installed, they can only be a small
part of any solution *and will tend to create the wrong impression about the
problems of cyclists and divert attention away from the problems which mass
motoring poses to other road users and society in general.*

Personal experience of cycling in areas of Northern Switzerland provides an illustration of this difficulty: a tradition of engineering for cycling has provided a cycle-friendly — and pedestrian and local resident-friendly — environment in parts of many urban areas; which, because of available spare capacity and resources would be exceptionally unlikely to be implemented in Britain. But, perhaps the real problem is that when making necessary journeys by bicycle outside those areas specially designated for bicycles, motorists unused to the presence of cyclists (unwelcoming to people straying outside "their" area?) tend to behave even worse than in countries where such cycle-friendly engineering is common.

If segregation is to work, it has to occur alongside a changed attitude on the part of motorists, such as appears to be the case with more careful motorist behaviour at junctions on some Danish schemes. Also, as part of a full and integrated road transport policy, it must involve a re-allocation of road space where space is lost from private motorists to the benign modes. This is not an impossibility, as *some* examples from Denmark, Belgium, the Netherlands, Switzerland and West Germany suggest. Nor, however, is even such very well installed provision the solution that many campaigners appear to think it is. While they have been increasingly confident at informing engineers, planners and politicians that cycle facilities need to be good and extensive — and in that sense they have made the point that something is not better than nothing — the points made above do not seem to have been placed properly on the agenda.

Cars and lorries — a case of motorway madness

Special roads for motorists, later to become motorways, were first thought of in much the same way as motorists were later to think of cycle tracks — as a device for getting a problem group out of the way. For this reason motorists in the early years of the century *opposed* them in the same way that cyclists were to become wary of segregationist proposals "for" them. Writing before the First World War, the chairman of the Motorists' Union stated:

> **"I am totally and entirely opposed to taking the motorist and placing him on the heights of fame with a special road to himself, or in the depths of infamy as a being who is not fit to be allowed on the ordinary roads of the country... Once allow us to be put on separate roads and there will be an increasing outcry to keep us on those roads and to forbid access to the ordinary roads of the country."[20]**

Ironically, the idea of special roads for motorists was supported by the Cyclists' Touring Club, which called for the establishment of "special highways designed to facilitate rapid transport and reserved for the use of high-speed (then thought of as over 30 mph) traffic".[21]

The motorists need never have worried that motorways would erode their power and privilege. On the other hand, cyclists and pedestrians, some of whom still think that motorways can help to "get the problem out of the way", *should* have been worried.

In the event, the provision of fast roads for motorists encouraged motoring which would not otherwise have occurred, filling up not only those motorways where there was sufficient untapped pressure for motoring — the M25 being the most obvious recent example — but the surrounding roads feeding them, which also contain other road users.[22] This disbenefit of extra traffic has to be set against those cases where traffic has been diverted away from the shared roads without extra traffic generation; but with today's pressure for driving this is increasingly rare. As with other forms of segregation, it is a question of which road user group is powerful enough to secure space, as well as the fact that some forms of transport are far greedier for space than others.

Apart from generally becoming part of a more heavily motorised and dangerous society, motorways are exceptionally space consuming, particularly when compared with the requirements of rail links. Environmental destruction spreads beyond the space taken up, to areas where materials are extracted for construction. Claims for job creation stimulated by motorway building are exaggerated.[23] The process of choosing sites for motorways and building them has been anti-democratic and contemptuous of the lives and environment of local residents.[24] In fact, from their illogicalities of cost-benefit analysis through to their generation of traffic, motorways are an archetypal example of how things go wrong when motorists are pandered to. Their safety record has signally failed to meet expectations and is a classic case of risk compensation and officially inspired confusion.

Motorway safety

According to the engineers' book, motorways should have a good safety record. They are, after all, *safer roads*. They have long sight lines, no right turns and an absence of less visible road users moving at much slower speeds (cyclists, moped riders, pedestrians). From tricky junctions through to children appearing from behind parked cars, motorists do not have to worry as much about danger as they do on most other roads. *And this is precisely why the accident record is poor*, or at least a lot worse than the pro-motoring lobby would have us believe.

The high speeds on motorways — the reason why a higher proportion of accidents result in fatality than on other roads — are, of course, partly to blame. Motorways were built for speed as well as for safety. But this misses the point: traditional ways of engineering roads for safety *produce* speed, just as they decrease motorist vigilance and alertness. Similarly, the amount of freight travelling on motorways is a feature of a transport system centred on roads, not an unfortunate chance occurrence contributing to accidents.

In the Department of Transport's guidelines on road safety policy into the next century, we are reassured that "motorways have a generally superior record to all other types of road... motorways are eight times safer than other roads".[25] This kind of figure — between six and nine — is constantly repeated by Ministers. It is an example of abuse of statistics which should not fool anybody, distorting in the following ways the picture of chances of being hurt (particularly being killed) on motorways.[26]

First, the figure is arrived at by adding up all the reported casualties and dividing them by total vehicle mileage. 38 per cent of the people killed on Britain's roads — pedestrians, cyclists and moped riders — are not on motorways. Motorcycle users, who make up some 12 per cent of fatalities, are much less likely to use motorways as a proportion of their total mileage than car users. *So about half the people killed on Britain's roads are from vulnerable road user groups who are either less likely to be, or are in most cases never, there anyway.* So in terms of the chances of car users — the main road user group — being hurt or killed or motorways the safety figure comes down by about a half.

Second, because of the higher speeds involved on motorways, the chances of being killed once a crash has occurred are far higher than on built-up roads (and about the same as on other non-built-up roads). The chances of being killed — the most important kind of casualty — per mile travelled are about four times higher on other non-built-up roads *but the same as on built-up roads.*

Third, all this uses *vehicle mileage* as the denominator or measure of exposure. But do real people think of exposure to risk in terms of their vehicle mileage? Do they not think of their chances per *journey*, or in terms of the time taken on it (per *hour*)? Looked at this way, motorways become distinctly bad in their record compared to other forms of road, particularly built-up urban roads. The point is that motorway journeys are much longer than urban journeys; the average car journey time is some 21 minutes,[27] but motorway journeys take much longer. The average speed of all car journeys is 20 mph,[28] but the average speed on motorways is considerably higher.

All this can be summarised by applying it to a part of the DTp's defence of motorways: "[I]n terms of journeys of similar length, one on a motorway will be safer than one on another type of road. Put another way, the chance of an accident in a journey of 200 kms on a motorway is the same as a chance of an accident on a journey of 20 kms in a built-up area."[29] This differential factor of 10 is reduced to 2.8 for serious injuries and *disappears for deaths.* If casualty rates are calculated per *hour* rather than per *mile,* given average urban journeys at less than 20 mph and motorway journeys at some 40-50 mph, we can divide these figures by two or three times if we consider *time* as the important denominator. This shows motorways as two or three times *worse* for deaths, and about the same for serious injuries, in terms of the time spent travelling. *The chances of car users dying or being seriously hurt per hour travelled on a British motorway are worse and no better respectively than on typical urban roads.* In terms of those *journeys* which are longer in time on motorways compared to built-up urban roads, the motorway accident record would be even poorer, with the serious injury figure becoming worse as well as the fatality figure.

The picture is admittedly different on non-built-up roads, so any desire to use them instead of motorways for long-distance travel may be mistaken. But, even there the balance is not clear cut in favour of motorways. People may not have made car journeys at all by the previous alternatives to motorways, and the advantage of removing traffic from non-motorway roads has to be set against the role of motorways in encouraging extra car travel in the first place. The casualties involving those additional journeys cannot be found in any official statistics.

Motorways play an important part in generating longer journeys.[30] While Britain's programme of inter-urban motorway building is mainly complete, motorway-style building or widening existing motorways is still on the agenda. Using vehicle miles, rather than a more faithful indicator of human experience as the denominator in a safety index or safety record, paints a falsely rosy picture in the statistics produced by the DTp to back up its support for motorways.

Much of this has been known for some time. A leading theorist of risk compensation wrote about it in the 1970s.[31] It may have even entered the minds of the engineers and public figures who enthusiastically supported the first motorways, namely those roads which were such an important part of the ideology and war economy of the Fascist states. (The close links between the British road lobby and the Nazi transport authorities, who were only too keen to entertain such people, was to become embarrassing later.)[32]

But a full acceptance of the root cause seems as far away as in any other branch of "road safety". In September 1988, a motorway driver with previous speeding convictions killed two women after driving into their almost stationary car at nearly 90 mph. He escaped a prison sentence after evidence was given on his behalf that he had suffered from "highway hypnosis". The claim that this "trance-like state" led him to ignore warning lights was made by a prominent figure in the road safety lobby,[33] although there was no hard published evidence of this condition. In a rare falling-out of allies, the AA suggested that the problem was due more to over-familiarity, boredom and other effects of driving for a long period of time.

Out of the confusion over the precise state of mind of this individual and others like him, three certainties emerge. First, there will be a string of conferences to establish links between different kinds of visual and other stimuli and psychological states measured by different psychologists in different kinds of experimental situation, with more or less invalid evidence being produced after a number of years (courtesy of funding from the car and insurance industries) which may or may not be accepted by the authorities. Second, the motoring organisations will continue to give occasional injunctions to motorists not to drive when they are tired, or on journeys which are too long; they will do so in the full knowledge that these injunctions will be ignored on a massive scale. Third, any changes in design or in education will be absorbed, as usual, by the behaviour of the dangerous at the expense of the vulnerable; and the origins of our society's motorway madness will be studiously disregarded.

Traffic Calming

Announcing changes in road hump regulations in April 1989, Minister for Roads Peter Bottomley spoke of "road humps, sleeping policemen, and raised junctions, etc, designed to make drivers think 'I am a worm, and I have to give way to everything else', rather than, 'I am the master'."[34]

Traffic calming does not appear to be a segregationist approach. It can include measures which definitely reduce the danger and other adverse effects of motor vehicle use, re-allocating road space in a genuinely beneficial way. However, even if traffic calming is widely introduced in Britain, its benefits are likely to be

restricted to certain kinds of area. It can also be used as an excuse for building more roads, if the need to reduce road capacity is ignored. In the sense that it can be restricted to certain parts of "the hierarchy of roads", traffic calming typifies the problems of segregationism.

(i) Defining traffic calming

Denmark, the Netherlands and West Germany have led the way with traffic calming. The practice can be seen to have developed from three ideas: [35] pedestrianisation; the Dutch *woonerven* (shared space in mews-type residential areas with vehicles travelling at very slow speeds and the distinction between carriageway and footway abolished); and the "environmental areas" mentioned in the Buchanan Report. [36] The term "traffic calming" applies to any scheme where physical changes in the road environment — such as road humps, traffic islands and footway extensions — have been introduced for one or more of the following purposes:

≣ Speed restriction (for accident or environmental reasons);

≣ Extending the space available for pedestrians and/or cyclists by reclaiming it from the carriageway; this includes catering for "non-traffic activities" such as children's play;

≣ Creating a more pleasant environment which, along with less traffic noise and pollution, is also more visually attractive.

This presents us with an image of a street where cars have been slowed down by physical mechanisms which are not dependent on law enforcement or education. It has more space for pedestrians to gather and talk in an environment which has become more attractive with less noise and pollution, and perhaps the provision of plants or other vegetation. Space may be provided for a cycle track, and/or a narrower carriageway can make it easier to cross the space allocated for vehicles. There can be an emphasis on how things *feel*; in fact, this is one area where safety is beginning to be talked about in terms of the legitimacy of people's perceptions of danger, with the possibility of at last moving away from discussing safety in terms just of accidents. [37]

A large range of measures can be taken on a variety of roads as part of different transport policies; and this is where the problem exists. One definition — "traffic calming refers to all traffic control and construction measures to produce changes in streets and the adjacent private property likely to attenuate the negative effects of motor vehicles on traffic conditions, on urban development and the environment" [38] — is based on avoiding "the extremes of isolated local measures and universal traffic policy measures". Right at the start of the discussion then, issues are raised concerning how traffic calming differs from traditional environmental traffic management, how much restraint is involved, what kinds of road can be treated and what kind of broader transport policy is implicated.

In one approach traffic calming actually becomes defined as an *overall transport policy*, with general promotion of walking, cycling and public transport. In other words, a modal shift away from car use:

Traffic calming in such a wide sense will include a combination of transport and, as important, land-use policies which will reduce both the number, and even more desirably the *need* for motor-vehicle trips in built-up areas. The traffic calming concept is manifested in a combination of transport policies intended to alleviate the adverse environmental, safety and severance effects motor vehicles have been [imposing] and continue to impose on both the individual and society at large.[39]

In Britain at present, as with cycle facilities, the most notable feature of traffic calming schemes is their absence. Where they exist, lack of guidance from the Department of Transport on official practice leads to a haphazard approach from local authorities. If schemes are narrowly implemented, without being part of a process with traffic calming in the above wider sense as its objective, then yet another smoke screen may be successfully created. "Traffic calming" has become a fashionable phrase to use: it is absolutely vital to make it clear from the start what is meant by it — and what its possible effects may be.[40]

(ii) Problems of limited traffic calming

The worry about traffic calming is that it has a palliative[41] or smoke screen[42] effect by being able to coexist with or even encourage increased car use. Sometimes it provides more car-parking space; or it may be used as a bargaining counter for new roads which will increase car use; or it may simply give the impression that problems associated with mass car use are being solved.

Proponents of the smoke screen theory argue that there should be no increase in car use for a variety of environmental and transport policy reasons. The very arguments which win over British engineers and planners to traffic planning schemes — that they need not interfere with capacity — are precisely the ones worrying the smoke screen theorists. If increases in pollution and public transport problems fit in easily with such ideas about traffic calming, there is a serious problem.

Unless the problems of increasing (or existing) levels of car use are dealt with, even limited traffic calming can fail. Whitelegg reports from his experience in West Germany of how the failure to deal with car-parking means that road space supposedly allocated to pedestrians or cyclists becomes blocked with parked cars;[43] an increase in car use can mean that initial danger reduction is eroded for pedestrians, particularly in neighbouring areas which are not traffic calmed.[44]

As with cycle planning, there is a question of how far traffic calming can proceed. There are some 4,000 converted streets in North Rhine Westphalia alone, but what happens outside these areas? Although space and facility can be taken from motorists on main roads and in shopping areas as well as residential streets, such moves are likely to be resisted because they counteract motorist privilege. Most roads are not traffic calmed even in these places where traffic calming is fashionable; in particular, rural roads will continue to pose massive problems to cyclists and pedestrians. And what if danger on them actually *increases* as motorists relax and speed up, when departing from a traffic-calmed zone, in response to the lifting of restriction?[45]

Whatever the engineering measures, motorists bringing a hostile attitude with them will not be easily civilised. Features such as chicanes can be played with or humps disregarded by the (company car?) driver unconcerned with the vehicles structure.

Even the smoke screen theorists allow traffic calming a "walk-on part" in the move towards a better road environment. It shows how slower speeds can dramatically alter the severity of accidents and reduce pollution. [46] But the importance of considering the wider context of car hegemony remains paramount. Road speed could be automatically controlled by, for example, the installation of speed governors in cars. Governors with different limits for different road types are already used in prototypes in Germany; [47] their settings could be regulated by electronic apparatus at the boundaries of each type of road (residential, urban, motorway). Instead, engineers make piecemeal local efforts, achieving far less speed reduction over a far longer time period.

(iii) A summary of problems

Whether traffic calming is meant to ameliorate the adverse consequences of mass car use or not, it contains problems which flow from the central difficulty outlined in this book: danger, and the other problems of mass car use, can not be solved by easy ways out which fail to confront the issues at source. If engineers are unwilling to deal with the issues, they should be: if they are, then they must honestly present them to the public. The problems otherwise are that traffic calming may:

≡ Not be intended to actually reduce danger or other car problems anyway, but increase parking and/or road capacity.

≡ Be intended to help, but cause problems as particular road user groups suffer from the disbenefits of measures designed for others — the classic example is of road narrowings or central refuges which might assist pedestrian crossing but squeeze cyclists. [48]

≡ Be intended to deal with problems, but be unable to do so because of the failure to control demand for cars — one transport planner claims that problems such as noise, emissions, danger and congestion could *increase* even in traffic calmed areas as a consequence of traffic calming. [49]

≡ Act as a smoke screen. Traffic and traffic-related problems may be pushed on to neighbouring sites. It may be used as a bargaining counter for new road building or as a more general idea that "something is being done". This effect can therefore occur in both an immediate physical way as well as at a broader ideological level.

Without society-wide changes in attitude and policy, we would have what has been described as squeezing the hosepipe without closing the tap. [50] It is certainly necessary to deal with the problem at source: it may be that the limited "walk-on part" played by traffic calming could be helpful (although perhaps better fulfilled by some other means such as variable speed governors), but it would have to fit in with the major changes required and not divert attention away from them. Even those measures associated with traffic calming which deliberately aim to restrain and reduce traffic in towns may fail to reach targets necessary for the solution of the global problems which they are (supposedly) aimed at. Needless to say, such limited restraint can co-exist with an increase in non-urban traffic danger and related problems.[51] At the end of the day, a muck-shifting exercise shifts muck elsewhere: it does not deal with the problems of having muck there in the first place.

Segregation, traffic calming and the Buchanan legacy

"What about 20 mph in designated areas (including all towns and villages and scattered residential areas) and a 60 mph limit on all main roads?... The benefits from a general slowing down would be enormous."[52]

So speaks the most influential figure in post-war transport planning in Britain, Sir Colin Buchanan. From the president of Volvo[53] to leading transport academics[54] the message is the same. Whether it be the danger or environmental damage caused by cars and lorries, it is time to create a road environment characterised by planning which is restrictive of at least certain kinds of car use. However much traffic calmers are keen to claim that they are not engaged in "a witch-hunt policy against the car",[55] an erosion of motorist privilege is on the agenda.

Restriction should not be seen as a harsh sacrifice made as an act of benevolence by motorists. It has to be understood in terms of the problems that motorists have always been able to get away with inflicting on others. After all, current debates on attempts to deal with commuting traffic have only just started — some 30 years after it was obvious that inner cities and their transport systems could never cope with the majority of commuters travelling by car. The proper re-allocation of road space, taking account of safety and other requirements, demands a very different approach from many (if not most) of those taken in the past.

Many of today's difficulties stem from problems arising with the publication of the Buchanan Report in 1963. The approach of the report owed much to segregationist ideas introduced during the war by Alker Tripp.[56] Buchanan described the advantages of mass car use, and the necessity of transforming the layout of towns and cities to accommodate it.[57] The question of how far traffic should be restricted, or how far road building should be facilitated, was left unspecified. For some, Buchanan provided an indication of the need to restrict traffic,[58] others gained from it the impetus to design massive road schemes (since criticised for their inhuman scale).[59] In the intervening period, however, environmental concerns have become dominant. Academics involved in assessing (promoting?) car use 20 years ago have moved towards emphasising its negative effects much more forcefully. Even those pushing for more road building feel obliged to pay lip-service to potential environmental disbenefits.

Whichever way Buchanan is assessed — pushing towards universal car use or warning against its potential disbenefits — there is a feeling that the agenda of discussion about increasing car use was fairly drawn up:

> The report accepts the maximum possible use of the motor vehicle, poses possible solutions to its movement in towns and asks what price the citizens are prepared to pay for greater or lesser freedom of car movement. That dilemma has still to be resolved, but, the validity of the question remains.[60]

But the way the dilemma was posed, however, was wrong. Buchanan has been criticised for over-emphasising the levels of car ownership that would be achieved and under-estimating the importance of walking as a mode of transport.[61] Accessibility was defined in too limited a way. Similarly, environmental areas were defined in too restricted a way to allow for an understanding of the effects of traffic on the people in them: "no more and no less than a method of arranging buildings for motor traffic".[62] Indeed:

> Closer examination [of the consequences of applying the concept of 'environmental areas' to existing urban areas] would have shown the outcome to be inequitable, not only entailing restriction on movement — especially on foot — between the areas because of their girdle of traffic, but also exposing people living on the peripheral roads to an even more unfair share of the nuisance generated by traffic than they had experienced previously.[63]

Other criticisms were made by radical transport theorists about the implications of encouraging car transport — the effects on public transport, equity, energy, more recent concerns with pollution and others considered in Chapter 14. A central flaw of Buchanan's approach is revealed in a statement he made some years after the report: "The signs all seem to me to point in the direction of people being prepared to put a high price to their mobility, and being ready to sacrifice other things first."[64] The trouble is that *other people pay that price* — people with less power. Whether elderly, disabled or child pedestrians, or cyclists suffering danger, or the poor and powerless both nationally and globally, this power relationship is not adequately theorised. And given the tendency of motorist power to grow, the need to counter-balance it is all the stronger.

This failure to grasp the dynamics of power erodes the best strategies for allocating road space. Segregation has to allocate areas for road users to be able to move in safety without threatening others. This has always been difficult for pedestrians (particularly in rural areas) and very difficult for cyclists; it is not helped by the advanced development of motorways. Even where there is space for adequate environmental areas, the dynamics of motorist power with its immense greed for space mean that the threat of danger and other car-produced problems do not go away up to another level of the "hierarchy of roads", but tend to expand on that level and permeate down.

Conflict in the struggle for space to provide for the ever increasing car population.
Environmentalists protest at the threat to an important natural habitat at Twyford Down in Hampshire.

Part Four

Danger and the way we get about

14.

One or two problems with cars

ACCORDING TO an article in The Times *newspaper, Los Angeles has more cars than the whole of China, India, Pakistan, Bangladesh and Indonesia combined. As the smog sits over the Californian city, in spite of catalytic converters and lead-free fuel, it doesn't take much imagination to foresee the environmental disaster that awaits us all if car ownership levels in the developed countries are repeated in the Third World. More than this, is it a coincidence that it was this, the most car-oriented city in the world, that erupted into arguably the most catastrophic rioting the United States has ever seen?*

We have seen that the problems created by mass car use, in terms of the danger posed to others, have never been properly addressed or tackled. Ordinary citizens are allowed, even encouraged, to endanger the lives of their fellows without anything more than minimal or pseudo restrictions. Insofar as an anarchic system of spontaneous adaptation gives much (although by no means all) of the motoring public a reasonable trade off between risk and freedom, this may be satisfactory. Looked at from the point of view of the more careful motorists and all non-car users, however, when compared even remotely to standards of occupational safety, this situation fails to meet a reasonable level of civilised or decent values.

Might this not be inevitable? Is it not the price we have to pay? There are two objections to the proposition that we have simply to accept the present dangers as necessary. Before stating them, it is worth repeating that the "we" who pay the price is often not the group responsible for the danger; those who are more likely to suffer are also less likely to be dangerous. Thus the displacement of danger generated by a particular road user group on to all of "us" in "our" society obscures the situation.

The first objection to the inevitability/necessity proposition is that, however necessary car domination may be, it does not warrant the current absence of control over car use. There are examples of institutions and practices whose existence is considered socially necessary where far stricter safety controls operate, at least in principle.

The second objection is that this kind of domination is *not* necessary. Mass car use has brought with it a variety of problems, all of which were brought into focus by the Government's 1989 White Paper, *Roads for Prosperity*. This document promised an additional £12.4 billion to be spent on increasing the road network capacity by some 2.0 per cent to provide for an estimated growth in car mileage of between 82 and 134 per cent by the year 2025.[1] This means an extra 15 to 24 million cars. How this increased number of cars would be accommodated is hard, if not impossible, to say.[2] If it is undesirable or impossible to allow all those entitled to drive to do so, the question arises: how do we decide who should and who shouldn't be a driver? There might be a case for squeezing a few million more cars onto the roads if mass car use were an unalloyed benefit, but it is not. Current levels of use generate a variety of serious problems, of which danger is just one.

According to the chief statistician at the Department of Transport in 1987:

"Road accidents are a manifestation of social behaviour, and society and individuals have to learn to live with increased volumes of motor traffic."[3]

The consideration below of the adverse effects of mass car use reveals many reasons why we should *not* be expected to live with increased — or even current — volumes of motor traffic, even before danger is put properly on the agenda.

A. Not just a dirty story — cars and pollution

In early 1989 a rather strange story appeared in the *Wolverhampton Express and Star*:

West Midlands Police is to 'go green' in a major move towards helping protect the environment. The force is looking to buy lead-free bullets to protect firearms officers from pollution.[4]

Whether this report, which was still circulating some months later, was a hoax or not is not of concern here. The notion of environmentally friendly bullets is certainly a trifle bizarre, and symbolises the way the nature of pollution is misunderstood.

In Britain at present, incomplete and much delayed steps have been taken to reduce one of the many pollutants — lead — from vehicle emissions. Action to deal with the other pollutants, which cause the vast majority of vehicle emission problems, is proceeding dangerously slowly and is impeded (or possibly even outweighed) by increasing volumes of traffic. One minuscule aspect of a major problem has been dealt with, while almost all of it has stayed the same or got worse.

It might be thought pessimistic to suggest that the removal of lead from petrol and the introduction of catalytic converters are only a smoke screen. However, the benefits of such measures are utterly trivial compared to the pollution problems posed by motor traffic. It is not just that petrol stations and oil companies bombarding us with images of fuels that "burn green" or "clean up the environment" grossly distort reality; nor even that when the fuel is burned in such dangerous pieces of technology the process is far from rational and peaceful. The fact is that there is no such thing as a clean car. Cars and other vehicles based on the internal combustion engine emit pollutants which need to be reduced by controls which eventually must require some restrictions on use.

Forms of pollution

(i) Greenhouse gases

Global warming — the exacerbation of the "greenhouse effect" through the accumulation of chemicals in the atmosphere as a result of human activity — is widely agreed to have begun. Exactly how much of a part vehicle emissions may play in changes which are fundamentally transforming life on this planet is difficult to predict. Nevertheless, we know that vehicle emissions are a big part

of a big problem. Cars and light vans produce about 18 per cent of global carbon dioxide emissions when in use, with an additional amount produced in their manufacture, and carbon dioxide is implicated in about half of the greenhouse effect.[5] Nitrous oxide, one of the nitrogen oxides emitted, is a greenhouse gas. So too are surface and tropospheric ozone (as opposed to the ozone in the ozone layer), which can be generated by the nitrogen oxides. Carbon monoxide contributes to the destruction of hydroxyl radicals, which play an important part in reactions which clean the atmosphere of pollutants; it may also contribute to elevated levels of tropospheric ozone.[6] Worsening concentrations of gases in the "greenhouse cocktail" are the major pollution problem emanating from vehicle exhausts.

217

(ii) Smogs and acid rain

Nitrogen oxides can turn to nitric acid in the atmosphere and fall as acid rain. They react with other chemicals in sunlight to form photochemical smogs. Smogs contain ozone which destroys billions of dollars' worth of crops in the USA and elsewhere and has other damaging effects on plants and materials.[7] The nitrogen oxides in smog irritate the mucous membranes with serious adverse effects on human health, particularly for those with respiratory ailments. [8]

(iii) Hydrocarbons

Benzene and polycyclic aromatic hydrocarbons are implicated in causing cancer.[9]

(iv) Smoke

Particles in vehicle emissions large enough to be seen as smoke, particularly in diesel emission, can have carcinogens adsorbed to them. The higher temperature at which diesel burns produces less of some of the noxious pollutants, so the defence of cars by pointing to the use of diesel in buses is therefore ill founded. [10] However, the additional health and other problems of diesel exhaust suggest no reason to advocate the car diesel engine.

(v) Spillage and leakage

Leaking or wrecked oil-tankers at sea, and vehicle oil poured and washed down drains, cause persistent pollution.

(vi) Noise

Although relatively universal, noise is the forgotten pollutant, a low priority even for people generally worried about pollution. Vehicle noise invades the home, upsets social intercourse outside and causes a variety of health problems which can be properly addressed only by reducing noise at source. The National Society for Clean Air reports that "Noise from road traffic is the largest single source of environmental noise nuisance in the UK, with 23 per cent of people in Britain 'bothered' and 8.0 per cent 'seriously bothered' by it."[11] An OECD estimate gives figures of 16 per cent of people exposed to "unacceptable" (above 65dB[A]), and over 50 per cent to "unsatisfactory" levels of noise.[12]

What has been done

Evidence on the harmful potential of leaded petrol emerged in the 1960s and 1970s. Regulations to control emissions of lead from petrol were passed in the USA in 1975. Discussions started at EC ministerial level in 1983 have led to the introduction of unleaded petrol and later to agreement (in June 1989) on a package of emission control regulations applying in the EC, with the implementation date of 1992.

The campaign over lead-free petrol indicates that sophisticated, media-conscious campaigners have to struggle for a long period to secure simple objectives in the face of manufacturers with long production lead times — even over an issue which does not affect the ease of motoring. (Although recommendations from campaigners to reduce pollution by more careful driving patterns appear to be difficult for some motorists to accept.)[13]

What needs to be done

The easiest problems to solve involve controlling noxious emissions through the installation of catalytic converters, which can reduce many or most emissions, and through the introduction of more efficient engines and lighter bodies to double fuel efficiency. Motorists would not be inconvenienced. However, catalytic converters do not have a beneficial effect on the production of CO_2 and leave open the question of increased pollution in the short- and medium-term until all vehicles are fitted with them. There is also the suggestion that catalytic converters do not function when cold, possibly on up to 20 per cent of a typical urban car journey.[14] The same short- and medium-term wait applies to more efficient fuel consumption. Manufacturers are unlikely to see an incentive for introducing such vehicles until fuel becomes significantly more expensive.

Any serious attempt to deal with the greenhouse effect and air pollution should require the restriction of vehicle emissions, particularly in the context of Third World car ownership coming remotely near levels in Western countries. This means not only changes in the kinds of car driven (with increased fuel taxation to stimulate the move towards more efficient fuel consumption), but also a stabilisation of, or more likely a reduction in, existing, let alone predicted, car mileage.[15]

Pollution is an issue of increasing concern. After years of failure to deal with the danger, loss of public transport, environmental destruction, and other problems arising from mass car use, many motorists have at last started questioning part of their behaviour. There is, however, something glaringly wrong with such "green consumers" discussing how alternative fuels can make life better for everyone when car use has so many other drawbacks.[16]

The consequences of global car use remotely reaching current European levels will be intolerable, even with increased fuel efficiency, catalytic converters, and so on. The West will have no authority to demand emission reductions from Third World countries if "we" ourselves fail to act.

Alternative fuels create problems as well. Liquid hydrogen needs electricity to freeze it, as well as involving storage and safety problems. As with electric vehicles, it demands an expensive fuel whose generation usually produces CO_2. Alternative sources of electricity are expensive, but should be used in future for those other more urgent energy needs at present served by nuclear power or fossil fuels. New dream technical fixes such as hydrogen fuel cells or cold fusion are not only exceptionally expensive and distant prospects: the problem is that their introduction would not just replace existing technology but displace it on to the Third World, in much the same way that tobacco's loss of markets in the metropolitan countries has been displaced. Engineering the road environment to produce more free-flowing traffic also fails to reduce pollution.[17] A more basic approach is needed.[18]

Everything points to emissions needing to be reduced through restriction, in the first instance by way of higher fuel prices that will push car manufacturers into producing more fuel efficient and/or alternative-fuel-using cars, and also to reduce car use overall. Even with cars that emit less pollution, there will still be no such thing as a "green car". They will still (like lead-free bullets) be dangerous. They will also be space hungry, in competition with more benign and equitable forms of transport, environmentally destructive, expensive, and so on.

B. Mass car use and health

Exacerbation of social and health inequalities, separation from directing health protective amenities and social isolation, as well as health damage by physico-chemical pollution... it is arguable that these factors may account for more years of life lost annually than do road traffic accidents.[19]

Using a broad definition of health, such as that exemplified by the World Health Organisation *Health for All by the Year 2000* strategy, and used by the new public health movement, all the problems generated by mass car use have health implications. Specifying them is hampered by the relatively late concern with transport and its relationship with health, compared to the work done on relating health to diet, unemployment and housing. Also, the medical establishment's credo of individualism and its acceptance of the transport *status quo* have allowed discussion to be trivialised and distorted. The long-term effects of land use planning — including features such as out-of-town retailing and the community severance caused by new roads, the decline of public transport, changes in access to health care and the maintenance of social support networks — do not get much attention. Instead we are offered self-help suggestions: that individuals walk or cycle for their health, presumably independently of traffic and other environmental conditions. This may be accompanied with trivialising irrelevancies, with an element of supposed humour, such as the debate about "erectile impotence" in male long-distance cyclists.[20]

Despite the predominant ideology, health problems generated by our current transport system can, and should, be highlighted. These include:

≡ The discovery that increased chances of death among elderly people may be due not just to hypothermia in poorly heated accommodation, but also to exposure to prolonged cold outdoors. Responding to interviews, a group of elderly people revealed that the biggest single reason for getting cold is waiting at bus-stops for decreasingly adequate bus services.[21] When published in the *British Medical Journal*,[22] the research implied no difference between walking (which produces bodily warmth and is normally regarded as healthy exercise by doctors) and waiting in the cold for up to 40 minutes at a bus-stop — an example of the kind of unenlightened medical thinking which impedes an assessment of the links between health and transport.

≡ The prospect of poorer diet for inner-city dwellers without cars and, therefore, without access to out-of-town hypermarkets, as local shops raise prices and otherwise show a decline in services as a consequence of competition.[23]

≡ The loss of access to health care with changes in health provision which may discriminate against those unable to make longer journeys (by car) as health centres become more centralised in location. Access for women, in particular, is inadequate.[24]

These issues, rarely mentioned until recently,[25] exist alongside the more obvious health questions:

(i) Accidents

Accidents and the fear of danger can cause additional health problems — inhibiting the mobility of the elderly, the disabled and child pedestrians, and placing additional burdens on parents organising transport for children who cannot be allowed to walk or cycle.

(ii) Pollution

Insofar as car manufacturing and use play a role in the depletion of the ozone layer, they are implicated in health problems, particularly skin cancers, in those areas of the world most immediately affected. The long-term worldwide effects of global warming are implicated in potential famine and migration phenomena which may make other health problems appear insignificant. As for noxious emissions, carbon monoxide (CO) and nitrogen oxides (NOx) can cause respiratory irritation and health problems. CO can cause coronary damage. Photochemical smogs and tropospheric ozone, produced by the reaction of NOx and CO with hydrocarbons, irritate mucous membranes in the eyes and elsewhere.

Carcinogenesis is a complex process involving mutagens and inducing agents (promoters). Understanding it requires knowledge of concentrations of material, of how it is taken up, and of other elements of epidemiological work. Research into a link between emissions and cancer is as yet fairly thin on the ground. If such work is carried out, mass car use may well be significantly implicated as causing a large number of cancers. Airborne polycyclic aromatic hydrocarbons alone are held responsible for 30 new lung cancers each year in Sydney.[26] Benzene is implicated in some 600—1,900 new cancers every year in the USA,[27] where concentrations are lower than in Britain. One estimate for Britain gives a figure of a possible 5,000 new cancers caused by hydrocarbons every year.[28] Other evidence points to diesel emissions as a possible carcinogen.[29]

(iii) Mobility and access

Less tangible, but equally (or more) important, are the effects of *loss of mobility* for non-car-users, and the wider *access problems* for all exacerbated by mass car use.[30] Loss of access to health care, poorer diet and other effects of changes in local retailing, loss of green space and general community severance are worsened by heavier traffic flow, road building, pollution, and so on. What would once have been regarded as the most simple and basic of journeys, such as those made by children and elderly people crossing the road to visit friends and relatives, become less frequent.[31] The associated stress is hardly acknowledged, although occasionally mentioned with regard to the driving experience. As the loss of social support networks occurs,[32] we see the worsening of general health problems which already disproportionately effect particular social groups, notably low-income inner-city dwellers. The most disadvantaged within these groups suffer most of all.[33] Another problem of increased motorisation is the reduced access to health services for non-drivers occurring over time.[34]

Perhaps the most unhealthy aspect of this unhealthy picture is the lack of interest on the part of the medical establishment and others in doing research on a scale which would equal the sophistication of the number crunching performed on road-accident and other traffic phenomena.[35] But this is because official accident statistics are produced purposely to justify more road building and other features of current transport policy; equivalent resources are unlikely to be devoted to those who suffer from it. If any such work is done without there first being a radical change of perspective, material will be produced either to justify the use of limited technological fixes — such as hoods on the nozzles of pumps at petrol stations to reduce concentrations of benzene[36] — or to slot into another programme of justification for maintaining the *status quo*.

The untold story: mass car use and cancer

The few studies that look at the possible link "suggest strongly that residential traffic density is a substantial risk for cancer, even taking smoking behaviour and socioeconomic characteristics into account".[38] This does not mean that smoking is not a cause of cancer. But it does mean that mass car use may be also a major cause, or a co-promoter with smoking. Because the origins of the debate involved studying *either* environment *or* smoking in the causality of cancer,[39] environmental causes were studiously neglected. One of the few researchers looking at the link between benzene from petrol and cancer suggests that: "one might... speculate that the more widespread, common-place and 'normal' a chemical exposure is perceived to be, then the less likely it will be that the exposure is recognised , let alone considered to cause cancer." In such ways the experts fail to see the wood for the trees.

But this is true for all dangers posed by a car-dependent society and it is not just the difficulties of seeing things in the wider context which complicate the issue. It is a question of the difficulties of confronting powerful interests (with the motor, roads and related industries far more powerful than the tobacco industry) and of confronting one's own privilege.[40] In such ways have "experts" taken apparently easy ways out at the expense of motorisation's victims.

C. Sabotage — cars and public transport

A conventional view, held even by those who would usually be wary of any competition with public services, runs as follows: bus use and other public transport are inherently inferior to car use; therefore car use should be encouraged; public transport will remain as a second-rate alternative for those too incompetent or unfortunate to drive.

It is a dangerous view. Car use cannot be universal, and there are good arguments for a substantial reduction in car use. A public transport system has to exist. The assumption that it should not be supported indicates an inability to conceive of the needs of non-car-users and of the impossibility of reaching a state of car saturation. But even those advocates of car use who would like public transport to be well funded fail to confront the basic problem that *mass car use inevitably reduces the possibilities of public transport provision.*

Some countries which are heavily dependent on cars do have good-quality public transport. The erosion of public transport in Britain in the 1960s and 1970s, when nearly a third of the 17,000 miles of railway and two-fifths of the country's 4,200 stations were closed down,[41] was a needless onslaught. Nevertheless, a decline in public transport provision is a basic consequence of mass car use, which tends to sabotage public transport in three ways: through the allocation of funding, competition for space and loss of ideological support.

(i) Funding

Public transport passengers, excepting those with fare concessions, pay. In 1988 passenger revenue earned by Britain's buses and trains was £2.58 and £2.19 billion respectively.[42] When people leave public transport to make their journeys by car they reduce this source of revenue.

In addition, public transport requires subsidy by the taxpayer. In 1988 this was £750 and £606 million for buses and trains respectively[43] — about one-fifth of public transport's total income. It can therefore be argued that when a small number of passengers stop using a bus, they take revenue away from the bus service; if sufficient of them leave, provision can be reduced (by having fewer buses) and taxpayer subsidy reduced as well. But the reduction of provision will then have adverse effects on those who still want to use the service. It is therefore reasonable to see the movement away from buses to cars as constituting a withdrawal of finance, and to count this in the monetary costs of car use.

Those people dependent on public transport because they are poorer than car users are more in need of subsidy than car users. Yet, as shown below, the level of subsidy to cars is probably far higher than that to a form of transport which has far fewer antisocial and anti-environment effects and should therefore be in receipt of far more support.[44]

(ii) Space

Cars compete with buses for space, and car use is much more wasteful of land than rail, bus or tram provision. It also competes directly by slowing down public transport. One bus or coach carries, on average, the passenger equivalent of 22 cars, taking up about a seventh of the space for the same amount of passenger use.[45] Of people going to work in central London by road, between 50 to 100 per cent more go by car than by bus — in some 130,000 cars as opposed to only 3,000 buses.[46]

(iii) Ideology and political support

Ideology is the least-mentioned destructive effect of mass car use on the prospects for public transport. When the most articulate and powerful passengers desert buses and trains, important potential support for the provision of public transport is lost. This is not limited to lobbying for more resources. If cars are seen as superior or more desirable than public transport, the latter will always be at a disadvantage.

Though intangible, attitudes are important. There is a lack of imagination about the kind of service that public transport could give were the motoring option reduced, and were demand, finance and space made available for buses and trams. Location of stops near home; more regular, cleaner, personally more secure and less expensive services; greater accessibility for disabled people — these are only the beginning. Ultimately, forms of demand-led "public transport" approximating to cars could be created.[47] Innovative and committed thought is hardly given to these possibilities, because of the car fixation. Many people think that they do public transport a favour simply by using it. By contrast, people with disabilities have claimed that, until they have access, we do not have a genuinely *public* transport system because so many members of the public are excluded from it. Indeed, one can extend this idea by stating that, unlike the relatively trivial opposition offered by walking or cycling, mass car use has impeded *the very possibility* of a proper public transport system.

D. Counting the cost of cars

Motorists continually complain that they have "paid for the roads" or at least paid far more than other road users.[48] This kind of statement bolsters unwarranted feelings of indignation and self-pity when the negative effects of mass car use are pointed out. The amount of taxation concerned is in fact very small compared to other taxes, and payment should not in itself constitute justification for anything: car and other taxation is not, and never was, meant to give specific exclusive entitlement to road space over non-car-users.

In fact, *the costs of car and associated vehicle use are far greater than the taxation paid by motorists.* Motoring is subsidised out of the public purse. People who walk or cycle instead of driving cost less than motorists, *even after the contributions of motorists are counted.* Cyclists and pedestrians in effect subsidise motorists, not the other way round.

Some words of caution: counting the social costs of anything is a dubious business. The categories used to assess costs and benefits, as well as the very business of placing monetary values on environmental destruction and human experiences such as the bereavement caused by accidents, are contentious. The arbitrary nature of categories and the values attached to them, the problems of effects on those less able to pay or on future generations, the inequities of adverse effects on minorities, the difficulties of assessing the full effects of policies or their alternatives are referred to above.[49] In particular, where waste and obsolescence appear to be almost endemic features of the economic system, it appears that costs can also appear as benefits. Indeed road crashes generate forms of economic activity (such as in the important insurance sector), and can therefore appear on both sides of the cost-benefit balance. As with accident statistics, the political purpose of the presentation of statistics on congestion, road building, car taxation etc by the road and car lobby is to argue for yet more money to be spent on roads and motoring.

Nevertheless, a consideration of costs can be revealing. The costs most usually referred to are congestion, accidents, and road building and maintenance. But this is too limited. We can also consider costs of loss of revenue to public transport, stress and health costs, policing, and a variety of environmental and social effects.

One problem in assessing costs and contributions of different kinds of vehicle is that cars are categorised along with light vans and taxis which may have more valid reasons (business or semi-public transport) for being there. It is also difficult with limited space to deal with relatively minor matters such as the contribution to congestion of the different classes of two-wheeled motor vehicles relative to the different amounts of vehicle taxation they pay. The biggest analytic problem involves isolating the costs and contributions of lorries from those of cars. While the cost of maintaining roads for goods vehicles (the track costs), particularly for those of more than 3.5 tonnes, is some 30 per cent of the official total of track costs, there is some sense in linking it with the cost of cars. This is because much of the need for road freight — such as the lack of cheap rail freight alternatives and the use of car-oriented retail outlets — is one of the consequences of a car-dominated transport system.

Assessing the full costs of private motor vehicle traffic in the three traditional areas would lead to the following estimates.

Congestion

Congestion is difficult, if not impossible, to quantify. If it is assumed that I have the right to drive at a speed I regard as desirable from a home anywhere in Britain to work in central London, then any delay can be counted as a congestion cost. The road lobby uses this kind of thinking to argue for even more subsidy to motoring to recompense those who are the principal cause of congestion in the first place. Some costs, however, such as loss of time for carriage of goods and services, should be considered.

The most thorough estimate is of costs of some £3 billion for the seven major British conurbations for 1987-8.[50] Allowing for inflation and growth in traffic since that time, this could now be more like £4 billion, with allowance for other conurbations leading to a nationwide figure of £4.5 to £7 billion. A figure of £2 billion for additional accidents produced by congestion, and the cost of delay while debris is removed from them, also needs to be considered. The Institution of Civil Engineers gives a figure of £10 billion, including the £2 billion extra accidents

ONE DAY, SON, WHAT REMAINS OF ALL THIS WILL BE YOURS....

figure.[51] The CBI's report on congestion in London in 1989 gave a figure of £15 billion.[52]

Allowing for a degree of exaggeration from the CBI, and deleting the cost of extra accidents (dealt with below), the figure would be between £7 and £12 billion. Some congestion costs may be attributed to buses, pedestrians and cyclists. Allowing £1 to £3 billion for these costs, we have a final total of *at least £4 billion, and more probably £11 billion*, due to private motor vehicles, mainly cars.

Delay affects emergency vehicles. Between 1975 and 1988 the average speed of ambulances attending emergencies was reduced, largely by increasing congestion, from 25 to 12 mph.[53] I can find no estimate of financial costs attached to this.

Accidents

The official estimate for costs of accidents is about £5 billion for 1987.[54] Costing accidents is one of the most contentious areas, partly because of the issues surrounding the costing of pain, suffering and bereavement, and partly because the monetary benefits due to the alleged "saving of accidents" can fit all too neatly into yet more plans for road building. Also, if one is moving away from the narrow "accident reduction" objective of "road safety", financial savings are not the objective to be concerned about.

However, a use of official criteria again indicates that even by its own standards car use is heavily subsidised. If inflation is allowed for, with accident numbers remaining more or less constant, the cost in 1990 should be about £5.5 to £6 billion. If costing were to include long-term disability following road traffic accidents, this figure would be likely to rise again to over £6 billion.[55] If motorists are to be considered responsible for all the accidents they are exclusively involved in, and about half of the rest, it seems that 60 to 80 per cent of the cost should be attributed to them, that is, *£3.6 to £4.8 billion.*

An alternative method of costing accidents involves comparing costs of road and rail.[56] By costing loss of production, policing, processing in the legal system, insurance premiums, medical treatment and mental and physical pain (partly included in the British estimates), it gives figures of some 2.5 per cent of GDP in Belgium and West Germany for costs of road accidents, with costs of rail accidents some 300 times lower. Transferring these estimates to Britain _ making a rough comparison of accidents per head of the population — we have a cost of some *£12.5 billion* — substantially higher than official estimates.

A study of motor vehicle crashes in the USA in 1988 gives an estimate of no less than $334 billion in costs, which given the high level of cars in the traffic mix can be largely attributed to cars. Translated to the British car population this would amount to some £30 billion, to the British number of crashes approximately £35 billion.[57] I will stay with the lower British and German estimates.

Road building and maintenance

The total cost of capital and current costs of national and local roads is approximately £4 billion.[58] It can be argued that some of this is "for" pedestrians and cyclists. Yet much road surface maintenance, for example, does not meet the needs of these groups, and one could add an additional cost for maintenance at a higher level on to the cost of motoring, because motor vehicles are a principal cause of the deterioration of road and footway surfaces. Also, the reason for provision of facilities such as pedestrian crossings is arguably motor vehicle use. Yet here I will take a more conservative stance and stay with the *£4 billion* figure, although plans for road building issued in 1989 calling for an extra £6 billion to be spent would be additional costs.[59]

Other costs

Loss of revenue to local public transport

If it is agreed that good local public transport is necessary to a civilised society, made available as a service alongside public health and education provision, then the cost of mass car use competing with it should be included.[60] A proportion of these "lost fares" that would have been paid by motorists if some or all their car journeys were made by public transport should arguably be counted as a cost of motoring. At an average of 10,000 miles per car per annum, with a public transport cost of approximately 10p per mile, the full cost would be some £1,000.[61] With reduced journeys and lower fares this would amount to some £600—£700 . One might subtract an amount to allow for the cost relative to cyclists and pedestrians, who travel less miles than motorists and thus compete less effectively, of some £150—£250. However, it could also be argued that these modes do not involve the energy use and pollution of all motorised transport, and even that cycle use should receive direct subsidy, so that there should be zero subtraction. Without allowing for the passengers in cars, for these estimates (£350—£700 per car in 1989) this produces a total of *between £6.3 and £12.6 billion*.

Policing

The cost of policing and use of traffic wardens is about £330 million a year.[62] A small part of this may be attributed to non-motorised road users, but these more vulnerable road users are apparently not receiving the protection they need in terms of the curtailment of dangerous driving and pose less of a threat to others. If such an increase in enforcement — whether by human or automatic means — took place, the costs would surely rise. Were the possibilities of being caught for serious road traffic offences endangering other road users to rise from the 'tiny' to the 'very small', the cost of policing — even allowing for the non-motorised road users' contribution — would probably increase by at least £1 billion. This does not include the very considerable use of police and court time in dealing with the theft of vehicles and other crime relating to cars. As owners of very expensive consumer goods left in public places, it seems reasonable to suggest that motorists should pay back some of this cost.

Health

This is particularly difficult to assess, because research on the effects of air pollution is only just beginning and is difficult to quantify. Problems of smoking-related illnesses, for example, may be exacerbated by levels of certain kinds of air pollutants: we just do not know to what extent this is true. Similarly, stress has been estimated as costing some £5 billion in sickness absence. Other costs of stress such as reduced work performance have not been quantified. It seems reasonable to suggest that at least 20 per cent of stress is related to motoring (for motorists), danger, delays and poor service on public transport related to a car-centred transport policy, thus giving a cost of £1 billion.[63]

Specific environmental problems related to health have been costed as follows:

Air pollution

Quinet's survey for the OECD suggests that this costs on average 0.4 per cent of GDP.[64] Teufel gives a figure of some £7 billion[65]: Apel estimates the cost in Berlin close at approximately £150 million.[66] Quinet's figure based on the cost of car use in Britain would be £1.7 billion (at 1990 constant market GDP). Estimates are therefore £1.7—£7 billion.

Noise

Estimates from these authors are as follows: Quinet[67] 0.1 per cent GDP or over £4 billion, Apel[68] and Teufel[69] both suggest costs twice as high as air pollution.

Given Quinet's overall cost, these estimates — based on relative costs of noise as compared to air pollution — are £4 billion — £14 billion.

It has been suggested that the intangible costs of road building and car use — loss of independence of children travelling by foot, community severance, pollution, vibration, noise, visual intrusion, and so on — should be included.[70] This would add significantly to the cost which we can say motoring incurs. While the costs of global warming are still unknown, there are estimates for car emissions, as well as for some of the other intangible costs:

Cost of escorting children to school

This is based on costing the hours lost to parents taking children by car on journeys which children of the same age made by foot or by bicycle some 20 years previously. The cost is a staggering £10—£20 billion.[71] One might allow a reduction in this as parents might still wish to accompany children travelling by the benign modes, but a figure of £5 *billion* might still be arrived at.

Taking up space

Whether in terms of taking up space on the public highway when parked, or of use of internal building space (garages) which could be used for people to live in, this is one of the great hidden costs. Apart from visual intrusion and loss of garden space in residential parking, car parks replace vast amounts of potential commercial or residential buildings. Calculated in terms of the costs of rental of space and rating of domestic dwellings, I cannot come up with any estimate less than some £250 per vehicle, or *£4.5 billion*.

Adding up the costs

Congestion:	£4 to £11 billion per annum
Accidents:	£3.6 to £12.5 billion
Roads (without the "Roads to Prosperity programme):	£4 billion
Policing (without general car theft etc.):	£1 billion
Public Transport revenue loss:	£6.3 to £12.6 billion
Stress:	£1 billion
Air pollution:	£1.7 billion to £7 billion
Noise:	£4 billion to £14 billion
Children's escort time loss:	£5 billion to £20 billion
Space:	£4.5 billion
Total Costs:	**£ 35.1 to £87.6 billion**

Table 5.

It should be repeated that this does not include costs such as the loss of agricultural land, greenhouse gas emissions, defence costs for protecting oil supplies, and various adverse social effects. One of the biggest costs could be loss of working hours and health care for people suffering bad health (from cancers and other problems caused by pollution) which have not been costed here.

Amounts paid

The total of specific road user taxes paid by all private vehicle users is about £11.5 billion, which is below the lower estimate of conventional costs alone. [72] Adding on VAT (cyclists also pay VAT on bicycles) can bring this figure to just below £17 billion. This figure is below the upper estimate of conventional costs, and below the mid-range of the wider costs — which still exclude the costs of intangibles. It also excludes taxation costs of freight carriage by road which would otherwise be passed on to consumers. The amounts paid by motorists, even including the VAT, come to about £12 to £13 billion, only just above the lower estimate for the limited conventional costs.

In addition, one can argue that were motorists to drive less or otherwise spend less money on driving, they could spend the saved money on alternatives which are also taxed, principally through VAT. This makes the amount spent by motorists on tax appear even less impressive, and their deficit even greater.

This means that if hypothecation — the payment back of what they see as excess taxation demanded by the roads lobby — occurred, motorists would, in fact, have to pay additional money back to the Exchequer to come up to the level of cost that pedestrians and cyclists now incur. The amount to be paid would be between £21 billion and £75 billion, or approximately £1,200 and £4,200 per car.

This may seem a large sum, and it certainly amounts to a quite staggering cost, but it fits in with other estimates from abroad. While Germany has a more extensive motorway network (and much more investment in the rail alternative), it has similar population and road network densities and proportion of distances travelled by rail, bus and car.[73] Its population is some 10 per cent larger, and accident numbers tend to be higher. Bearing this in mind, Teufel's calculations[74] of costs of 110 billion DM (with state revenues of 30 billion DM), and considering the time at which these figures were given and the ensuing fluctuation of exchange rates, these figures amount to costs equivalent to *£35—£50 billion per annum.*[75]

In fact the deficit costs per car as worked out for Germany by Teufel, the USA by Renner[76] (whose estimate for total car deficit is less than the total cost of auto crashes quoted above for the USA), and the California Department of Transportation[77] are in the region of $2,000—$2,500 per annum. These costs do not include some of the social costs I have estimated.

All this depends on assumptions about the way an economy should operate. It might be argued that the car industry, which has received taxpayers' support through the years, should be subsidised anyway. One can suggest that smashing bridges by using heavy lorries is one way of stimulating the economy by requiring the building of new bridges. It would give one more reason for the road builders and the lorry operators to unite in the British Road Federation. It gives an appropriate illustration to Keynes' remarks about an economy functioning with men being paid to dig holes in the road and fill them up again. But one could equally argue that shifting resources to the alternatives of public transport construction and operation — or indeed other sectors of the economy — would provide the same employment and fulfil the needs of the economy.

None of this means that, if motorists were to pay back what is in effect a subsidy to bring them into line with cyclists and pedestrians, *they should not pay a tax as well.* This could be a tax on pollution to pay for the effect of greenhouse gas emissions. Of course, people living in parts of the world most immediately affected by drought or flooding, and, where congestion is a factor, those most immediately affected by ambulance delays, would be more likely to put a higher cost on such disbenefits than those who cause them.

Meanwhile the pervasive myth of motorists "paying for the road" persists. For a recent Minister of Transport: "There is nothing subsidised about motoring in Britain today."[78] Yet his own department, in a brochure about the Transport and Road Research Laboratory, gives a figure of costs of traffic, which, despite being a severe underestimate, is higher than specific road taxes paid by private vehicle users.[79] Then there is the additional subsidy of tax relief for company cars.[80] Beyond this, payers of taxes, community charge and business rates fork out enormous additional amounts of subsidy for the purchase of parking places and mileage allowances for local and central government staff. Since allowances are calculated on the basis of fixed costs which would be paid by the car owner anyway, this constitutes one of the more expensive institutionalised perks in contemporary British society.[81]

The myth of motorists "paying their way" is dangerous in road safety terms as it supports unjustified feelings of being discriminated against with respect to non-motorists. It is therefore particularly wrong for figures in the road safety lobby, such as Murray Mackay of PACTS, to support the myth.[82] Relative to other road users such as cyclists and pedestrians, motorists *most certainly do not pay their way*.

E. Cars and congestion

The summer of 1988 saw the beginning of a rash of media reports and discussion on the problem of traffic congestion in Britain's cities, particularly London. One somewhat cynical comment was that the rush of concern was stimulated by editors caught in traffic jams on London's orbital M25 motorway, or else perturbed at the limitations on commuting into central London by car.[83] Of course there are problems with congestion: there have been traffic jams since pre-war days. However, most of the people suffering in the commuting crawl into central London are not in private cars — only 16 per cent travel by car[84] — although the problem frequently appears to be defined in terms of inconvenience to the private motorist.

Congestion problems don't just affect motorists. Increased congestion implies delayed public transport users, additional costs to the public in goods and services, additional pollution, possible additional danger, disturbance of residential streets by people taking short-cuts, and so on. These are problems which affect far more than the minority of people going to work by car. Meanwhile motorists take up a massive amount of room compared to the other modes of transport, particularly buses,[85] and in this sense bear prime responsibility for congestion.

There is another more compelling reason to see motorists' problems as at best marginal, and to see motorists as the cause of the problem, rather than just another group suffering from congestion. It is that *there are no solutions to congestion which can pander to the desire of commuters to drive to work*. Any attempts to do so, namely those centred around road building and provision of extra parking space, not only have severe disadvantages; they just do not work in solving the problem as it is officially defined.

So what's the problem?[86]

As with "road safety", defining how congestion is a problem, and hence its causes and solutions, depends on your interest or viewpoint. Some might suggest that a cause of congestion is the persistent refusal of motorists to share car use (the average occupancy rate is 1.2—1.5 people per car[87]). Car sharing has been applied as a solution to traffic problems in parts of the USA, although the advantages of access to faster priority lanes reserved for high-vehicle occupancy is of limited relevance in Britain. Its main relevance is probably to have produced an amusing indication of motorist unwillingness to behave responsibly: the system is said to have been abused through the use of inflatable dummies passing as occupants. It has limited benefits, and if passengers are prepared to abolish privacy, full-blown public transport seems more rational.

On the other hand, it is sometimes argued that the tendency of people to want to cross the road is a cause of congestion. A Los Angeles planning report states: "The pedestrian remains the single largest obstacle to free traffic movement."[88] As with "road safety", people are a problem to be got out of the way, and buildings are also something of a difficulty. Of course it is still possible to squeeze some more cars into cities — but at what cost? In 1963 Buchanan calculated that if 9,000 residents, 50,000 staff and 115,000 shoppers in London's Tottenham Court Road all used cars, six ten-lane motorways would be needed.[89]Engineering and technological changes (for example, in junction design and computerised signalling systems) have increased capacity to allow more vehicles to be squeezed less painfully than such a prediction would have allowed, and in that sense a quart has been put into a pint pot. A gallon will be more of a problem.

Anyway, whatever the cause or the precise solution, it has generally been accepted that there was a "congestion problem" which we all opposed, and whatever the limitations might have been, more roads were built to do at least something about it. What happened?

The road building experience

In areas where there is suppressed demand for car transport, however, new roads *generate* new traffic rather than relieving congestion. The prospect of new road building, road widening or similar "improvements" simply shifting the jam further on down the road has long been pointed out by objectors to such schemes. It has been very much in evidence on London's M25. The academic attempt to wrestle with the prospect of new roads generating new traffic, and trying to build this into forecasting techniques, is relatively recent,[90] although it was shown in the early 1980s that the building of the Westway had generated traffic.[91]

The best-known work on the subject is that of Mogridge, which centres on the relationship between overall traffic speeds and the speed of public transport.[92]The key to speeding up traffic is not the provision of more road space for cars, which fills up with more cars and reduces support for public transport. It is to take space away from cars to provide more space for buses which can attract people away from cars and move people faster. Just as nature abhors a vacuum, available road space is taken up by those modes which appear most attractive.

This idea is a product of the same kind of common sense thinking as the risk compensation hypothesis. It assumes that human beings tend to adapt to changed circumstances. Like risk compensation it is ignored if it offends the dominant ideology surrounding the private car.

Motorists have always been able to blame problems associated with motoring as inevitable, trivial, or caused by something other than motoring. It is a different story with congestion. When we look at attempts to solve congestion problems however, even looking at them from the view of traditional criteria which may be wrongly biased towards car use, the indicators point away from cars. Unless they involve a programme of reducing car use and supporting alternatives to it, any of those attempts are simply incompatible with the existence of what we now recognise as our cities.

But what is the problem?

Even in terms of achieving an aim of fast-flowing vehicular traffic (which would not be achieved by road building and would require a shift away from car use as a necessary pre-condition), problems of land use and pollution might increase:

> Higher average traffic speed appears to spread the city, creating lower density land use, a greater need for cars, longer travel distances and reduced use of other less polluting or pollution-free modes. The benefits gained in terms of less polluting traffic streams appear to be overwhelmed by the sheer amount of extra travel and the resulting bulk of emissions.[93]

If the aim of a transport system is to enable as many motorists to drive into a city centre as possible, then building more roads would be (to some extent) the appropriate transport policy. West London's Westway motorway cost an enormous amount of money, severed a community, brought massive visual intrusion, noise and other pollution and accelerated a trend towards declining public transport, but it *did* allow more motorists to share in the experience of commuting in their cars, even if congestion at the end of the Westway and elsewhere in London remained the same. For some motorists this is the desired objective. Consequently, increasing parking space and road space for cars (both of which generate more traffic as well as being extremely expensive) may be seen as the way forward. To increase the number of motorists sharing in the congestion experience at the expense of others and the environment would only be a further extension of what has been happening since the onset of mass motorisation anyway.

What is required is a fuller understanding of what transport and environmental rights citizens should have. I could argue that if my 'right' to commute in my car from one end of England to another is not easily available (because there are insufficient door-to-door motorways allowing me to drive at 200 mph easily), that

I have been "delayed" by "restrictions" which could "cause congestion" if I persist in excercising this 'right' with other motorists. After all, the figures used to calculate the cost of congestion and assess its size are criticised even by establishment transport planners for their arbitrary nature.[94] I would go further and repeat the criticism made elsewhere in this book that the calculations are not so much arbitrary as arbitrary *within an ideologically constructed framework designed to support an inequitable status quo.* Defining transport needs in terms of the requirement for a sustainable economy, minimal environmental impact, public health, easy access and safety for those outside cars, would give us a different agenda.

With that agenda adhered to, and with the non-car user not discriminated against, we would have a reduction of car use which would lead to a decline in the kind of problems now associated with congestion. But defining congestion as a problem in the way it is now, even with the realisation of the need not to build new roads as a solution, does not take the discussion far enough.

F. Other problems

(i) Other environmental damage

The environmental damage caused by mass car use is huge. The word "environment" is too bland to describe the surroundings intruded on, eroded and destroyed by modern motorised societies. The damage extends beyond the noise, noxious pollutants and greenhouse gases produced by vehicles, and the massive amount of energy consumed.

Vast amounts of non-renewable resources are consumed in the manufacture of cars. Enormous tracts of land are taken up by road building — up to 4,000 acres of rural land, including valued parts of the countryside, each year in Britain, with another 35,000 due to disappear if the new roads programme is fulfilled.[95] Car-parks, quarries dug for road-building materials, and the disposal of spoil from construction take more land.

Inner cities and town centres are weakened or torn apart by the urban sprawl created by road building. A look at photographs taken before the impact of mass car use reveals the full extent of the intrusion.

Many of the changes that matter are difficult to separate out from each other, or too subtle to notice as they encroach gradually over a period of time. They are harder still to assess and cost for a number-crunching cost-benefit analysis. But they are real enough.

(ii) Alienation and inequality

The car promises an *essentially private control over public space.* Most of the problems in dealing with the adverse consequences of car use stem from this; when people feel that the use of the car is essentially their personal business, it is difficult to approach it in the way required, as something with profoundly *public* effects. The ownership and use of cars also generate a kind of individualistic separation of

234

members of society from each other.

A look at an urban bus queue usually reveals society's less powerful citizens; they are likely to be poor, elderly or women and children. Since the prospect of everybody, or even all adults, being car owners is a myth, the idea of a car-borne democracy is also a myth. As the society becomes more attuned to car use, those with cars benefit more. Households lower down the income scale find it difficult to have a car; and within one-car families, those who already have power (usually the man) will have first call on the car.

(iii) Talking about it?

These disbenefits multiply. As people use cars, they become dependent on them. Dramatic changes in society are generated over the span of no more than a few decades, assuming a natural or permanent appearance. The change may be the transformation of childhood, with the loss of independence of movement. It may be the desertion of streets that become more threatening to the remaining pedestrians. Whatever the change, its very appearance as natural impedes the search for, or creation of, alternatives. We cannot talk about life in modern societies properly unless we fully recognise the impact of cars. None of this points necessarily to the abandonment of car use; but it should be considered as problematic and open to discussion in the same way that other features of modern society, many of them more permanent, are.

Do you sincerely want people to drive cars?

If the average non-car-owner is asked if they would want a car, or even the householder with one car whether they would want another, most would answer yes. If you describe the consequences of such wishes coming true and ask people if they would enjoy living in the world that resulted from it, you would get a different answer. Cars are fine for you if you belong to a restricted population allowed to use them.

Consider again the forecasts in the White Paper *Roads for Prosperity*, around which the contemporary transport debate centres.[96] Before growth stops, we are told, there will be another 27.5 million motor vehicles in Britain. If all motor vehicular traffic increased at the upper limit, this would swell to an additional 32 million vehicles. Adams' calculation of the space required merely to park these extra vehicles arrives at either a new 257-lane motorway from London to Edinburgh with stationary vehicles parked on it, or an area the size of Berkshire. If parking space is required at destinations, as well as at home, this area needs to be doubled. Any approach to such future forecasted levels would require a massive increase in the miles of road for these cars to move in between their parking places. With just a fraction of the forecast numbers, the amount of road space in Britain would have to be increased well beyond the present programme just to keep congestion at present levels. Solving the problem by reducing on-street parking rather than building more roads would exacerbate the parking problem. Coping with increased traffic at junctions would mean junction "improvements" involving grade separation and enlargement — a world of Hanger Lane-type gyratory systems. The cost would vastly outstrip the £20 billion in the current programme. A less pessimistic outlook by a mainstream transport planner still presents us with an unpleasant and expensive vision of a future, should the forecast be realised.[97]

Amenities for people without access to cars, who would still number in the millions, would become even less available than at present. Public transport would decline further, and there would be less safety for those using the vulnerable modes of transport. Pollution problems would also worsen.

The Los Angeles example

Los Angeles is probably the most car-oriented city in the world.[98] Its history is instructive for anyone wishing to pursue the path of motorisation further.

The Los Angeles region has more miles of freeway- and motorway- type roads than the whole of Britain. An initial view, before the contemporary congestion problem, would suggest all the supposed advantages of car use: cars moving quickly along roads specially built for them. Yet this conceals the central difference between *access* and *mobility*. Los Angeles has a population density half as high as London's, and this figure diminishes to one-tenth in the outer parts of its urban sprawl. Thus the extra speed is required to travel the additional distance — which has been created in the first place by building a city around the car. If access is considered, rather than mobility, the city's inhabitants are not necessarily any better off; few journeys are short enough to be comfortably walked or cycled, and local amenities are not favoured. Bus transport is unattractive or non-existent. Longer journeys mean increased energy use and pollution. The notorious Los Angeles smog remains despite the introduction of catalytic converters.

Even the speed of the freeways cannot be relied on. The phenomenon of "suburban gridlock" has been generated, and traffic engineers have given up the possibility of a totally congestion-free system, despite the $61 billion road-building programme announced in 1988. Methods of restricting access on freeways are now being tried, diverting cars back on to the roads they were supposed to relieve. Add on massive social polarisation between separated rich and poor, and you have a vision of the car-dominated future that is already here.

This may be just the beginning. Los Angeles has more cars now than the whole of China, India, Pakistan, Bangladesh and Indonesia combined.[99] Third World countries are in some cases developing their own car industries; virtually all are increasing their car ownership rates per head of population far faster than the West is. There are now some 400 million cars in the world. Allowing for population growth, a world with British levels of car ownership would have perhaps six times as many cars. The depletion of natural resources required to build these vehicles and the roads for them, the amounts of energy needed to fuel them and the emissions from them (whatever technological fixes were introduced) would dwarf today's problems.

236

But perhaps, as with all the problems of mass car use, the real problem will always start from the inability to properly place the issue on the agenda. After the 1992 Los Angeles riots the suburban middle class were shocked to learn the real feelings of inhabitants of the same city, visible through a controlled gate of contemporary media, but not from actual human contact. The culture of fear is a vicious circle started as soon as mass car use begins, with the first flight from community and the simultaneous private colonisation of public space. The privatisation of space in Los Angeles is carefully described in the American Social Science Association's Best Book Award Winner of 1990, *City of Quartz*.[100] It was justly praised for its detailed sociological, historical and geographical account, with one exception. There is no reference to the role of the car in the geography or culture of the most car-centred city in the world: neither "car" nor "automobile" make it to the index.

The non-democratic car

While the effects of greenhouse gas emissions have come into the debate only recently, many of these issues were publicly discussed more than 20 years ago. Mishan indicated how:

There can be no socially acceptable solution to the traffic problem that aims to accommodate the private automobile.[101]

A few years later Illich pointed out the non-democratic nature of car use, and its inappropriateness for answering transport problems in the Third World.[102] The 1974 report by the Independent Commission on Transport stressed the difference between accessibility and mobility.[103] The impossibility of universal car use and the scale of environmental devastation involved in trying to achieve it were described by the then Guardian motoring correspondent in 1972.[104]

Despite these warnings, motorisation has increased. This chapter has raised the question for each motorist: if motoring cannot be universal, and yet there is vast demand for it, what makes you so special?

Essentially this question of asking motorists to justify the basis for their privilege, and particularly its restricted nature, is an extension of the questions concerned with safety. It is simply asking people with vast potentially (or actually) destructive power *to account for themselves.*

That motorists have been able to get away from this responsibility is an indication of the scale of the problem. This is partly because of the weakness of motorisation's victims. They are the same groups discussed with regard specifically to safety issues, and on a global scale they include potential victims of the effects of global warming (such as coastal flooding or famine) who are predominantly the poorer members of Third World countries.

But on top of this the ideology surrounding car use allows motorists to continue to escape their responsibilities. Examining this requires a look at how motorists see themselves.

15.

The view from the driving seat — motorist attitudes

IF YOUR VILLAGE has been cut in two by fast cars, what can you do? The people of Theydon Bois, near Epping Forest, bought their own Home Office approved radar speed gun, but couldn't convert their recordings of up to 54mph over the speed limit into private prosecutions. Part of the problem facing communities like these is that motorists now believe the road to be theirs. As Winston Churchill correctly predicted, they have assumed "moral ownership" of roads which once performed a social function in small communities, rather than providing a relentless source of danger.

❖❖❖

This book has set out to revive the pre-war idea, which has never entirely disappeared, that the problem of traffic accidents is a problem of (motor) traffic. The principal responsibility for danger must therefore be seen to lie with those who make the roads dangerous in the first place — motorists. But do not the motorists have something to say for themselves? They do, and it reveals the nature of the ideology supporting excessive use and abuse of cars. The words and phrases used to legitimate their actions, the "techniques of neutralisation"[1] employed, are more than mere defences. Their use, on those rare occasions when motorists are asked to account for themselves, prop up the structure of motorist hegemony.

Most important is *the absence of serious talk about the use of cars in modern society*. Media discussion about transport issues is limited to the occasional nod in favour of public transport, or muttering about how bad "it" or "the traffic" is. Safety is hardly mentioned, and then only in the language of the road safety lobby, or in terms of how specific groups of motorists might be dangerous. Any suggestion that mass car use is implicated in the loss of public transport is virtually absent: contrast this with discussion of the impact of private health or education on the public sector.

The Marie Antoinette syndrome —"Let them drive cars"

There has been some discussion in the media implying that car use might not be totally desirable. We are asked: "Could you live without your car?"[2] The respondents of the question discover a strange world of inadequate public transport and other difficulties for non-car users. Like Victorian visitors slumming it in the netherworld, they find out how the other half lives, and it is not very nice. The "other half" indeed. Or rather the one-third of households without cars, the one-fifth of men and half of women without driving licences and the half of all journeys that are not made by car.[3] Many motorists are amazed to learn of the existence of such people.

Ignorance is only part of the motorist self-centredness syndrome. The modern car user enjoys, as did the naive princess, a position at the top of a hierarchy of power and privilege. As in her case, this system (and those at the top of it who benefit from their advantage) is *largely responsible for* those problems such as inadequate public transport which face those at the bottom — in this case the non-car users.

In addition, motorists do not want, at least in urban areas, these others to become car users. Their comfort as car users depends on their numbers being limited: they do not really want the peasants to eat cake.

With accidents, the attitude is more one of the suffering victim, although this approach also applies to any suggestion that motorist privileges should be restricted. The justifications given are that:

"I pay a tax for the road."

Some 70 years ago, Churchill correctly anticipated what the effect of the Road Fund tax would be:

It will be only a step from this for them to claim in a few years the moral ownership of the roads their contributions have created.[4]

The "tax" never gave motorists special legal rights on the road, particularly with respect to other road users. Now a car or vehicle excise tax, it is no longer "for the road" anyway. It does not cover the costs of catering for motorists: indeed the non-car user is effectively subsidising the motorist.[5] It is a relatively small amount of money — even with combined taxation on items such as petrol — compared to income tax, VAT, or the council tax or business rates. Yet people who do not otherwise feel they can

LOOKING AT THE WORLD THROUGH CAR SUPER-STRUCTURED GLASSES

buy privilege, let alone with such non-existent justification, will use this defence.

"I take a test."[6]

Motorists are not genuinely trained how to drive. They drive more or less properly once for half an hour before systematically infringing the rules and regulations they have learned about. They are allowed to drive after passing a "test" which is set up to let the vast majority of those who want to drive do so. These people then develop a sense of pride as a consequence of having gone through this rite of passage — and then they claim that doing so should give them special rights.

"I have to obey the Highway Code."

Motorists are supposed, like everyone else, to obey the Highway Code. Unfortunately, they don't, and neither do they obey laws on speed and so on.[7] Rule infractions occasionally lead to minor "punishments", with slightly harsher ones for a minority of these occasions creating the illusion that rule-breaking is taken seriously. But motorists do not really have to do what they are legally supposed to, and never have done.

Other petty pseudo-restrictions apply:

"My car has to have an MOT."

This is not only inadequate,[8] but the idea of risk compensation suggests that it has no significant effect on motorist danger anyway, because motorists adapt to more efficient braking systems and so on. There is no evidence to suggest its introduction led to any reduction in accidents.

"I have to have third party insurance."

Third party insurance — originally opposed by the motoring organisations — is another supposed control which I would suggest decreases the need for care on the part of motorists.

One further illustration typifies the cosmetic nature of restraints on motorists. Motoring organisations originally opposed the registration of motor vehicles and the use of number plates as an unwarranted infringement on their freedom, and for a longer period the 30 mph speed limit.[9] Their current official history[10] still proudly describes the way in which AA "scouts" would warn motorists of speed "traps" set by the police ahead of them — a move which led to a senior Home Office official of the time to describe them as "like an association of burglars employing scouts to warn them which houses are and which are not watched by the police".[11]

In 1990 residents of a village just outside London took the extraordinary step of purchasing a Home Office approved speed detecting machine as part of a campaign to protect themselves from high speed through traffic. Attempts to have traffic calming measures installed had failed because the road they live on is a through route — too high up the "hierarchy of roads" which determines whether such measures can be taken. The police refuse to allocate police officers because the "accident rate does not justify it"[12] — since it is reported that villagers are not only scared to cross the road, but even to walk on the pavement, this is hardly surprising. However, despite recording vehicles reaching 84 mph in their 30 mph speed limit area with their radar speed gun, the campaigners have been unable to secure any private prosecutions. The police point out that the Data Protection Act prevents them from giving names and addresses from the computer which holds the registration numbers.

So while the motoring organisations normally (but not always) present a more respectable image, this presents no change in their determination to protect their members from genuine attempts to control the danger they present to others. The legislation they proudly flaunted and fought against in the pre-war years was never really going to restrict them anyway. It consisted largely of pseudo-restrictions, not real restrictions, which were possibly worse than nothing because conceding to them made the motorists appear responsible.

Victim blaming

The above techniques of neutralisation are most often used when comparison is made with the road users who do not share these pseudo-restraints — cyclists and pedestrians. Such comparisons have a long history, going back to the first complaints about motorist danger. They may be seen as an example of what psychologists call *projection* as a defence mechanism;[13] or just an attempt to divert attention away from the problem.

An early example is one of the first segregationists, H Alker Tripp.[14] He claimed that "when he (the cyclist) comes to harm, the fault is more often his own than somebody else's". Yet his own figures only barely suggest this to be so, and all the published British figures since indicate precisely the opposite. The most recent work, by the AA Foundation for Road Safety Research, claims that of all road user groups, cyclists were the least likely to be at fault where accidents had occurred (in 27 per cent of cases);[15] in a study in Oxford where a bicycle was involved in a crash with a motor vehicle, the cyclist was the main person at fault in 25 per cent of cases, and only 17 per cent where the cyclist was an adult. The only other post-war study was carried out by the Metropolitan Police and gave the main blame to adult cyclists in 31 per cent of cases.[16]

One variant of this victim-blaming is to become concerned about cyclist/ pedestrian conflict. For Alker Tripp, this problem was:

by no means negligible: in some places the accidents of this kind have been more than 5 per cent of the total accidents of all kinds.[17]

Yet in view of the fact that, at the time Tripp was writing about (the late 1930's), more miles were travelled by bicycle than car[18] — this indicates a low proportion of accidents. Nowadays the DTp gives the relative likelihood of a cyclist being in a crash with a pedestrian resulting in the death of the pedestrian as being about five times lower for each mile travelled than for car drivers.[19] Yet — another example of the distortion these statistics can give — about 90 per cent of cyclist distance travelled, as compared to about 50 per cent for motorists, is on the built-up area roads where pedestrians are much more likely to be than on rural roads. So in terms of a real comparison where proximity of pedestrians is brought in to consideration, the figure should be more like 10 times less. But the lack of threat posed by cyclists may be even more marked than this. Common sense tells us that pedestrians pay less heed to cyclists than cars — indeed this is one area where pedestrians actually pose a threat themselves — thus pushing the differential, in terms of *danger*, even higher. Also, responsibility for the fact that cyclists ride on pavements because they fear for their safety may partly be placed on motorists for making the road environment dangerous. And the reason for relative lack of vigilance on the part of pedestrians towards cyclists is part of a culture where the dangerous are deferred to and the less dangerous and more vulnerable are neglected.

Individualism and irresponsibility —"Other people are far worse"

Apart from the vulnerable road users, other motorists are blamed. As explained in Chapter 1, motorists tend to appraise the general standard of driving as bad while refusing to describe themselves as bad, and rate themselves as above average. Sometimes the ability of drivers with convictions for dangerous driving to blame others for being "the cause of accidents" is unnerving. [20]

This is not simply the natural human inability to accept one's own failures, or the projection of one's own incompetence on to others, or the tendency to blame groups other than the ones we belong to (old drivers if we are young, men if we are women, and so on). While all these features may be present, the crucial element here is the *failure to accept responsibility*.

At the core of the motorists attitude is a special kind of individualism and personal pride. What people do in their cars is seen as the *personal business of the motorist* involved. This is the central characteristic of driving and its importance in the understanding of the death and injuries inflicted on hundreds of people daily, and other problems, just cannot be over-estimated. The root of all the problems associated with car use is that people are encouraged to think of an essentially public activity — and the most potentially dangerous to others that the majority of us will ever regularly engage in — as an essentially private one.

People use cars to express their individual psychologies. [21] The roles of family man, "independent" woman, "dynamic" young man and so on, are played out in the public arena. The idea of a car users behaviour as private and personal creates an almost impenetrable ideological fog around discussion of transport safety and related issues. We are not allowed to ask even basic questions about what motorists regard as fundamental human rights. Breaking through that barrier, and initiating a serious discussion on the kinds of car use that may be thought appropriate in a civilised society, means looking at such questions.

Consider the irrational defences of motorists' privilege described above. They are often made explicitly in comparison to other road users. Yet it is precisely in comparison to other road users that they are revealed as irrational. Alker Tripp made his attack on cyclists arguing that the:

club member who takes a pride in his cycling, very seldom comes to grief; the majority of cyclists, however, are not of that calibre, so very many of them being young, venturesome and casual.

He also notes, specifically by way of comparison, that:

In the case of motor vehicles, registration and licensing were an initial and fundamental measure for ensuring orderly and lawful use of the road. [22]

But, according to Tripp's own figures, responsibility for accidents cyclists had involving motorists was that of the motorist in about half of all cases (and virtually all studies since have placed legal responsibility on motorists in the same or higher proportions, at least with adult cyclists). It is therefore dubious if their involvement was only seldom: certainly their organisations and media were concerned about their members being killed in incidents that were far from seldom.

What is being argued — along with a combination of victim blaming and encouragement for club cyclists to congratulate themselves without looking too hard at the origin of the danger — is simply a defence of motorists. It is based on the idea that the minimal restrictions placed on motorists had actually worked. But there is no indication that any of the measures taken in the Thirties *did* actually have any definite effect on reducing danger. "Orderly and lawful use of the road" by motorists in the full sense of following the Highway Code has never happened. The idea of risk compensation suggests one of the reasons why this did not happen: describing what he noticed from the driving seat in the first days of the 30 mph speed limit, Alker Tripp remarked on another occasion that "he noticed that driving was extraordinarily comfortable". [23]

Fatal road accident casualties 1927 to 1940

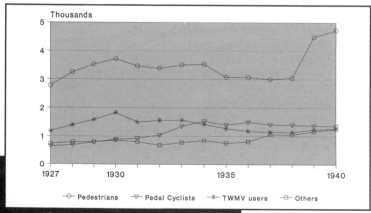

Figure 5.

Pedestrians   Pedal Cyclists   TWMV users   Others

Source: Transport Statistics GB 1988

243

This opinion comes from one of the most influential figures in transport planning: the same views are aired regularly. A motorist writing to a cycling campaign's magazine[24] complains that some cyclists "appear to believe that the Highway Code does not apply to them". What is interesting about this comment is not that — unless he is very unusual — the correspondent very likely breaks the rules of the Highway Code and the law himself, or indeed that in doing so he could be implicated in much more damage to other human beings, or even "causes of accidents". No, what is interesting is that he can get away with accusing others of his own faults so easily. This is not an example of human frailty, but something specific to the ideology surrounding car use.

Giving a name to it — the concept of car supremacism

Previous chapters have described how mass car use has brought with it a variety of problems for society as a whole, in particular for the non-car user. The severity of these problems is increased because the use and abuse of cars is not met by any significant moderating or countervailing force. Such a force is absent because of the division between the groups suffering at the hands of motorists: pedestrians, cyclists and public transport users. These groups are further weakened by being among low status, low power groups in a contemporary society — elderly people, people with disabilities, children and people on low incomes. The ideology surrounding car use further strengthens car hegemony and prevents any rational discussion of transport needs and related issues. One part of this ideology is the contemporary ideology of "road safety", with all its victim blaming and mystifications. We need a way of talking about car use that restores, to what is assumed to be a personal and private pursuit, its genuinely public nature.

This might be achieved, I suggest, by arguing that there is a kind of *supremacism* which car use tends to involve. All car use has negative effects: the moment any motorist gets in a car there is removal of support for public transport, increased danger for others, use of scarce resources, and so on. Exactly where the power of the car user becomes excessive or intolerable is a matter of debate: the fact that all car use has negative effects does not mean that anything like all car use should be stopped. (Indeed, a typical example of unthinking — and sometimes almost hysterical — prejudice is the immediate assumption, once the inherent dangers are referred to, that the only possible remedy is a ban of all motor vehicles in all circumstances.) But it is necessary to realise that there are inevitable adverse consequences, particularly if left unchecked, and with the additional problems of imbalance of power and ideological distortion this is even more true.

The word "supremacism" is deliberately borrowed from its use in attempts to understand discrimination and oppression by race and sex. This might seem somewhat extreme. Admittedly, the problems of danger from car use should really be seen as Health and Safety problems, and we are dealing with problems that are

— in some ways — more limited and less brutal than those of racism and sexism. Nevertheless, the concept is needed if we are to escape from the idea that road danger is due to individual deviants.

It is also needed because we all approach issues with a set of prejudices and ideological distortions which need to be *positively* identified and dealt with, rather than just left to good intentions which may, or may not, exist. In fact, it can be argued that it is *much more* necessary to see car use as something which requires checking, than attitudes on gender or race: the very fact that even particularly careful motorists can kill through a moment's negligence makes this in some ways *more* of a necessity than the examination of power and ideology surrounding other social issues. It is quite possible to think of human beings as naturally benign and co-operative; but when they are in positions of power which have a high level of inherent danger to others, control is required.

The concept of car supremacism implies a need for social policies that borrow from Equal Opportunities (or even positive discrimination) ideas and practices in the approach to transport and other policies involving car use. But surely there are cases where car use actually is superior: where, unlike preference to people of one race over another, one can argue that car use is superior to walking or public transport ? The analogy with other forms of discrimination may break down here — but it also breaks down in the opposing direction. There may indeed be (limited) benefits from using cars for those who use them (with disadvantages from car use for others). But in terms of their availability and accessibility, and their relative absence of adverse effects, one can argue that *the benign modes of transport are in many ways superior* to car use. Besides, *any* car use at all already involves a degree of discrimination against non-car users: thinking of allowing it to occur without genuine controls amplifies this. The fact that it is desirable makes it more, not less, of a problem.

There are other reasons for the supremacism/equal opportunities analogy applying more fruitfully to the transport situation than to other divisions in society. The existence of organised groups of women and people of ethnic minorities etc is more apparent than that of the victims of car hegemony who are more likely to suffer from the divide-and-rule policy of the transport and road safety establishments. What is more, divisions between men and women, for example, are rather more long-established than the problems generated over the last few decades by mass car use. And it is not as easy for men to rape women inadvertently as it is for motorists to injure and kill through a little avoidable — and criminal — negligence.

Consider the following examples of the supremacist ideology. I am constantly told by motorists that they do not *want* accidents. (With this particular technique of neutralisation the emphasis is clearly on "want", frequently with a tone of pained or bewildered indignation.) But the reality in terms of law and rule infractions, of inadequate training in the first place, of the inevitable "mistake" or "error of judgement" even in terms of what the motorist happens to feel is correct, is hardly one where people behave as if they were doing *all they could* to avoid accidents.

245

If motorists were in a situation where they knew there was a real chance of being caught for rule infraction (even with existing penalties), or of suffering financial hardship through paying for the consequences of such rule infraction in the event of crashes, or of suffering far more physical harm in a crash; if motorists were in a position where their own loved ones were walking or cycling round the next corner (and could not be "got out of the way"); if large financial incentives for rule obeying, and genuinely painful financial or custodial punishments for rule breaking existed; if all this were so, or just some of it, motorist danger would still exist, but would be considerably less than it is now. Motorists may not want accidents, but with some 10,000 crashes occurring every day, we can say that they — all of them — tend to not want them to an inadequate degree.

The point is that the level at which danger is acceptable should not be left to motorists to decide, which is effectively the case now, both on a general and individual level. Motorists simply do not have the incentive to behave properly, or the disincentive not to. Any motorist can be asked about the times when they have been too tired (to take just one example) to drive within the kind of criteria described above: they may say that in normal circumstances they would not drive when it is dangerous to do so, but nevertheless, they have done so, and will continue to do so again until a deterrent exists.

The prospect of backlash

All this means that any genuine move away from excessive danger, environmental nuisance and antisocial behaviour will be met by a backlash. Because motorists see their privilege as, first and foremost, one which cannot be put in question — to even be talked about as a problem — let alone have any move taken to even moderate or reduce it, the reaction is often hostile. There is an interesting similarity here between racist or other supremacist defences, and the defences of car supremacism. Anybody can examine these defences by engaging in a useful piece of do-it-yourself sociology by questioning motorists about their behaviour, basing their approach on the assumption that they know the motorist is dangerously antisocial.

Responses will vary. Some motorists are quite happy to accept, or even celebrate, the danger they pose to others. Another approach is the somewhat more tolerant view that others should get out of their way for their own good and in the interests of "road safety". At the less obviously vicious end of the spectrum we get a shrug of the shoulders indicating that *they* cannot see themselves as a problem, or a more wounded and shocked denial with a response reminiscent of the denials of prejudice wherever prejudice exists: "I am not anti-pedestrian", the motorist equivalent of "some of my best friends... ". Pushing the criticism further will, as with all criticisms, run the risk of the wounded innocence turning into straightforward nastiness. This can happen through the use of the car supremacist "joke".To take one from London's Time Out magazine:

cyclists need not know the Highway Code. You score extra points belting them

with your wing mirror — bonus if you run over their skid lids.[25]

This is not just sick humour but a particularly vile celebration of the danger that even the most careful motorist possesses. Such jokes are, in fact, a particularly inadmissible form of behaviour. In a climate where racist jokes or jokes about rape are unacceptable, and where there is a generally agreed upon need to be aware of potentially antisocial behaviour, such "jokes" should be less acceptable. After all, the easiness for endangering others, and the consequent requirement for positive commitment to avoid doing so, is higher for the individuals concerned.

Plainly discrimination against people by gender or ethnic origin permeates more aspects of their lives, and a case can be made for some car use in society: but we are not just inventing another "ism" for intellectuals or the so-called "chattering classes". "Car supremacism" describes a great deal of suffering and inequality which in some ways is more important than other issues covered by equal opportunities and similar ideas. And which is a lot less likely to be talked about.

Conclusion

Conversations with motorists and analysis of coverage of transport in the media, tell us more than innumerable academic analyses. There is simply no point specifying solutions to transport problems if we are prevented from discussing them properly. Unfortunately that happens — even to the exclusion of defining what the problems are in the first place — because of the refusal of motorists to consider that they may not in fact have a basic right to drive. Until we have sorted out what their obligations are, and how they have been avoided, there is no prospect of a "level playing field" for participants to debate the future.

We need to think of society as pervaded by a "car supremacist" set of power relations and ideology because of:

≡ the very attractiveness of the motoring option, particularly when motorisation has made alternatives unattractive.

≡ the institutional weakness of those groups suffering from the adverse effects of motorisation.

≡ the tendency for motor danger or other adverse consequences of motorisation to be pushed sideways after supposedly being controlled: popping up elsewhere after it has simply been pushed temporarily underground.

≡ the ease with which negative behaviours, particularly with regard to danger, can occur, and need therefore to be approached with a positive commitment to deal with the issue.

16.

"Road safety" or danger reduction?

IN OCTOBER 1990 the President of the Institute of Road Safety Officers and President of the Medical Commission on Accident Prevention, Prince Michael of Kent, caused a minor controversy by presenting the annual "road safety" awards named after him a few months after receiving the fourth in his tally of convictions for speeding and careless driving. While there are different sections of the road safety industry, with some genuinely opposed to such apparent hypocrisy, his behaviour is in many ways not qualitatively different from their own.

❖❖❖

The case of the problem Prince

Trying to deal with the most obvious examples of motor danger tends to obscure less visible problems which may be more important; and there is the likelihood of motorists compensating for any control of danger in one area by maintaining or increasing it elsewhere. For these reasons the process of pinning down what needs to be done about what JS Dean called the "motor slaughter" involves carefully stripping away a layer of "road safety" mystification, often to reveal another beneath it. Consider three aspects of this particular episode:

(i) Speed

The awards in question are sponsored by the Institute of the Motor Industry, which at the time had a number of its car manufacturer members under censure from the Advertising Standards Authority for promoting the ability of their cars to be driven at illegal and dangerously high speeds. But the ASA itself is criticised for only having a voluntary code of practice which is referred to after advertisements have appeared. And what difference does advertising make anyway? The availability of such vehicles in the hands of those attracted to the possibility of high speeds in them is surely more important than debate about advertising: yet while the demand for speed governors has been made by some for over 50 years, it is hardly raised as an issue by the road safety industry, and then either on a voluntary basis or for motorway speeds only. Instead we have discussion of limited speed reduction in some residential areas.

The official view is that most (80 per cent) urban roads are eligible, although only a tiny minority are likely to be treated by techniques which, in any case, are of questionable use in reducing speeds.[1] The average cost of these engineering treatments is £40,000 per kilometre and if work began on all those roads considered eligible, there would have to be allowances for some £4.8 billion, and 57 years in order to complete the project.[2] But this does not refer at all to the problems of speed on rural roads where those outside cars are particularly at risk.

This may all be dependent on increasing road building, and might spread speeding vehicles to other parts of the network where they will still be dangerous. Even where speeds are reduced, with a necessary and desirable reduction in destructive potential, motorists who do not receive additional controls may compensate by relaxing more at the slower speeds. And if elderly or child pedestrians take advantage of slower speeds on their roads to make more journeys, even if there are fewer casualties per journey made by them, it is possible that there could be more casualties overall. Traffic engineers would be unable to gain financial support from the DTp on safety grounds because of "an increase in accidents", or otherwise would oppose introducing such schemes themselves.

(ii) Training

One of the two main "Prince Michael Road Safety Awards" presented was to a woman who had successfully campaigned for the legal age at which a motorist can accompany a learner driver to be raised to 21. There is none of the following:

≡ Evidence that this has any effect on casualty levels or danger on the road, yet this move has been greeted with approval by "road safety" pundits such as motoring correspondents, generating yet more complacency among them.

≡ Consideration, typically in the context of law- and rule-breaking as typical, as to how this measure is to be enforced.

≡ Assessment of the importance of altering ages and the prevalence of accidents among learners, which constitute a minuscule proportion of all crashes.

≡ Consideration of how such a move might divert attention away from the question of restricting accompanying journeys to trained instructors.

≡ Question of the need for genuinely learning how to drive, and of the fact that "the test" is either useless as a means of control of danger, or not much better than useless.

But the layers of misunderstanding do not end there. For even real training leaves motorists with massive dangerous potential, and may even stimulate worse behaviour from those who have acquired "undue proficiency". Indeed, one reason given for the royal tendency to acquire speeding convictions is their special driving instruction on how to drive away from terrorist attacks — fast.[3] Teaching people to be nicer than they wish to be is a somewhat futile activity, largely introduced to have voluntary measures as opposed to necessary controls. The main advantage of any real training and testing would be to reduce the numbers of people entitled to drive. This would be offset by increased pride and would be opposed by motorists' organisations as soon as significant reduction in motorist members appeared as a prospect.

(iii) Cycle helmets

The other main award went to a campaigner for bicycle crash helmet wear, with Prince Michael making a particularly strong appeal for parents to buy their cycling schoolchildren helmets.[4] Of course, against a motorist driving at well over the legal speed limit (the reason for one of Prince Michael's convictions), helmets make as much sense for cyclist protection as chocolate fireguards do against fire.

The question of hypocrisy

Is the rest of the road safety lobby much less hypocritical? The DTp manages a system which has always been car and lorry oriented to an even greater extent than its continental counterparts. Local authority road safety officers support an educational system based on obscuring the relative lack of danger of cyclists and pedestrians as compared to motorised road users. In so doing, this urges the vulnerable to accept and defer to unnecessary danger. Vehicle engineers, supported by doctors and other sections of the road safety lobby, have pursued a safety level for motorists which is consumed as a performance benefit, generating even more motor danger.

"Road safety" has colluded with or generated what is nothing less than a system of institutionalised violence.[5] This may occur directly through a move such as seat belt legislation. It may be through the activities of personnel moving between the motoring lobbies and road safety, such as the former head of Road Safety Division at the DTp becoming a senior RAC official (another senior official has been Prince Michael). It may be through more general cultural shifts whereby certain groups — the oppressed — acquire "problem" status, while others — the dangerous — lose it. A great deal of the way in which the solutions become part of the problem is diffuse, and intangible. It may be unintentional on the part of some "road safety" practitioners, but if we are to regard certain standards of behaviour on the part of motorists as unacceptable, why should they be any less so from those who set themselves up to speak for safety?

Looked at in terms of the role of the road safety lobby, perhaps the really important point is that the antics of those such as Prince Michael *are not really hypocritical at* all. After all, there is a sense in which he can claim to be acting for safety by demanding that other road users simply try and get out of his way. My argument against this is justified not by the gut reaction that his ideas are unjust, inequitable and victim-blaming, but that ultimately if there is to be a reasonable chance for human beings to get about in safety, danger has to be controlled at source. This will back up the initial gut reaction, but it is important to be clear about the rationale for it. It also means that we get a clear idea of the power structure which underlies the discussion about safety on the road. This has profound consequences for the possibility of debate: it is questionable whether it is worth the effort to discuss the issue with such people as if they were on the same side as those of us genuinely committed to reducing motor danger. Consider how we should approach just the last of the above issues.

The wrong end of the stick with helmets...

We could argue that:

1. More lives are lost from head injuries by car occupants who could more easily wear helmets, and of a tougher design as well. But why should gross numbers be important? After all, gross numbers of deaths on the road have been reduced ("lives have been saved") as a relatively safe environment has been transformed into a sort of motorised dodgem circuit with a smaller proportion of journeys being made by

the vulnerable. Besides, looking at things from the viewpoint of the greatest number will always tend to benefit the majority, which (albeit narrowly, in terms of journeys) is nowadays those road users who have created a dangerous environment in the first place.

2. In terms of the *chances* of being hurt or killed, the car occupant helmet would seem about as feasible. But this may still repeat a central error of placing the onus on those who are least capable of bearing it. Moreover — and this cannot be repeated too often — those who are most vulnerable are in the main those who are not only always dependent on what motorists are allowed to get away with, they are not the source of the danger.

3. The evidence, with bicycle or motorcycle helmets or other measures, suggests that the supposed aim of safety measures ("saving lives") is not being achieved anyway. But that has never stopped such measures from being advocated, even when there was more definite data than there is in this case, and even when lives were taken as much as saved by them.

THE ULTIMATE SAFE CYCLIST....

4. Any measure (even without an element of discomfort) is inequitable unless car passengers do it as well. But then the *status quo* is basically inequitable anyway.

So, using the arguments of the road safety industry may be tempting; it is certainly useful to expose its contradictions. But ultimately these arguments are either irrelevant to what actually happens, or can be used to further the oppression of the victims of motorisation.

...and some other issues

Meanwhile, the road safety lobby continues to get hold of the wrong end of the stick not just once, but twice over. The debate on helmets does not just point the finger at the victims and potential solution to a problem instead of the problem, it is also derived from a way of thinking which got it wrong when motorists had been considered for helmet wear. For through the fog of mystification one image shines through. It is the modern rally driver: highly trained, well belted and of course helmeted in the cause of what we have come to know as "safety".

And the mechanisms whereby motorists adapt to attempts to control them (by accident migration, risk compensation, increased pride, smoke screening or whatever) are gradually being recognised by the road safety industry — which then draws exactly the wrong conclusions. Consider the case of the former Greater London Council Chief Engineer (Traffic) and leading figure in the road safety industry in Britain, Ken Huddart. In 1984 he was critical of evidence for the phenomenon of accident migration arguing that "it could reduce road safety workers' confidence in their work".[6] In 1986 he pressed the National Secretary of the Cyclists' Touring Club to refrain from voicing its worries about the effects of the seat belt law.[7]

By 1990 however, he was arguing that accident migration *did* happen in the case of motorway chevrons. (These are painted along the carriageway every 40 metres and signs urge drivers to keep two chevrons between them and the vehicle in front). According to Huddart[8] the effect of getting motorists to change to this behaviour (which, according to the Highway Code, they should be doing anyway) would reduce accidents as headways lengthened on the motorways — but road capacity would be reduced, resulting in motorists choosing alternative roads which happen to have higher accident records, thus increasing overall accidents.

In his calculations there is no mention of what would happen if motorists were dissuaded from long distance travel by having to pay the full costs of motoring, or having to take proper driver training, or being subject to real law enforcement. The possibilities of such travel being made unnecessary by location of jobs and amenities locally, or by long distance travel occurring by the far safer means of rail, do not figure.

When it comes to the figuring of cost benefit analysis, we are confronted with its discriminatory basis by Murray Mackay. Discussing the costs of casualties, he claims that motorcyclists are subsidised by other road users because:

> motorcycling does not bear the full burden of the risks and attendant casualties which come from having motorcycling in the traffic mix.[9]

These costs do not include the harm caused to others by motorcyclists, or the harm which would have been caused if the motorcyclists had been driving cars. Furthermore, it does not allow for the fact that most of the crashes leading to motorcycle injury where other vehicles are involved are the fault of others: one might think that they shoud pay the costs incurred. Such reasoning is grotesque and pernicious. It is doubly wrong because it holds that not only are the vulnerable more of a problem ("cost"), but the dangerous — who I think are a problem — are not.

What can we do with the road safety industry?

Can we campaign successfully for the road safety lobby to mend its ways? Could we argue for cost-benefit analyses, for example, to fully charge their costs to motorists? I am dubious about such an attempt. Even if we could calculate the full range of costs, including the costs of resource wars involving oil-greedy countries and the effects of global warming on inhabitants of Third World coastal plains, the information would not be used properly. The use of cost-benefit analyses is ultimately determined by over-riding political considerations, where at present car hegemony decides. Besides, minorities like rural pedestrians and cyclists will always tend to lose out even if this bias is overturned.

When it comes to road safety advice and regulation, even those who realise its smoke screening function sometimes argue that "the baby should not be thrown out with the bathwater".[10] But the fact that there is an element of truth in an argument (in this case it is recommending bicycle crash helmets, but it can apply elsewhere) is precisely what makes it so dangerous. The problem is that the disadvantages of advocating helmet use (such as the passing over of other measures, as well as the more intangible — but very definite — identification of cyclists as a problem) which we are bound to see, may outweigh any genuine benefits.

The precise mechanisms differ, but the ways in which the central issue is avoided are so many and varied, their surrounding ideological fog so dense, and the weakness and diversity of the groups suffering from car hegemony so pronounced, that only a radical break from the "road safety" paradigm will do.

There is simply no point in arguing about alternative ways to "save lives" when the concept is so weak, when it may be achieved by creating more dangerous conditions for the vulnerable and when evidence about the effect of ways of achieving this is not properly available. This supposed aim of saving lives is not genuinely believed in anyway — it is one of the reasons why measures are endorsed for which there is no real evidence of "accident reduction" in the first place. Most of all, when what we want is danger reduction and not "accident reduction", or perhaps even "accident rate reduction", we require a fundamental break from the "road safety" tradition.

The alternative — danger reduction

The aim of attempting to reduce road danger is to reduce it at source, by restricting the capacity of those with a tendency to hurt others in collisions. Initiatives should only be encouraged if they do not increase the spread of danger to vulnerable road users. Although it appears to inevitably endanger those outside cars, safety for car occupants can be supported so long as such measures protect the vulnerable as well. Safety for car passengers should involve genuine controls on the motorised, instead of measures such as increasing vehicle crashworthiness. If the risk of being hurt is reduced, it must be replaced by the risk — which should exist properly in the first place — of legal punishment and ultimately far greater social disapproval for behaviour which poses a threat to others.

Insofar as technologies may be available to reduce the capacity of the dangerous to hurt others they need to be used: the point about such technologies though is that in a car supremacist society they will not be used for that purpose. Technologies do not develop and exist independently of power and ideology.

Assessment of safety should be made in terms of the experience of the road user. In the first instance this means using an appropriate denominator to produce a rate based on the experience of the road user concerned; qualitative assessment of the perceived danger should also be included. If pedestrians provided with superior crossing facilities have a reduced casualty rate per crossing or journey, that can count as an improvement even if overall casualties increase. It may even count as an improvement if the quality of life is assessed as superior even if the rate does not decrease — decision making should move more into the hands of those most immediately affected, rather than professionals'.

A criminological example

Contemporary work on personal security and crime points out the negative effect of fear of crime as well as crime itself. Actually measuring the size of a problem, even given the difficulties of non-reporting, is made difficult by being unable to assess the relative importance of different occurrences. While professionals should be on hand to inform local residents of what appears to be the real crime level, the fear itself has to be understood and respected.

As with "road safety", it appears that removing potential hazards does affect people's behaviour. Design initiatives such as superior street lighting may encourage people to move around more and thus be more exposed, but their chances of being assaulted per journey do not necessarily increase, and besides they report that their quality of life has improved.[11]

The prospect of the road safety establishment dealing with such issues is intriguing. As we have seen before, safety might be increased for those endangering others (bullet-proof vests for gun licence holders?) or a decrease in the numbers of elderly women being assaulted because their fear inhibits them from moving outdoors might be welcomed. Our record would be hailed as being superior, and women would no doubt be recommended to wear chastity belts as a way of preventing rape.

Of course, this last analogy may seem misplaced: women are not responsible for rape, which requires a high degree of intention on the part of the offender. Yet, while high levels of individual punishment such as long-term prison are not called for, a lower level of intent should not be an excuse. Indeed, *precisely because* it is easy to endanger others lives on the road, there is more of a need to control motorists than members of the male sex. The potential for harm, after all, is much more readily exercised. As for the question of victim responsibility, admittedly the analogy fails. But insofar as accident avoiding behaviour by cyclists is to be encouraged, the use of "safety aids" is the opposite of what is needed. And, above all, those advocating helmet use are generally responsible for the danger created, either by their own motoring, by their collusion with the car supremacist *status quo*, by exacerbation of the danger through the use of seat belts etc, or, as in the case of the speeding Prince, by being more directly responsible for danger.

255

Research and pseudo-research

Meanwhile the task of studying safety according to the criteria of danger reduction and the experience of road users, particularly the vulnerable, has hardly begun. We could, for example, study the effects of "local safety schemes" allowing for regression-to-mean and accident migration phenomena, along with consideration of macro-social factors. Traditional research, even when performed properly, suffers from the usual fault of this kind of positivism in the social sciences of not being sensitive to changes occurring within the wider society, which affect the object of study. What we know about society-wide risk compensation is just forgotten about in virtually all of what passes for road safety research. Looking at risk compensation with regard to specific measures, we also need to remember that, even with data of good quality which do not yet have, the results of studies will suffer from being on particularly small populations, and that we have to go back to what we know from previous episodes which are better documented, such as seat belts. We should also take a fresh look at road safety interventions not just in terms of what has happened, but also by reference to what would have happened had there been far more users of the benign modes — as would have been the case with a better transport policy — in the area studied.

But apart from throwing virtually all official work into question, we have to consider how research has a destructively confusing effect. Research can do this:

≡   By re-circulating knowledge which is either known about already, obvious or plain irrelevant, in a way which delays consideration of real issues. This may serve the purpose of bodies funding research, such as government departments or insurance companies who want to appear to be supporting "road safety".

≡   By presenting findings in a way which confuses an already confused issue. In a road environment where motorist behaviour is characterised by persistent breaking of the Highway Code, the AA Foundation for Road Safety Research chose to examine the extent of the breaking of the code — by cyclists. In fairness, the study did suggest that only 2.0 per cent of those failing to comply with the Code actually put themselves at risk by doing so, but the message that the advice in the Highway Code for cyclists may be wrong is not necessarily the one that reaches public consciousness. Proper research is limited by looking at parts of the car-dominated whole, constituting a divide-and-rule approach where the object isolated for study becomes seen as the problem — especially in a climate where the *status quo* is so unquestioned.

≡   By "research" being largely a backing up process for policy recommendations which have already been decided on. In the most important "research" on cycle safety in recent years,[12] "cyclist conspicuity" is assessed as contributory in many cases where motorist responsibility could well be described as the contributory factor, and then only regarded as relevant in a fifth of accident cases. While more recent research has suggested that road design at notoriously hazardous situations such as roundabouts is implicated in motorists not noticing cyclists,[13] this idea is not mentioned. Yet "cyclist conspicuity" is still in the report's recommendations, as it would have been whatever the results would have been. The majority of accidents with adult cyclists and vehicles are ascribed as being the legal responsibility of motorists in a clear majority of cases, yet the recommendations are for training of cyclists and mere "publicity" for motorists.

≡ By the hiding or misreporting of "wrong" answers which result from genuine research or academic work. Here I refer to the covering up of results which do not support the received ideology, as happened with the Isles Report. Organisations that fund research generally have set ideas about what they want to prove and will not be interested in publishing results that set their cause back. Furthermore, financial restrictions on obtaining statistics from the DTp also make life harder for bona fide researchers operating outside the ideology of the road safety industry. Subtle misrepresentation is just as important. In July 1990, a conference on health aspects of cycling featured a number of medical experts. Despite the fact that helmets were given only a small amount of attention, and described as being of minimal importance, the apparently descriptive report of the conference in the *British Medical Journal* devoted a significant proportion of its report to helmet endorsement.(An accompanying piece on "safe cycling for schoolchildren" contained four items, three of which described unquestioning support for helmets.) An objection about such misrepresentation from one of the conference speakers went unpublished.[14] The "research" on helmet compulsion in Victoria simply refuses to consider risk compensation to explain its results.

The mythology of road safety is hard to dislodge, particularly when it forms part of a powerful ideology which assumes so much which is wrong to be natural. Yet it should be persistently questioned by, among other things, criticism of the isolation and definition of problems, methodology, and presentation.

Meanwhile, a dissertation by a Road Safety Officer on cycle helmets (which does not properly consider the actual experience of helmet wear) wins the 1991 Fina award, with the Fina fleet (company car) manager on hand to see it presented by the RSO's President, Prince Michael of Kent. [15] Texaco's campaign to shift responsibility for "being seen" yet further away from motorists onto children, when they would be in an excellent position to deal with motor danger at source [16] if they really wanted to see a civilised approach to safety, receives a Prince Michael Road Safety Award — part of a scheme initiated by the Institute of the Motor Industry (President, Prince Michael of Kent). [17] BP Oils recent campaign to "get them young" is called *"Living with Traffic"*. Of course, no oil company would seriously be interested in reducing traffic danger at source, nor would it be interested in reducing oil consumption to reduce the biggest global problem of all: a point worth remembering for those interested in advertising bans. However, we should not have to accept their message, whether it comes from them or from those with less oily hands.

Accusing the road safety lobby

All of us try to avoid accidents as far as is humanly possible. [15]

Television advertisement for Audi cars, November 1990.

This statement is untrue, or more accurately, is meaningless, since it is the essence of being human that *we do not* always do our best to avoid accidents. The road safety lobby, by denying this essential truth, has facilitated car advertisers' and others' ability to collude with or encourage the risk-taking of the dangerous at the expense of safety on the road. Simultaneously, the non-violent behaviour of the vulnerable has been subject to criticism and regulation.

Locating problems away from the source of road danger involves a kind of "divide and rule" mechanism whereby relatively trivial differences of interest between different user groups are exploited to mask the over-riding domination and danger of mass car use. Lectures from any road safety "experts" who are drivers will involve some hypocrisy, even if their law breaking is less obvious than that of speeding Princes. Whether from royalty or not, they all embody a kind of feudal ideology whereby the best the vulnerable can expect is the benevolence of their supposedly natural betters. This feudal ideology places the same responsibilities on the dangerous and non-dangerous: Prince Michael criticises drivers *deliberately* trying to push cyclists off the road, but says that cyclists who in some unspecified cases might delay motorists overtaking them are equally to blame. [18]

The road safety lobby is suffused by a relentless "feel good" mentality: the potentially dangerous and their supporters in the road safety establishment congratulate themselves on alleged progress, while their potential victims comfort themselves with whatever attempts they can make to avoid danger. But we need to get real progress, not feel good. Until there is a genuine commitment to see the capacity to hurt others as the central problem, there can be no decent way to work with the road safety industry. Safety has been turned on its head into "road safety". It needs to be put back on its feet.

258

17.

Conclusion — getting about in a civilised society

THIS BOOK presents a view of safety and other transport questions which argue an alternative to the dominant way of thinking. It does this by returning to the original idea of danger on the road as being essentially a problem which is created by mass car use, and that we have to go back to that idea to come up with any kind of decent or civilised approach. Similarly, more general transport questions have to be looked at from the starting point of the problems created by mass car use.

A neatly arranged recipe of solutions is not presented, although suggestions for future action are aired. There are good reasons for this. I argue that the simple numerical criteria, used by the road safety establishment for assessing success, are either inadequate or downright wrong. There are ways in which we can get an idea of whether things are improving, but the kind of numbers used at present play only a part in assessment. The real problems come when we look at the overall context of the transport system. This must involve basic background assumptions about the rights of different road users which inevitably decide the limits of what is possible. If these parameters change, so does the whole nature of the debate. Numerical criteria such as targets for emission reduction and minimum standards for bus provision, upper limits for car mileage etc can be used — but these are quite different to the traditional kinds of target.

Indeed, the transport debate is apparently changing. Since 1989 the official willingness to attempt to pander to the demand for ever increasing car use has — so it seems — been transformed by awareness of congestion and pollution problems. Under the banner of the "new realism"[1] transport academics and policy makers are united on a new consensus where the car will be given less rein. But as I suggest in this book, there are some fundamental questions which have not been answered.

We hear an injunction from a Government Minister to use cars less,[2] when the Government is aware that alternatives are not properly available and when they continue to actively encourage car use. But this kind of hypocrisy extends further to all approaches which do not deal with the adverse consequences of mass car use. The idea of car use as a more or less basic human right is a part of the untheorised and unquestioned ideological baggage of mass car use. It will be more than dishonest to call for a shift away from the private car while this pervasive ideology goes unopposed.

There are two basic reasons for not simply adding one more "shopping list" of

259

suggestions.

The first reason is that there is no point *advancing solutions until we know what the problem is*. I do not accept establishment definitions of safety or congestion problems, and see the question of the right to transport in access terms which oppose the car mobility criteria of contemporary debate. As a broad general aim, I would argue that we should see the problem, apart from wider environmental problems, as one of *discrimination against non-car users* — whether it be in terms of inadequate local public transport, danger, or amenities inaccessible to non-car transport. In one sense that discrimination will exist with any significant amount of car use: nonetheless, it is possible to consider quite high levels of car use as tolerable and acceptable if the general idea of anti-discrimination is remembered. There *are* problems — from alienation to global warming — which adversely affect all of us: indeed, many of these can be solved by an approach which is an extension of a kind of enlightened self-interest. Nevertheless, their effects are not equally distributed and their solutions are not easily soluble on an individual level. What is more, as with all cases where some people oppress others, appeals for all of us to simply work together, irrespective of who is actually implicated in the cause of the problem, are likely to fail.

The second reason refers to a question which hangs over any discussion of policy and is particularly a factor where safety is concered. Time and again it is raised: "Is something better than nothing?" J S Dean's words from 40 years ago

stand just as true now as they did then:

> In trying to end the motor slaughter we are perpetually chasing a factor we never catch. It is a problem we cannot solve because X changes with every attempt at a solution.[3]

Unless there is a genuine commitment to the idea of danger reduction, the nature of risk-taking is such that if it is pushed out of the window it tends to return through the back door. The same point applies to transport policy elsewhere, where a more general motorist "factor X" impedes a genuine move away from the excesses of mass car use. This may involve cars moving into space freshly vacated by some others, or the problem of backlash. It is likely to be particularly acute in this area of campaigning because the attachment to cars has been so great, and the movement on behalf of motorisation's victims so lacking in unity, political power, and an articulated set of beliefs opposing the ideologies surrounding car domination.

These two related points need to dominate all consideration of policy.

Democracy, equal opportunities, and decisions

> I really do question whether we can go on catering for the understandable but somewhat selfish interest in mobility whilst society as a whole continues to pick up the cost... We must get back to thinking about the needs and objectives of users and society.[4]

If we are complaining about a state of affairs which we should have known was bound to happen, then both as a rhetorical question and as a start to serious inquiry we have to ask: How did we get to this state of affairs? The questions asked about our society need to be basic — and come up with equally basic answers.

Similarly, the statement about "needs and objectives" begs a whole range of fundamental questions. Whose needs take precedence, and at whose expense are they to be fulfilled? If the needs are economic, what kinds of growth and what levels of sustainability are involved, and in what sectors ? "Needs" are generated by the very technologies and infrastructures which are supposed to meet the needs in the first place — with the experience of expensive new roads filling up with the traffic they generate being the most obvious example. But the real issue is whether people who have decided that they "need", for example, to commute from the Midlands to London by car, should be allowed to inflict the adverse consequences in terms of safety, pollution, etc on everybody else. What happens to the people who suffer, particularly in terms of safety, but in all the other ways as well, and who are always likely to be particularly powerless to resist this damage?

Easy...

To some extent the resolution of car generated problems can be easy and acceptable. There is evidence that a reversal of increased car use and restrictions on its danger would be supported by large proportions, or even majorities, of the population. Surveys indicate:

261

☰ High levels of acceptance for methods of traffic reduction, including reduction in road space available for cars and fixed charges to travel in central London, and willingness to shift from cars to public transport if services were improved.[5]

☰ About a third of car users would use cars less if public transport were better, with one in six not finding it difficult to adjust their life style without their cars — even with no change in the provision of alternative modes. A third think the driving test is ineffective, and the vast majority support more controls like wheel clamps, random breath tests and cameras at traffic lights — with nearly half supporting prison sentences for drivers over the legal limit for drinking and driving.[6]

☰ There is majority support for additional regulation and/or better law enforcement.[7]

There is also a long history of grass roots campaigns for pedestrian crossing installation which seems to have extended to interest in some kinds of traffic calming.

A look across the Channel reveals that governments can rely on the support of the people for pedestrianising large areas of cities, introducing traffic calming and reducing the road space available for motorists in cities like Nuremberg and Freiburg, and in smaller towns throughout Northern Europe.[8] Vienna, Florence and Milan have had effective traffic restraint systems and cars banned from city centres. The Dutch are beginning to demand that new developments above a certain size must have public transport facilities in order to avoid additional traffic generation. Some of these measures fail to tackle long-term trends in car ownership and use, but others claim to try. In Bordeaux, France's fourth biggest city, the administration is described as having "declared war on the car".[9] A variety of measures are to be employed to restrict car use and access to city streets, with priority on many to be turned over to pedestrians and cyclists. The city representative responsible for implementing the plan states:

The idea that one can adapt a town to suit the car is absurd and the equivalent of killing off a city.

The Dutch former Transport Minister talks of how her previous commitment to road building was misguided — "like all dreams, the illusion proved finite" — and of the need to reduce the distance travelled by motor vehicles.[10] The chairman and chief executive of Volvo has argued for a "more or less total ban on cars" in Swedish inner cities, with cars replaced by public transport — "and we can start now".[11] Policies in Europe involve encouraging bicycle use at levels not seen in this country outside cities like Oxford and York. Pedestrians can cross city streets in safety in Zurich. Parents can allow their children to play outside in residential roads in the Dutch town of Delft, and cyclists enjoy a high level of respect from motorists in much of rural France.

A European Commission green paper calls for " a significant shift in the balance of modes of transport". The EC Commissioner comments:

> We consider independent transport a personal freedom. In the meantime we are committing suicide. We are crazy rats.[12]

...not so easy...

Although no less desirable, the shift away from excessive motorist hegemony appears to become more difficult in other cases.

An example constantly raised is that of women and personal security. Cars — in the short-term — provide women with a greater degree of personal security than public transport does. Yet the increase in car use means that public transport becomes more neglected in terms of provision of guards and security systems, and more dangerous for non-car using women. Similarly, the numbers of people walking about decrease as more women use cars, contributing to an increasingly hostile environment.

Indeed, this extends to the future for those women who drive: a look at at the massive car parks in the United States, even where security systems are provided, hardly presents a very safe environment. And entering suburban homes means walking in deserted streets at the mercy of assailants hidden, of course, behind cars. Apart from the consequences for others, the prospects for a life entirely sheltered by personal capsules are either of limited attractiveness or impossible.

There is no prospect of all women over the age of 16 driving their own cars; as the number of those who do moves up over the half way mark, those who are left behind will become even less secure. It is these people, let us remember, who are more likely to be particularly vulnerable: the elderly or disabled, or the poor, along with under-17-year-olds.

Similarly, the trend away from allowing children to walk unaccompanied to school, and the use of cars to take them there, places an extra burden on parents and guardians (who are particularly likely to be women). Meanwhile, it creates a more dangerous environment for those children who do walk or cycle to school and reduces the prospect of public transport provision.[13]

Along with congestion reduction achieved by shifting away from car use to public transport, these examples show how the individualist selfishness of car use inhibits collective approaches which could solve at least some of the problems only partially "solved" by car users at the expense of others.

This leads to an absolutely fundamental principle. Solving the problems of mass car use is ultimately something which has to be done collectively. As the ideas put forward by the notion of the *Tragedy of the Commons*[14] and *The Prisoner's Dilemma*[15] suggest, if decisions are only made in terms of individual self-interest, we end up with a situation which is bad for humanity, including those self same individuals. Alternatively, thinking of long-term solutions collectively gives genuine possibilities of individual, as well as social and environmental, interest being served. This does *not* mean avoiding individual responsibility — indeed confronting individuals directly is important — but it *does* mean insisting on policies and beliefs being changed at a society-wide level.

...and difficult

But much of the move towards civilised policies involves some things which motorists are just not prepared to countenance. Very often precisely because such simple, rational and convenient solutions are still opposed by motorists, we have to come to a simple conclusion: a large proportion of motorists — often people who are otherwise opposed to dangerous behaviour and selfishness — just do not want to fulfil their transport responsibilities and behave in a civilised way.

Consider the feasible alternative to our car-dominated roads. With few private cars (or even none at all) it would be possible to have uncongested roads and a high level of demand for public transport systems. These could be tram, bus, semi-public systems like taxis etc, and many of the desirable features of car use could be replicated by using modern technology to summon additional vehicles on demand, place stops near to home and create privacy in separate vehicles or mini-carriages. Walking and cycling could be less hazardous, necessary goods and services could be moved more easily; there would be less noise and other pollutions, and, therefore, less cost. The alternative of moving further down the path of car dependence will exacerbate existing problems and is intolerable at best. At worst, it is just plain impossible.

What we are talking about is a situation where self-interest can be served, but only by a collective self-interest which supersedes and actively opposes the individual selfishness of the motorist. If a few motorists decide to commute to central London, the adverse effects on them and the rest of the community need not be great. When the numbers increase, everybody suffers. In the reversal of this trend, not only do certain groups greatly benefit, but the so does the community as a whole.

We are therefore confronted with an important and inevitable conclusion. Motorists simply cannot be allowed to use or abuse the power they have at present. They must be denied access to the kind of power they now have in the first place. Motoring is too important to be left to motorists, who currently, whether in terms of safety or otherwise, do not have adequate incentive to behave decently, or disincentive not to.

While rational discussion is required, the persistent refusal to behave in a civilised fashion, including the use of a hidden agenda to prevent such discussion, demands a radical alternative to the status quo. This means appealing to the fact that the needs of minorities tend to be forgotten in the name of democracy. In fact genuine democracy requires positive action on their behalf wherever discrimination is built in to the system. Besides, on a global level, the need of the majority requires an urgent reduction in CO_2 emissions. Pessimists may argue that humanity is inherently bound for global ecological disaster, but the existence of a significant proportion of people, albeit a minority, who have no desire to be "crazy rats" removes the justification for that cynicism. The precondition for serious debate is acceptance of guilt and humility on the part of those supporting the car supremacist *status quo*. The fact that it will be difficult to achieve is no argument against demanding it.

What we are left with, then, is a contradictory situation. There is a widespread desire for change, particularly among the groups which suffer particularly badly from car supremacism. On the other hand, we have a great deal of wilful selfishness made worse by a refusal to even consider the issues, or to have them presented properly, in the first place. Consider two issues:

1. Pricing and equity

The idea of motorists paying their way has been aired in the debate over Electronic Road Pricing (ERP). There is some public support for this, even from some motorists, as it accords with the "polluter pays" principle, and could lead to resources being allocated to public transport. But it is still based on inadequate definitions of congestion as a problem, has a number of practical problems associated with it,[16] and falters at the notion of "equity": that is to say that the system of control seems to discriminate unfairly against poorer motorists.

This just indicates the poverty of the debate. The following points need to be made about the real issues of equity. There is:

≡   Discrimination against the impoverished of the world who will suffer appallingly as a consequence of global warming to which car dependence makes such an important contribution.

≡   Discrimination against benign mode users who suffer danger (if they walk or cycle) and inadequate bus services, and against local residents, who could all benefit by the restriction of traffic, and who might get additional revenue for public transport, and other support for alternative modes, by having additional costs paid back by motorists.

≡   A situation where motorists are subsidised already,[17] quite apart from the additional subsidy to company cars. Taxation on non-subsidised alcohol at a high level has been happening for years without complaint about "equity".

≡   The need to state that we do not want car use to be universal and that therefore the principle that poorer people should not miss out is simply absurd. Even if we did accept universal ownership, opposing proper taxation would only make any sense if there was no differential in spending power at all in society: unless that situation obtains some people will always be able to spend more money than others.

But try arguing that we should no more sponsor motoring than expensive clothes or luxury goods. Working through the idea that motoring is already subsidised is bad enough: the problem is that it is simply not accepted that cars should not be owned as a basic right (although the idea that *other* people should not drive is).

2. Rural Areas

The rights of the cyclist, pedestrian and bus user have been most threatened in rural settings. This continues to be an area of virtually no debate.[18] The loss of genuine local community through long-distance commuting, and severance by busy roads should not be underestimated. Furthermore, if we are to provide any kind of example to the largely rural Third World in order to discourage motorisation and curtail greenhouse gas emission, we must restrain our own patterns of high mileage.

There is a great deal to be gained by tackling car supremacism: quiet country lanes and local communities with local amenities easily reached by local buses, cycling or walking in safety.[19] Even where higher costs and other controls on cars push car addicts away, lower house prices would create the possible conditions for local people to remain if they wish.

Despite the scale of the problem and the desirability of the alternative, this is one area that is virtually off the agenda. When it does occasionally get discussed, motorists demand uncontrolled privilege again: apparently *their* own needs as motorists are special.

Where car use is concerned we must not forget that we cannot have our cake and eat it. We cannot expect to see non-globally destructive patterns of development taken up in the developing world if we disregard them ourselves. If we in the industrialised countries restrict car use only in the urban setting, leaving motorists a free rein elsewhere, then the largely rural non-industrialised nations may view this as a precedent for a massive (if nevertheless non-urban) motorisation programme. Yet the principal environmentalist organisation's response to traffic problems in 1992 is one which accepts an *increase* in rural traffic.[20]

"Sail before steam"

A general attitude which would characterise road use in a civilised society would be the adoption of the "sail before steam" dictum. This is only a rough guide, and apparently no longer strictly applies in nautical law or routine practice. But it encapsulates the notion that the onus of responsibility should be placed on those who are both more dangerous and less vulnerable. It would place the burden of responsibility, whether legally, or in engineering or education, on those at the top of the hierarchy, demanding their accountability for the destructive effects of their activities on those below them and society and the environment as a whole. It would mean considering walking, cycling and public transport before car use in any transport policy. There are difficulties. Where, for example, do vulnerable but potentially dangerous motorcyclists fit in? But the principle should be clear.

266

Part of the legal expression of this approach involves the making of collisions involving cyclists and pedestrians an offence of strict liability, as described above.[21] Indeed this is the expression of more a civilised basis to safety on the road.

It is vital to destroy the myth that we all just have roles to play and simply need to get on with doing so. This profoundly corrupting myth stands at the heart of contemporary ideology. It is essentially just like arguing for the kind of relationships that exist in a feudal society: everybody is allowed to break rules to some extent, but some are allowed to do so far more dangerously than others, with the less violent also being the ones who are most at risk from the violence of others. This central relationship has not been changed beneficially to any significant extent by road safety interventions.

Some proposals

The central argument is that progress can only be properly made by addressing the adverse consequences of the transport status quo in a radical fashion. It should not be up to advocates of alternatives to promote, for example, public transport provision in a way which satisfies motorists. Rather, it should be up to motorists to indicate that their privilege does not have too adverse an effect on public transport. The equal opportunities perspective demands that the problems of car hegemony are dealt with as the priority.

Also, the awareness of problems tending to crop up elsewhere in the system means that simple "shopping list" approaches should be treated warily. Although sometimes apparently similar to my recommendations, there is a central difference between such piecemeal approaches assuming progress without side effects, and my integrated systemic approach. Although time-scales can mean lengthy periods of implementation, the different elements in the system have to be introduced more or less simultaneously to avoid adverse migratory effects.

The need for transport

Transport, with the exception of walking or cycling, should be seen as a regrettable necessity, rather than something which is desirable in its own right. Employers can be encouraged to give financial assistance to those living locally, for example. Other steps, like land use planning, should be taken to encourage the siting of amenities and employment within local communities. In this way, a large proportion of journeys would be short ones which could be walked or cycled.

Public transport

The general perspective can be informed by a view of local public transport as a necessity, rather than a cost-effective business to be run where possible. The emphasis should be on local journeys, accessibility, personal security, and the meeting of minimum requirements: stops within easy distances of dwellings, maximum intervals between services etc.

Design of public transport can include the introduction of technologies to support demand-led features: homes can be linked by telecommunications to stations so that additional or special carriages etc are provided when required.

Ultimately individual vehicles could be included on automatic grids, retaining privacy but generating safety and allowing for more equity.

Car use should be seen as competing with public transport. Car users should meet the cost of the lost revenue and other costs incurred as a result of competition.

It is no longer feasible to use the blanket term "public transport" to describe all the alternatives to car use. The aim of sustainable transport is not altogether compatible with such forms of "public" transport as Concorde or faster inter-city rail. The success of rail has to be seen in terms of supporting local communities, not encouraging long distance commuting.

Walking

Walking should be seen as the priority mode. Facilities such as crossings can be determined more in accordance with pedestrian need.[22] As with cycling, maintenance of highways to basic standards could be legally enforceable, without the need for the present buck passing between local authorities and public services.

Cycling

Contemporary encouragement of cycling is restricted to road space allocation. A whole range of schemes to encourage this mode can be taken: reduction of prices on breathable waterproof rainwear, removal of VAT, educational campaigns in schools aimed at encouraging cycle use etc. The main form of encouragement is simply to reduce the danger from motor vehicles.

What happens to the three Es?

The new approach argues against separating elements of opposition to danger into different categories. Insofar as it is possible to discuss the traditional three Es of intervention, they should all be seen as interdependent and based on a commitment to reduce danger at source.

Engineering

Cars might carry equipment to record the circumstances of crashes and allow for attribution of guilt. This might involve cyclists having to carry some kind of sensor device which could link in with the technology employed on cars. Essentially this is simply an extension of current aircraft black box or lorry tachograph technology. If a leading car manufacturer can propose an "intelligent" road network where sophisticated electronic systems prevent cars speeding and over-running junctions, and keeps them in line on corners, similar technology ought to be available to stop them from damaging other road users.[23] While this is likely to be objected to as being the hand of Big Brother, it is only an invasion of personal liberty in the same way that health and safety legislation invades the liberty of employers — a group which is responsible for less danger than motorists. Information from such devices can be used in a legal system of enforcement.

Enforcement

The strict liability provision should be introduced for crashes with vulnerable road users.

Education

In a more civilised society children would be informed more of their rights and less of the need to defer to the dangerous: the principle of "sail before steam" as described above could then be introduced to children at an early age.

Targets?

Policy makers are likely to want some kind of target to replace the inequities and mystifications of Cost Benefit Analysis. The current Dutch Government is aiming to cut projected increases in car use by half to stabilise CO_2 emissions from the transport sector.[24] This involves a country whose inhabitants' per capita emissions of CO_2 are substantially higher than those in the Third World, and when the main prescription for targets of reduction has been a 60 per cent reduction of CO_2.[25] It would involve having about one car for every 2.5 people, which on a global level would increase car ownership by about five times, at least doubling CO_2 emissions from the transport sector if vehicles and their manufacture were two or three times more fuel efficient. And this target is more stringent than anything discussed in Britain. Bringing us into line with the target level set by the United Nations' Intergovernmental Panel on Climate Changes would involve an 80 per cent reduction, at least, from the road transport sector.[26]

This, along with so much else, points to a need for a reduction in current levels of car ownership and use, achieved in the first instance by massive increases in taxation on petrol[27] and annual car taxes, and backed up by other restrictions such as tougher law enforcement and more difficulty in obtaining driving licences. But everything depends on a more fundamental radical ideological change without which the "backlash" reaction from car users and the car lobby will prove insuperable.

Meanwhile, my local newspaper — always a good source for the student of road danger — records the case of a motorist who drives his Mercedes on the wrong side of the road and into another car , killing the occupant.[28] The motorist responsible has two previous endorsements in the previous two years for careless driving and a pedestrian crossing offence. He is fined £200 and banned for 6 months.

We end as we began.

The outrage we feel at such an astonishing show of leniency is worth nothing unless we act to control not only those cases where harm is done, but also the appalling potential for danger which all motorists present to their more vulnerable fellow road users. It is not too melodramatic to remember the victims and their loved ones, often unaware of the background to the tragedy, and even worse, prone to self blame. This book hopes to let them and others see their anger as justified, and show them where this anger can be directed.

Appendix

The astronomer from General Motors

A review of *Traffic Safety and the Driver* by Leonard Evans

LEONARD EVANS is one of the most famous "road safety" workers in the world. He has received numerous awards from the road safety establishment and is a prolific author of "road safety" titles, of which this book[1] is the latest. Regarded as "invaluable" by the reviewer in the British road safety practitioners' magazine,[2] it is more than just an enormous summary of an even larger amount of published work on road safety. It represents the state of the art in "road safety" thought and practice. Criticising it involves going beyond the work of an individual, to the heart of an ideology.

❖❖❖

Traffic Safety and the Driver goes further than most "road safety" text books by referring to a central idea that I present in this book. That is, the common sense notion that road users adapt to the conditions they find themselves in, in ways at least partly dependent on how they perceive the risks presented to them. Evans is sometimes forced to admit the truth of this notion, and what flows from it, but at the same time he adheres to the mythology of the road safety industry. We are therefore left with a continually and persistently flawed work which mirrors those contradictions. Revealing these flaws is a necessary part of the process of demythologising a dangerous set of beliefs.

Danger and accidents

Probably the main example of risk compensation (or whatever we might wish to call the process of adaptation to perceived risk of various kinds) is the decline of pedestrian deaths, particularly among children, over the last 60 years. Even where the chances of being hurt or killed per crossing or walking journey appear to have increased — ultimately danger *will* result in actual harm occurring — these chances have not increased as much as the increase in vehicular traffic would at first have suggested. As Evans correctly puts it:

> ...the main mechanism which reduces the number of children playing in the road is the very increase in danger brought about by increased traffic. It is

270

another example of a perverse effect in which factors adverse to safety generate safety increases because of large human behaviour responses on the part of the children and their parents.[3]

Of course this effect, working on other benign mode use as well as just children's play, is not "perverse" at all. It is an obvious feature of human behaviour. What we need to remember is that if people are scared away from danger, we do not have a "safety increase". We have a decline in one kind of accident because of danger: using the phrase "safety increase" to describe this experience is a perversion of language and an insult to the victims of motor danger. If the number of women sexually assaulted in public places declines because women are scared to venture out, we do not talk about "safety increases".

Saying that danger is different from, and to a large extent inversely related to, collisions, is a crucial element of my common sense notion. As Evans is opposed to it, he has to oppose the correct use of the English language. Indeed, he makes this clear when he sews up the argument against risk compensation before it starts, on page 9 of the book:

increased safety generally implies reductions in such quantities as the number of crashes, injuries, or deaths.

For Evans, the contemporary dodgems circuit type of traffic system has increased (or at least kept at a roughly similar level) safety compared to previous stages of motorisation because of the lowering (or at least stabilisation) of injuries or deaths. Of course, the massive increase in crashes has occurred: but there is still "more safety" because there are fewer and generally more careful benign mode journeys made, and the dangerous have been hugely protected from the consequences of those increased crashes. I think this means that there is more danger around if one is concerned about it at source, and to be clear about it, I would call this an increase in motor danger.

Let us consider specific features of motor danger which Evans gets the wrong way round. Sometimes, as part of his self-contradiction, he gets them the right way round as well.

A. Insurance

All drivers I have questioned admit they would drive more carefully if their vehicles contained high explosives set to detonate on impact... I suspect that the potential embarassment of losing my own crash-free record has further increased my own driving caution.[4]

and:

Increasing the cost of crash involvement tends to reduce the likelihood of crashing: purchasing collision insurance very likely increases crash risk...[5]

This is nothing more or less than a statement of how, if more is at risk (whether monetary loss or expert reputation), more care will be taken. It is a clear guide to designing control of danger and explaining how more crashworthy vehicles have contributed to motor danger: both these conclusions are either opposed or not considered.

B. Education

Many studies have failed to show that crash rates are influenced by car driver education, training, or knowledge... Driving is essentially a closed-loop compensatory feedback process in which the driver makes control inputs to what is perceived.[6]

The higher [crash] involvement rates of younger, and male, drivers seem more related to how they are choosing to drive, particularly their propensity to take driving risks, than to their abilities at the driving task.[7]

The problem of traffic crashes is much more one of drivers doing things that they know they ought not to do, than of drivers not knowing what to do.[8]

In other words, there is little point in doing anything other than thinking of deterrent procedures to stop motor danger, rather than trying to impart knowledge which people already have, even if it involves genuine careful driving techniques rather than the acquisition of extra ability to drive as racing drivers.

Indeed, with the lower risk associated with the moves supported by Evans (seat belts, more crashworthy cars etc) being inserted into the closed-loop compensatory feedback process, everything he is working for will increase the motor danger. Despite all this, Evans still suggests that educational initiatives which attempt to get motorists to be more concerned about others might contribute to making them more careful.

C. Road engineering

If a hazardous section of roadway is rebuilt to higher safety standards (sic), it is likely that drivers will travel this section faster than before the improvement, or with reduced care.[9]

I have already referred to Evans' review of engineering methods and their failure.[10] The failure of motorway building methods to achieve anything like the casualty reduction rates that they would without risk compensation, has also been commented on.[11] Evans ends his chapter on engineering by saying: "Nearly all attempts to examine engineering and environmental factors encounter larger driver behavior influences."[12] The point is that as common sense, risk compensation and one part of Leonard Evans' thought process tells us, the driver behaviour is actually modified by those engineering approaches themselves.

However, when it comes to certain aspects of road safety the evidence is too threatening to entertain at all properly, and straightforward — albeit somewhat over the top — denial occurs. This occurs with:

(i) Helmets

The work of Adams on the American motorcycle helmet wearing experience is mentioned in passing, but none of the findings seriously considered or examined. The British experience, which Evans could have investigated to complement his many articles on helmets, is also ignored.[13]

(ii) Seat belts

Seat belt legislation is the flagship of the road safety movement. How does Evans deal with its failure to meet its officially stated objectives? Comparing the Durbin-Harvey estimates of benefits with what should have happened, Evans compares his prediction of a 26 per cent decline in fatalities for drivers with the 18 per cent actual decline, describing it as "in reasonable agreement".[14] The calculation he uses in this book is more complex than the one of his which I use, but comes up with a very similar value. It is not in reasonable agreement, it is 31 per cent out. Evans evades this by — completely without justification — weighting the 18 per cent figure to 20 per cent. Even so it is still 23 per cent out.

None of this includes consideration of the alcohol factor: that is to say the apparent decline in deaths among drivers who were drunk, associated with a change in relevant legislation since claimed as responsible for this phenomenon by the road safety lobby, at the same time as the introduction of the seat belt law. This would reduce the claims made by Durbin and Harvey still more, and make the discrepancy even greater. It is not referred to at all by Evans. Nor is the effect the law had on pedestrians or cyclists, as discussed by Durbin and Harvey, seriously considered. Nor is the work of Adams. The Isles Report and the work of Janssen are not mentioned.

Evans deals with the 27 per cent increase in (mainly unbelted) rear seat passengers killed following the law by drawing on very scanty evidence to suggest migration from front to rear seats. He justifies this by claiming that:

≡ He knows of one (sic) specific case where this occurred.

≡ The 27 per cent increase compared to an 18 per cent decline for belted drivers implies an unrealistically high seat belt effectiveness in crashes. It does not. The shortfall between an 18 per cent decline and a predicted decline of 26 per cent implies an increase in tendency to crash by newly-belted drivers of the same order.(If anything it is greater.)

≡ "The consistent finding of higher fatality reductions for passengers than drivers for essentially similar use rates, implying higher when-used effectiveness for passengers."[15] But earlier Evans claims that the fatality reducing effectiveness of seat belts is less for front seat passengers than for drivers.[16]

And his thesis depends on claiming behavioural response to road safety legislation against the aims of that legislation: this contradicts what he generally suggests happens (although he spends a great deal of his book tacitly or openly accepting his idea).

273

Considering adaptive behaviour — a note on philosophy

Evans' book is peppered with references to compensatory behaviour by motorists.
To give one more:

> Human behavior feedback, or user response, to changes in safety systems may
> greatly alter safety outcomes. In some cases the outcome may even be of an
> opposite sign to that which is expected... improved braking or handling
> characteristics are likely to lead to increased speeds, closer following, and
> faster cornering. Safety (sic) may also increase, *but by less than if there had been
> no behavior response*.(my emphasis)[17]

Evans also considers that the positivist approach to at least one feature of the
traffic safety scene is not flawless:

> ...driving is more than a collection of specific steps — it is more of a holistic
> process not explainable in terms of a collection of reductionist details.[18]

Indeed. That irreducible process consists of a huge variety of personal characteristics which interact with the effects of widely different experiences in
numerous different situations over a lifetime. It is affected — adversely, for the
vulnerable — by the measures advocated by such "experts" as Evans: greater
physical protection for motorists and a refusal to see dangerous driving as a
problem. This is made worse when instead of confronting the issue head on,
motorists are pandered to by the suggestion that they should voluntarily change
their ways.

While Evans seems to believe that driving can't be broken down into different
parts, he still maintains that driver behaviour has to be seen as separate from
environmental factors. But if we are to look at the process of driving as an
irreducible whole, why not extend this approach to one of social holism, as
(generally implicitly) suggested by Smeed, Minter, Adams and others?

There is a long history of this kind approach being made by sociologists and
anthropologists. Evans, however, with strident declarations that the superiority of
his work is based on its scientific status, simply can not cope with this. It is
impossible therefore to relate concepts like economic activity to fatality levels
because "the mechanism" implicated can not be identified. The point is that teasing
out a separate, reducible factor from a morass of interdependent features may just
not be possible. Evans can not follow his partial scepticism about reductionism
through.

Without necessarily having to change paradigm, Evans should treat this
socially holistic view as a possible alternative. Instead he criticises it using criteria
which themselves have been partially accepted as faulty.

There are three other criticisms that can be made:

≡   It is still possible to state that a proper explanation should be aware of
    macro-social factors, even without using a philosophy which holds that
    the whole is more than the sum of its parts. One would think that without

some form of macro-sociological explanation it becomes difficult to talk about beliefs in society, whether as general attitudes, social mores, or ideology. Indeed, Evans' conclusions include the following:

> **Because engineering and medical changes alone seem incapable of explaining such large effects (in fatality rates) especially as some of the safety benefits of engineering are consumed in mobility increases and increased driver risk taking, it is concluded that human behaviour changes have made the larger contributions... the human behaviour component judged to have had the largest effect is a general evolution in social norms pertaining to driving.** [19]

But theorising concepts like "social norms" fits uneasily (or not at all) with the number crunching Evans carries out elsewhere.

≣   Even where a traditional positivist approach is advocated, [20] it is necessary to be critical in order to be scientific. Evans, however, takes a view which either implicitly or explicitly, accepts the car supremacist *status quo*. This relates to the next point:

≣   Scientists should be able to account for their own activity, and be able to make a statement about the origin of their own belief system. This problem is discussed below, but first one question needs to be asked.

Does it matter how much adaptation there is?

For me, if there is any significant compensatory behaviour which increases motor danger, there is a serious problem. The case of the anti-depressant drug Prozac, which caused widespread relief of frequently suicidal depressive states of mind, but which was allegedly implicated in the cause of a very few cases of homicide, is instructive. The central theme of the debate, as with other discussions about beneficial drugs and their side effects, was that an otherwise benign move had to be re-considered if there were even a relatively small number of malignant consequences. In the case of policy moves such as compulsory seat belt wear, the apparent adverse effects are of a similar order to the beneficial ones.

For Evans, there is no problem at all. Compensatory behaviour, which exists everywhere else, can not exist here, or in a number of other interventions where human beings apparently stop being human. The evidence is simply distorted in ways I have indicated in this book. But even if the negative effects were not so great, *there would still be a problem*. Instead of seriously considering this, all we get is a facetious comment about possible negative effects which shows an utter contempt and disregard for road users outside cars. [21]

Number crunching covers up the fact that some endanger others. Evans carries this tendency to extremes: I think that decency and civilised values — let alone the fact that the safety of those outside cars ultimately depends on reducing motor danger at source — demand that we oppose it.

Homeostasis

Evans misses out on certain examples of safety interventions which fail to meet their promise (such as skid resistant surfaces)[22], and denies obvious evidence on others (motorcycle helmets and seat belts). However, he spends some of the book accepting the obvious facts of adaptation with some interventions (features of highway design, driver education, better braking and other vehicle characteristics) and the same effect with danger increases (icy road conditions, increased traffic for child pedestrians and the change of the rule of the road in Sweden). He also accepts the idea of some sort of collective response to change and accident migration from treated black spots.

The emphasis of these essentially common sense ideas in road safety literature is most commonly associated with Adams and Wilde, originally under the banner of something called Risk Homeostasis Theory (RHT). Evans refers to RHT in extreme terms, resenting discussion of it in learned journals. Why?

≡ RHT does not give a clearly quantified description of changes to be expected after road safety interventions. It states that adaptation may occur over different periods of time, that it may occur more with later interventions if it has occurred less with earlier ones, and that changes in risk taking in the road environment may be balanced by ones outside it.

≡ RHT involves notions of collective, as well as individual, adaptation to perceived risk.

≡ RHT gives a central role to a concept of risk of danger to life and limb which is inadequate to explain changes in road user behaviour.

Evans criticises each of these features forcefully — but at various parts of his book virtually contradicts himself on the relevant points at issue. He does indeed protest too much, and we learn a lot by looking at his self-contradiction.

Quantifiability

Evans regards quantifying as the central aspect of scientific endeavour. But discussion on the nature of social science has always been sceptical about the possibility of doing so without distorting the nature of the human experience. This is particularly so when we talk about the interdependence of the very many virtually indefinable experiences which are constantly changing in the road environment. The only reliable measure of crashes is deaths, but individual deaths are experienced in quite different ways by members of society. When we talk about the other features of danger we are talking about the virtually immeasurable (danger) to the more measurable (injuries) which either will not or can not be counted properly, and which mean quite different things to those involved. On top of this Evans gives — quite correctly — a central role to cultural change or "social norms". How are these to be quantified? Beyond this, Evans' failure to use the rules of his own brand of science when dealing with the seat belt and helmet experiences hardly inspires confidence.

Collective change

As well as stressing the importance of social norms, we read that: "Societies react to the total number of fatalities, whereas individual drivers cannot..."[23] But the work of Minter and Adams is criticised because the individual mechanisms allegedly at work can not be identified. As mentioned above, this is essentially a tautological argument. Even so, the idea of inevitable casualty reductions occurring from experience, if not the fully macro-sociological idea of social learning, is accepted.

Risk

Evans argues that fear for life and limb can not be the dominant factor. Indeed not: social norms are also obviously involved. Stating that surveys show people being more worried about risks which are small (such as Alar poisoning from apples) does not mean that people are not accurately assessing risk: it means that they regard some as more important than others.

But all this is an argument for pointing out that interventions may tend to fail, and that fear of harm (or at least breach of formal or informal rules) is important. Evans picks up this idea, accepts much of it, violently criticises the largely irrelevant parts of it, and then moves on. Once again, why?

Are things getting better all the time?

Accepting that risk compensation or adaptation to perceived risk occurs, and that ordinary human beings have an individual and maybe collective capacity to do this spontaneously has certain consequences. The fact that it occurs is obvious. The fact that when motorist protection is involved there can be adverse consequences for the non-car user is evidently regarded as unimportant by Evans. But on top of this, we have a picture of why change has occurred which is not complimentary to either the road safety lobby or the great motoring public.

When he refers to the wider social change in driving behaviour which has happened, Evans is describing an alleged amelioration of driving behaviour which has been added on to the efforts of the road safety industry. In fact, what has happened is that motorists have become more careful *because of the presence of more danger from increased traffic*, a phenomenon noted by Smeed in specific locations, as well as society-wide.[24] The benefits of these behaviours seem often to have been *eroded* by changes in vehicle crashworthiness and other measures.

This presents a less complimentary picture. Even without the adverse effects of increases in motor danger, and the moral implications for even individual cases of endangering others, this view contradicts the positive view of the way things are going. The idea that "road safety" has not done much good (change would have occurred anyway), but at least something is better than nothing, simply does not hold if some things have become worse and/or if danger is colluded with.

This does not mean that "we can do nothing", simply that attention should be directed at reducing danger at source, rather than pandering to it. Why Evans should be inclined to take his view involves consideration about the role of the researcher.

Looking from afar?

Evans sees his position as a "traffic safety scientist" as having more in common with that of an astronomer than a biological or physical scientist.[25] Of course, even regarding biology or physical science as easily applicable to social science runs into certain basic problems of meaning and causality. One subject wrestled with by philosophers of social science is about the position of the scientist in society with regard to the object of study.

Leonard Evans is a Principal Research Scientist at General Motors Research Laboratories. I do not for a moment suggest that he has no scientific integrity, or that he has been bought off by his employers. What I am suggesting is that it would be very difficult, if not impossible, for him to come to the kind of conclusions that I have, and retain the position which allows him time to write, publish, visit conferences etc.

He would not be able to suggest that road safety interventions made to protect motorists are morally reprehensible (or should at least be given a lower order of priority than measures to control motor danger at source) because of the additional motor danger presented to the non-car users in the road environment. Such statements about the effects of changes in vehicle design might make it difficult for him to be a recipient of his Volvo Traffic Safety Award.

His positioning of traffic safety as a public health problem does not involve consideration of the related health danger arising from pollution from vehicle exhausts, or global warming and vehicle emissions. In September 1991 the *Wall Street Journal* revealed that the Coalition for Vehicle Choice, which has some 50 Washington lobbyists fighting prospective US legislation to increase vehicle efficiency, was financed by Ford, Chrysler — and General Motors.

As for congestion, this will sort itself out, albeit with a degree of imperfection that comes from market equilibrium processes.

What about the other problems outlined in Chapter 14?

It seems to me there is no more a natural limit on vehicle ownership than there is a *natural* limit on the ownership of radios, televisions, bathrooms, shoes or houses.[26]

None of these items incur as much direct damage in terms of pollution or greenhouse gas emission (except with the possible exception of energy use in homes) as car manufacture and use does. Pollution or global warming are not referred to anywhere in this book, published in 1991.

Conclusion — Supporting motor danger

At the end of this massive book, what does its author have to say in terms of positive recommendations? We have only one actual policy demand: the increase in taxation on alcohol. Controls specifically on drink-driving are not on because, presumably, the (American) motorist does not want them. As pointed out in Chapter 12, drunk driving is just one type of motor danger which can be used to detract attention away from others, and which needs to be controlled by perceived deterrent measures. Evans wants to see de-glamourising of anti-social driving as depicted on television. This is a purely voluntary measure which (apart from not having any of the scientific evidence Evans praises) has no relevance to everyday negligence and is hardly likely to impinge very far, if at all. Finally, we have an appeal to the old cop-out "encouragement of courtesy in driving": a solution to the abuse of power which asks the powerful to try and be nicer.[27]

In other words, it is business as usual: voluntary measures which will not decrease, or even slow the increase in, motor danger which the road safety lobby has been implicated in. Although apparently contemptuous of the non-motorised road user and negligent of other adverse effects of motorisation, Evans is aware of a lot of the truth of motor danger. But he is blind to it, because there are none so blind as those who will not see.

⚞ Notes

Introduction

1 Pettifer, J and Turner, N, Automania, Collins, 1984, p. 219.
2 Plowden, W, The Motor Car and Politics 1896-1970, Bodley Head, 1971, p. 81.
3 Walk (Pedestrians' Association), spring 1990, pp. 6, 10.
4 Pettifer and Turner, op cit.
5 For a discussion of under-reporting, see Chapter 1.
6 Department of Transport, Road Accidents Great Britain 1988, HMSO, 1989.
7 Havard, J, "Drinking and driving: ten years on from Blennerhasset; keynote address, " BMA Conference, London, 1985, p. 2.
8 See OPCS data quoted in Adams, J, Risk and Freedom: The Record of Road Safety Regulation, TPP, 1985, p. 8.
9 Paulos, J, Innumeracy: Mathematical Illiteracy and its Consequences, Viking, 1989.
10 See Plowden, op cit, for a history of this period.
11 See Chapter 6, note 30.
12 For an account of the involvement of the motoring organisations and the British Road Federation see Dean, J, Murder Most Foul, Allen & Unwin, 1947. The links between the DTp and the roads lobby are explored in Hamer, M, Wheels within Wheels, Routledge, 1987. (The Department of Transport has been abbreviated to "DTp" for most of my career, with "DoT" being a reference to the Department of Trade: although "DoT" now appears to be coming into official fashion for the Department of Transport for no stated reason, I retain "DTp" throughout this book).
13 DTp, National Travel Survey 1985/86 Report — Part 1, HMSO, 1988, table 2.10.
14 Ibid, table 2.17.
15 Ibid See tables 3.2 and 8.1.

1. Playing it by numbers

1 DTp, Road Accidents Great Britain 1990, The casualty report (RAGB). HMSO, 1991, Preface, p. 1.
2 See eg Cicourel, A, The Social Organisation of Juvenile Justice, Heinemann, 1976.
3 See eg, Adams, J, "Evaluating the effectiveness of road safety measures, " Traffic Engineering and Control, June 1988.
4 DTp, "Review of surveys to business and local authorities: Stats 19 road accident report form, " Statistics Bulletin (88) 31, 1988.
5 See Chapter 4 on the suppression of the Isles Report on seat belt effectiveness in Europe. For further evidence of DTp reticence on potentially embarrassing statistics see Adams, J, Road safety: Problems of Evaluation, London Centre for Transport Planning Seminar, March 1988.
6 See Langley, J, "The need to discontinue the use of the term "accident" when referring to unintentional injury events, " Accident Analysis and Prevention, 20, 1, 1988.
7 Probart, D (executive member, Campaign against Drinking and Driving), interview, 10/3/90.
8 RAGB 1987, p. 5.
9 A figure of seven-eighths is given by RAGB 1987, p. 52.
10 RAGB 1986, section 9.
11 RAGB "Definitions and symbols and conventions" (each issue).
12 Pedder, J, et al, "A study of two-wheeled vehicle casualties treated at a city hospital, " Proc. 6th Int. Conf. IRCOBI, 1979.; Bull, J, and Roberts, S, "Road accident statistics — a comparison of police and hospital information, " Accident Analysis and Prevention, 5, 1973, pp. 45-53;

Hobbs, C et al. "Classification of injury severity by length of stay in hospital, " Transport and Road Research Laboratory (TRRL) LR 871, 1979.
13 Hepworth, J, McDonald, M, & Hall, RD, "Accidents to cyclists: a pilot study of levels of reporting and severity, " University of Southampton, Dec 1984. Another recent study (Mills, P "Pedal cycle accidents — a hospital based study", RR220, Transport and Road Research Laboratory (TRRL), 1989) has the figure of 61 per cent unreported serious injuries. The important point is perhaps that reporting is affected primarily by the involvement of a motor vehicle. Non-reporting increases for the kind of accident typically involving child cyclists falling off while playing: this is of interest to those in the road safety lobby who wish to use such evidence to detract attention away from danger posed by motorists
14 Guille, G (Guernsey Fire Service), personal communication, March 1990.
15 Saunders, RA and Wheeler T, "Reported accidents and the GP, " Highways and Transportation, Dec 1987.
16 British Medical Association (BMA) memorandum submitted to the BMA's Board of Science and Education to the House of Commons Transport Committee, second special report, Road safety: (inquiry not completed) (appendix 37, No. 275), 1983.
17 Grattan, E and Hobbs, J, "Permanent disability in road traffic accident casualties." TRRL Report 924, 1980.
18 RAGB 1990, Table 26, for this section's figures.
19 DTp: Road Safety: The Next Steps. DTp, 1987.
20 Brownfield J, (Head of Road Safety, GLC), Ways to Safer

Cycling, conference proceedings, DTp, 1985, p. 3.
21 RAGB 1987, table 6a.
22 Disabled Persons Transport Advisory Committee: Annual Report Mobility Policy for Britain's Entire Population" 1990
23 National Travel Survey 1985-86, DTp, 1988, part 1, p. 39.
24 Central Statistical Office, Social Trends, HMSO, 1990.
25 RAGB 1987, para. 6.1.4.
26 See Chapter 10, note 11.
27 Morgan, JM, "How many cyclists and how many bicycles are there in Great Britain?, " TRRL WP (TP) 36, 1987.
28 Scott, C and Jackson, J, Accidents to Young Motor Cyclists: A Statistical Investigation (SS. 277B), Central Office of Information, 1960.
29 See Plowden, S, "Reducing Motorcycle Accidents", p. 10.; Road Safety: What Next?, Policy Studies Institute conference, 1985.
30 Broughton, J "The relation between motorcycle size and accident risk", TRRL, RR 169, 1988.
31 Survey of 70 TWMV casualties in Saunders, R, "Road Safety Management: interviewing casualties", Journal of Social Health, April 1989.
32 See Chapter 2 on crashworthy cars. The DTp does now collect data on different types of car with specific reference to crashworthiness (see DTp, Transport Statistics Report "Car and Driver: Injury Accident and Casualty Rates. Great Britain: 1990". Government Statistical Service, April 1992), however it only deals with the minority of crashes involving reported injury, and no attempt is made to even consider whether greater crashworthiness increases danger to others.
33 See Chapter 2 on the Smeed law and the difference between "expected" and actual increases.
34 RAGB 1987, para 1.2.
35 RAGB 1987, para 6.1.6.
36 RAGB 1990 table 23. There is still a popular prejudice that cyclists and pedestrians significantly endanger car occupants. Well before the modern crashworthy car: "In personal injury accidents involving a pedal cycle and a four-wheeled vehicle, 99 per cent of the casualties were cyclists" (Starks, J & Lister, R"Some safety aspects of pedal and motor-assisted cycles" Road Research Technical Paper No.38, Road Research Laboratory, 1957)
37 Broughton, J, "The variation of car drivers" accident risk with age." TRRL Report RR 135, 1988. The problems involved are reduced

sensory ability, limitation of necessary movement, reduced channel capacity and dementia. (see Bull, J & Raffle, P "Editorial" Journal of the Royal Society of Medicine, 85, p.p188-9, April 1992.)
38 Accident rates rise to a peak a year or two after young drivers receive their licence and do not level off until drivers are around 25 to 30 years old. See Pelz, D and Schuman, S, "Are young drivers really more dangerous after controlling for exposure and experience?", Journal of Safety Research, 3, 1971, pp. 68-79.
39 Broughton, op cit
40 See Evans, L Traffic Safety and the Driver, Chapter 2, VNR, New York, 1991.
41 Guardian Women's Page debate on driving, Jan 1989.
42 Quoted in 50th National Road Safety Congress, RoSPA, 1983.
43 The Lex Report on Motoring, Lex Motoring Plc, 1989.
44 Gallup, for General Accident survey amongst motorway drivers, June 1988: 39 per cent of those surveyed had "nodded off" on the motorway, and two-thirds of those surveyed underestimated safe stopping distances.
45 A recent example is McCormick, I et al, "Comparative perceptions of driver ability — a confirmation and expansion, " Accident Analysis and Prevention, Vol. 18, No. 3, 1986, p. 205.
46 Campbell, B, "Accident proneness and driver license programs," First Int. Drivers' Behaviour Research Assoc., Zurich, Switzerland, 1973. Similarly, the idea that particular individuals ("the accident-prone") are the major group of people involved in crashes, let alone the idea that they can be properly identified, or prevented from driving by suitable tests and legislation, is successfully opposed by Whitlock, F, Death on the Road: A Study in Social Violence, Tavistock, 1971.
47 An esential tradition in the sociology of deviance stresses this point. For a recent attempt to show that a "social problem" (alcohol abuse) has to be seen as related to what the average member of society does, see Rose, G & Day, S: "The population mean predicts the number of deviant individuals" British Medical Journal, 301, 1031 -1034, 3 Nov 1990.
48 Kirby, J, I didn't see him, Assoc. of Optometrists, 1987.
49 See Chapter 9.
50 Katz, I Guardian Crescendo snoring, 16 Nov 1991.

51 "Danger doze is cause of M-way crashes", Care on the Road, December 1989. Also see note 44 above.
52 RAGB 1988, para 4.1.
53 Evans, L op cit 85 -89.
54 See Table 15 RAGB
55 Codling, P "Weather and road accidents" in Holdings, D & C (eds) Climatic resources and economic activity. Newton Abbot, 1974,
56 RAGB 1987, para 7.4.
57 DTp, International Comparisons of Transport Statistics 1970-1985. Part 2: Road Accident Deaths, HMSO, 1989, table 8.
58 Booth, K Characteristics of Urban Motorcycle Accidents, Institute of Motorcycling, April 1989, London.
59 RAGB 1987, chart 7g.
60 DTp, International Comparisons of Transport Statistics, op cit Chart 13
61 Ibid , table 11.
62 Because it is often simply equated with changes in allocation of road space, which as Chapter 13 shows is inadequate.
63 Bracher, T, (IVU), Policy and Provision for Cyclists in Europe, European Cyclists' Federation, 1988.
64 Tight, M and Carsten, O , "Problems for vulnerable road users in GB, the Netherlands and Sweden, " Drive programme report V1031, Institute for Transport Studies, Leeds University, 1989.
65 DTp International Comparisons of Transport Statistics, op cit. Summary Table 6. Britain's decline was about 37 per cent to an average of 36 per cent.
66 DTp, "International comparisons of transport statistics 1970-1985. Part 1: intermodal, " Statistics Bulletin (88) 38, 1988, tables 3, 2.
67 Ibid , tables 5, 4.
68 Sixth Bi-annual Report, European Commission on the Economics and Financial Situation of Railway Undertakings, 1988 (applying to 1985-86).
69 Rails for Sale, Transport 2000, 1989, p. 8. For another indicator of Britain's relative decline in travel by public transport (use declines where other European countries' use increases) see Roberts, J, "Autolatry: A Detumescent Force?", PTRC Summer Conference 1986, p. 243.
70 Harman, R "European Railways: Financing and Planning" Transport 2000, 1991.
71 RAGB 1990.
72 See eg, the claim of 2, 500 accident victims saved referred to in "Accidental injury, " British Medical Journal, 298, 11.2 1989, p. 349.
73 See the work by West-Oram, F : Chapter 10, note 18 and "The one-

third reduction target". Traffic Engineering and Control, 359 — 363, July/August 1991.
74 RAGB 1988, table 7.b.
75 Morgan, J "Cycling in Safety?", Safety 91, 1 -2 May 1991.Transport and Road Research Laboratory. Page B2. Despite this retrospective reduction, there was still an increase in the rate of over two thirds. This should also be seen in the context of superior medical facilities and a probable decline in the proportion of cyclists who are children and therefore particularly vulnerable, in terms of susceptibilty to bodily insult and probable ineptitude in traffic. Of course, insofar as there has been a significant rise, one can also comment that because it is lower than the rise of danger (as indicated by insurance claims), cyclists deserve credit for having coped with massively deteriorating conditions.
76 See Figure 1.
77 Carsten, O et al , "Urban accidents: why do they happen?", AA Foundation for Road Safety Research, 1989. For the other evidence see Chapter 15 Note 16.
78 Comments by Malcolm Rifkind quoted in Care on the Road (RoSPA), Feb 1992.
79 Rifkind, M interviewed in BBC Radio 4's "Today" programme, 21 October 1991.
80 Adams, J , Hillman, M & Whitelegg, J, One False Move: A study of children's independent mobility, Policy Studies Institute, 1991.
81 Martin, P Response to Adrian Davis (Friends of the Earth) letter of 25/10/91, 30/10/91. Despite this technical ease of doing such research, he also thought "it unlikely that we can do much more to get to the bottom of this".

2. A question of adaptation: risk compensation

1 Dean, J , Murder Most Foul, Allen & Unwin, 1947, p. 20.
2 Hansard, 10 April 1934.
3 Quoted in Plowden, W , The Motor Car and Politics 1896-1970, Bodley Head, 1971, p. 277. This also has a full and accessible account of the debates of those years.
4 In terms of deaths per hour travelled. See Chapter 13 on motorways.
5 Durkheim, E , The Rules of Sociological Method, Free Press, 1964. Also Durkheim, E , Suicide, Routledge, 1963.

6 See eg, Rock, P , The Making of Symbolic Interactionism, Macmillan, 1979; Filmer, P et al , New Directions in Sociological Theory, Collier Macmillan, 1972. This is a somewhat simplified overview of different traditions: for example, there are forms of macro-sociological explanation which are unacceptable to the latter approaches, yet not in the tradition of social holism.
7 An exception is Laurence Ross' work on drinking and driving; Ross bemoans the lack of sociological enquiry, yet his approach accepts a discriminatory status quo. See Chapter 12, notes 18, 53.
8 Smeed, R , "Some statistical aspects of road safety research, " Journal of the Royal Statistical Society, series A, part 1, 1949.
9 See Campbell, D , Mackay, GM et al , Reducing Traffic Injury — a Global Challenge, Royal Australasian College of Surgeons, Melbourne, Australia, 1989, p. 12.
10 Ibid.
11 Mackay, G, interview, 31 July 1989.
12 See Road Accidents Great Britain 1990, The Casualty Report (RAGB), 1990, HMSO, 1991, table 2.
13 Cases are given in Chapter 4 and Part 3, also see the evidence in Adams, J, Risk and Freedom: The Record of Road Safety Regulation, Transport Publishing Projects (TPP), 1985, pp. 30-7.
14 Ibid, Chapter 7.
15 The mean percentage change annually is + or — 4.4 per cent over the last 30 years, with the only figure bigger than 8 per cent in this period being 12 per cent in 1963-4: RAGB 1990, table 2. Since some changes are positive and some negative, the mean could be expressed as even lower than this.
16 Evans, L, "An attempt to categorise the main determinants of traffic safety." (Abstract) Int. Symposium on Driving Behaviour in a Social Context, May 1989, Paris.
17 See Adams, J, op cit, pp. 141-3.
18 A recent attempt at research into assessing ways of correcting motorists' overestimation of their skills failed because motorists were unable to accept making even the most obvious driving errors: McKenna, F, Personal Communication, 15 March 1990. See also Chapter 1, note 43.
19 Lennox-Boyd, A, foreword to RSGB 1952, HMSO, 1954.
20 For example, the law on speed and Rules 51, 105, 65, 66, etc. See the evidence in Chapter 7.
21 For example, Janssen's

experiments with non-seat belt-wearers using seat belts. See Chapter 4, note 20.
22 Rumar, K et al, "Driver reaction to a technical safety measure — studded tires, " Human Factors, 1976, pp. 443-54. See discussion in Adams, op cit, pp. 41-4.
23 See Chapter 6.
24 See eg, Lund, A, Williams, A and Zador, P, "High school driver education; further evaluation of the Deklab County study, " Accident Analysis and Prevention, 18, 4, 1986, pp. 349-57.
25 See Chapter 6.
26 Smeed referred to this survey (Tanner, J "Accidents at rural three-way junctions"Journal of the Institution of Highway Engineers, 1953, 2, 11, 56 -57) in Appendix 1 of Smeed, R "Methods Available to reduce the Numbers of Road Casualties", 1964 International Road Safety Congress.
27 Smeed, R ibid.
28 This is particularly apparent in the myth of the "improving rate" as discussed in Chapter 1.
29 See Chapter 4.
30 See Chapter 11.
31 See Chapter 12.
32 Wright, C and Boyle, A, "Accident "migration" after remedial treatment at accident black spots, " Traffic Engineering and Control, May 1984, pp. 260-6.
33 John Cohen in Cohen, J & Preston, B, Causes and Prevention of Road Accidents, Faber, 1968, p.17. See Chapter 8, note 8.
34 The effect was recognised by Sir Francis Galton. The modern work originates from Hauer, E, "Selection for treatment as a source of bias in before-and-after studies, " Traffic Engineering and Control, Vol. 21, Nos. 8/9, 1980, pp. 419-21. Also Hauer, E, "On the estimation of the expected number of accidents, " Accident Analysis and Prevention, 18, 1986, 1, pp. 1-12.
35 Wright, C and Boyle, A, "Road accident causation and engineering treatment: a review of some current issues, " Traffic Engineering and Control, Sept 1987, p. 475.
36 Maher, M, "Accident migration — a statistical explanation?, " Traffic Engineering and Control, Sept 1987; also the debates in the letters columns of the same journal in Jan and July/ Aug 1987 issues include the idea that increase at neighbouring sites could be due not to accident migration from a treated site but regression-to-mean at these neighbouring sites: this is discounted in the most thorough piece of work by Mountain, L &

Fawaz, B"The effects of engineering measures on safety at adjacent sites6, Traffic Engineering and Control, pp. 15-22, Jan 1992.

37 See Mountain, L and Fawaz, B, "The area-wide effects of engineering measures on road accident occurrence, "Traffic Engineering and Control, July/Aug 1989. See Chapter 5 for discussion.

38 An early claim, complete with alleged financial benefits, is in Smeed, R 1964, op cit.

39 RAGB 1990. "Vehicles skidding in road accidents".(By Ho, Y-S), p.49.

40 For a sceptical view of the benefits of road engineering from within the road safety establishment see Evans, L, Traffic Safety and the Driver', VNR, 1991, p.85: "Surprisingly, the influence of such devices..on safety is not all that clearly established."See Appendix and Note 10 in particular.

41 Albery, D, Partial Progress, Pluto, 1984, p. 13.

42 Gibson, J, and Crooks, L, , "A theoretical field analysis of automobile driving, " American Journal of Psychology, 51, 1938, pp. 453-71.

43 Smeed, R, 1949: op cit.

44 For the history of the risk compensation debate see Adams, op cit, chapter 8.

45 Quoted ibid, p. 129.

46 Quoted in Transport Retort, (Transport 2000), 11 July 1988.

47 Adams, op cit; more recent work includes: "Seat belts, drink and statistics, " Financial Times, 20/12/ 1985; "Risk homeostasis and the purpose of safety regulation, " Ergonomics, 31, 4, 1988, pp. 407-28; "Evaluating the effectiveness of road safety measures, " Traffic Engineering and Control, June 1988, pp. 344-52; "Safety, risk and human fallibility: From Chernobyl to Clapham" (unpublished), March 1989; "Three Homos and Homeostasis: Some Speculations, " First European Congress of Psychology, July 1989.

48 A summary of Wilde's views is Wilde, G, "Beyond the concept of risk homeostasis: suggestions for research and application towards the prevention of accidents and lifestyle-related disease, " Accident Analysis and Prevention, 18, 5, 1986, pp. 377-401.

49 Smeed, R, "Some factors affecting visibility from a drivers seat and their effect on road safety, " British Journal of Physiological Optics, 10 (2), 1953, p. 63.

50 See Chapter 13 on motorways.

51 See Adams, J, Transport Planning: Vision and Practice, " Routledge, 1981. More recently Adams, J: "The Transport Dilemma: pull the ladder up or climb back down?", University College London, 1990.(unpublished).

52 See Adams, J, op cit, note 13 and op cit, note 47, July 1989.

53 Wilde, op cit.

54 Ibid, p. 380, Fig. 1.

55 Broughton, J, "Predictive models of road accident fatalities, " TrafficEngineering and Control, May 1988. This is a critique of Adams and also of a similar approach by Minter, which uses the concept of "social learning" to account for adaptive change to increased motorisation. See Minter, A, "Road casualties — improvement by learning processes, " Traffic Engineering and Control, Feb 1987.

56 See, eg, the critique of Broughton by Andreassend, D, Letters, Traffic Engineering and Control, Nov 1988, p.587.

57 Lund, A and O'Neill, B, "Perceived risks and driving behaviour, " TIMS/ORSA meeting, May 1985, IIHS.

58 Ibid., p. 8.

59 For some of these objections and others see Mckenna, F, "Do safety measures really work?", Ergonomics, 28, 1985, pp. 489-98; "What role should the concept of risk play in theories of accident involvement, " Ergonomics, 31, 1988, pp. 469-84. They are also answered in Adams, op. cit., note 40, July 1989.

60 This attitude was revealed in our work on pedestrian crossings (see Chapter 10). The director of transportation for Cambridge County Council claimed that the introduction of cycle facilities in Cambridge could generate "a sense of false security among cyclists." His other well-known contribution to the Ways to Safer Cycling conference in 1985 was to say: "Can I finish with a message to the general public: if you are thinking of cycling in a busy city, then don't' — Bicycles Bulletin (Friends of the Earth), 33, 1985. (This was left out of the official record.)

61 See the discussion above on the nature of risk; and Adams, op cit, note 47, July 1989, responding to Summala et al.

62 Sabey, B remarks at summing-up session, Eurosafe 1988. Similar remarks were made by her at the Transport and Health Study Group Meeting, London, 1988.

63 Alexandersson, S, "Some data about traffic and traffic accidents, " Swedish Road Safety Office, 1972.

See also the comment in Adams, op cit, note 12.

64 See note 59.

65 This position appears to be taken by McKenna and was taken by Smeed in his 1953 paper.

66 See Chapter 4.

67 For a good indication of how the "multi-causal nature of accidents" prevents easy identification of successful control strategies see Friedland, M et al, "Regulating traffic safety: a survey of control strategies, " Law and Economics Workshop, University of Ontario, Oct 1987.

68 "Yes Minister" (interview with P Bottomley), Bicycle Action, 5, 5, Feb 1989.

3. Accidents, Danger and Accident Causation: the Politics of Road Safety

1 The remark is attributed to JS Mill, but can be seen as a recurring theme in ethics for centuries. It may be wiser to see it as basic theme of natural justice rather than link it specifically to Mill's utilitarianism, particluarly in view of the utilitarian underpinning of modern cost benefit analysis.

2 Haight, F, comment in discussion on Road Safety Seminar (presented by Hillman, M and West-Oram, F), PTRC Summer Conference, 12 Sept 1989.

3 Wilkinson, P, "Drivers protest at life in the new fast lane, " The Times, 20/11/89, reporting the M40-M42 link.

4 Jackson, J, Guardian Motoring, 20/ 2/88.

5 Adams, J, "Risk homeostasis and the purpose of safety regulation, " Ergonomics, 31, 4, 1988, pp. 407-28.

6 Campbell, D, Mackay, GM et al, Reducing Traffic Injury — a Global Challenge, Royal Australasian College of Surgeons, Melbourne, Australia, 1989, p. 12.

7 DTp, RAGB, 1988, HMSO, 1990, table 48. Over previous years it has tended to be around 20 per cent higher.

8 See the previous two chapters and section "Saving lives" and the meaning of death on the streets.

9 The exception being motorcycling.

10 The danger posed by the benign user groups is minimal, but frequently remarked on. See Chapter 15, Note 19

11 Evans, L, "Driver behavior revealed in relations involving car mass, " in Evans, L and Schwing, R

(eds), Human Behavior and Traffic Safety, Plenum Press, 1985.
12 This view is stated from time to time by engineers ie, Mackay, GM, interview, 31/7/89.
13 Davis, R, "An end to road deaths?", New Society, 22/4/88. For an indication of the approach involved see Lawson, S, "Cushioning the impact" Surveyor, 21 March 1991 Knocking down roadside trees etc is likened to putting insulating wire on electric cable by the author, now employed by the AA. See also Rattenbury, S, and Gloyns, P: "Accident patterns in rural access and scope for countermeasures: vehicles and highways", Traffic and Engineering and Control, October 1992. Not only trees but stumps "as these can still be aggressive" (p. 541) should be removed, as well as fences since these are "a particularly aggressive form of man-made structure" (p. 544).
14 Hass-Klau, C, An Illustrated Guide to Traffic Calming, Friends of the Earth, 1990, p. 2.
15 See Chapter 13 on traffic calming.
16 Ibid, see note 41.
17 Household, G, Rogue Male, Penguin, 1984, p. 98.
18 Hillman, M, personal communication, 11/3/90.
19 Transport and the Environment, DTp, 1988.
20 Willesden and Brent Chronicle, 8/3/90.
21 See Chapters 6 and 7.
22 Howarth, I, "Interactions between drivers and pedestrians: some new approaches to pedestrian safety, " in Evans and Schwing, op cit.
23 Black, S, Man and Motor Cars: An Ergonomic Study, Secker & Warburg, 1966.
24 See Chapter 14.
25 The term refers to the benign effects on the environment, relative lack of danger, accessibility, low cost etc. of walking and cycling.
26 See Chapters 4 and 11 in particular.
27 Stewart, D & Chudworth, C, " A remedy for accidents at bends", Traffic Engineering and Control, pp. 88-93, February 1990.

Part Two. Introduction

1 See, eg, Jackson, J, "In defence of the careful drinking driver, " Guardian, 20-26/12/88.; Harry, R, "Gremlins at the Wheel, " Guardian, 10/6/85.
2 The numbers of these bodies represented on the PACTS General Committee are, respectively, 4, 3, 5, 6, 7 and 5.

3 See Chapter 1, Note 12.
4 See Chapter 17 on pseudo-research.
5 The most obvious is the creation and initial total control of the Prince Michael Road Safety Awards by the Institute of the Motor Industry. But also, for example, in 1990-1 PACTS received sponsorship from the Society of Motor Manufactures and Traders, Total Oil Great Britain Ltd, Volvo Concessionaires etc (PACTS AGM July 1991).
6 See Chapter 2, Note 60.
7 A good overview is "What are Roads Worth?", Conference sponsored by Transport 2000 and New Economics Foundation, 1991, London.
8 Pearce, D et al, Sustainable Development, Department of the Environment, 1989.
9See Plowden, S, Transport Reform: Changing the Rules, Policy Studies Institute, 1985, which describes how COBA might be modified.
10 My criticisms are not based on a simple opposition to consideration of monetary value per se. Ideas put forward by, for example, Barde, J-P, & Pearce, D(eds). "Valuing the Environment: Six case studies"(Introduction), Earthscan, London , 1991 are certainly legitimate.
11 See Chapters 4 and 11.
12 See Barde, J-P & Pearce, D: op cit.
13 See Adams, J "The Appraisal of Road Schemes: Half a Baby is Murder" Universities Transport Study Group, 6 January 1977, Glasgow. These arguments are also in Adams, J: Transport Planning, Routledge, 1981, appendix 1; and London's Green Spaces, Friends of the Earth, 1989.
14 Dalvi, M, "The value of life and safety: a search for a consensus estimate, " DTp, 1988.
15 Adams, J, ;Hillman, M & Whitelegg, J, "One False Move: A study of children's independent mobility", Policy Studies Institute, 1991.
16 See section on health in Chapter 14.
17 Cole, S: "Applied Transport Economics", p. 193, Kogan Page, 1987.
18 This section should be read with the section on Costs in Chapter 14.
19 See Jacobs, M: "Can Monetary Values be Assigned to the Environment" in "What are Roads Worth?" op cit, and in a longer form, Jacobs, M "The Green Economy: environment, sustainable development and the politics of the future", Pluto, London, 1991

20 For example, given the choice between buses and cars described in Chapter 17.
21Heller, J, Catch-22, Jonathan Cape, 1962.
22 See the failure of skid resistance measures in terms of their officially stated aims, and also motorway construction for "safety" in Chapter 2, Notes 38 -40.
23 See Section on Motorway Madness in Chapter 13.

4. Clunk-Click Cover-Up: Seat belt Myths and Realities

1 Moore, JO, Cornell University Automotive Crash Injury Research Group, 1957
2 Hansard, vol. 906, 1 March 1976, col. 948.
3 Ibid, col. 928.
4 Dr Stanislaw Gebertt, quoted in The Times, 1 July 1981.
5 Boyd, H, "Educating the Road User, " VeloCity Conference, London, 1981.
6 Irwin, A, Risk and the control of technology: public policies for road traffic safety in Britain and the US, Manchester University Press, 1985.
7 The lowest figure is that of "at least 40 per cent" in Grime, G, "The protection afforded by seat belts, " SR449, Transport and Road Research Laboratory (TRRL), 1979. Most of the figures, eg, those reviewed in Adams, J, Risk and Freedom: The Record of Road Safety Regulation, TPP, 1985, seem to be over 50 per cent. The kind of figure regularly quoted in th 1960's , for example by leading figures in the road safety community like Reuben Smeed (see Smeed, R "Methods Available to Reduce the Numbers of Road Casualties", 1964 International Road Safety Congress, London, 21-26 September 1964.) was "a 73 per cent reduction in fatal injuries" suggested in Lister, R, & Milsom, B: "An Analysis of the Injuries Sustained by Car Occupants", Practitioner, 332 40, 191, 1963.
8 Lancet, 11/1/86, p. 75.
9 The second kind of objection was considered with much less seriousness, on those rare occasions when it was considered at all.
10 See the review of material in Simson, JNL, Editorial, Journal of the Royal Society of Medicine, 82, March 1989. The fullest list of articles dealing with this aspect of seat belt use is in Zuppichini, F, Le cinture di sicurezza nei traumi stradali, Verona, 1986, chapter 6.

11 See the superficial discussion in Moore, op cit.

12 Hansard, 20 Jan 1986.

13 DTp, Road Accidents Great Britain 1987, HMSO, 1988, table 8b. In 1982 the claim rate varied from 18.35 per cent per vehicle for comprehensive insurances, through 12.2 per cent for non-comprehensive, to 29.4 per cent for "fleet" vehicles.

14 Evans, L and Wasielewski, P, "Do accident-involved drivers exhibit riskier everyday driving behavior?, " Accident Analysis and Prevention, vol. 14, no. 1, 1982, pp. 57-65.

15 O'Neill, B, et al, "Mandatory belt use and driver risk taking: an empirical evaluation of the risk-compensation hypothesis, " in Evans, L and Schwing, R (eds), Human Behavior and Traffic Safety, Plenum Press, 1985.

16 Similarly, under a voluntary regime, people wear belts more when they perceive the risk to be higher. See McCarthy, PS, "Seat belt usage rates: a test of Peltzman's hypothesis, " Accident Analysis and Prevention, 18, 5, 1986.

17 Mackay, GM, "Reducing car crash injuries: folklore, science and promise, " Foley Memorial Lecture, Pedestrians' Association, 1982.

18 Mackay, GM, et al, "Seat belts under a voluntary regime, " IRCOBI, 1982. See also examples of this kind of study reviewed in Bragg, BW and Finn, PF, "Influence of safety belt usage on perception of the risk of an accident, " Accident Analysis and Prevention, 17, 1, 1985.

19 Ashton, S, Mackay, GM and Camm, S, "Seat belt use in Britain under voluntary and mandatory conditions, " 27th Annual Proceedings, Association for the Advancement of Automotive Medicine, 1983.

20 Janssen, W, "Working paper on results of seat belt study." Soesterberg, TNO Institute for Perception, 1989.

21 Collett, P and Marsh, P, "Seat belts in Europe, " report to the Rees Jeffreys Road Fund, 1984.

22 Ibid, p. 32.

23 Collett, P and Marsh, P, "Driving passion: the psychology of the car", Jonathan Cape,1986, p. 178.

24 Mackay, op cit.

25 Janssen, W, "The effect of seat belt legislation on fatality rates in a number of West European countries, " Soesterberg, TNO Institute for Perception, 1989.

26 See Adams, op cit, chapter 5, and epilogue (also pp. 111-115, although superseded by later work). The main work on seat belts was originally,

"The efficacy of seat belt legislation: a comparative study of road accident fatality statistics from 18 countries, " Dept of Geography, University College, London, 1981; and "The efficacy of seat belt legislation, " Society of Automotive Engineers, SAE Transactions, 1982. Also see "Smeed's law, seat belts and the emperor's new clothes, " in Evans, L and Schwing, R (eds), Human Behaviour and Traffic Safety, Plenum Press, 1985. Other material, particularly on the British experience, is referred to below.

27 Mackay, GM, op cit.

28 See Adams, op cit, pp. 53-4.

29 Isles, JE, "Seat belt savings: implications of European statistics, " DTp (unpublished), April 1981.

30 Hamer, M, "Report questions whether seat belts save lives, " New Scientist, 7/2/85.

31 DHSS, Research Report No. 13: The Medical Effects of Seat Belt Legislation in the United Kingdom, HMSO, 1985.

32 See Chapter 2 on the Smeed law.

33 See Adams, op cit, pp. 41-5.

34 Scott, P and Willis, P, "Road casualties in Great Britain during the first year with seat belt legislation, " TRRL Research Report 9, 1985.

35 See Chapter 1.

36 Durbin, J and Harvey, A, "The effects of seat belt legislation on road casualties in Great Britain: report on assessment of the statistical evidence, " in Compulsory Seat Belt Wearing: Report by the Department of Transport, DTp, October 1985.

37 See Broughton, J and Stark, D, "The effect of the 1983 changes to the law relating to drink-driving, " TRRL Research Report 89, 1986, fig. 8.

38 "A summary of responses to arguments presented against the indefinite continuation of compulsory front seat belt wearing, " PACTS briefing paper, January (date in January not given) 1986.

39 RoSPA briefing paper, January 1986.

40 Evans, L: "Evaluating Fatality Reductions from Increased Safety Belt Use", Risk Analysis, p.50. 7, 1, 1987

41 See Hansard (Lords), 20 Jan 1986, 45-70, and (Commons) 14 Jan 1986, 89, 35, 877-96, on the specific areas of contention. All quotes from MPs and Lords in the debate come from these sections of Hansard.

42 PACTS briefing paper, January 1986 (see note 36).

43 Durbin, J and Harvey, A, "The effects of seat belt legislation on British road casualties: a case study

in structural time series modelling (with discussion), " Journal of the Royal Statistical Society, 149, 3, 1986.

44 "Transport and Road Research Laboratory", 1988, " DTp, 1988, p. 13.

45 DTp, "Transport statistics for London, " Statistics Bulletin (88) 51, 1988, p. 12. See also the digest of the TRRL Report by Broughton, J, "The Variation of Car Drivers' Accident Risk With Age, " RR 135 (TRRL), 1988. "Significant reductions occurred in 1983, when seat belt wearing was made compulsory and the law relating to drink/driving was amended."

46 Roger Moate, MP, in the House of Commons debate, 14 January.

47 Rattenbury, S, with comment by Adams, J, in PACTS seat belt briefing document, op cit Appendix 2.

48 Mackay, M, interview on Radio 4 Woman's Hour, 6 September 1985.

49 Irwin, op cit, pp. 165, 168.

50 Hansard, vol. 89, no. 35, col. 895, p. 462. This quotation was selected by RoPSA to headline their report on the debate.

51 "A summary of responses... ." RoSPA briefing paper, January 1986.

52 Care on the Road, RoPSA, March 1987.

53 RAGB 1988, table 23.

54 Adams, J "Risk and Freedom" op cit, Chapter 9.

55 On this specific case, see, for example, McCarthy, M, "The benefit of seat belt legislation in the United Kingdom", Journal of Epidemiology and Community Health, 218-222, 43, 3, 1989. The thesis tends to be accepted to at least some extent by those more sympathetic to the victims of this legislation. In my experience members of the road safety community who do not deny the reality of what happened are likely to be evasive or circumspect about the truth. Some will frankly accept the truth with regret, but only in private, others with a cavalier disregard for the victims.

56 See Chapter 15 for figures on modes of transport used for travel. As explained in Chapter 3, the fact that a large proportion of casualties are outside cars should not be the basis for concern: the fact that vulnerable and non-violent minorities like this should have their rights protected , particularly when they are environmentally benign etc, should. I only mention the proportion to show the car-centred arrogance of the road safety lobby.

57 Mackay, GM "Vehicles and

Accidents" in Leeming, J ed: "Road Accidents: Prevent or Punish", p.111. Cassell, 1969,

5. The Engineer's Tale

1 Mackay, GM, "Reducing car crash injuries: folklore, science and promise, " Foley Memorial Lecture, Pedestrians' Association, 1982.
2 Mackay, op cit.
3 Mackay, GM, "Vehicles and accidents, " in Leeming, JJ (ed), Road Accidents: Prevent or Punish?, Cassell, 1969 .
4 Aldridge, "Ways to Safer Cycling, " conference proceedings, 10/4/85, DTp, pp. 33-5.
5 See Chapter 10.
6 Leeming, op cit, p. 71.
7 See Chapter 15.
8 Leeming, op cit, p. 71.
9 Leeming, op cit, Introduction.
10 See statement by Pehr G. Gyllenhammer in Svenska Dagbladet, 25/6/89
11 Leeming, op cit.
12 Mackay, "Vehicles and accidents, " note 2, p. 111.
13 Mackay, GM, interview, 31/7/89.
14 Ibid.
15 See Chapter 13, note 47.
16 Mackay, GM interview, op cit.
17 Ibid.
18 See Hauer, E, "On the estimation of the expected number of accidents, " Accident Analysis and Prevention, 18, 1, 1986.
19 Boyle, A and Wright, C, "Accident "migration" after remedial treatment at accident blackspots, " Traffic Engineering and Control, May, 1984.
20 Mountain, L and Fawaz, B, "The area-wide effects of engineering measures on road accident occurrence, " Traffic Engineering and Control, July/Aug 1989. Also Chapter 2, Notes 36 — 37
21 Ibid.
22 Streff, F and Geller, E, "An experimental test of risk compensation: between-subject versus within-subject analyses, " Accident Analysis and Prevention, 20, 4, 1988.
23 Mackay, GM, "Towards a unified traffic science, " International Scientific Initiatives on Road Traffic, First Round Table, October 1989.
24 Mackay, op cit.
25 See Chapter 10, Section on Pedestrian Crossing Criteria Survey.
26 Wright, C, and Boyle, A, "Road accident causation and engineering treatment: a review of some current issues, " Traffic Engineering and Control, Sept 1987.
27 Ibid, vol. 28, no. 9, pp. 475-80.

28 See Mackay's dismissive review in Accident Analysis and Prevention, 17, 3, 1985, of the discussion of the need to reduce speeds, according to traditional engineering criteria, in Hillman, M and Plowden, S, Danger on the Road: The Needless Scourge, 1984, Policy Studies Institute, chapter 3.
29 Despite claiming scientific credentials, and feeling free to lobby for their chosen solution, senior engineers may still sneer at opponents for being academics and lobbyists. See Huddart, K, letter to Traffic Engineering and Control, July/Aug 1987.

6. The Educator's Tale

1 Plowden, W, The Motor Car and Politics 1896-1970, Bodley Head, 1971, p. 96.
2 OECD, Effectiveness of Road Safety Education Programmes, Paris, 1986.
3 Personal communication, 1991 — speaking in a personal capacity only.
4 Evans, L, Traffic Safety and the Driver, VNR, 1991, p. 105.
5 Road Safety: The Next Steps, DTp, July 1987.
6 One of the largest studies of driver education shows how young people receiving driver education use it to acquire driving licenses earlier and end up with more crashes: Lund, A; Williams, A, and Zador, P "High school driver education: Further evaluation of the DeKalb county study", Accident Analysis and Prevention 18: pp. 349-357, 1986. This only seems to be a subject of concern for road safety professionals with skills learned by cyclists: see Note 7/92 "Notes on the Annual Meeting of Road Safety Members", RoSPA 10 March 1992.
7 See Adams, J, Risk and Freedom: The Record of Road Safety Regulation, TPP, 1985, p. 124., also Evans, L op cit p.105 — 107.
8 For an example of this, see Williams, A, and O'Neill, B, "On-the-road driving records of licensed race drivers", Accident Analysis and Prevention, 6, 263-270, 1974
9 OECD, op cit, p. 52.
10 Pettifer, J and Turner, N, Automania, Collins, 1984, p. 201.
11 Ibid, p.202.
12 Plowden, op cit.
13 A prominent Labour activist like MP Alfred Salter would speak on behalf of ramblers, cyclists and pedestrians, but there is no evidence of road safety being officially advanced as a class issue, and articulating it as such had to wait for

the work of JS Dean. In the 1950's some commentators such as Barbara Wootton would criticise the lenience of motoring offender sentencing as lenience for the middle or ruling classes.
14 See Chapter 7.
15 The Times, 12/8/89, reported a survey of more than 2000 motorists by Devon and Cornwall police showing that almost nine-tenths of motorists do not recognise basic road signs. They were asked to identify 10 signs within two minutes; only 23 managed all 10; the average was 6 out of 10. In another survey (The Times, 16/8/90, p. 1), 30 per cent of motorists could not identify a "keep left" sign, and 70 per cent did not know the Highway Code's recommended gap between their vehicle and the one in front.
16 The driving licence is reapplied for at the age of 70, with no necessary requirement to retake "the test."
17 See Fitzgerald, P, "Road Traffic Law as the Lawyer Sees It, " particularly pp. 169-72, in Leeming, JJ, Road Accidents: Prevent or Punish?, Cassell, 1969. See also Chapter 15.
18 Paper given by Wells, P, at 'New Insights into Driver Behaviour', organsied by PACTS, 21 October 1991, London.
19 For research indicating minimal benefits of advanced driver training see Lund, AK and Williams, AF, "A review of the literature evaluating the defensive driving course, " Accident Analysis and Prevention, 17, 6, 1985.
20 Hoinville, G et al, "A study of accident rates amongst motorists who passed or failed an advanced driving test, " Transport and Road Research Laboratory (TRRL) Report LR 499, 1972.
21 Brown, I, "Prospects for improving road safety, " Ergonomics, 29, 12, 1986. p. 1500.
22 Maggie Baxter (RoSPA Advanced Drivers Association), personal communication, 6/10/89.
23 Beck-Burridge, M and Lyon, J, The Porsche Driving Book, 1988.
24 Ibid, p. 23.
25 Ibid, pp. 37.
26 Ibid, pp. 38, 85, 87.
27 Ibid, p. 22.
28 Plowden, op cit, p.331.
29 Christie, N, and Downing, C "The effectiveness of the 1988 police national motorway safety campaign" RR268, TRRL, 1990.
30 Dean, J, Murder Most Foul, Allen & Unwin, 1947, pp. 50-8.
31 Plowden, op cit, p. 332.
32 Dean, op cit.

33 Flick Rea (Secretary, Pedestrians Association), personal communication, 10/10/89.

34 Oakley, W, The Winged Wheel: The History of the First Hundred Years of the Cyclists' Touring Club, Cyclists' Touring Club, 1977, p. 135.

35 Quoted in McGurn, J, On Your Bicycle: An Illustrated History of Cycling, John Murray, 1987, p. 155.

36 It is difficult to assess this accurately, as the normal problems of inadequate mileage counts for cyclists are exacerbated by their non-existence prior to 1938. In 1938 the distances travelled by cyclists and motor vehicles were respectively 17.2 and 29.2 x 109miles. (Derived from Tables A 1.2 and A 1.3 in Stores, A., "Cycle ownership and use in Great Britain, " LA 843, TRRL, 1978.) This includes all motor vehicles — buses, and lorries as well as cars — so that we can assume that the total of car mileage in 1938 was certainly not more than 50 per cent higher than that of bicycles. In 1934 there were less than half as many cars registered than in 1938 — some 1.3 as opposed to 3.1 million (see Plowden, op. cit., Appendix B), with no suggestion that there were significantly less bicycles. It therefore seems safe to assume that less miles were travelled by car than by bicycle in 1934.

37 McGurn, op cit, p. 156.

38 See the account of opposition to a drink-driving poster campaign in Plowden, op. cit., p. 332.

39 Dean, op cit, p. 59.

40 Downing, C, "The education of children in road safety, " TRRL, Healthy Community Symposium, Stockholm, 1987.

41 Ibid, p. 12.

42 Singh, A and Spear, M, "Road safety education in schools and colleges, " TRRL, CR 133, 1989.

43 Many of Hardy's photographs belong to the Hulton Picture Library; Marzaroli, O, Shades of Grey, Mainstream Publishing, 1986; Baker, S, Street Photographs: Manchester and Salford, Bloodaxe, 1989. Also see some of the photographs in Ward, C "The Child in the City", The Architectural Press, 1978 and Chapters 12 and 13.

44 "City Streets: Sharing urban space and the detailed design of road" (presentation by Paul Jansen), seminar at Oxford Polytechnic, 4/7/88.

45 Howarth, C, "Streets safe for children?", Walk, Nov 1983.

46 Howarth, C and Lightburn, A, "How drivers respond to pedestrians and vice versa, " in Osborne, D & Lewis, J (eds), Human factors in Transport Research, Vol. 2, Academic Press, 1980.

47 Dean, op cit, p. 72-6.

48 Gallup, Report on findings: Pedestrian survey, March 1989, p. 56.

49 Sometimes the anti-pedestrian theme of education is open: "Give the motorist a free rein in a car which is safe (sic) and it is the pedestrian who in the end will have to toe the line." This is to be achieved, for drivers as well as pedestrians, "by careful instruction at an early age: " Black, S, Man and Motor Cars: An Ergonomic Study, Secker & Warburg, 1966, p. 91. For blind enthusiasm for early driver training see Austin, M, Accident Black Spot, Penguin, 1966: "it is becoming increasingly necessary for young people to be trained, from an early age, in the use... of vehicles." (p. 170).

50 An example of integrating education for children with traffic calming on residential streets is Howarth, C and Lightburn, A, "A strategic approach to child pedestrian safety, " in Foote, H et al (eds), Road Safety: Research and Practice, Praeger, New York, 1981.

51 For some common faults, see Brown, op cit p. 1499

52 See Section on Cost in Chapter 14.

53 See Chapter 15.

7. The Lawyer's and Policeman's Tales

1 This Chapter draws on Davis, R "Safety or smokescreen?, " New Law Journal, 17/2/89. My thanks to JR Spencer of Selwyn College, Cambridge, for his assistance in commenting on drafts of that paper and this chapter.

2 A classic defence of motorists privilege, with this message implicit in the title, is Leeming, JJ, Road Accidents: Prevent or Punish?, Cassell, 1969.

3 See Plowden, W and Hillman, M, response to review of Danger on the Road: The Needless Scourge, Policy Studies Institute, 1984, by Boston, R, Guardian, 5/5/84.

4 DTp/Home Office, Road Traffic Law Review: Report, HMSO, 1988. Henceforth referred to as "North."

5 Home Office/DTp/Scottish Office, The Road User and the Law: The Government's Proposals for Reform of Road Traffic Law, HMSO, Feb 1989, Cm 576. Since then, this has now become, with little or no change, the 1992 Road Traffic Act.

6 See eg, Guardian editorial 13/4/89.

7 North, op cit, p. 11.

8 See the letter issued by Northamptonshire police, ibid., p. 313.

9 Ibid., p. 315.

10 The Road User and the Law, op cit, p. 2.

11 North, op cit, p. 316.

12 The Duke of Westminster, by Chester Magistrates in January 1990. He also received a £250 fine for speeding on 29 October 1992.

13 Ibid, p. 336.

14 Ibid, p. 336.

15 Tables 13 and 14 in Home Office: "Offences relating to motor vehicles England & Wales 1988. Supplementary Tables", Government Statistical Office, London.

16 North, op cit, p. 332.

17 Ibid, p. 331.

18 Ibid, p. 331.

19 Highway Code, HMSO, 1987, Rules 51, 105, 65, 66.

20 New Law Journal, editorial, 6/1/89, gives a figure of 2 million drinking drivers; see Chapter 12, note 16; some 7 per cent and 20 per cent of women and men drivers claim to drink and drive at least once a year, and about 1 per cent and 5 per cent respectively claim to do so more than 3 or 4 times a year.

21 See Chapter 9.

22 See Chapter 12.

23 The evidence in 1984 was collected in Plowden and Hillman, op cit, p. 93. In a recent survey three-quarters of drivers said they do not stick to speed limits in built-up areas: see Jones, P, "Traffic quotes: public perception of traffic regulation in urban areas, " DTp, 1990.

24 See the section on "the dangerous Prince" in Chapter 16

25 Guardian, 31 July 1990.

26 See Chapter 3.

27 See Plowden and Hillman, op cit, p. 93, n. 48.

28 In a survey by British Car Rental, reported in Care on the Road (RoSPA), October 1991.

29 This legislation was supported by a Guardian editorial, 31 May 1989. Also see my letter in response on 7 June 1989.

30 Social Surveys (Gallup), "Survey amongst motorway drivers, " June 1988, General Accident.

31 Care on the Road, Dec 1989.

32 See Chapter 1; 90 per cent of insurance claims do not involve crashes where there was personal injury.

33 See Road Traffic Act 1972, sections 25, 166.

34 "Traffic accidents — the law and police action, " 23/6/86.

35 Information in this section from Graham Buxton, former head of West

Mercia CID, interview, 1 December 1989.
36 See North, op cit, annex K/5-K/7, for a comparison with the number of charges for homicides, etc. This book compares road danger with occupational danger. While the numbers of deaths involved in industrial accidents are about three times less, this is an area which has always been regarded as a legitimate concern for action by the trade union and labour movements. Of course, the danger on the road is presented by fellow citizens rather than irresponsible employers — but that could be an argument for more, not less, concern. Also, one could argue that some kinds of industrial activity with a degree of inherent danger are socially necessary, to an extent which the level of car and lorry use is not. See Chapter 14 & 17.
37 See Introduction to Part Two : The Economists' Tale.
38 See Chapter 14, section on costs.
39 There is a substantial literature on the philosophy of punishment. For one summary see Honderich, T, Punishment: The Supposed Justifications, Hutchinson, 1969.
40 See Chapter 6.
41 See Chapter 12 on the experience of the introduction of the breathalyser in Britain.
42 See Chapter 15, Note 3.
43 Quoted in Willett, T, Criminal on the Road, Tavistock, 1964, p. 6.
44 A summary of the relevant points is in Fitzgerald, P, "Road traffic law as the lawyer sees it, " in Leeming, op cit. His arguments are only extreme versions of those made by others and are referred to in some degree by North.
45 For an account of this school of thought in academic criminology see Taylor, I, Walton, P and Young, J, The New Criminology, Routledge, 1973, chapter 2.
46 Despite a good introductory discussion on the nature of motoring offences and crime, the one major study of motoring offenders in British academic criminology, Willett, L, op cit, then falls into precisely the trap of examining their criminality by comparing their offences with traditional criminal offences.
47 See note 42.
48 See Chapter 12, Note 12 on drink-driving controls, for example.
49 See DTp, Transport Statistics Great Britain 1975-1985, HMSO, 1986, tables 7.2, 6.5.
50 See Chapter 14; not least the difficulty or impossibility of car use for all those entitled to driving licences who may want it.

51 See Chapter 14 on congestion.
52 See eg, the rather lenient view, in discussing the legitimate extent of the use of strict liability for traffic offences, in Williams, G, Textbook of Criminal Law, 2nd edn, Stevens, 1983, p. 321. A more favourable view is given by Honderich, op. cit., p. 170.
53 As does Fitzgerald, op cit, in supporting Leeming; and also Williams (who claims to be very knowledgeable about vehicle design).
54 See Dix, M, and Layzell, A, Road Users and the Police, Police Foundation, 1983. There was no clear evidence that motorists' experience with the police had soured their attitude towards them; the belief that this does happen is "an important and influential myth" (p. 137).
55 Increasing support for random breath testing (see Chapter 12, Note 12) could be an example of this.
56 North, op cit, puts it in full: "It is in principle anomalous that the enormous resources of the automobile industry are devoted to designing, producing and marketing vehicles to travel at well over 100 mph, and the criminal justice system is then directed to preventing drivers using them accordingly" (p. 44). The failure of North to accept the logic of this and push for automatic controls is picked up in Spencer, J, "Road traffic law: A review of the North report, " Criminal Law Review, Nov 1988.
57 North, op cit, p. 16.
58 Ibid, p. 18.
59 Ibid, p. 25.
60 The Road User and the Law, op cit, para 2.8.
61 Ibid, para 2.7.
62 Spencer, op cit.
63 Ibid.
64 As was specified by Articles 175 and 176 of the Penal Code in Albania: private cars were illegal (although cars were used by senior party officials), and motoring was restricted to bus, lorry and van drivers; if children under the age of 14 were hit there was no question of mitigation, with the assumption being that motorists were supposed to drive slowly enough to avoid any children who might run into the street. Also see Kodi Rrugor, Tirana, 1988. Political changes in this part of the world have now made this obsolete.
65 Spencer, op cit, quotes a figure of 20 per cent for disqualified drivers who carry on driving.
66 Dean, J "Murder Most Foul", p.34. Allen &Unwin, 1947, London.
67 Eurosafe 1988 conference at the

Guildhall, July.
68 Quoted in Transport Retort 13, 1990, Transport 2000, London.
69 See the views of Isaac Foot, MP quoted in Plowden, W "The Motor Car and Politics, 1896 — 1970, , p.277. London 1971, although he might have only be arguing for the onus of proof to be placed on the motorist — which makes the hostile reponse to him all the more remarkable.
70 See North, op cit, p. 74. It is also interesting that this comment becomes a tacit acceptance of risk compensation: "we believe that a cycle is inherently less dangerous to other road users than a motor vehicle — not least because a cyclist is more vulnerable than a motorist if an accident occurs". Cyclist only are referred to because pedestrians were not included in North's brief.
71 The St. Christopher's (sic) insurance scheme. An earlier version specifically for convicted drunk drivers was made illegal: the relative lack of concern for non-drink driving offences from the medical profession and other parts of the road safety lobby is interesting (See Chapter 12.)

8. The Doctor's Tale

1 Mackay, GM, Transport Safety — towards a European Perspective, All Party Transport Safety Group, July 1989. As well as involvement in PACTS, there are specifically medical inputs into the other bodies such as RoSPA, and their "own" Medical Committee on Accident Prevention.
2 Karpf, A, Doctoring the Media: The Reporting of Health and Medicine, Routledge, 1988, chapter 7.
3 Ibid.
4 See Crawford, R, "You are doing harm to your health": the ideology and politics of victim blaming, " International Journal of Health Services, 7, 1977, p. 663.
5 Cameron, D and Jones, I, "An epidemiological and sociological analysis of the use of alcohol, tobacco and other drugs of solace, " Community Medicine, 7, 1985, pp. 18-29.
6 See Ashton, J and Seymour, H, The New Public Health, Open University, 1988, p. 125.
7 Ibid, p. 157.
8 Cohen, J and Preston, B, Causes and Prevention of Road Accidents, Faber, 1968, p. 17. Unfortunately, despite a promise in the introduction to raise this issue later in the book in the light of initiatives such as seat

belts, this does not occur.
9 Transport and Health Study Group
Health on the Move: Policies for
health promoting transport" Public
Health Alliance, 1991. See also the
work of Wolff referred to in Chapter
14.
10 See the claim of 2, 500 deaths
after injury a year (which includes
non- road-crash injuries), from
Irving, M, quoted in BMJ 298, 11/2/
89, p. 350; also Rinke, C, "Concepts
in emergency and critical care;
Preventable trauma deaths, " Journal
of the American Medical
Association, 254, 23-30/8/85. Also
Trunkey, D, "A time for decisions, "
British Journal of Surgery, 75, 1988.
pp. 937-39; Trunkey quotes the
Royal College of Surgeons
Commission on the Provision of
Surgical Services (the Irving Report),
which suggested that the
"preventable death rate" from
injuries due to the absence of proper
trauma care was about one-third.
11 See the section on post-injury
management in MacKay, GM,
Effective Strategies for Accident and
Injury Reduction, Rees Jeffreys
Discussion Paper 13, Transport
Studies Unit, Oxford, 1990.
12 Godlee, F & Walker, A:
"Importance of a healthy
environment", BMJ, pp.1124 -1125,
303, 2 November 1991.
13 British Medical Association:
"Cycling: Towards Health and
Safety", Oxford University Press,
1992.
14 See my review of the BMA report
in London Cyclist May/June 1992.
The criticism about no mention of
CO_2 emissions is, however,
unfounded.
15 Report of annual BMA meeting in
Nottingham in BMJ, 305, p.192. 18
July 1992.
16 See Chapter 12.

9. "Sorry, mate... " The conspicuity con

1 Oakley, W, Winged Wheel,
Cyclists' Touring Club, 1977, p. 34;
an account of the cyclist
organisations' campaigns on the
lights question occurs throughout this
book, as it does in Plowden, W, The
Motor Car and Politics 1896-1970,
Bodley Head, 1971.
2 For a discussion of this principle
see Chapter 16.
3 The Cyclists' Case against
Compulsory Rear Lights, National
Cyclists' Union, Nov 1922.
4 McCaghrey, G, in Optometry
Today, 14/3/87. Also Kent, M, Daily
Mail, 16/5/88.
5 Guardian, 29/8/87.
6 See Well, Drive Safely, Association
of Optometrists, c. 1986.
7 Kirby, J, "I didn't see him, "
Association of Optometrists, 1988.
8 Local Transport Today, 15/11/89,
p. 7. evidence for this is in Epstein,
D et al "Low luminance myopia"
Acta Ophthalmologica 59, 1981
9 Road Safety: The Next Steps, DTp,
1987, p. 33.
10 Observer 25 August 1991
11 Andrew Raffle, Chair of RoSPA's
Technical Committee (and trustee of
Medical Commitee on Accident
Prevention), quoted in Heath, J
"Afraid of the Dark" Care on the
Road (RoSPA) Nov 1988. The
comment is justified by a dubious
reading of one limited survey.
12 House of Commons, First Report
from the Transport Committee on
Road Safety, session 1984-5, paras
42-5.
13 Beck-Burridge, M and Lyon, J,
The Porsche Driving Book, 1988,
chapter 4.
14 Ibid, p. 84-6.
15 Ibid, p. 87.
16 See Cole, B and Hughes, P, "A
field trial of attention and search
conspicuity, " Human Factors, 26,
(6), 1984. Also Johansson, G and
Backlund, F, "Drivers and road signs,
" Ergonomics, 13, 1970.
17 "Most subjects with homonymous
defects cannot compensate for their
deficiencies" — Lovsund, P, et al:
"Effects of driving performance of
visual defects: A driving simulator
study" Accident Analysis and
Prevention 23, 4, 1991.
18 See the section on Motorway
Madness in Chapter 13
19 Kalberg, V-P, "The effects of
reflector posts on driving behaviour
and accidents" PTRC Summer
Conference 1991
20 See the work quoted in Evans, L, :
Traffic Safety and the Driver pp. 86
— 88, VNR 1991
21 Prower, S, "Daytime lights-on
laws for motorcars and motorcycles,
" British Motorcyclists' Federation
research paper, 1985. See also
Minter, A, "Case not proven, '
Motorcycle Rider (journal of the
BMF), 2, 19, Nov/Dec 1985.
22 Prower, S, "Why motorcyclists
using daytime lights will still have
accidents, " workshop presentation,
3rd Int. Conf. on Vision in Vehicles,
Sept 1989. Prower, reviewing a study
where accidents were disaggregated
by type relevant to use of daytime
headlamps, estimates that even if
there were no risk compensation by
either motorists or motorcyclists, or
any long-term risk compensation, and
daytime lights were to prevent one-
third of the 9 per cent of accidents
described as being within their scope,
this would still leave 97 per cent of
all motorcycle accidents unaffected.
23 See Chapter 11.
24 Leonard, J, "Lights out!, " Road
Rider (USA), 1974, pp. 48-50.
25 Fulton, E, Kirkby, C and Stroud,
P, "Daytime motorcycle conspicuity,
" TRRL SR 625, 1980.
26 Watts, G, "Bicycle safety devices
— effects on vehicle passing
distances, " Transport and Road
Research Laboratory SR 512, 1979;
and "Evaluation of pedal cycle
spacers, " TRRL Report 820, 1984.
27 Watts, G, "Evaluation of
conspicuity aids for pedal cyclists, "
TRRL Report 1103, 1984.
28 Aizelwood, J, "Conspicuity aids, "
Cycletouring, Dec/Jan 1984-5.
29 Letter to D Roberts, Ref RS 6/9/
024, dated 21 November 1984
30 Boyd, H, "Safety aids for riders, "
paper given at Bikesafe Conference
(Australia), 1986, p. 7.
31 Lund, H, "Cycle Accidents in
Lighting-up Time — an Analysis of
92 Accidents in Copenhagen",
Danish Council for Road Safety
Research, Notat 2, 1985.
32 Avon County Council, joint road
safety advisory sub-committee, 4/7/
84, para 2.4.
33 Boyd, op cit.
34 Ibid, p. 2.
35 Ibid.
36 Ibid.
37 Ibid, p. 2. But see Prower, op cit,
note 15, for a critical view of the
Swedish experience.
38 Conspicuity is one of the central
points argued for (without evidence)
in Pedestrian Safety: New Proposals
for Making Walking Safer, DTp,
April 1989. See Chapter 10.
39 "Man, 21, killed on way to dance,
" Willesden & Brent Chronicle,
1988.
40 "Motorist banned", Independent,
29 July 1992 (One column inch)
41 The case of George Glynn made
the Daily Mail and Daily Mirror front
pages (but not some of the
broadsheets) on 21 January 1992.
42 Boyd, op cit, p. 2, refers
specifically to cyclists, but the point
applies to all those outside cars.
43 Daily Mail, medical page, 26/12/
89.

10. "Does Someone Have to Die First?" Problems for Pedestrians

1 House of Commons debate on Road Safety, Hansard, vol. 159, no. 167, 595-96, 3 Nov. 1989.
2 Dean, J, Murder Most Foul, Allen & Unwin, 1947, p. 41.
3 Particularly if wheelchair users are included as "walkers." Also, those with visual and other disabilities are less able to drive.
4 National Travel Survey 1985-86, DTp, 1988, part 1, p. 39.
5 See Chapter 7.
6 See Chapter 7.
7 Daor, E and Goodwin, P, "Variations in the importance of walking as a mode of transport, " GLC research memorandum RM 487, 1976. Quoted in Goodwin, P, "Walking: the paradox of public opinion, " Foley Memorial Lecture, Pedestrians' Association, 1984.
8 See Note 43 Chapter 6.
9 See Chapter 13 on traffic calming.
10 See Chapter 13 for problems of segregating roadspace "for" pedestrians.
11 See Gallup Report on Pedestrians Survey, March 1989. Some 10 per cent of respondents claimed to have been involved in accidents as pedestrians. Assuming a respondent's mean age which is mid-life, a figure of up to 20 per cent can be arrived at.
12 NTS 1985-86, op cit, p. 39.
13 See the discussion in Hillman, M, "The neglect of walking in UK transport and planning policy, " Proceedings of the "Feet First" Symposium at City University, 19 May 1989, City University and Transport 2000.
14 Table 5 in DTp, Road Accidents Great Britain 1990, HMSO, 1991
15 See Gallup Report, op. cit.
16 This can be seen in the change between NTS 1975-76 and NTS 1985-86, and one can assume this to be a trend which started earlier. See Hillman, op cit, p. 1.
17 Adams, J, ;Hillman, M & Whitelegg, J, "One False Move: A study of children's independent mobility", Policy Studies Institute, 1991.
18 This point has been made in West-Oram, F, "Street Credibility, " Consumer Voice, (National Consumers' Council), spring 1988. And in "Danger on the road — the cover-up, " Transport Retort (Transport 2000), July/Aug 1987.
19 See Chapter 1.
20 See Adams, J et al op cit for a

comparison between the English schoolchildren studied and children in Germany. The German children were allowed to cross roads on their own at a much earlier age.
21 Pedestrian Safety: New Proposals for Making Walking Safer, DTp, April 1989.
22 David Worskett (Head of Road Safety Division, DTp), interview, 11/1/89. Despite recent emphasis on 20mph speed limits and traffic calming in certain urban areas, this philosophy has not changed. The permanent secretary at the DTp has stated that funds will only be available for traffic calming on casualty saving, not environmental improvements or anxiety relief criteria. (Quoted in Adams, J: "Safety in Numbers", Surveyor 16 April 1992.
23 Hillman, op cit p. 1.
24 Hillman, M and Whalley, A, Walking Is Transport, Policy Studies Institute, 1979.
25 See Roberts, J, Talking about Walking: A Literature Review, TEST, March 1989, for a bibliography. An excellent combination of photographic material with text discussing the loss of freedom to children is Ward, C, The Child in the City, Architectural Press. 1977. (For other photographs, see note 10 above)
26 Hillman, op cit, p. 8.
27 Pedestrian Safety, op cit.
28 See Chapter 12.
29 See Chapter 14, section on Pollution.
30 See Chapter 13
31 See Chapter 14, section on Cost.
32 What's Wrong With Walking, National Consumer Council, 1987.
33 This section is based on Davis, R and Donnellan, M, "Flow criteria or community need? Alternatives for installing pedestrian crossings, " PTRC Summer Conference, 12/9/89; reprinted in Walk, (Pedestrians' Association), Spring 1990.
34 DTp, Highways and Traffic, "Design considerations for pelican and zebra crossings", Departmental Advice Note TA 52/87, 1987.
35 Ibid, para. 4.3.1 (j).
36 Griffiths, J, Hunt, J and Marlow, M, "Delays at pedestrian crossings, " Traffic Engineering and Control, vol. 25, nos. 7/8 and 10, 1984, pp. 365-72 and 505-10; vol. 26, no. 5, 1985, pp. 277-82. The first calculations were published in Research on Road Traffic, Road Research Laboratory, 1965, p. 402. There is continuing work in this area; see TRRL Leaflet LF 1050, June 1987.
37 Cresswell, Griffiths, J and Hunt, J

quoted in Heraty, M, "Review of pedestrian safety research, " TRRL Contractor Report 20, 1986.
38 See Crompton, D, "Pedestrian delay, annoyance and risk: preliminary results from a 2 year study, " PTRC, 1979.
39 Gilbert, D, personal communication, Jan 1989.
40 Goldschmidt, J, "Pedestrian delay: its measurement and response to changes in traffic patterns, " Universities Transport Study Group Conference, 1976.
41 See Roberts, op cit.
42 Todd, J and Walker, A, People as pedestrians, OPCS, 1980.
43 See Chapter 2 on accident migration.
44 See the discussion in Chapter 2.
45 see the discussion in Chapter 3.
46 Institution of Highways and Transportation with the DTp, Roads and Traffic in Urban Areas, 1987.
47 This is the suggestion put forward as lying behind the lack of importance accorded by planners and others, by Goodwin, op cit, p. 4.

11. On Your Head Be It: Helmets

1 For the concept of "cause of accidents" see Chapter 3.
2 An example — one of many, most of which are more subtle — of this is the comment by one MP attending the 1991 Select Committee on Transport that methods of slowing vehicle speeds in residential areas would not have to be attempted if cyclists wore helmets. See Bingham, K: "MP's say nowt", Cycling Weekly11 January 1992
3 Adams, J, Risk and Freedom: The Record of Road Safety Regulation, ' TPP, 1985, p. 96. The US and some less important material is reviewed in Chapter 5 of "Risk and Freedom".
4 Figures were given by the junior minister, Keith Speed, in the Parliamentary debate on compulsion. See Hansard (Commons), 5 April 1973, cols 770-1.
5 See DTp, Road Accidents Great Britain 1973, HMSO, 1974, review of RTAs in 1973, para 5.
6 The figure of 35 per cent was given by the best known road safety academic of the time, Reuben Smeed. See Smeed, R "Methods available to reduce the numbers of road casualties", 1964 International Road Safety Congress, September 1964.
7 Tables calculated from editions of RAGB (and its predecessor Road Accidents); also DTp, Transport Statistics Great Britain 1974-1984

and 1975-1985. The figures are given for riders, as passengers' exposure rate is not counted.

8 See the report in "Comment, " Motor Cycle and Cycle Trader, 1/5/71.

9 For a full account of this see Harris, M, Bikers: Birth of a Modern Day Outlaw (sic), Faber, 1984.

10 Thompson, H, Hells Angels, Penguin, 1967.

11 Cohen, S, Folk Devils and Moral Panics, Paladin, 1973.

12 Editions of Road Accidents Great Britain 1987 — 1990, table 23.

13 See Plowden, S, "Reducing Motorcycle Accidents, " Road Safety: What Next ?, Policy Studies Institute, proceedings of conference, 1985, p. 10. The latest publicity on this from the DTp (DTp: "Accident Fact Sheet Number 7: Motorcycle Injury Road accidents: great Britain 1990: The Facts", DTp, 1992.) gives a figure of motorcycles being three times more likely than cars to hit pedestrians. This is not corrected for age or other relevant variables, and legal fault is not considered.

14 Certainly regarding fatality rates. See RAGB, 1982, Essays.

15 Cohen, J and Preston, B, Causes & Prevention of Road Accidents, Faber, 1968, see table J in the section by Preston; also Hobbs, F, Traffic Planning and Engineering, 2nd edn, Pergamon, 1979.

16 Figure 4 is based on OPCS Series DH4 No. 12, 1986. Mortality Statistics England and Wales, accidents and violence. Codes 800-4. Fracture of skull, and 850-54 Intracranial injury, excluding 800-4, together are what are counted as head injuries. (A contemporary examination of car passengers' head injuries is in a study of single vehicle only (SVO) accidents: "The head is the body are most frequently sustaining life-threatening injuries, so protection of the head is of great importance." [Rattenbury S, and Gloyns, P: Traffic Engineering and Control, Oct 1992, P.544] The solution advocated is not helmet wear, but removal of roadside trees and fences. See Chapter 3, note 13).

17 See Adams, op cit, p. 150, on Swedish small-scale studies.

18 Downing, C and Bennett, M, "Safety helmets for pedal cyclists — a pilot study amongst children, " TRRL Supplementary Report 283, p. 1.

19 Tunbridge, R, Everest, J et al, "An in-depth study of road accident casualties and their injury patterns, " TRRL, RR 136, 1988. Figures 3 and 4 are derived from table 4 and tables

2 and 4 respectively.

20 Letter from Charles Coin, Cycling, 9/6/84.

21 See below on "The danger from Victoria" and the criticism of the Victorian seat belt legislation in Chapter 4.

22 Juden, C, "That's a lie, " Cycletouring, April/May 1988, p. 136.

23 Downing and Bennett, op cit.

24 Worrell, J, "Head injuries in pedal cyclists: how much will protection help?, " Injury, 18, 5, 1987.

25 Morfey, C, "Bicycle helmets — how effective are they in real crashes?, " University of Southampton, Feb 1988.

26 A widely quoted piece is Thompson, R et al, "A case-control study of the effectiveness of bicycle safety helmets, " New England Journal of Medicine, 320, 21, 1989, p. 1361.

27 Wasserman, R et al., "Bicyclists, helmets and head injuries: a rider-based study of helmet use and effectiveness, " American Journal of Public Health, 78, 9, 1988, p. 1220.

28 Wood, T and Milne, P, "Head injuries to pedal cyclists and the promotion of helmet use in Victoria, Australia, " Accident Analysis and Prevention, 20, 3, 1988, pp. 177-85.

29 Rodgers, G, "Reducing bicycle accidents: A reevaluation of the impacts of the CPSC bicycle standard and helmet use, " Journal of Products Liability, 11, 4, 1988, p. 307.

30 Bicycle Federation of Washington Newsletter, 1988/89 (undated), editorial. On a similar note, see "From the editor, " Bicycle Forum, summer/fall 1989, published by Bikecentennial, Missoula, MT, USA.

31 Vulcan, A, P et al.: Mandatory Bicycle Helmet Use: Experience in Victoria, Australia, Accident Research Centre, Monash University, August 1991. (Draft) Now published in World Journal of Surgery 16, 3, May-June 1992.

32 Peter Vulcan, Personal Communication, 15 June 1992.

33 Vulcan, A et al op cit, p. 15. These are the figures derived from Transport Accident Commission Claims. The figures are 47 per cent and 30 per cent for admissions to public hospitals.

34 ibid, p.15

35 ibid, p.14

36 Sullivan, G: "Initial Effects of Mandatory Bicycle Helmet Wearing Legislation" Road Information Services, Vic Roads, July 1990

37 See Shepherd, R: "Helmet Law Discourages Cycling", Australian Cyclist p.18, Oct/Nov 1991. On the

Great Victorian Bike Ride, Clarke, C: Personal Communication, 3/11/91

38 Morgan, M et al: "Bicycle Helmet Usage Rates in Victoria 1990 -91". Report GR 91 — 9, Vic Roads, Victoria, 1991.

39 Vic Roads — Road Information Services (1991). Table 1;Road Traffic Accidents Involving Casualties, Victoria 1983 to 1990.

40 About 6 — 8 per cent of all fatalities in Victoria have been cyclists: the approximately 1 in 3 decline noted would yield the 2 points.

41 Bicycle Helmet Safety Institute: Bibliography of Helmet Documents, 19 December 1991, BHSI, Washington. The Rodgers paper is referred to obliquely in a review of the CTC's position, without any consideration of it's content.

42 Bicycle Helmet Safety Institute, Proposal for a Bicycle Helmet Safety Project, 1989.

43 Cycle Trader, Nov 1989.

44 Stalnaker, R, et al, "Driving point impedance characteristics of the head, " Journal of Biomechanics, 4, 1971, p. 127. Also see Gurdjian, et al, "Tolerance curves of acceleration and intracranial pressure and protective index in experimental head injury, " Journal of Trauma, 6, 1966, p. 5. Both are quoted in Bicycle Helmet Safety Institute, The Helmet Update, Washington, 1989.

45 Keighley, J, "Helmets: unfashionable gear, " Climber and Hill Walker, vol. 28, no. 12, Dec. 1988, pp. 43-4.

46 See the items on the CTC position paper and Mathew, D, "The road to helmets — paved with good intentions, " Bicycle Bulletin (Friends of the Earth), July-Dec 1988 in The Helmet Update, op cit. In an attempt to condemn and ridicule the British approach, the BHSI claim that the US cyclist casualty rate is lower. The sloppiness of the manner of this claim is in stark contrast to the sophisticated scientism of work on impedance characteristics etc. Britain and the USA have roughly similar cyclist fatality rates measured per head of the population, although our reported casualty level is 5 times lower than those admitted to hospital — not all of the difference is likely to be accounted for non-reporting. However, the important difference is that there are about twice as many commuter cyclists — who do the majority of cyclist miles in Britain — per head of the population in Britain compared to the USA. See Bicycle Institute of America: "Bicycling Reference Book 1989', Bicycle

Institute of America, Inc. These figures, which would suggest that the USA cyclist casualty rate per mile travelled, is significantly higher than Britain's, are eschewed in favour of a denominator consisting of the number of people who own bicycles.
47 McCroy, J "The Headbangers Survival Kit", Mountain Biking UK, Summer Special, July 1991.
48 Aya, R, "The legacy of "Pete" Snell, " Snell Memorial Foundation (undated).
49 This description is based on my own reading of the meaning of helmet wear, and also on Clarke, A (government relations officer, League of American Wheelmen, now of the Bicycle Federation of America — in personal capacity), personal communication, 26/1/90.
50 Cyclists can endanger pedestrians and vice versa: no doubt members of each group can also bump into each pother. The point is that these dangers are trivial compared to the motor danger threatening both groups. The current interest in, for example, pavement cycling is more indicative of the inability to properly discuss danger on the roads than anything else. See the discussion in Chapter 15. Figures are given in Chapter 1, also see Davis, R. Great Motoring Myths No. 5 London Cyclist March/April 1992, and response to Letter in July/August 1992 edition.
51 The European Cycling Federation adopted the Cyclists' Touring Club, "Cycle helmets position paper."
52 See eg, "In a nutshell; are helmets a good idea, " London Cyclist, Jan / Feb 1990; and "Hard-headed look, " CTC DA News, 3, April/May 1989.
53 See Chapter 4.
54 Derived from Vic Roads — Road Information Services figures for 1983 -1990 and Tables 2 and 5, RAGB 1990
55 See Anderson, P, Montesin, H and Adena, M, "Road Fatality Rates in Australia 1984-5, " Federal Office of Road Safety, June 1987, compared with RAGB 1990 and 1985, table 26, and RAGB 1987, table 6a).
56 Boyd, H: "Knocking the problem on the head", Safety Education, p.6-7, Summer 1988.
57 For the appropriateness of this analogy see Chapter 16.
58 Vulcan, AP et al "Evaluation of mandatory bicycle helmet use in Victoria, Australia", 36th Annual proceedings, Association for the Advancement of Automotive Medicine, Illinois, 5 October 1992.
59 Calculated from graph 5 in Vulcan, AP et al, Oct 1992, op cit.

60, 14 and 36 per cent declines among adults and children cyclists respectively. "Govt survey shows decline in cycling", Australian Cyclist, Aug-Sept; 1992).

12. Drink Driving as a Road Safety Problem

1 British Medical Association, Report of the Board of Science and Education, The Drinking Driver, March 1988, p. 9-10.
2 This is a general point about road safety education made in Chapter 6 but is particularly applicable here. See Havard, J, "Drinking and driving: ten years on from Blennerhasset, " keynote address, BMA Conference, London, 1985.
3 Borkenstein, R et al, "The role of the drinking driver in accidents, " Department of Police Administration, Indiana University, 1964.
4 Allsopp, R, "Alcohol and road accidents: a discussion of the Grand Rapids study, " TRRL RRL 6, 1966.
5 Blood alcohol content (BAC)is measured in milligrams of ethanol per 100 millilitres of blood (or mg per cent).
6 For example, The Medico-Legal Investigation of the Drinking Driver, British Medical Association, 1965.
7 Quoted in Dunbar, J, "A quiet massacre: a review of drinking and driving in the United Kingdom, " Institute for Alcohol Studies, Oct 1985.
8 See Chapters 4 and 6.
9 For an account of these see Havard, op cit.
10 The classic explanation of this is Ross, L, Deterring the Drinking Driver, Lexington Books, 1984.
11 This view is constantly reiterated. For a typical statement see Action on Drinking and Driving, Review of Policy on Drinking and Driving, Institute of Alcohol Studies, April 1988.
12 An example is the second annual Lex Report on Motoring, (MORI), 1990. Also see those quoted in Action on Drinking and Driving, op cit, p. 10.
13 DTp, Road Accidents Great Britain (RAGB) 1988, HMSO, 1989, table 3f.
also DTp, RAGB 1990, HMSO, 1991, table 1n.
14 DTp, RAGB 1988, HMSO, 1989, section 3.3, .
15 "The facts about drinking and driving, " TRRL, 1986.
16 The Lex Report on Motoring, op cit, gives figures of 11 per cent and 4 per cent for men and women on the

last six months, which is close to the OPCS survey result of 22 per cent and 7 per cent annually. See Goddard, C and Ikin, C, Drinking in England & Wales in 1987, OPCS, HMSO, 1985, chapter 5.
17 Goddard, and Ikin, op cit.
18 Ross, L, "Social control through deterrence: drinking and driving laws, " Action on Alcohol Abuse Seminar, London, 29/5/85.
19 From 52 to 781 (index), Table 2, RAGB 1990, HMSO, 1991.
20 Ibid. Table 1k and RAGB 1988, HMSO, 1989, table 3b.
21 Statement by Chair of Traffic Commitee of Association of Chief Police Officers, reported in The Guardian 4 December 1991.
22 See Note 50 below, and Chapter 4
23 For a statement of this and other arguments for random breath testing see PACTS, "Arguments against random breath testing at roadside checkpoints and some rebuttals, " Jan 1989.
24 See Evans, L, "Traffic Safety and the Driver" VNR, 1991, p.195.
25 Adams, J, "Legal restraints on drunken driving: comment, " Eurosafe '88, London, 1988.
26 Youngman, J, "Alcohol and Road Crashes, " Road Crashes — the Alcohol Factor Seminar, Melbourne, 21 Oct 1987.
27 See an account of this episode in Havard, op cit.
28 See Youngman, op cit.
29 See Ross, op cit, note 18. for an indication of chances.
30 Dunbar, op cit, p. 2.
31 For example, Robinson, D, (ed), Alcohol Problems: Reviews, Research and Recommendations, MacMillan, 1979.
32 See Chapter 8
33 See Gusfield, J, "Categories of ownership and responsibility in social issues: alcohol use and automobile use, " Journal of Drug Issues, Fall 1975.
34 See Dunbar, op cit, pp. 13-22, for a summary.
35 Raffle, P, "Interrelation between alcohol and accidents, " Journal of the Royal Society of Medicine, 82, March 1989.
36 Ibid, p. 135, for an account of the biochemical and other changes in the response to trauma caused by alcohol.
37 Evans, L op cit p.163, 170-172
38 Havard, op cit.
39 For example, see only one page in Evans, L op cit (p.175-176) for discussion on "Other drugs, illness and sleep deprivation" out of 57 pages on drink-driving.

40 House of Commons Transport Committee, Report on Road Safety, 1984-5, para 89.

41 Irving, A, "The international attitude to drug/driving problem: legislation and countermeasures, " Medico-Pharmaceutical Forum and TRRL joint meeting on Medicines and Traffic Safety, June 1986.

42 Lesch, O et al, "Medication and drug abuse in relation to road traffic safety, " Pharmatherapeutica, 5 (5), 1989, pp. 338-54. Proportions given are 4 per cent and 0.3-0.6 per cent respectively, with the British car numbers at that time at around 18 million.

43 Interview with Professor M Lader (National Addiction Centre), Face The Facts, BBC Radio 4, 28 September 1991.

44 Ulrich, L et al, "Hüfigkeit von Medikamenten in Strassenverkehr. Eine Pilotstudie an Verkehrsteilnehmern in der Schweiz, " Z-Rechtsmed, 93 (2), 1984, pp. 95-110. The most recent figures for Britain found 4 per cent of dead drivers had blood concentrations of medicinal drugs likely to affect the central nervous system, with another 2.5 per cent having concentrations of hedonistic drugs ("drugs of abuse") such as cannabis (see Everest, J, Tunbridge, R and Widdop, B, "The incidence of drugs in road accident fatalities in England and Wales, " TRRL, PA 1570/88, 1988). A survey of 800 serious crashes in Melbourne, Australia indicated that a third of all casualties had been taking psychotropic drugs (see report by Mason, I. Care on the Road August 1991)

45 Figure quoted in Spencer, J, "Road traffic law: a review of the North Report, " Criminal Law Review, Nov 1988.

46 For example, Sabey, B in "Drinking and driving — ten years on from Blennerhasset, " BMA Conference, London, 1985.

47 Robinson, op cit, p. 8.

48 PACTS, op cit, p. 5.

49 See discussion in Chapter 7.

50 See Chapter 4.

51 PACTS briefing paper, "A summary of responses to arguments presented against the indefinite continuation of compulsory front seat belt wearing, " Jan 1986.

52 PACTS, op cit, p. 1. Also, see Chapter 4, note 42 for other official volte-faces

53 See Chapter 1 on SVOs; also the final paragraph of Ross, op cit, note 18.

54 Recent comments along these lines have come from Minister for Roads Peter Bottomley at the 1989 AGM of the Pedestrians' Association and his successor Robert Atkins (ICE, "Walking into the "90s', 6/6/90).

55 See Chapter 7, also Chapter 15

56 See Guardian "Tip-offs on drink-driving backed by High Court", 1 February 1991.

13. Getting Out of Whose Way? — Segregation, traffic calming and the struggle for road space

1 Whitelegg, J, "Traffic calming: a "green" smokescreen, " London Borough of Ealing Conference on Traffic Calming, Jan 1990.

2 Roberts, J, User Friendly Cities, TEST, 1989.

3 Franklin, J, "Campaigning for what?, " New Cyclist, 8, Winter 1989-90.

4 See Chapter 14.

5 An estimate of some 3 million casualties caused annually to pedestrians from defective footway surfaces is made in National Consumers Council, What's Wrong With Walking?, HMSO, 1987.

6 See Chapter 10.

7 See section on Pedestrian Crossing installation criteria in Chapter 10. A mass market book referring to contemporary transport problems refers to crossings as for motorists, rather than for pedestrians: see Elton, B: "Gridlock", Macdonald, 1991.

8 Atkins, S, Critical Paths: Designing for Secure Travel, Design Council, 1989, pp. 58-9.

9 Birmingham Women's Video Group, Paradise Circus, 1988.

10 See TEST, Quality Streets: How Traditional Urban Centres Benefit from traffic calming, Transport and Environmental Services, 1988.

11 A current example in Britain is Lancaster, where the pedestrianised city centre is surrounded by a fast moving giratory system, and road building is on the agenda to increase accessibility to the centre by car

12 See Chapter 6, note 36.

13 See Chapter 15.

14 Oakley, W, Winged Wheel, Cyclists' Touring Club, 1977, p. 53.

15 Watkins, S, "The user's response to cycling schemes, " Cycle '83, National Bicycle Conference, 1983.

16 Hall, P, "Planning for a Golden Age, " RTPI 75th Anniversary Conference, The Planner, 10 Nov 1989.

17 Milton Keynes Cycle Users' Group, "The Milton Keynes Redway: a comparison of design specifications, " 1988. Also see Cycletouring, June/July and Aug/Sept 1990.

18 See Chapter 14.

19 See McClintock, H, "Cycle planning: a comprehensive bibliography, " Nottingham University, 1989 (2 vols). A good short summary of the advantages and disadvantages of planning for cyclists is Clarke, A, "Riding against the flow, " Bicycle, May 1987; also Davis, R, "Improving the status of London's cyclists, " Cyclist Monthly, Oct 1982.

20 Quoted in Plowden, W, The Motor Car and Politics: 1896-1970, Bodley Head, 1971, p. 92.

21 Oakley, W, op cit, p. 53.

22 See Chapter 14 section on Congestion. An illustration of how road improvement can generate traffic is Mackie, P & Bonsall, P, : "Traveller response to road improvements: implicatiuons for user benefits", Traffic Engineering and Control 29, 411-416, 1989. Also See interview with Tony May, Local Transport Today, 1/11/89.

23 These claims have been criticised since the Leitch report in 1977. See Davis, R, "Motorway madness, " New Society, 8/4/88. For the fallacy of the economic generation argument see Vancke, J, "The effect of major roads upon the local economy: a study of industrial location and its effects, " unpublished Ph.D thesis, University of Aston, 1990. For an examination of the immediate environmental effects see Secrett, C and Cliff-Hodges, V, "Motorway madness: roads and their impact on the natural environment, " Friends of the Earth, 1986. For the process whereby economic arguments fit into the justification see Tyme, J, Motorways versus Democracy, MacMillan, 1978; Mathew, D, Capital Schemes?, Friends of the Earth, 1987, p. 43.

24 See Hamer, M, Wheels Within Wheels: a study of the road lobby, Routledge, 1987, chapters 4, 6.

25 DTp, Road Safety: The Next Steps, 1987. Despite this assertion being persistently criticised for its misleading nature, the "eight times safer" phrase continues to crop up. See the speesch by the Minister for Roads and Traffic, Robert Atkins, House of Commons debate on road safety, Hansard, 3 Nov 1989, vol. 159, no. 167, col. 580.

26 All figures used here are from

DTp, Road Accidents Great Britain 1990: The Casualty Report, 1991, principally table 26.
27 National Travel Survey, 1985-86, table 3.16
28 Ibid, table 3.17.
29 RAGB 1987, para 11.5. (I use the more recent figures in RAGB 1990 in my argument here: there is little difference between them and those in RAGB 1987).
30 See note 22
31 Wilde, G, "The risk compensation theory of accident causation and its practical consequences for accident prevention, " Österreichische Gesellschaft für Unfallchirurgie, Salzburg, 1976. The point about long sight lines increasing motor danger was made by JS Dean in Dean, J, "Murder Most Foul", Allen & Unwin, 1947. Good visibility for motorists at junctions can increase the chances of car/cyclist accidents (Henson, R and Whelan, N "Layout and Design Factors affecting cycle safety at T-Junctions". Traffic Engineering and Control, October 1992.
32 See Hamer, op cit, chapters 4, 6.
33 Dr Ivan Brown; see report in The Times, 29/9/88.
34 The Independent, 20/4/89.
35 Hass-Klau, C An Illustrated Guide to Traffic Calming, Friends of the Earth, 1990. For some time the main guides to the debates surrounding traffic calming have been Bowers, T. et al in Built Environment, Oxford, 1985, 12, 1-2; Hass-Klau, C (ed), New life for city centres, Anglo-German Foundation, 1988; and Whitelegg, J, "The principles of environmental traffic management, " in Tolley, R (ed), The Green Modes, Bellhaven Press, 1990. A recent summary of ideas is in Traffic Calming — Ways Forward, seminar at London Borough of Ealing, 1990. This area gives "practitioners" a massive opportunity to display their ideas and practice: a sub-section of their industry is producing a lot of new material, although the basic features will remain the same.
36 Traffic in Towns, HMSO, 1963, known as the Buchanan Report, discussed below.
37 See discussion on this in Chapter 3. An example of this tendency is Nishimura, T and Takai, H, "A study on the evaluation method for physical environment in residential areas by using conscious measures, " PTRC Summer Conference, 1989.
38 Keller, H, "Three generations of traffic calming in the FDR, " PTRC Summer Conference, 1989.
39 Hass-Klau, op cit, p. 1.

40 This point is well made by Brindle, R, "Traffic Calming in Australia: A definition and commentary", Australian Road Research, 21 (2), June 1991.
41 Roberts, J, User Friendly Cities, TEST, 1989, pp. 45-6.
42 Whitelegg, op cit, note 1, p. 9.
43 Ibid.
44 Whitelegg, J, "West Germany — the slow road to success?, " Annual Conference of British Geographers, 1989.
45 This appears to be the case from preliminary stages of research in the Netherlands on speed outside residential areas in Rotterdam. Rene Kohler (Dutch Ministry of Transport), personal communication, April 1990.
46 Hass-Klau, op cit, pp. 2-3.
47 See Institut fir Landes- und Stadtenwicklungsforschung des Landes Nordrhein-Westfalen, City-Paket und Geschwindigkeits-schalter, 1989.
48 See Cleary, J: "Cyclists and Traffic Calming", Cyclists' Touring Club 1991.
49 Collins, M: "Traffic Calming and Environmental Management", PTRC Summer Conference, 1990.
50 Brindle, R op cit.
51 An important document is Pharaoh, T: "Less Traffic, Better Towns: Friends of the Earth's illustrated guide to traffic reduction", FoE.London, 1992. As Figure 2, p.5. shows, this strategy involves more rural traffic.
52 Buchanan, C, letter to The Times, 13/12/89.
53 Gyllehammer declaration, in Svenska Dagbladet, 25/6/89.
54 See Hall, op cit.
55 Hass-Klau, op cit, p. 1.
56 Tripp, H, Town Planning and Road Traffic, Arnold, 1942.
57 See the discussion on Buchanan in Wistrich, E, The Politics of Transport, Longman, 1983, chapter 4.
58 Roberts, J, personal communication, Jan 1990.
59 Wistrich, op cit, p. 68.
60 Ibid, p. 69.
61 For these and other criticisms see Hillman, M, "The wrong turning: twenty years on from Buchanan, " Built Environment, 9, 2, 1983.
62 Ibid p. 106.
63 Ibid p. 105.
64 Buchanan, C, "Transport for society, " Institution of Civil Engineers, Conference on Transport for Society, London, 1975.

14. One or Two Problems with Cars

1 The limits were based on upper and lower estimates of economic growth. This figure has now swollen to about £20 billion with the addition of new schemes.
2 See later in this chapter. For a fuller discussion of what the forecasts imply in environmental and other terms see Adams, J, "Car ownership forecasting: pull the ladder up or climb back down, " Chartered Institute of Transport, May 1989. A much more optimistic account, although still regarding the forecast possible increase in car use as posing an intolerable strain on the environment and society, is given in Goodwin, P et al: Transport: The New Realism, Transport Studies Unit, Oxford, March 1991
3 Dale, W, letter in Traffic Engineering and Control, July/Aug 1987.
4 Reported in "This England, " New Statesman and Society, 21/4/89.
5 See Boyle, S and Ardill, J, The Greenhouse Effect, New English Library, 1989, p. 27.
6 For this and other material on pollution see Whitelegg, J, "The Future of Public Transport, " Public Transport Users Association, Melbourne, November 1989.
7 See Pearce, F, Turning Up the Heat, Bodley Head, 1989, chapter 10.
8 Dockery, D et al: "Workshop on Health Effects of Atmospheric Acids and their Precursors", American Lung Association, March 1990.
9 See section on mass car use and health for this and other health effects of pollution, also Whitelegg, J, "Traffic calming: a "green" smokescreen?, " London Borough of Ealing Conference on Traffic Calming, Jan 1990. On bezene see Note 28.
10 See OECD, Environmental Effects of Automotive Transport, Paris, 1986, for a discussion of diesel particulate emissions.
11 Stansfield, S, "Aircraft noise and health, " Radical Community Medicine, 38, summer 1989; and National Society for Clean Air, Pollution Handbook and Pollution Glossary, 1989.
12 Barde, J-P, & Button, K: Transport Policy and the Environment, P.3. , Earthscan, 1990. See also the costs of noise referred to in Notes 63 -65.
13 Dunmore, J, personal communication, Aug 1989..
14 See Roberts, J: User Friendly Cities, back cover, London, 1989

15 The level to which emissions should be restricted depends on the target level of CO_2 specified. If this level is to be in line with stopping the increase in global warming, we appear, even with far more fuel efficient cars, to be talking about reduction. See note 18.

16 For an example of such "concerned" talk see Hutchings, V, "Learning to love the milk float, " New Statesman and Society, 2/3/90.

17 Newman, P et al "Does free-flowing traffic save energy and lower emissions in cities?", Murdoch University, Nov 1988; see also section on congestion.

18 For a similar analysis and conclusions see Earth Resources Research and World Wild Fund for Nature, Atmospheric Emissions from the Use of Transport in the UK, vols 1 and 2, WWF, 1989-90; also Flavin, C, "Slowing global warming: a worldwide strategy, " Worldwatch Institute, Report 91, Oct 1989. Also see Bailey, R, Road to the Future, Green Party, 1991, for a carefully calculated "trend-breach" forecast of why car use needs to be cut by 50 per cent to the 1970 level. The basis is the target of 60 per cent cut worldwide called for in IPCC, "Intergovernmental Panel on Climate Change: Report to IPCC from Working Group" June 1990. In addition bodies like the Global Commons Institute (See GCI, "Carbon Energy Intensity: Target and timetables for sustainable systems and global rights", GCI, 1992, forthcoming) have argued that the target is unobtainable unless the OECD countries like Britain cut by a higher amount to achieve a level of emissions per head of the global population which is equitable, in order to be able to negotiate succesfully with non-OECD countries to get them to cut their emissions. This means an 80 per cent cut throughout the British economy over the next decade or two: a target accepted by the Green party, but not Friends of the Earth. An alternative is to consider the global implicatiuons of Third World/South countries have the same level of car use in similar geographical areas that we do: either way substantial reduction of car use (as opposed to reduction in increase) is required.

19 Wolff, S, "Public health versus public policy: an appraisal of British urban transport policy, " Laboratory of Toxicology, University College, London, 1990 (unpublished).

20 Desai, K and Jingel, J, "Hazards of long distance cycling, " British Medical Journal, 298, 22/4/89, pp. 1072-3.

21 Hamer, M, "Death waits at the bus stop, " New Scientist, 4/12/86.

22 Keatinge, W, "Seasonal mortality among elderly people with unrestricted home heating, " British Medical Journal, 293, 20/9/86, pp. 732-3.

23 Morton, S and Hannah, J, "Within minutes of the M62" — major retail development proposals for Greater Manchester, " Radical Community Medicine, 38, summer 1989.

24 Hamilton, K and Gregory, A, "Women, transport and health, " Radical Community Medicine, 38, Summer 1989.

25 See Transport and Health Study Group: "Health on the Move: Policies for Health Promoting Transport, Public Health Alliance, 1991. A good short statement is Wolff, S: "Straight Talking on Transport and Health", Health Visitor, February 1992

26 Freeman, D and Cattell, S, "The risk of lung cancer from polycyclic aromatic hydrocarbons in Sydney air, " Med. J. Aust., 149, 1988, pp. 612-15.

27 See Carhart, B and Walsh, M, "Potential contributions to ambient concentrations of air toxics by mobile sources, " 80th Annual Meeting APCA, New York, 24/6/87. Also Carrey, P and Somers, J, Air Toxics Emissions from Motor Vehicles, US Environmental Protection Agency, 1988.

28 BBC 2 TV, Public Eye, 10/11/89. See also Wolff, S, Letter, Nature, 346, 9/8/90, p. 517., and at more length: Wolff, S: "Correlations between car ownership and leukaemia: Is non-occupational exposure to benzene from petrol and motor vehicle exhaust a causative factor in leukaemia and lymphoma?", Experientia, March 1992

29 For this and other general indications of health problems see Whitelegg, J, "The future of urban transport, " Public Transport in Crisis Conference, Melbourne, Nov. 1989, and Rowell, A et al "Populations at Risk", Earth Resources Research, July 1992 (extracts published in "Gasping for Change", Greenpeace UK, London 1992.)

30 See discussion on mobility/access difference in section on "The Los Angeles example".

31 See Appleyard, D and Lintell, M, "The environmental quality of city streets: the residents' viewpoint, " AIP Journal, March 1972, which has assumed classic status.

32 See Morton, & Hannah, op cit Also Berkman, L and Syme, S, "Social networks, host resistance and mortality: a nine year follow-up study of Almeida county residents." American Journal of Epidemiology, 109, 1979, pp. 186-204. This shows that low levels of social support are linked to an increased mortality rate.

33 Children in social class 5 are seven times more likely to be killed as pedestrians than children in social class 1. See Office of Health Economics, Accidents in Childhood, Briefing No. 17, OPCS, 1981.

34 Hillman, M & Whalley, A, "Walking is Transport", pp. 91 — 94, Policy Studies Institute, 1979.

35 Although some data do exist if looked for, see Note 29 for examples.

36 BBC 2 TV, Public Eye, op cit, note 28.

37 For example, the way noise nuisance is supposedly quantified in cost-benefit analyses. See Adams, J Transport Planning: Vision and Practice, Routledge, 1981.

38 Wolff, S: Letter, American Journal of Epidemiology, March 1992. In particular, see notes 7 — 10 in this letter.

39 Ibid.

40 See Introduction to Part Two. This may also involve revising the classic positivist method, at least to incorporate an understanding of risk compensation, and an awareness of the needs of the less powerful and more vulnerable in terms of the planning and execution of research programmes.

41 See Hamer, M, Why We Have to Control the Car, Friends of the Earth Transport Paper, No. 1, 1984.

42 DTp, Transport Statistics Great Britain 1978-88, HMSO, 1989, p. 29.

43 Ibid., p. 141 (rail) and p. 32 (buses). The £750 million for busesis made up of capital sums for local public transport, current revenue support to public transport and grants for concessionary fares.

44 See section on cost. The estimates of subsidy vary from about 0 per cent, at the lowest level of counting for conventional costs without any estimate for social costs, to the higher estimates, particularly with the figures used by Teufel in Germany, of some 80 per cent, with my calculations (without environmental or similar costs) going up to some 60 per cent.

45 Buses and Coaches Council, Briefing Sheet 6, 1989.

46 See Hamer, op cit.

47 See Chapter 17.

48 See Chapter 15, , on attitudes to tax.

49 See Introduction to Part Two on cost-benefit analysis. Costs are at 1990 levels unless otherwise stated.
50 Lavelle, D, The Way Ahead: The Cost of Congestion, " British Road Federation, June 1989. (Unless otherwise stated, all costs here are per annum for Great Britain.)
51 Infrastructure Policy Group, Congestion, Institution of Civil Engineers, 1989.
52 Transport in London Task Force, The Capital at Risk, Confederation of British Industry, March 1989.
53 Report in The Times, 20 December 1988
54 Road Accidents Great Britain 1987, HMSO, 1988, p. 35.
55 See Galasko, C et al, "Long-term disability following road traffic accidents, " Research Report 59, 1986.
56 Dubus, P, "Safety and quality of service, " Int Transport Workers Federation Symposium on Railway, Environment and Transport Quality, Geneva, Feb 1990.
57 Report prepared for the Federal Highways Administration by the Urban Institute, Washington. See reference in Pro Bike News, Bicycle Federation of America, October 1991.
58 £3.812 billion is the figure given for 1988-9 in Basic Road Statistics 1989, British Road Federation.
59 Roads for Prosperity, op cit.
60 See Section C. above
61 At 1989 costs.
62 "Allocation of road track costs 1988-9, " DTp.
63 The figure was originally produced by the Post Office Chief Medical Officer in the 1970's, and reproduced by the Health and Safety Executive. It would be quite possible to massively increase the value of the cost by considering the variety of effects on work performance by stress and stress-induced illness. Colin Mackay, Principal Psychologist, HSE, Personal Communication, 21 January 1992.
64 Quoted in Quinet, E: The Social Cost of Land Transport, OECD, Paris 1990
65 Table 8.7 in Whitelegg, J: "Till the Pips Squeak; Ecological Taxation reform", in Whitelegg, J "Traffic Congestion: Is there a way out?", Leading Edge 1992
66 In Schulz, W & E "The Federal Republic of Germany" in Barde, J-P & Pearce, D eds: "Valuing the Environment: Six case studies", p.30Earthscan, 1991.
67 In Barde, J-P, & Button, op cit.
68 See note 66.
69 See note 65.
70 Plowden, S, Transport Reform:

Changing the Rules, " Policy Studies Institute, May 1985.
71 Adams, J, Hillman, M, and Whitelegg, J: "One False Move: A study of children's independent mobility", Policy Studies Institute, 1991
72 Basic Road Statistics 1989, op cit, table 33.
73 DTp, "International comparisons of transport statistics 1970-1985, " Statistics Bulletin (88), 38, HMSO, 1988
74 Ibid. Figures for 1988 at 1986 prices.
75 Teufel, D et al, "Okosteuern als marktwirtschaftliches Instrument im Umweltschutz. Vorschlage fir eine Steuerreform". UPI Bericht NR, 9, . Heidelberg, 1988.
76 Renner, M: "Rethinking the Role of the Automobile", Worldwatch Institute, 1988.
77 Quoted in Zuckerman, W: "End of the Road", p.214, Lutterworth, 1991.
78 Cecil Parkinson, BBC TV On the Record, 25/2/90.
79 The figure of £15 billion is given in Transport and Road Research Laboratory 1988, DTp, 1988, introduction, although there is no indication of how this figure is arrived at.
80 The estimated cost of company cars in the London area alone is £800 million. See Haringey Council, Blueprint for Transport, Nov 1988.
81 A variety of other forms of subsidy can exist, such as loan schemes.
82 Mackay, GM, review of Hillman, M and Plowden, S, Danger on the Road: the Needless Scourge, in Accident Analysis and Prevention, 17, 3, 1985, pp. 273-4.
83 Transport Retort, 11, 8, Nov 1988, p. 2. This section refers to London, but the lessons are relevant for other major conurbations.
84 Transport in London, DTp, 1981. Also see TEST, The Big Choke, 1989, p. 4, where a figure of 14 per cent is given.
85 For example, Harris, P: "Moving in the right lane", Surveyor 7 September 1989, claims that buses are 4 — 15 times as efficient in carrying people per hour on a single lane road. See also Note 45.
86 For a more detailed explanation of the issue of defining congestion and it's critical role in discussing "solutions to congestion", see Davis, R: "Congestion: So what's the problem?" in Whitelegg, J (ed): "Congestion: Is there a way out?", Leading Edge, 1992.
87 These figures vary by time of day (higher outside the peak) and location

(higher for cars crossing the outer cordon, which roughly approximates to the M25). See Greater London Council, Transport Data for London, GLTS 81, 1984; and Baker, L, "Company cars and their effect on journeys to work in central London, " Traffic Engineering and Control, 28, 1987, pp. 530-7.
88 Gruen quoted in TEST, The Big Choke, op cit, p. 21.
89 Buchanan, C quoted ibid, , p. 3.
90 For example, Bonsell, P and Mackie, P, "The generation gap?, " Local Transport Today, 23/8/89.
91 Purnell, S, "The effects of strategic network changes on traffic flows, " PRA Note 4, Transportation and Development Department, GLC, 1985. The implication is also that congestion at the end of the Westway (Marylebone Road) was not diminished.
92 Mogridge, M, "Jam today, jam yesterday, and jam tomorrow, " University College, London, 1985.
93 Newman, P et al, "Does free-flowing traffic save energy and lower emissions in cities?, " Murdoch University, Nov. 1988.
94 See Goodwin, P et al op cit, p.42.
95 Some of these issues are addressed in a statement opposing the White Paper Roads to Prosperity produced by nine environmental groups: Roads to Ruin, London, 1989.
96 See the discussion in Adams, J, "Car ownership forecasting: pull the ladder up or climb back down?" Traffic Engineering and Control, March 1990.
97 Goodwin, P et al, op cit p.80 — 82.
98 Adams, J, "Car ownership forecasting: pull the ladder up or climb back down?" Traffic Engineering and Control, March 1990. p. 138; see also Hamer, M, "Splitting the city, " New Internationalist May 1989.
99 Adams, J, "Broken down on the bypass, " The Times, 2/3/90.
100 Davis, M "City of Quartz" Verso, 1990.
101 Mishan, E, The Costs of Economic Growth, Penguin, 1979, p. 130.
102 Illich, I, Energy and Equity, Calder & Boyars, 1974.
103 Independent Commission on Transport, Report, Coronet Books, 1974.
104 Breach, I, "Can you give up your car?, " Guardian, original article 1972, repeated in amended form 13/10/89.

15. The view from the driving seat — motorist attitudes

1 For a discussion of techniques of neutralisation see Taylor, I et al, The New Criminology, Routledge, 1973, p. 176.
2 Granada TV, World in Action, March 1990, had two programmes with this title.
3 DTp, Transport Statistics Great Britain 1991, (TSGB) HMSO 1991, Table 2.15 (a): in 1988 -1990, 78 per cent of adult men and 48 per cent of adult women, 1.e. 62 per cent of the adult population had driving licences. As recently as 1980 just under half the adults surveyed (in TSGB 1975-1985) had driving licences. National Travel Survey 1985-86 , HMSO. reports 38 per cent of households without a car owner living in them in 1985 (Para 2.12). On journeys, 80 per cent of the short (under 1 mile) journeys, which are 33 per cent of the total, are walking journeys, (Para 8.1); therefore figures in Table 3.2 are only 75 per cent of non-walking journeys. these involve 69 per cent being by car, ie, 69x75 = aproximately 50 per cent.
4 Plowden, W, The Motor Car and Politics 1896-1970, Bodley Head, 1971, p. 201.
5 See Chapter 14 on costs.
6 See Chapter 6 on "the test".
7 See Chapter 7.
8 See Which?, April 1989, for a criticism.
9 Plowden, W op cit for a history.
10 "AA: The Concise History, 1905 — 1980's", Automobile Association.(no date)
11 Plowden, W; op cit p. 99.
12 Annells, J "Gun law on the B172' Evening Standard, 1 October 1990, London
13 In approaches derived from Freud. See Hall, C, A Primer of Freudian Psychology, Mentor, 1954, pp. 89-91 for a brief explanation.
14 Tripp, HA, Town Planning and Road Traffic, Edward Arnold, 1942, p. 28-30.
15 Carsten, O et al: "Urban Accidents: why do they happen?", AA Foundation for Road Safety Research 1989
16 Mills, P, "Pedal cycle accidents — a hospital based study, " TRRL RR 220, 1989. is the Oxford study; the police report is Metropolitan Police Report B5/14/75, 1975. One American study gives the similar figure of 1 in 3 cases being adult cyclists' responsibility (Williams, A

"Factors in the initiation of bicycle-motor vehicle collisions"American Journal of Diseases in Children, 370-377, 130, 1976.)
17 Tripp, A, op cit p. 29.
18 See Chapter 6, note 36.
19 Motorists in crashes killing 351 times as many pedestrians as cyclists over some 60 times more miles. Figures derived from RAGB 1990, tables 1, 23. Also, in 1989 the London Accident Analysis Unit reported that cyclists were involved in only 0.7 per cent of accidents with pedestrian casualties, despite constituting a much higher proportion of vehicular traffic. In another example of prejudice, Time Out (no. 1042, 5/8/90) drew attention to the "problem" of cyclists endangering pedestrians in the only article it had carried dealing with pedestrian safety in more than twenty years.
20 See the accounts in interviews in Parry, M, Aggression on the Road, Tavistock, 1968.
21 Marsh, P and Collett, P, Driving Passion, Cape, 1986.
22 Tripp, A: op cit p.29, including note 1.
23 Tripp, A: "20mph Limit in Blackout", The Times, 1 February 1940, London
24 Letters, London Cyclist, 2, Spring 1990
25 "London's Hated Hundred", Time Out, 951, 9 — 16 November 1988, p.21.

16. "Road safety" or Danger Reduction?

1 See Chapter 13 section on Traffic Calming.
2 The figure of 80 per cent was given by Minister for Roads and Traffic, Christopher Chope in the Second Reading of the Traffic Calming Bill on 24 January 1992 in the House of Commons. This applies to some 120, 000 kms of urban road. Basic treatment costs £25, 000 per km, and twice as much with basic environmental works: hence the approximate figure of £40, 000. The number of years quoted is based on the current amount of Transport Supplementary Grant (TSG) donated by central government (the DTp) to local authorities for traffic calming and similar schemes — although the role of TSG is basically to support road building and other capacity increasing "improvements". Personal communication, Adrian Davis (Friends of the Earth), 26/2/92, also Letter in Local Transport Today, 20/2/92

3 Barker, D: The Guardian "Royal saga of life in the fast lane". 23/10/1990.
4 In similar fashion, at about the same time the traditionally pro- road building Institition of Highway Engineers gave it's road safety prize (sponsored by Mobil) to a scheme encouraging cycle helmet wear.
5 It is not necessary for a high level of intention to be in evidence for the dictionary definition of "violence" to apply.
6 Quoted in Adams, J: "Risk and Freedom: The record of road safety regulation", TPP, 1985, p.150.
7 Communication from Alan Leng (formerly National Secretary, CTC) March1988.
8 See News section, Local Transport Today, 19 September 1990
9 Mackay, GM: "Effective Strategies for Accident and Injury Reductions", Rees Jeffrey Road Fund Discussion Paper 13, Oxford, Jan 1990.
10 Boyd, H(former National Bicycle Safety Officer, RoSPA). "There is a danger of throwing out the baby with the bath water.(but)...I agree entirely that helmets are a red-herring... "Cycling and the Healthy City" Papers from a conference organised by Friends of the Earth, 27 June 1990.
11 See eg, Painter, K "Lighting and crime prevention for community safety: the Tower Hamlets study; first report", March 1989, Middlesex Polytechnic Centre for Criminology.
12 Mills, P: "Pedal Cycle Accidents — A Hospital Based Study", RR220, TRRL, 1990.
13 Allott & Lomax: "Cyclists and roundabouts: A review of the literature", Cyclists' Touring Club, 1991
14 Communication from M McCarthy, August 1990.
15 The press advertisement running concurrently compares Audi's philosophy to that of top class boxers trying win fights: it points out the advantages of "safety aids" allowing drivers to sustain crashes, which allow "the capacity of the vehicle to acelerate very fast, "So you live to fight another day" Guardian 1/12/90, p.7.
16 "Care on the Road", August 1992, p.15.
17 "Care on the Road", April 1992, p.9. Presumably by checks on motorists for eyesight (but see Chapter 9 for potential smokescreening problems with this)
18 "Care on the Road", August 1992, p. 16.
19 See report by Woodland, L "New Cyclist" Winter 1990, p.7.

17. Conclusion: getting about in a civilised society

1 Goodwin, P et al: "Transport: The New Realism", Transport Studies Unit, Oxford, 1991
2 Roger Freeman, Minister for Public Transport, Woman's Hour, Radio 4, 5/10/90.
3 Dean, J, Murder Most Foul, Allen & Unwin, 1947, p. 20.
4 Interview with Tony May, Local Transport Today, 1/11/89.
5 Gallup, "Public attitudes to traffic restraint, " Metropolitan Transport Research Unit (London), Nov 1989; also "North-east London public attitudes survey, " Feb 1990. See also the survey in Which?, Oct 1990, indicating that the majority of people support stricter traffic regulation enforcement, more bus lanes, cycle lanes and pedestrianised streets and banning cars from congested areas, even if motorists are inconvenienced.
6 Lex Report on Motoring, Lex Plc, 1990. Also see Pharaoh, T "Less Traffic, Better Towns", Friends of the Earth, London, 1992 for a summary of public opinion.
7 See DTp, "Traffic regulation in urban areas — the public view, " TAU, April 1989. See also work by Dix and Layzell cited in Chapter 7, note 54.
8 See Danish Road Directorate, "Consequence evaluation of environmentally adapted through road in Vinderup, " Report 52, 1987; as an example, and Chapter 13.
9 Paul Webster reporting in Guardian, 25/7/89.
10 See report in Cycle Touring, April 1990, pp. 26-7.
11 Interview with Pehr Gyllenhammar, Svenska Dagbladet, 25/6/89.
12 Johnson, B, reporting in Daily Telegraph, 7/6/90.
13 Parents may feel that their presence reduces the risk of abduction; yet the Gallup Pedestrians poll, March 1989, indicated that they worry about their children being hurt in road accidents just as much; the chances of the latter are far greater.
14 Hardin, G: "The Tragedy of the Commons" extracted in Dobson, A, ed: The Green Reader, Andre Deutsch, 1991.
15 For an example of how this applies to transport see: Adams, J: "The Transport Dilemma: pull the ladder up or climb back down?", University College London, 1990 (unpublished).
16 Summarised in Adams, ibid.

17 See Chapter 14.
18 For example, in Cresswell, R "Rural Transport and County Planning", Leonard Hill, 1978, there is no mention of cycling and walking is mentioned once. The more recent Banister, D: "Rural Transport and Planning: A bibliography", Mansell, 1983 cites only five references on cycling, one of which refers to Holland, and two of which are on cycle hire schemes. There are only four works on walking, one is Norwegian.
19 For a list of disadvantages for those who do not "like running two cars" in rural areas, see the comments from the Head of the Rural Unit of the NCVO, Town and Country Planning, July/August 1988, p. 233
20 Pharaoh, T op cit.
21 See Chapter 7.
22 See Chapter 10.
23 Peugeot, reported in Lewin, T, "Drivers with death in mind, " The Sunday Correspondent, 18/11/90.
24 De Loor, H: "The Netherlands National Environmental Plan" at Town and Country Planning Association annual conference, 27-28 November 1990
25 Intergovernmental Panel on Climate Change, "Report to IPCC from Working group 1: Policymakers summary of the scientific assessment of climate change, " June 1990. See Chapter 14 "Not just a dirty problem".
26 See de Loor, H, op cit (The projection is actually for vehicle distance: nevertheless the general point remains the same, that the level of car use replicated globally would be utterly unsustainable for even the biggest optimist.)
27 For a discussion on how this sort of target might be achieved, involving a cut of car mileage by 50 per cent, (lorries by 60 per cent and doubling bus usage) see Bailey, R: "Road to the Future: Global warming, congestion and transport — the solutions", Green Party, London, 1991.
28 North West London Press, 10/8/84.

Appendix. The Astronomer From General Motors

1 Evans, L: "Traffic Safety and the Driver" Van Nostrand Reinhold, New York, 1991.
2 Care on the Road, August 1991
3 Evans, op cit p.367.
4 Ibid, p. 327

5 Ibid, p. 330
6 Ibid, p. 128
7 Ibid, p. 136-7
8 Ibid, p. 158
9 Ibid, p. 60
10 "Surprisingly, the influence of such devices (traffic engineering methods, such as installing traffic signals or stop signs) on safety is not all that clearly established. There is a general theme in the traffic engineering literature that traffic control devices enhance safety, but sefinite evidence is difficult to generate). Ibid p.85
11 See the section on Motorway Madness in Chapter 13.
12 Evans op cit p.95
13 See Chapter 11.
14 Evans op cit p. 265
15 Ibid, p. 265
16 Ibid, p. 229
17 Ibid, p. 306
18 Ibid, p. 305
19 Ibid, p.355
20 For a defence of the methods of traditional (perhaps positivist) science for analysing society see Gellner, E: "The scientific status of the social sciences" in Gellner, E: "Relativism and the Social Sciences" Cambridge University Press, 1985. Commenting on his ideas, his editors describe a "commitment to empiricism. It is the matter of placing the wells of truth...under the control of no group and of no interested party".
21 Evans op cit p. 265
22 See the work on skid resistant surfaces in Chapter 2.
23 Evans op cit p. 355
24 In 1964 Smeed referred to Tanners 1953 survey (Tanner, J "Accidents at rural three-way junctions"Journal of the Institution of Highway Engineers,1953, 2, 11, 56 -57) in Appendix 1 of Smeed, R "Methods Available to reduce the Numbers of Road Casualties", 1964 International Road Safety Congress as follows: "the number of accidents involving collisions between vehicle son two arms of 3-way junctions tended to be proportional to the square root of the product of the flows on the two arms, rather than than to the product of the flows as would be expected if the behaviour of the drivers was unaffected by the flows" (my emphasis) Also throughout this paper Smeed refers to evidence that suggests: "in some circumstances at any rate — behaviour is affected by the amounts of traffic on roads".
25 Evans op cit p. 11
26 Ibid, p.371
27 Ibid, p388

⟨≜⟩ Index

299

Organisation for Economic
  Cooperation and
  Development   106, 107,
  218, 228
Ottaway, Richard   90
ozone layer   221

P

Parish Council   135
Parliamentary Advisory Council for
  Transport Safety   61, 85,
  87, 90, 231
Parliamentary Advisory Council on
  Transport Safety   138,
  194
Parry, Bob   90
Paulos, John Allen   8
Pearce   65
pedestrian crossings
  official criteria   162
Pedestrian Safety
  New proposals for...   161
pedestrians   21, 61, 156–164
  accidents to   22
  chance of being hurt   158
  fatalities   28
  killed annually   24
  traffic   20
Pedestrians' Association   8, 90,
  113
Pedestrians' Association for Road
  Safety   35, 109, 135
police   112, 119–137
  Devon and Cornwall   145
  Leicestershire   124
  Metropolitan   241
  motorcyclist   150
  north of England   120
  training   125
Policing
  cost of   227
Policy Studies Institute   161
Pollution   221
population density   29
Porritt, Lord   90
  75
Porsche   112
Powell, Raymond   90
prematurity   8
prescribed medication   190
Prosecutions   121
Prozac   275
Public transport   222, 267
  funding   223
public transport   28
PV²   162

Q

Quinet   228

R

Rail investment   29
random breath testing   187
rear-seat passengers   84
Redmond, Martin   90
Renner   230
Rifkind, Malcolm   33

risk   8
  ambient   103
  compensation   36, 256
  homeostasis   46
  taking   24, 41
Risk Homeostasis Theory   276
Road Accidents Great Britain   15,
  27, 82
  1987   22
  1990   16
road building   22
Road Research Laboratory   162
road safety   8, 9, 23, 72, 106,
  251
  education   106–119, 108
  legislation   89
  lobby   53
  Motorways   205
Road Safety Act, 1967   72, 184
Road Safety: The Next Steps   107
road tax   224, 239
road traffic
  offences   120
Road Traffic Act, 1930   190
Road Traffic Bill, 1934   35
Road Traffic Law Review
  Report   119
Road Transport Lighting (Cycles) Act,
  1945   144
Roads for Prosperity   216, 235
Robertson, George   91
Rodgers, William   88
Ross, Stephen   88
Roundabouts   49
Royal Automobile Club   56, 61,
  109, 251
Royal Society for the Prevention of
  Accidents   10, 61, 111,
  113, 152, 181, 187
rule of the road   48
Rutherford, William   81

S

Sabey, Barbara   56
"Safe" cars   54–55
Safety First   62
safety index   8
schoolchildren   158
Scott/Willis report   82
seat belts   42, 49, 71
  Legislation   78
  segregation   196
Sheerman, Barry   87, 90
skidding   44
Skinner, Dennis   90
Smeed, Reuben   38, 45, 274, 277
  Smeed Law   38
Smog   218
Snell, Pete   179
  Memorial Institute   179
snorers   26
Social Survey   112
Social Trends   21, 158
Society of Motor Manufacturers and
  Traders   113
Somers, Lord   127
speed   55
speed governors   211
speed limit, 30mph   35, 109

speed limits   122, 240
Spencer, John   133
statistics   14
  inaccurate   17
Stats 19   15, 18, 22
stress   228
studded tyres   42
subways   157, 199
supremacism   244
Sweden   48
Sydney   221

T

teachers   115
Teufel   228
Texaco   257
That's Life   174
Theydon Bois   238
Third World   237, 253
  car ownership   219
Trades' Union Congress   106
traffic calming   196, 209–210
traffic engineering. *See* engineers
Training   107
  advanced driver   111
Transport 2000   90
Transport Act, 1981   72, 81, 194
Transport and Road Research
  Laboratory   *see*
  Department of Transport
Transport Statistics Great
  Britain   158
trauma care centres   142
Tripp, H Alker   212, 241, 242
tyres   42

U

United States of America   52, 157
  Consumer Product Safety
  Commission   152
  National Highway Traffic Safety
  Administration   166

V

Vauxhall   113
victim blaming   113, 241
Victoria   175, 179
Volvo   55, 72, 212
  Traffic Safety Award   55, 278

W

walking journeys   158
Wall Street Journal   278
weather conditions   27
wheel mounted reflectors   152
Wilde, Gerard   45, 276
women   24
Wood and Milne   175
World Health Organisation   220
  *Health for All by the Year
  2000*   220
Wright and Boyle   103
Written warnings   120

Y

young drivers   114

☰ Useful organisations

The aims of the following organisations tend to be restricted: whether because of their sectional interests, or the effects of pro-car ideology which extend even into otherwise radical groups. Nevertheless, whether through the provision of local groups or publications, they represent potentially useful contacts:-

Campaign Against Drinking and Driving
83 Jesmond Road, Newcastle upon Tyne, NE2 1NH, tel 091 281 1581
Campaigns on drink-driving, but offers support to the relatives of people killed in all kinds of road crashes.

Council for the Protection of Rural England
Warwick House, 25 Buckingham Palace Road, London, SW1W 0PP, tel 071 976 6433
Producer of useful reports and has some local groups.

Campaign for the Protection of Rural Wales
Ty Gwyn, 31 High Street, Welshpool, Powys, SY21 7JP, tel 0938 552525
Sister organisation of the CPRE.

The Countryside Commission
John Dower House, Crescent Place, Cheltenham, Gloucestershire, GL50 3RA, tel 0242 521381
Deals with rural transport issues.

Cyclists' Touring Club
69 Meadrow, Godalming, Surrey, GU7 3HS, tel 0483 417217
Bi-monthly magazine, occasional publications, technical advice notes and national lobbying.

Environmental Transport Association
The Old Post House, Heath Road, Weybridge, KT13 8RS, tel 0932 828882
Insurance and other services for motorists with a conscience. It opposes the road lobby, in which other motoring organisations play a major role.

Friends of the Earth
26-28 Underwood Street, London, N1 7JQ, tel 071 490 1555
Occasional publications dealing with traffic reduction, emissions etc.

Greenpeace UK
Canonbury Villas, London, N1 2PN, tel 071 354 5100
Newly involved in car problems. Limited scope for local activity.

Keep Death Off Our Roads
95 Upper Brents, Faversham, Kent, ME13 7DL, 0795 536917
Campaigning and helping the bereaved.

Pedestrians' Association
1 Wandsworth Road, London, SW8 2XX, 071 735 3270
Useful information in regular publication *Walk,* and some local groups.

RoadPeace
PO Box 2579, London, NW10 3PW, 081 964 1021
Launched in 1992 to campaign for a legal response to dangerous driving and to help families of accident victims.

Transport and Health Study Group
c/o Dr S Watkins, Department of Public Health Medicine, Stockport Health Authority, Bramhall Moor Lane, Hazel Grove Lane, Stockport, Cheshire, SK7 5AB

Transport 2000
Walkden House, 10 Melton Street, London, NW1 2EJ, tel 071 388 8386
Traditionally a pro-rail alternative to the roads lobby. Publisher of *Transport Retort.*

Railway and transport books

from Leading Edge

The Great Railway Conspiracy

Few books on railways in recent years have stirred so much controversy and wide interest as David Henshaw's extraordinary account of the Beeching Years which touches many raw nerves in road haulage, and broader political circles. "Henshaw tells the tale well and uncovers much skulduggery," The Daily Mail.
£14.95, hardback.

Traffic Congestion: Is there a way out?

A remarkable collection of papers which blows apart surviving myths about road-building as a solution to congestion. Edited by leading public authority, Dr John Whitelegg. "The expert contributors advance some radical solutions to the dead-end street that the road lobby is forcing us down," Transport Review.
£9.95, paperback

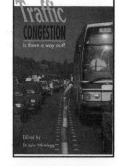

The Wensleydale Railway

Christine Hallas tells, in remarkable detail, the story of an English country railway, whose future is now topical, as the subject of ambitious reinstatement plans. "A splendid publication and good value for money," Push and Pull magazine.
£5.25, paperback

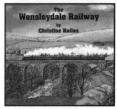

The Line that Refused to Die

In this revised and updated version of their best-seller, Stan Abbott and Alan Whitehouse tell the story of the successful campaign to save the Settle & Carlisle line -- and add some words on the ongoing story of this and Britain's other rural railways. Features a foreword by Michael Palin. "The authors have a remarkable story to tell, of intrigue in high places, of U-turns, of hopes dashed and deferred, of leaks and nods and whispers and labyrinthine negotiations," The Yorkshire Post. £7.99, paperback.

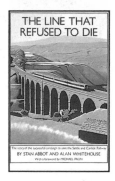

Leading Edge, Old Chapel, Burtersett, Hawes, N. Yorks, DL8 3PB.

Postage and packing charges — orders over £2, add 75p; over £6, add £1.

☎ (0969) 667566

With the ETA breakdown service you get everything...

	ETA 'Roadrescue'	AA 'Relay/Homestart'	NBRC 'Total Protection'	RAC 'New Recovery'
Roadside assistance	✔	✔	✔	✔
Recovery	✔	✔	✔	✔
Home rescue	✔	✔	✔	✔
Legal advice & expenses	✔	✔	✔	✔
European cover	✔	✗	✔	✗
Replacement car	✔	✗	✗	✗
Personal accident cover	✔	✗	✗	✗
Message service	✔	✗	✗	✗
Road lobbying	✗	✔	✔	✔
Price* (1992)	£66	£77	£72	£82

...except membership of the road lobby

You pay more as a member of the AA, RAC or NBRC (National Breakdown) *and* they spend your money lobbying the government for more roads.‡
The environment pays too – more motorways means more destruction of the countryside and more pollution.
The Environmental Transport Association, backed by the World Wide Fund for Nature, provides a breakdown service second to none *and* campaigns for environmentally friendlier transport.
The ETA also provides roadrescue for cycles.

Join today for a safer and greener tomorrow

Phone 0932 82 88 82 anytime

ETA, The Old Post House, Heath Road, Weybridge, England. KT13 8RS

*Prices are as at 1.4.92 and do not include joining fees, special payment discounts or older car supplement. ‡ The AA and RAC both lobby the government directly, and all three motoring organisations are members of the British Road Federation which campaigns energetically for more motorways and main roads.